COUNT LEO VON CAPRIVI

GERMANY
AFTER BISMARCK

THE CAPRIVI ERA
1890–1894

J. ALDEN NICHOLS

HARVARD UNIVERSITY PRESS

Cambridge, Massachusetts

1958

Publication of this book has been aided by a grant from the Ford Foundation

Library of Congress Catalog Card Number 58–11554

Printed in the United States of America

TO MY WIFE

PREFACE

During the preparation and writing of this book I have frequently been questioned by friends and acquaintances of kindly intent as to the subject of my labors. My reply, that I was working on the "Caprivi Era," almost always produced the same reaction, varying with the strength of the acquaintance and the courage of the questioner from a polite "oh," to a blunt "Who is Caprivi?" The explanation that Caprivi was the man who succeeded Bismarck and headed the German government for four years during one of the most crucial periods of the history of the Second Reich almost always produced mild surprise. The impression had been that it was Kaiser William II who succeeded Bismarck, that there had been other forgotten or vaguely remembered chancellors — Bülow and Bethmann-Hollweg, for instance — and then had come the war, one of the primary causes of which had been the rash removal of Bismarck and the resulting "personal rule" of the "wild young Kaiser." Considering the great notoriety of the Kaiser during his lifetime and the fact that the two world wars turned the attention of scholars to foreign policy, this view is natural enough. Recently, with the histories of Ziekursch and Eyck, a beginning has been made toward modifying and correcting it. Yet even Dr. Eyck, in his *Das persönliche Regiment des Kaiser Wilhelms II* — as, indeed, the title implies — tends to find in the personality of William II the perfect scapegoat for all of Germany's prewar ills. But this concept is too simple. Personal rule for William II was impossible on the face of it. Who did rule, then? It is this question to which I have applied myself, and it is hoped that, as regards the critical years 1890–1894, at least a beginning toward an answer has been indicated.

It has not been my intention to write a complete history of the Caprivi Era. The present study is meant to be only a political sketch, an attempt to probe after the lines and sources of political power, to outline the regime that followed Bismarck's dictatorship in Germany. Attention, therefore, has been paid to economic and cultural questions only when their bearing on the political development has been too direct, too obvious to ignore. To establish some sort of clarity of outline it has been felt necessary both to utilize considerable detail and to sacrifice it. Narrative and an essentially chronological arrangement have been used in order to present movements, developments, and personalities in their correct sequence and to demonstrate their interrelationships. At the same time specific aspects have been summed up briefly or passed over in an attempt to concentrate on the total picture. To preserve a balanced perspective it was necessary to incorporate periodic summaries of foreign affairs, since the connection between the foreign and domestic fields, especially in the case of the trade treaties, was a very close and real one.

Any study of the domestic scene in the Germany of William II runs the danger of degenerating into a recital of court gossip. Much of this sort of thing has been produced, especially in the host of personal memoirs. Consequently, there seemed to be no need to emphasize this aspect. Some of the more relevant incidents and anecdotes have, of necessity, been included, but there is much that has deliberately not been included. In contrast to this attempt at restraint where the Kaiser is concerned, I cheerfully confess to having given the widest possible coverage to the activity and personality of the chancellor, Caprivi. To try to resurrect this obscure and forgotten man would, perhaps, be a valid enough excuse. But I have also found that his personality and policies were much more important to the era than might be suspected, that the tragedy of his personal failure is closely interwoven with the tragedy of Germany. Also, believing with Caprivi that history does not need to be dull, I have tried to suggest some of the drama inherent in the unfolding of both tragedies. I have no illusions, however, as to how much of it has escaped me.

In writing a history of Caprivi and of the Caprivi Era it has perhaps been inevitable that the net product should have turned out to be, in a sense, another essay on Bismarck. It should, therefore, be explained that the Bismarck who is depicted here is the latter-day Bismarck, the fallen giant, and, more importantly, the lengendary Bismarck. Admittedly, this is only part of the story and only a partial view of a phenomenal personality. A total and balanced judgment of the man and of his career was obviously not within the bounds of this study and was not attempted. Others, notably Dr. Eyck, have already done well by this formidable assignment. My conclusion, as expressed in the "Epilogue," is meant as a judgment of Bismarck not as a man but as a German institution, from the special point of view of the fateful years following his fall, of the subsequent history of the German nation.

I owe a debt of gratitude to the staffs of the Columbia University, Yale University, Wesleyan University, and New York Public Libraries for the use of their collections and facilities and for their friendly coöperation and assistance; through Inter-Library Loan to the staffs of the Harvard University, University of Chicago, Princeton University, Ohio State University Libraries, and the Library of Congress for the use of important books; to the Committee on Research of Wesleyan University for generous financial assistance; to the Hauptarchiv, Berlin, for furnishing me with microfilm copies of the Caprivi papers in their collection; to Dr. Leo von Caprivi of Eckendorf for kind advice; to Professor Norman Rich and M. H. Fisher, editors of the *Holstein Papers* (Cambridge University Press, 1955–   ) for gracious permission to study and to quote from the Holstein *Diaries* in page proof and the *Correspondence* in the German typescript; to many friends and colleagues who at various stages have freely given advice, criticism, and encouragement; to Professors John H. Wuorinen and Henry L. Roberts of Columbia University, who read the original manuscript and made valuable suggestions; and to Professor Carl E. Schorske of Wesleyan University for his very helpful criticism.

The present version of this study results from a considerable reworking of the original, presented to Columbia University in 1951 for the Ph.D. degree. There has been a general reorganization; some parts have been reduced, others expanded; and important new material has been added, especially that drawn from the *Holstein Papers*, recently published, and from the small collection of Caprivi papers in the possession of the Berlin Hauptarchiv. The author, of course, accepts complete responsibility for the contents.

Thanks are due to the following publishers for permission to quote from their publications: to Deutsche Verlags-Anstalt, Stuttgart, for *Denkwürdigkeiten des General-Feldmarschalls Alfred Grafen von Waldersee*, edited by H. O. Meissner (1923), and *Rudolf von Bennigsen*, by Hermann Oncken (1910); to Eugen Rentsch Verlag, Erlenbach-Zürich, for *Bismarck* (1941–1944) and *Das Persönliche Regiment Wilhelms II* (1948), by Erich Eyck; to Harper and Brothers, New York, for *German Diplomatic Documents*, translated by E. T. S. Dugdale (1928), and *The Kaiser vs. Bismarck*, by Bismarck (1921); to Alfred A. Knopf, Inc., New York, for *Philip Eulenburg: The Kaiser's Friend*, by Johannes Haller (translated by Ethel Colburn Mayne, 1930); to K. F. Koehler Verlag, Stuttgart, for *Zwischen Kaiser und Kanzler. Aufzeichnungen des General-adjutan-*

ten Grafen von Wedel aus den Jahren 1890–1894, by Carl, Graf
von Wedel (1943); to The Macmillan Co., New York, for *Memoirs of
Prince Chlodwig of Hohenlohe-Schillingsfuerst,* edited by Fr. Curtius, translated by G. W. Chrystal (1906), and *Letters of the Empress Frederick,* edited and translated by Sir Frederick Ponsonby
(1928); to Meyersche Hofbuchhandlung Verlag, Detmold, for *Johannes von Miquel,* by Hans Herzfeld (1938); to Putnam and Co.,
Ltd., London, and Little, Brown and Co., Boston, for *Memoirs of
Prince von Bülow,* translated by F. A. Voight (1932); to Reimer Hob-
bing Verlag, Berlin, for *Der Neue Kurs,* by Otto Hammann (1918),
and *Denkwürdigkeiten des Botschafters General von Schweinitz*
(1927); to G. Schirmer, Inc., New York, for the first stanza and
chorus of "Die Wacht am Rhein," translated by Henry G. Chapman,
in *Songs of Germany,* edited by Max Spicker (1904); to Verlag
Ullstein, Berlin, for *Friederich von Holstein Lebensbekenntnis in
Briefen an eine Frau,* by Helmuth Rogge (1932).

Braintree, Massachusetts   J. Alden Nichols

CONTENTS

List of Illustrations

As the light of the setting Bismarck-sun dispels the storm clouds of the 8-hour—6-hour—5-hour—3-hour—2-hour—no-hour day, Caprivi-Wotan leads Germania across the New Course rainbow bridge, inscribed with "Sunday Work," "Workers' Protection," and a sign pointing toward Valhalla. Windthorst-Loge seems to be coming along, too. In the foreground lies the dead giant, Anti-Socialist Law, with his banishment-paragraph club, while the Social Democrat-Nibelungs rejoice at the left, and the three Rhine Maidens—the *Münchener Allgemeine Zeitung, Kölnische Zeitung,* and *Hamburger Nachrichten*—sing "Whither are we tending?"

This and the cartoons following are all from *Kladderadatsch; humoristisch-satirisches Wochenblatt,* Berlin, 1848—.

"You will never get him this way; he's too deep down."

Caprivi takes the army-bill horse, containing the Greek-agrarian enemy, into the city, while Miquel looks on with satisfaction.

"Not the shadow of a disagreement exists between Caprivi and Miquel, if one believes the assurances of the official press and doesn't look too closely at this picture."

PROLOGUE

Happy the land to which fate has once granted a statesma[n]
great that after his departure all future generations look
longingly to his era as to an heroic age.

Preussische Jahrbücher, J[u]

It is my fate to stand always in the shadow of the

Capriv[i]

Chapter I

THE GREAT MAN

When utopias are attempted and the Throne strains after popularity, then that leads to parliamentarism and to the downfall of monarchical authority . . . He had expected other things from the Kaiser.

Bismarck

The question at issue was . . . whether the Hohenzollern dynasty or the Bismarck dynasty should reign.

William II

1

BISMARCK AND EUROPE

THE old man had been speaking for over an hour to a Reichstag which, except for occasional bursts of applause, hung breathless upon his words. And well it might, for this towering figure in the cuirassier's uniform with the high black boots, with his white hair, bushy eyebrows, deep-set brooding eyes, and drooping mustache, was the almost legendary Prince Otto von Bismarck — the man who by ruthless cleverness and strength of will had solved the riddle of the Sphinx, the thousand-year-old "German Problem," had won over Russia with kindness, had defeated the two empires of Austria and France in brief and glorious wars, and had succeeded, by this policy of "blood and iron," in organizing the traditional chaos of Central Europe, had set up in the heart of the continent a powerful second German Reich.

This marvel of political virtuosity had been accomplished in 1871, and, since then, for seventeen years the great manipulator had kept the peace in Europe and had built up the position of his new empire economically and politically to a position of practical hegemony over the Continent. But now, for the past two years, the

European powers had come increasingly into conflict, and the international atmosphere had become tense with the threat of a general war. Russia, brooding bitterly ever since 1878 over the setback which the Congress of Berlin had caused to her ambitions in the Balkans, was threatening recalcitrant Bulgaria, and in the fall of 1886 had forced the Bulgarian ruler, Prince Alexander of Battenberg, to abdicate. To this threat to the Near East the empires of Austria and Britain had reacted with growing hostility. Even in Germany Prince Alexander had become a popular hero. And while tension had developed in the east, an ominous rumbling had arisen in the west, where Paris crowds were deliriously acclaiming *"le brave général"* Boulanger, minister of war, who looked so handsome upon his black horse and who was already rapidly becoming the embodiment of French national pride and the spirit of "revenge" against Germany.[1]

Against these menaces to his Reich from the east and from the west, the seventy-one-year-old Bismarck had acted with dispatch. In November of 1886 he had introduced a bill into the Reichstag to increase the size of the German army from 427,000 to 468,000 men. In February 1887 he had renewed the Triple Alliance of Germany, Austria, and Italy, which was the basis of his foreign policy. The same month, to further strengthen Italy against the lures of France, he had encouraged an agreement between Italy and England to preserve the *status quo* in the west Mediterranean. In March he had brought about a similar agreement between England and Austria for the east Mediterranean, the Balkans, and especially the Straits. Then, having lined up Austria, Italy, and England to check the Russian menace in the east, the following June Bismarck had himself concluded a secret treaty with Russia promising support in Bulgaria and the Straits.

By midsummer 1887 the old chancellor had thus completed his network of alliances. But in July the crisis had suddenly worsened, when Ferdinand of Coburg, an Austrian prince, had been elected to the throne of Bulgaria in defiance of the Russian tsar. By October, Russian troops had begun to gather on the frontier. In November Bismarck had driven Russian securities off the German exchanges; in December he had introduced new increases in the German army into the Reichstag; and finally, on February 3, 1888, he had pub-

---

[1]On Bismarck, see especially Erich Eyck, *Bismarck* (Erlenbach-Zurich, 1941–1944); A. J. P. Taylor, *Bismarck* (London, 1955). For the international crisis of 1886–1888 cf. W. L. Langer, *European Alliances and Alignments* (New York, 1931), pp. 323–453; E. M. Carroll, *Germany and the Great Powers* (New York, 1938), pp. 219–268.

lished the terms of his alliance with Austria, calling for German aid against a Russian attack.

Now, three days later, on February 6, 1888, Prince Bismarck was speaking to the Reichstag, ostensibly on the new army bill. Crowds assembled along the streets had cheered him as he had arrived at the Reichstag building. Inside, the hall was packed to the doors by members and visitors, including two Prussian princes, a grand duke, and several foreign ambassadors. For several days past the world had waited tensely for this speech. In reality Bismarck was speaking to all Europe, and all Europe was listening.

In the past year the master diplomat of Berlin had set up a system of alliances and guaranties which included every great power in Europe — with the exception of France. Republican France, the irreconcilable, obsessed with the loss of Alsace-Lorraine and with thoughts of revenge for the humiliation of 1870, was to be quarantined and isolated. With one hand Bismarck had supported Russian ambitions in the Balkans and Constantinople, with the other he had opposed them with the assistance of England, Italy, and Austria. By balancing east against west, and promising German neutrality or aid for each against the aggression of the other, he had put a premium upon the preservation of peace and had retained for Germany the decisive position of arbiter and judge. By means of the diplomatic net he had so skillfully woven about Europe, the clever old sorcerer had cast a spell which had reduced the Great Powers to a somewhat frustrated immobility. And he had kept all of them from aligning themselves with France. Now he had merely to bring his accomplishment to their attention and to remind them that Germany had the last word.

Masterfully, he sketched for his audience the diplomatic history of Europe since the Crimean War and, skillfully, at every point defended the policy of first Prussia and later his own German Empire. Now he was coming to the conclusion:

That is over and done with; we no longer solicit anyone's love, neither in France nor in Russia ("Very good!" enthusiastic "Bravo!"). The Russian press, Russian public opinion have shown us the door; old, powerful, and reliable friend that we were; we shall not force ourselves upon them. We have tried to restore the old intimate relationship, but we run after no one ("Bravo!" on all sides). . . . I do not believe a disturbance of the peace to be imminent . . . The threats that we are encountering — not from the governments, but in the press — are certainly an incredible nonsense (laughter); that one should consider it possible to intimidate a great and proud power, such as the German Reich, through some sort of threatening formation of printer's ink, through putting words together ("Bravo!") . . . We can easily be corrupted by love and good will — perhaps too easily — but by threats, absolutely not! ("Bravo!") We Germans fear God and nothing else in the world (enthusiastic "Bravo!"); and surely it is the fear of God that causes us to love and to cherish peace. But, nevertheless, he who breaks it will see for himself that the militant patriotism, which in 1813 called to the colors the whole population of Prussia, at that time weak, small and exhausted, is now the common property of the entire German nation, and that he who in any way attacks the German nation will find her united in arms and in the heart of every soldier the firm belief: "God will be with us!" (loud continued applause).

The master in Berlin had spoken; there would be no war. Gradually the crisis eased.[2]

2

BISMARCK AND GERMANY

Bismarck's handling of the international crisis of 1886–1888 is all the more impressive because he himself had deliberately created a large part of the international tension. Following a tried political precept, he had called up external dangers to exorcise what he conceived to be an internal threat to his own political position. For, since 1862, he had not only brought about German domination over Europe but, through the same process of divide and rule, had also brought about and maintained for twenty-five years his own personal domination over Germany.[3]

The wars of 1866 with Austria and of 1870 with France had solved the German problem, not by a slow, peaceful process of amalgamation, but by what amounted to a political and moral conquest of Germany by Prussia. These wars had been won by the Prussian army, the military vehicle of the Prussian Junker aristocracy, which, in consequence, dominated the new German Reich. But, inasmuch as the Prussian victories had been dedicated by Bismarck to the cause of German nationalism, a sizable portion of the liberal and nationalist German middle class had thereby also been won over to the support of the new German nation. Bismarck

[2]*Verhandlungen des Reichstages . . . Stenographische Berichte* (Berlin, 1871–1938), 1887–1888, II, 732–733 (hereafter cited as *Sten. Ber.*); *Schulthess' Europäischer Geschichtskalender* (Munich, 1860–1938), 1888, pp. 23, 40–42 (hereafter cited as *Schulthess*).

[3]Eyck, *Bismarck*, III, 477; Langer, *European Alliances*, pp. 379–380, 382–383; Carroll, *Germany and the Great Powers*, pp. 266–267.

had created his new German Reich on the basis of an antagonistic coöperation between the Prussian aristocracy on the one hand and the German middle class on the other, with the Hohenzollern king of Prussia representing — through the title of "German emperor" — the idea of national unity.[4]

The German Reich, as set up under Bismarck's constitution, was a curious combination of the sovereign princely states, represented by the Bundesrat (Federal Council); of the Prussian aristocracy, represented by the Kaiser (emperor), the army, and the bureaucracy; and of the German nation, represented by the Reichstag (Imperial Diet), whose members were elected by direct universal manhood suffrage. There was, as such, no real government of the Reich; only the chancellor who, appointed by the president of the Federation, the Kaiser, presided over the Bundesrat and represented the federated states to the Reichstag. Although he was assisted by various state secretaries, he alone was responsible for policy, not to the Reichstag, but to the Bundesrat and to the Kaiser. Whatever was the constitutional position of the Bundesrat, however, Prussia, consisting of two thirds of the area and population and practically all of the industry of Germany, actually and inevitably dominated the other states. And, since the king of Prussia was also the German emperor, it was only natural that the minister-president of Prussia, Bismarck, should also hold the office of Reich chancellor. Prussian policy and German policy thus were identified. And, finally, a particularist movement of the smaller states in the Bundesrat against Prussian leadership could always be opposed by appealing for support to the representatives of the nation in the Reichstag.[5]

The key to the whole structure was the position of the chancellor. Above the different forces of Prussian aristocracy, German particularism, and liberal nationalism stood the chancellor — Bismarck — in the position which he had so astutely created for himself, encouraging now one factor, now another, and by balancing them off, one against the other, thus maintaining his own supremacy over all.[6] In the Reich which he had fashioned there was only one whose authority potentially surpassed that of Bismarck: the German

[4]Cf. Arthur Rosenberg, *Birth of the German Republic* (New York, 1931), p. 1.

[5]For the governmental structure of the Second Reich see Loewenstein, "Germany," in *Governments of Continental Europe*, ed. James T. Shotwell (New York, 1942), pp. 311–333; A. L. Lowell, *Governments and Parties in Continental Europe* (Boston, 1896), I, 241–285; R. H. Fife, *The German Empire between Two Wars* (New York, 1916), pp. 101–113. For further discussion and explanation of the constitutional organization of the Reich, see below, pp. 37–38, 41–43, 183–191, 220–225, Chapter IX, section 1, Chapter X.

[6]Cf. Rosenberg, *Birth of the German Republic*, p. 4.

Kaiser, to whom he was constitutionally responsible. But William I owed him his position as Kaiser, and although in the past there had been differences between them, Bismarck had always won his point and maintained his control. In 1885, however, William I, at the age of eighty-eight, had fallen seriously ill. True, he had happily recovered, but who could count on his reaching his ninetieth birthday? And the Crown Prince Frederick and his wife, the eldest daughter of Queen Victoria of England, were noted for their liberal, anti-Bismarckian ideas. This was the threat which Bismarck faced, a threat made doubly dangerous by the hostile disposition of another power in the state — the Reichstag.[7]

To support Bismarck and his policies in the nation and the Reichstag, two parties had been formed out of the two elements of Prussian aristocracy and German middle class: the Free Conservatives (*Reichspartei*) and the National Liberals. At both extremes remained the uncompromising irreconcilables, the ultraconservative German Conservatives and the ultraliberal Progressives. In opposition there had also arisen with the years, beside the splinter parties of Danes, Guelfs, Poles, and Alsatians, the powerful Center party, welded together by the *Kulturkampf* and representing a continuation of the war of 1866, of Catholic particularism against the domination of Protestant Prussia. And also, the Social Democrats, the new threat from the left, had managed, despite the crippling effects of Bismarck's anti-Socialist law of 1878, to maintain and even to increase their representation in the Reichstag. The Progressives, united since 1884 with part of the old National Liberals into the German Radical party (*Freisinnigen*), were looked upon with particular favor by the heir to the throne and had been popularly labeled the "Crown Prince's party." [8] In 1886 the Radicals had 67 seats in the Reichstag, the Center party, 100; a combination of these two with other oppositional elements would produce a slight majority, which could support an anti-Bismarckian "Gladstone Ministry" for the future Kaiser. At the first hint of the inevitable clash between Frederick and Victoria and himself, Bismarck would be faced with the bitter alternatives to yield or to resign, one as impossible as the other to the dominating character of the old man.

Within the framework of his monarchical principles, there was nothing that Bismarck could do about the imminent succession of

[7]Eyck, *Bismarck,* III, 429–431.

[8]L. Bergsträsser, *Geschichte der politischen Parteien in Deutschland* (Berlin, 1932), p. 107; Rosenberg, *Birth of the German Republic,* pp. 12–18.

Frederick, but, if he could find an issue explosive enough, perhaps he could effect a change in the party line-up in the Reichstag. Only two issues could possibly do the trick: the internal threat of socialist revolution, and the external threat of war. The socialist issue had been momentarily disposed of in February 1886, when the Reichstag, in a compromise move by the Center, had renewed the anti-Socialist law for a period of two years. There remained the issue of national defense. The military budget had been fixed by the *septennat* of 1881 for a period of seven years, until March 31, 1888. Kaiser William I's ninetieth birthday, however, fell in March 1887; Bismarck could not afford to wait.[9]

In January 1886 General Boulanger had been appointed French minister of war. Two months later Bismarck was already attacking him and the French menace in the Reichstag and the press, although Boulanger had done nothing provocative as yet. In fact, Bismarck's attacks probably increased Boulanger's popularity with the French. The international situation during the summer of 1886, as has been seen, did provide Bismarck with sufficient reason for asking the Reichstag for an increase in the army. But the increase in size was, in fact, not the cause of the subsequent political crisis. Rather, it was the demand that the military budget be voted again for a period of seven years — although this very bill would end the old *septennat* prematurely at six years — that prompted the opposition in the Reichstag. Bismarck knew perfectly well that this oppositional Reichstag could not possibly give him a new *septennat*. One of the basic points of the 1884 fusion program of the constitutionally minded Radicals had been to fix a maximum limit of three years upon the life of the military budget — the length of the term of the Reichstag at that time. The Center party might be willing to compromise at some intermediate figure, but could never agree to seven years. Bismarck, however, insisted; a seven-year period would shelve the critical issue of the army budget until 1894, well past the coming change in Kaisers; and, besides, by insisting on the impossible he could provoke the Reichstag into rejecting the defense bill, could then dissolve it and order a new election, which might produce the majority favorable to himself which he so passionately desired. The battle with the Reichstag for the new *septennat* was in reality "a struggle to maintain his own political domination over the next German emperor."[10]

[9]Eyck, *Bismarck*, III, 431–432.
[10]Eyck, *Bismarck*, III, 448.

That this was Bismarck's prime motive is substantiated by the fact that in March of 1886 he appointed his oldest son, Herbert, secretary of state for foreign affairs at the age of thirty-six, and also that the two Bismarcks then proceeded to press their friendship upon the twenty-seven-year-old Prince William, whose antipathy to his parents was well known. They went so far as to introduce him into the working of the Foreign Office, not without an emphatic protest from his father, the crown prince, who wrote Bismarck: "Considering the unripeness and inexperience of my eldest son, together with his leaning toward vanity and presumption, and his overweening estimate of himself, I must frankly express my opinion that it is dangerous as yet to bring him into touch with foreign affairs." [11] In 1886, however, Bismarck was less interested in shaping the character of the future William II than in securing his support for the coming battle against his father; and the Foreign Office was an ideal place to accustom the impressionable Prince William to the idea that the Bismarcks, father and son, were absolutely indispensable to the continuation of the Reich. The crown prince might protest, but he was powerless to control the education of his son as long as Bismarck had the support of the head of the family, the aged William I.[12]

On November 25, 1886, the military bill was brought before the Reichstag. Bismarck, however, remained aloof on his estate at Friedrichsruh, leaving the handling of the bill on the floor and in commission to the minister of war, who was further instructed not to give the commission any information on the international situation and not to agree to any compromise reduction in the seven year time limit. Only after the bill had been reported unfavorably by the commission did Bismarck return to Berlin. His speeches in the Reichstag on January 11, 12, and 13, 1887, were conciliatory towards Russia and emphasized the danger of a French attack as the main reason for the army increase, attacking General Boulanger by name, thus further inflaming the French and rallying them to the support of their general. In order to reduce the danger inherent in the tense situation in the Balkans, Russian friendship was a must for Bismarck's foreign policy; he had, on the other hand, long since reckoned with the permanent hostility of France: as long as the French were diplomatically isolated he might provoke them with

[11]Otto v. Bismarck, *The Kaiser vs. Bismarck*, trans. Bernard Miall (New York, 1921; trans. of *Gedanken und Erinnerungen*, vol. III), p. 3.

[12]Eyck, *Bismarck*, III, 446–447. Cf. L. Bamberger, "Zum Jahrestag der Entlassung Bismarcks," *Gesammelte Schriften* (Berlin, 1913), V, 325–326.

impunity. The bill was then defeated; Bismarck dissolved the Reichstag; and the election battle was on.[13]

Despite the fact that the seventy-two-year-old chancellor was also, during January and February, busily conducting complicated diplomatic negotiations with Austria, Italy, and England, he nevertheless outdid himself in his conduct of the election campaign. First he formed a "Kartell" of the Conservative, Free Conservative, and National Liberal parties to work together in the campaign and to support each other as a bloc in the election. Then he threw his propaganda machine into high gear and overwhelmed the country day after day, with headlines and lurid colored posters depicting the horrors of an attack by the revengeful French upon helpless German women and children. He called up 73,000 army reserves for the French frontier. He caused panic in the stock exchange with the rumor that the government was about to request a war loan from the Prussian Landtag. Foreign newspapers, including *The Times* of London, joined in and added to the furor of the war scare. In France real apprehension began to spread. The dangers implicit in the tense international situation, however, meant nothing to Bismarck if only he might achieve his victory in the election. And this he did: "The German voter, who feared war just as much as the French peasant and townsman, believed that only passage of the *septennat* could prevent it, and voted for the Kartell." [14]

It was a brilliant victory for Bismarck. The Kartell parties had won the desired majority, and on March 11 the military bill was approved by the Reichstag. To be sure, before the expiration date of the new *septennat* in 1894, three new army bills were to be introduced, including the great Caprivi reform bill of 1892. But now Bismarck had his majority. And, most important of all, the Radical "Crown Prince's party" had been shattered, had in fact lost more than half its seats in the Reichstag. There could be no more threat of an oppositional "Gladstone Ministry." Now Frederick and his

[13]Eyck, *Bismarck,* III, 448–457. For the election campaign, see Eyck, III, 458–469; Bergsträsser, *Geschichte,* pp. 110–112; Carroll, *Germany and the Great Powers,* pp. 238–248. This discussion of the domestic aspects of the 1886–1888 crisis is based mainly on Eyck; the purely diplomatic aspect, as given above (pp. 3–6), on Langer, *European Alliances.* It is believed that the two points of view are less in conflict than they appear, since the German statesman was quite capable of resolving a really tense diplomatic situation by a brilliant *tour de force* that would also serve his private political interests. The essential point that Eyck emphasizes is that the manner in which the coup was accomplished, both in the double-dealing diplomacy and the inflaming of popular passions, although producing a temporary and brilliant victory, was in the long run irresponsible and dangerous. The author is in agreement with this view.

[14]Eyck, *Bismarck,* III, 463.

English wife could succeed to the imperial throne; they would be powerless. But here there was suddenly revealed a most ironical twist of history — it became known a few months after Bismarck's victory that the crown prince was already slowly dying of cancer of the larynx. In a helpless condition he succeeded his aged father in March 1888, to reign for only a brief and tragic ninety-nine days. On June 15, 1888, William II succeeded his father and grandfather as German Kaiser. It was, indeed, "only a shadow, a tragic shadow, against whom Bismarck had gained his last great domestic triumph." [15]

3

BISMARCK'S FALL FROM POWER

It is the fate of the successful opportunist continually to face new and complicated developments arising from his own past acts. Bismarck, in 1888, was at the height of his career. He had brought the Reichstag to heel. He had preserved peace in Europe. By his own cleverness and strength of will at the age of seventy-two, he had once more demonstrated his dual mastery over Germany and the European continent. Yet in exactly two years he was to be stripped of his power and even to be no longer chancellor of the German Reich.[16]

During his father's last illness William, then crown prince, had proposed a toast to Bismarck on his birthday, in which he had compared the Reich to an army which has lost its commander and whose next in command lies sorely wounded. "At this moment," he declared, "forty-six million true German hearts look to the flag in fear and hope and to its bearer . . . he leads the way, we follow him!" [17] A loyal, extremely self-effacing, and humble statement from the young man who was soon to become Kaiser, this would certainly seem to suggest that William had an exalted idea of Bismarck's

[15]Eyck, *Bismarck*, III, 465; cf. O. Stillich, *Die politischen Parteien in Deutschland* (Leipzig, 1908–1911), II, 310–311. For a careful consideration of the rather overoptimistic attitude of the Radicals towards Frederick III and of his actual political ideas and tendencies, see A. Dorpalen, "Emperor Frederick III and the German Liberal Movement," *American Historical Review*, 54:1–31 (October 1948).

[16]For the most complete accounts of Bismarck's fall see Eyck, *Bismarck*, III, 543–599; Egmont Zechlin, *Staatsstreichpläne Bismarcks und Wilhelms II, 1890–94* (Stuttgart, 1929), part I; for the day-to-day developments, see K. A. von Müller, ed., "Die Entlassung," *Süddeutsche Monatshefte* (Munich), 19(I):138–178 (1921) — reports of the Bavarian Ambassador Count Lerchenfeld; also Bismarck's own account in the third volume of his memoirs, *The Kaiser vs. Bismarck*.

[17]*Schulthess* (1888), p. 72.

importance. And, in fact, there was much good feeling between them in the first year of William II's reign. It did not, however, take long to evaporate. The twenty-nine-year-old William II, whom his best friend, Philipp Eulenburg, sadly described as "remarkably young for his years," [18] took his new position as German Kaiser extremely seriously. Indeed, Bismarck himself had encouraged him to believe in his divine mission and his own genius. William's quick energy, his weakness for applause and flattery, his impulsive self-confidence could be benevolently tolerated and even encouraged when, as prince, he was drawn by Bismarck into alliance against his father and mother. As German Kaiser, however, his actions began to be uncomfortable to the old man. He traveled too much and to the wrong places (Constantinople — it could make the tsar suspicious); he spoke too much and to the wrong people (after all, the chancellor was his adviser and responsible for policy); he made himself too prominent (who ruled Germany?). Above all, he thought he was the ruler; he gave orders. As long as it was a matter of correcting minor errors and preventing blunders, their relationship was not too difficult. When a serious difference arose there would be trouble.[19]

This difference developed in 1889 over the attitude of the imperial government towards the "social question." In May of that year there was a spontaneous and unorganized strike of some 170,000 coal miners in the Ruhr. Bismarck had no intention of interfering, but one day the young Kaiser suddenly appeared at a meeting of the Prussian Ministry and ordered it to compel the mine owners to make concessions to the strikers. Through his personal intervention the strike was finally settled on this basis. Here was a two-fold challenge to Bismarck, both in policy and in personal behavior.[20]

Since 1879, when Bismarck had adopted a policy of protective tariffs, Germany had, once again, after the slump of the seventies, been

[18] Philipp, Fürst zu Eulenburg-Hertefeld, *Aus 50 Jahren* (Berlin, 1923), p. 222.

[19] For a penetrating analysis of the character of William II, see J. Ziekursch, *Politische Geschichte des neuen deutschen Kaiserreichs* (Frankfurt a. M., 1925–1930), III, 5–8; of his relation to Bismarck, *ibid.*, II, 423–430. Cf. also B. Bülow, *Memoirs of Prince von Bülow* (Boston, 1932), IV, 609, 611, 682–683, 658–659, 673–674; General Alfred Graf v. Waldersee, *Denkwürdigkeiten des General-Feldmarschalls Alfred Grafen von Waldersee*, ed. H. O. Meissner (Stuttgart, 1923), II, *passim;* Sir Frederick Ponsonby, trans. and ed., *The Letters of the Empress Frederick* (London, 1928), *passim;* K. A. Müller, "Die Entlassung," pp. 172–173; H. Rogge, *Friedrich v. Holstein Lebensbekenntnis in Briefen an eine Frau* (Berlin, 1932), p. 151; Eyck, *Bismarck*, III, 556–559.

[20] Ziekursch, *Geschichte*, II, 432–433; Eyck, *Bismarck*, III, 560; H. H. Freiherr v. Berlepsch, *Sozialpolitische Erfahrungen und Erinnerungen* (München-Gladbach, 1925), pp. 22–24; William II to Emperor Francis Joseph, April 3, 1890, *Österreichische Rundschau* (Vienna, 1904–   ), 58:100 (hereafter cited as *Österr. Rdsch.*).

experiencing a rapid advance in industrialization, with all the usual accompanying dislocations and social ills. Bismarck himself had done much to meet the needs of the working man with his program of compulsory state social insurance for old age, accidents, and sickness. But he had balked at limiting the hours or conditions of labor; this would be interference with the rights of management. The Reichstag had long clamored for such legislation; almost everybody favored it but Bismarck.[21] After all, Great Britain had had its factory acts for more than fifty years. But by 1889 Bismarck had lost his interest in social legislation. His introducing it in the first place had not been the result of any "silly humanitarianism" on his part. He had elaborated his insurance laws deliberately to entice the working classes away from democratic socialism. And simultaneously he had acted in a negative fashion by suppressing meetings and publications of the Social Democratic party through an exceptional "anti-Socialist law." But neither paternalism nor oppression had worked. With the continuing forward march of industrialization came a rising clamor from the laboring classes, not only for better conditions but also for political power. The Social Democrats, who in 1875 had banded together on a mild Lassallean reform basis, since 1878 had reacted to Bismarck's repression by turning more and more to the ideas of Karl Marx and the proletarian revolution; and all the while they continued steadily to increase their representation in the Reichstag.[22]

Bismarck, in 1889–1890, was in no mood for concessions. Such further reforms as might be made, he declared, would only weaken the position of the government, increase the demands of the opposition, and lead eventually to a democratic parliamentary regime — the destruction of his monarchical, autocratic Reich.[23] In 1887 it had taken all the aroused emotions of a war scare to defeat the opposition and to produce a favorable majority. The resulting Kartell-Reichstag was now reaching the end of its term. In February 1890 there would have to be an election. It could scarcely produce better results for Bismarck than in 1887; it would probably be much worse. In October 1889, therefore, Bismarck introduced into the Reichstag a bill to make the exceptional anti-Socialist law permanent. Then he

[21]Eyck, *Bismarck,* III, 564–565; Bismarck, *Kaiser vs. Bismarck,* pp. 59–60; Rogge, *Holstein,* p. 152.

[22]See E. Anderson's neat summary of this Social Democratic development, *Hammer or Anvil: The Story of the German Working-Class Movement* (London, 1945), pp. 7–13.

[23]Cf. Bismarck to Lerchenfeld, February 10, 1890, in K. A. Müller, "Die Entlassung," p. 149; also January 16 report, p. 139.

retired to Friedrichsruh to think over the situation, let things work themselves out a bit, and to prepare a plan of campaign.[24] The life of the state can never stand still.

The old chancellor's withdrawal to Friedrichsruh at such a critical time was probably based on other motives as well. Perhaps he hoped that in his prolonged absence from Berlin the young Kaiser might become aware of his own inadequacy. There was, after all, little choice for him in his handling of William II. The forty-four years between their ages made it impossible for Bismarck to try to control William by continuously following him about. The only alternative was to let him alone and hope that he would stub his toe.[25] It was not an unsuitable approach to William II and might have worked very well in the long run. It was risky, however; particularly in a critical time. But Bismarck had not left the Kaiser completely unwatched. There were the various Prussian ministers and above all, the chancellor's oldest son, the foreign secretary, whom he was grooming to succeed himself. Count Herbert Bismarck was only too willing to take this opportunity, in his father's absence, to act as chancellor. He encouraged his father to remain in Friedrichsruh.[26]

On November 25, 1889, General von Schweinitz, the ambassador to Russia, reported to Bismarck at Friedrichsruh and found him conferring with the leader of the Reichstag Conservatives, von Helldorff-Bedra, over the party's attitude toward the anti-Socialist law. In the discussion of the bill a slight difference had developed between the Conservatives and the National Liberals. The latter, led by Johannes Miquel, objected to including in the permanent law the paragraph authorizing the police to banish socialist "agitators" from the scene of their activity. This clause had worked particular hardship upon individuals and families, and, in practice, had served, Miquel claimed, merely to spread the agitation into new areas. The extreme right wing of the Conservatives, however, who had never enjoyed coöperating with the National Liberals and were fundamentally antipathetic to the Kartell, firmly opposed making the slightest concession. Under the pressure of this element in his party, Helldorff sought assistance from Bismarck in trying to compose the difference between the factions. Bismarck, however, would give no

[24]Eyck, *Bismarck*, III, 561–562; Zechlin, *Staatsstreichpläne*, pp. 10–11; Ziekursch, *Geschichte*, II, 436.

[25]Cf. Ponsonby, *Letters of Empress Frederick*, p. 404; Ziekursch, *Geschichte*, II, 436.

[26]Cf. Friedrich Thimme, ed., "Bismarck und Kardorff," *Deutsche Revue* (Berlin), 42(I):52 (1917).

positive assurances. Maintaining that the Kartell was more important to him than the Socialist law, he nevertheless would make no concessions. This was no time for weak shilly-shallying, but for blood and iron. Perhaps, noted Schweinitz in his diary, Bismarck was right, and the "social question" should soon be solved by force.[27]

Meanwhile, in Berlin, William II was proceeding along quite different lines. He had decided that a law regulating hours and conditions of work, especially for women and children, was absolutely essential and had drawn one up. In the absence of the chancellor he had consulted with all sorts of people: his old tutor, Professor Hinzpeter; a Professor von Heyden, "an amiable man, a painter, who was a miner thirty years ago"; Count Berlepsch, governor (*Oberpräsident*) of the Province of the Rhine; and an obscure gentleman named Count Douglas.[28] Further, he had won over practically all the Prussian ministers to his side, as well as the king of Saxony and the grand duke of Baden. In fact, Herbert, playing his rôle of sorcerer's apprentice, had let the situation get quite out of hand.[29] On January 9, Dr. von Bötticher, vice-president of the Prussian Ministry and Reich minister of the interior, traveled to Friedrichsruh to try to persuade Bismarck to concede the labor-law reform and to return to Berlin. Both attempts were in vain; the old man would concede nothing, and Herbert still advised against coming to Berlin. Bismarck apparently felt quite sure of himself. It was ludicrous to think that his position in the Reich could really be threatened by a mere boy.[30]

William II, however, began to be impatient and through Bötticher peremptorily notified the chancellor on January 23 that there would be a Crown Council the next day, at which he was expected to be present. By various channels Bismarck discovered that the Kaiser intended to lay his labor-reform plans before the ministry. Arriving in Berlin ahead of time, he called a meeting of the ministers and arranged that they should accept the Kaiser's plans for consideration and discussion, thus deferring judgment.

At the meeting that evening the Kaiser introduced his reforms

---

[27]General H. L. v. Schweinitz, *Denkwürdigkeiten* (Berlin, 1927), II, 392; O. H. v. Helldorff-Bedra, "Fall des Sozialistengesetzes," *Deutsche Revue*, 25(I):275–277 (1900); Zechlin, *Staatsstreichpläne*, pp. 5–13; Eyck, *Bismarck*, III, 563; Ziekursch, *Geschichte*, II, 434–435.

[28]Ponsonby, *Letters of the Empress Frederick*, p. 405; Waldersee, *Denkwürdigkeiten*, II, 7; Bismarck, *Kaiser vs. Bismarck*, pp. 63–64; William II to Francis Joseph, *Österr. Rdsch.*, 58:101.

[29]Cf. Bamberger, *Gesammelte Schriften*, V, 326–327.

[30]Eyck, *Bismarck*, III, 566; cf. Waldersee, *Denkwürdigkeiten*, II, 54–56; Eulenburg, *Aus 50 Jahren*, p. 243; Taylor, *Bismarck*, pp. 234–235.

as expected, but with an extremely strong attack on the employers who, he said, squeezed their employees like oranges. The ministers, somewhat astonished, reserved judgment on the proposed legislation as agreed beforehand, and a conflict was avoided at that point. With the question of the anti-Socialist law, however, it was a different story. The day before, Helldorff had announced that the Conservative party would vote for the bill without the banishment provision if the government stated beforehand that it would accept the bill in this form. This move was a victory for the reactionary wing of the party and an attempt to force Bismarck's hand. Now the Kaiser declared that the government should give the requested assurance and accept the weaker law, which was better than nothing. This idea Bismarck bitterly opposed. If the government made such a statement it would bear the responsibility for the weaker law, and would be unable to introduce to the next Reichstag the even more severe measures which he believed would be necessary. Becoming greatly excited as he realized that the Kaiser remained unconvinced, he threatened to resign if his advice were not followed, and, finally, completely losing control, declared that if the law were not passed they would get along without one; they would "let the waves go higher," and if a conflict occurred, all well and good. The sooner they took a firm stand the less bloodshed there would be. To this the Kaiser replied that he did not want to stain the first years of his reign with the blood of his subjects and appealed confidently to the ministers, who, he knew, agreed with him. But the ministers, in conformity with the discipline of many years, meekly supported Bismarck. There was nothing the Kaiser could do; the chancellor's point of view was accepted. The government did not give the statement requested; on January 25, the Conservatives, therefore, voted with the opposition against the weakened bill, which did not pass. After September 30, Germany would be without an anti-Socialist law.[31]

Between the Kaiser and the chancellor, however, the fat was now in the fire. Bismarck had shown his hand; William II now knew the underlying purpose of his policy. Also the young Kaiser had been ignominiously and painfully shown that the ministers and the government were not his but Bismarck's. Such a bald and premature exposure of the underlying realities was unlike Bismarck. The old

[31]Eyck, *Bismarck*, III, 569–571; Ziekursch, *Geschichte*, II, 437; Karl Wippermann, ed., *Deutscher Geschichtskalender* (Leipzig), 6(I):11–13 (1890), and 6(II):60 (hereafter cited as Wippermann); Bismarck, *Kaiser vs. Bismarck,* pp. 61–68; K. A. Müller, "Die Entlassung," pp. 141–142; William II, *The Kaiser's Memoirs* (New York, 1922), pp. 35–36.

man, perhaps, had dominated unopposed for too long. With his advanced age he seemed to have lost his flexibility, his control. In the succeeding days he tried to make up for his crudity. He resigned from the Ministry of Commerce and suggested Berlepsch as his successor. He allowed the Kaiser to issue two proclamations announcing reforms in the labor question and inviting the European Powers to an international conference on the subject in Berlin. He even announced in various quarters that he intended to resign as minister-president of Prussia, and to keep only his office as chancellor, so as not to interfere with the Kaiser's reform plans.

All these steps, however, were mere tactical maneuvers; Bismarck had in no way given up his basic opposition to William II's social reforms nor his determination to remain in power. "The social question cannot be settled with rosewater; for that blood and iron are necessary," he told the Saxon ambassador.[32] He deliberately withheld his constitutionally necessary countersignature from the Kaiser's proclamations, and secretly tried to influence foreign governments to refuse the Kaiser's invitation to the international conference. His talk of resignation was calculated to raise protests and support for himself among the ministers, the general public, and foreign governments, which, however, much to his anger, it quite failed to do. Nor did he succeed in sabotaging the Kaiser's international labor conference. Rightly or wrongly, people were more favorable to the young ruler than to the old. The net effect of these maneuvers was to make William II lose all his confidence in Bismarck and to harden his resolve to get rid of him completely. In particular, Bismarck's intrigues against him with foreign ambassadors seemed to the Kaiser, with justice, an outright attack by the old man before all Europe on the prestige and integrity of the German crown.[33]

In the midst of these critical days occurred the election of February 20, 1890. For Bismarck's Kartell parties it had been an extremely difficult campaign. Since 1887 the Kartell Reichstag had accomplished little that was popular. Voters in the cities were especially resentful over the rise in the grain tariff and the consequent rise in the prices of bread and meat, and over the tax on

[32]Hubert Richter, ed., "Aus Kritischen Tagen," *Deutsche Rundschau* (Berlin), 190:156 (1922).
[33]Eyck, *Bismarck*, III, 573–579; Ziekursch, *Geschichte*, II, 438–449; Hans Herzfeld, *Johannes v. Miquel* (Detmold, 1928), II, 160–161; K. A. Müller, "Die Entlassung," pp. 142–152; *Documents Diplomatiques Français*, 1 ser., VII, 598–599, 603–606; 609–610, 616–618 (hereafter cited as *DDF*); Zechlin, *Staatsstreichpläne*, pp. 30–31; Richter, "Aus Kritischen Tagen," pp. 157–163.

liquor, measures for which the Kartell was responsible. The cost of living had increased, and the increase in the grain tariff made the Kartell especially vulnerable on this point. Also, the fiasco in the Reichstag over the fall of the anti-Socialist law suggested that the National Liberals and Conservatives were far from united. The Kaiser's labor proclamations had added to the confusion. They had created a real sensation in Germany, but had given joy mostly to the opposition parties — Radicals, Center, and Social Democrats. The reforms announced therein were clearly contrary to the policies both of the Kartell parties and of Bismarck. The obvious difference between Kaiser and chancellor in this matter made a positive campaign extremely difficult, especially for the Bismarckian "middle parties," the National Liberals and Free Conservatives. And, in addition, the electorate was conscious of having been intimidated in 1887.

The result was overwhelming and disastrous. The opposition, Center, Radicals, and Social Democrats, had banded together at the polls as a sort of anti-Kartell. Out of an approximate total of seven million votes cast, four and one half million — some 64 per cent — were cast for the opposition, against the Kartell and against Bismarck. Out of a total of 397 seats in the Reichstag the three Kartell parties dropped from 220 to 135. The Conservatives lost the least, falling from 80 to 73. The "middle parties," however, the Free Conservatives and the National Liberals, fell from 41 to 20 and 99 to 42 seats respectively. On the opposition side the Center gained 8 seats, bringing its total representation to 106, the largest single party in the Reichstag. The Radicals jumped from 32 seats to 66. The most impressive gain, however, was that of the Social Democrats, who, in spite of Bismarck's anti-Socialist law, raised themselves from 11 seats to 35 and increased their popular vote from 763,000 in 1887 to 1,427,000 in 1890, the largest number of votes polled by any party and, under the circumstances, as great a victory for this "outlawed" party as it was a defeat for the man who had outlawed it.[34]

If the German Reich had had a parliamentary form of government, Bismarck would have been compelled to resign his office at once in the face of such an overwhelming rejection of his policies by the electorate. But Germany's "constitutional" government was only

[34]For the 1890 election see Ziekursch, *Geschichte*, II, 442–443; Herzfeld, *Miquel*, II, 171–174; Fritz Hellwig, *Carl Ferdinand Freiherr v. Stumm-Halberg* (Heidelberg, 1936), pp. 408–409; Bergsträsser, *Geschichte*, p. 116; *Preussische Jahrbücher* (Berlin), 65:237–243, 346–351 (1890), hereafter cited as *Pr. Jbb.*, *Deutsche Rundschau*, 62:465–468 (1890), and 63:143; *The Times* (London), wkly. ed., February 28, 1890, pp. 1, 14; March 7, p. 12.

semiparliamentary; Bismarck's position did not depend upon the Reichstag alone. As long as he possessed the confidence of the Kaiser and king he could continue to rule. In the sixties he had successfully defied the Prussian Landtag and, with the support of King William I, had ruled — unconstitutionally, to be sure — for four years. He could do so again, if necessary.

The 1890 election, indeed, seemed to demonstrate the soundness of his own thinking during the winter as to the severity of the internal crisis and the immediate necessity for a new program of repression. He had originally granted universal suffrage to the Reichstag because he was concerned with the centrifugal particularistic tendencies of the federal states. He had been thinking of the past, and of the weakness and pettiness of the old German Confederation. The representatives of the nation would be content to follow his lead. But the Reichstag had turned out quite differently. The political parties which had arisen were more interested in following their own inclinations than in supporting what he, Bismarck, thought best for Germany. The tables had been turned: it was the Reichstag and universal suffrage which were now the threat and the federal states, rather, a support.

The only answer would be to change the suffrage. The 1871 constitution had been agreed to by the federal princes; they could, therefore, also agree to dissolve it. Then a new Reich and a new constitution could be created. With this oppositional Reichstag it would be easy to bring the situation to a head. Bismarck would introduce one or two severe measures which would be rejected; then the Reichstag would be dissolved, followed by a new election, another dissolution, perhaps several; it would be dangerous, but the sooner the crisis the stronger the government relatively, and the less bloodshed. It would be 1862 over again; once more he would defend the prerogative of the crown against the people, and once more, in the process, tie a second, younger — and inexperienced — William irretrievably to the continued necessity of Bismarckian rule. In the past year he had analyzed the situation correctly; this election, which seemed such a repudiation of his power, could very conceivably become just the necessary element for its continuation.[35]

[35]See especially Zechlin, *Staatsstreichpläne*, pp. 26–27, 35–67, and the minutes of the meeting of the Prussian State Ministry, March 2, 1890, in "Anlage 4," pp. 178–184; Ziekursch, *Geschichte*, II, 443, III, 3; Eyck, *Bismarck*, III, 580–582; Hugo, Graf Lerchenfeld-Koefering, *Erinnerungen und Denkwürdigkeiten* (Berlin, 1935), p. 240; K. A. Müller, "Die Entlassung," p. 172. Cf. Wippermann, 6(I):344, 346, 347; Taylor, *Bismarck*, p. 242.

The <u>1890</u> election had also impressed other persons in governmental circles. "The result of the election is worse than anyone expected," noted General Waldersee in his diary. "The Kartell has been blown up . . . We stand before an important turning point." [36] The defeat of the Kartell had been an especially hard blow for William II. In spite of his speeches, his proclamations, and his efforts to better the working conditions of the laboring classes, they had voted even more heavily for the enemies of the Reich, the Social Democrats. When the clever old chancellor, therefore, in an interview with William II on February 25 expressed doubt that the Kaiser would be strong enough to order extreme measures if the new situation eventually made them necessary, the Kaiser assured him emphatically to the contrary. In case of need, he would not flinch at anything.

Bismarck was the more able to persuade William II to adopt a strong policy because the new Reichstag seemed hardly likely to approve the huge increase in the army which the Kaiser had long had close to his heart. A bill had already been prepared authorizing an increase of 80,000 men — twice as large as that provided for in the 1887 bill. Bismarck now suggested that this army bill be introduced immediately to the new Reichstag, as well as a more severe anti-Socialist law. To this provocative program the Kaiser agreed, only with the condition that his labor-reform bill be introduced first. With the assured adoption by the Kaiser of his "conflict program" Bismarck could regard the labor bill as a comparatively minor concession, and readily assented. The reforms might come first, but then would come the two sure-fire issues of socialism and national defense and the inevitable battle with the Reichstag. After this there could be no turning back: "No surrender!" said Bismarck, closing the interview. To this battle cry the Kaiser seemed to agree. Bismarck went away believing that he had at last regained the Kaiser's support. Actually William II had long since not only lost all confidence in Bismarck's advice but also had ceased to regard his ideas seriously. By now he was merely humoring the old man. [37]

Habitually Bismarck had always liked to have at least two strings

[36] Waldersee, *Denkwürdigkeiten*, II, 106.

[37] Zechlin, *Staatsstreichpläne*, pp. 32–34; Eyck, *Bismarck*, III, 582; Ziekursch, *Geschichte*, II, 443–444; Waldersee, *Denkwürdigkeiten*, II, 106; K. A. Müller, "Die Entlassung," p. 154. Cf. the Kaiser's curious account to Emperor Francis Joseph, *Österr. Rdsch.*, 58:104; also Bill Bismarck's letter to Holstein, March 2, 1890, *The Holstein Papers*, ed. N. Rich and M. H. Fisher (Cambridge, 1955–), *Correspondence*.

to his bow. Forceful measures against the Reichstag might, after all, not be necessary. Through his "official press" he began sounding out the possibility of an alignment of the Conservatives with the Center party. At the same time he set about strengthening his position in the ministry by unearthing an old Cabinet Order of 1852, from the days of Frederick William IV, which specified that all business between ministers and king must be authorized by the minister-president.[38] Meanwhile, in the attention of the Kaiser the chancellor's influence had been effectively supplanted by the influence of a group of assorted advisers, all of whom warned urgently and incessantly against accepting a policy of conflict and crisis at this time. There was the Kaiser's uncle, the liberal-minded Grand Duke Frederick of Baden; there was the elderly and politically experienced National Liberal leader, Johannes Miquel; there was the chief of the general staff, the ambitious Count von Waldersee; there was the Kaiser's dear friend, Count Philipp zu Eulenburg; finally, there was the solitary and obscure old genius in the Foreign Office, Geheimrat (Privy Councillor) von Holstein. Some of them acted from personal ambition, almost all of them from patriotism. They were afraid that in the struggle to retain his power Bismarck might destroy his own handiwork. The Reich must be protected against its creator. For various reasons they all agreed (and collaborated toward this purpose) in warning William II that accepting a program of possible conflict with the Reichstag was not only dangerous in itself, but would mean placing himself irretrievably in Bismarck's hands, so that thereafter he would never be able to get rid of the domineering old man.[39]

Under the working of his own constitution it was not a complete disaster for Bismarck that, at the end of February 1890, he had lost the support of the nation, the political parties, and the ministers. Ultimately the one essential element for his rule was the confidence of the emperor-king. This he now thought he had secured, but in that he was mistaken. William II had neither the intention nor the capacity to swim against the stream. On March 4, after being advised by the Conservative leader von Helldorff that the Kartell parties were not in favor of such a bill, William II ordered Bismarck

[38] *Schulthess* (1890), p. 29; Eyck, *Bismarck*, III, 585.

[39] K. A. Müller, "Die Entlassung," p. 155; Herzfeld, *Miquel*, II, 172, 182–185; Waldersee, *Denkwürdigkeiten*, II, 113–114, and *Aus dem Briefwechsel des General-Feldmarschalls Alfred Grafen von Waldersee*, ed. H. O. Meissner (Berlin, 1928), *passim;* Kiderlen to Holstein, July 19, 1890, *Holstein Papers, Correspondence;* Zechlin, *Staatsstreichpläne*, pp. 71–76; Eyck, *Bismarck*, III, 597.

to abandon all thought of introducing an anti-Socialist law to the new Reichstag. To his great astonishment Bismarck immediately assented. What did it matter; there was still the projected big new army bill. But the Kaiser was now convinced that Bismarck was not holding to any consistent policy, only trying to remain in office at all costs.[40] His general excitement at this time and his specific reaction against the pressure which Bismarck was exerting on the ministers through the Order of 1852 is well illustrated by the following passage from a speech on March 5 to the Provincial Assembly (*Landstände*) of Brandenburg:

Just as [My grandfather] believed, so do I believe, and regard the people and country passed on to Me as a talent entrusted to Me by God which — as it says in the Bible — it is My duty to increase and for which I shall have to render an account . . . Those who wish to assist Me in this are heartily welcome, whoever they may be; those, however, who oppose Me in this work I will crush [*zerschmettern*]."

As Eyck remarks, "that this boasting by an untried young beginner did not turn all sympathy again toward the old statesman who could point to achievements of historic [*welthistorische*] importance, shows how very tired people were of his domination." [41]

Things now began to move more quickly. The old man sensed the presence of influences around the Kaiser hostile to himself. He suspected Bötticher, wrongly, and denounced him to the Kaiser, whereupon William II on March 9 bestowed upon Bötticher the Order of the Black Eagle, a most distinguished Prussian decoration commonly bestowed upon royalty. On March 12 Bismarck had a long but unprofitable conversation with his old enemy, the Center party leader, Ludwig Windthorst, from which the latter came away remarking, "I come from the political death bed of a great man." Friday evening, March 14, the Kaiser talked again with von Helldorff, who urged him to give up the army bill and denounced Bismarck's attempts to align the Conservative party with the Center.[42]

On Saturday morning, March 15, came the dramatic denouement. At nine o'clock the seventy-four-year-old Bismarck was awakened with the news that the Kaiser was awaiting him in the foreign secretary's villa in the garden at the rear of the chancellor's

[40]Zechlin, *Staatsstreichpläne*, p. 70; William II to Francis Joseph, *Österr. Rdsch.*, 58:104.
[41]Eyck, *Bismarck*, III, 586; *Schulthess* (1890), p. 34.
[42]Ziekursch, *Geschichte*, II, 446; Zechlin, *Staatsstreichpläne*, pp. 35–36, 77.

palace. The official notification of this audience had somehow failed to reach him the night before. Hurriedly he got out of bed, dressed, and walked across the garden to Herbert's villa. The Kaiser had come to tell Bismarck that he had changed his mind on the army bill, had decided to hold it down to proportions moderate enough to be acceptable to the new Reichstag. And he did announce this change of policy during the interview, "in the course of the conversation." But most of the interview was taken up by a heavy and blustering attack by the Kaiser on Bismarck's dealings with Windthorst and on the Order of 1852, which he demanded be repealed. How dared he make secret deals with an oppositional leader without the Kaiser's knowledge? If all business had to be transacted through the chancellor, how was this possible when Bismarck spent most of the year at Friedrichsruh? By concentrating on these subordinate issues William II spared himself the embarrassment of acknowledging how completely, first with the anti-Socialist law and now with the army bill, he had departed from Bismarck's "no surrender" policy. It was a tense scene, the old man and the young both angry, both losing control of their strained emotions. Bismarck finally went so far as to show the Kaiser a diplomatic report which stated that the tsar had called him "an ill-bred and dishonest boy [un garçon mal élevé et de mauvaise foi]." They parted coldly. What followed was anticlimax.[43]

Bismarck waited stubbornly and did nothing. The Kaiser, on the other hand, found waiting impossible; he sent various emissaries three times to Bismarck on March 16 and 17, requesting either repeal of the 1852 Order or his resignation. Finally, on the 17th, on the basis of reports of Russian armaments received from the Foreign Office, William II sent an excited note to Bismarck: "You ought to have drawn my attention long ago to the terrible danger threatening! It is more than high time to warn the Austrians and to take countermeasures." The old man's patience had borne fruit. He immediately started reports circulating in the Foreign Office and the ministry that he was resigning because he opposed the Kaiser's war plans against Russia. On the 18th he sent in his resignation, a long, carefully worded document dealing exclusively with the Order of 1852 and the issue of foreign policy, on which points he was able to present a very strong case. The resignation was obviously written

[43]Cf. especially Zechlin, *Staatsstreichpläne*, pp. 77–79; Eyck, *Bismarck*, III, 589–592; Bismarck's version in *Kaiser vs. Bismarck*, pp. 97–104; the Kaiser's version in K. F. Nowak, *Kaiser and Chancellor* (London, 1930), pp. 204–208; Eulenburg, *Aus 50 Jahren*, pp. 233–235; Prince Chlodwig zu Hohenlohe-Schillingsfürst, *Memoirs*, trans. George W. Chrystal (New York, 1906), II, 424.

for publication, and in it the old master "with all of his practiced skill told the Kaiser the strongest things in the most forceful way, yet without in any way violating the customary respectful phraseology." He had long since lost the battle, but intended to go down fighting.[44]

On March 20 Bismarck received the Kaiser's letter graciously accepting his resignation, which was published that evening in the official *Reichsanzeiger*. It ran as follows:

> With deep emotion I have perceived, from your request of 18th inst., that you are determined to retire from the offices which you have filled for many years with incomparable results. I had hoped that I should not be obliged to consider more closely the idea of parting with you in our lifetime. If I am nonetheless compelled, in the full consciousness of the grievous importance of your retirement, to accustom myself to this idea, I do it indeed with an afflicted heart, but in the confident expectation that the granting of your request will contribute toward sparing and preserving your life — irreplaceable to the Fatherland — and your energies, as long as possible. The motives of your resolve which you have put forward convince me that further attempts to persuade you to take back your offer would have no prospect of success. I therefore respond to your wish, in that I herewith grant you the requested discharge from your offices, etc.

The Kaiser then referred pointedly to "your wise and energetic peace policy, which I, too, am resolved, in future and out of complete conviction, to make the pattern of my own dealings." Thus, even in the act of finally severing their official connection he was once again forced to defend himself against the tenacious old man.[45]

For Bismarck himself it was difficult to believe that this was really the end. After so many great conquests it was bewildering that he could now be so easily and ignominiously defeated. It was a tragic moment, fully appreciated at the time only by himself. "Without the support of the Kaiser, without the support of his ministerial colleagues, the political parties and public opinion, Bismarck stood there, abandoned, completely isolated." [46] If he had had the nation — the Reichstag — behind him he could have confidently outmaneuvered William II as he had prepared to do with his father in

[44]Eyck, *Bismarck*, III, 595, 592–594; for Bismarck's own account see Bismarck, *Kaiser vs. Bismarck*, pp. 105–117, including the texts of the Kaiser's note of the 17th and Bismarck's letter of resignation. A brief and revealing summary of the whole crisis by the Kaiser is in J. M. E. Radowitz, *Aufzeichnungen und Erinnerungen*, ed. H. Holborn (Stuttgart, 1925), II, 316–317.

[45]Bismarck, *Kaiser vs. Bismarck*, pp. 120–121; DDF, 1 ser., VIII, 7.

[46]Ziekursch, *Geschichte*, II, 446. On Bismarck's isolation see Holstein's very interesting letter to Herbert Bismarck, January 24, 1890, *Holstein Papers, Correspondence*.

1887–1888; if he had had the Kaiser completely behind him he could have defied the Reichstag. But both the Kaiser and the nation had gone against him. He could not possibly have continued in power. History had played him false.

This German Reich was his handiwork; he had built it up; he had made the people believe in it, be loyal to it. But it had been his plaything. Behind the brave impressive façade he had manipulated the levers, pulled the strings. The officials, the generals, the ministers — yes, the Kaiser — were only puppets; he had made them dance. Now something had gone wrong. The show went on, but he himself, the master, had somehow become only a part of the act. It was his own magic that worked against him now, that made it appear that this puppet show was real, and he only an old villain to be quickly dispatched and dragged off the stage. It was a spell which rendered him powerless, and which he could not break.

When Bismarck came back from his farewell visit to the Kaiser on March 26 and again on his departure from Berlin, March 29, he was enthusiastically acclaimed by crowds of patriotic Germans along the way. When, during the same days, William II rode out on the street, he was enthusiastically acclaimed by crowds of patriotic Germans along the way. On March 18 the *Frankfurter Zeitung* editorialized: "The Bismarckian System falls; it withers before the fresh reality of a new age." [47]

[47] Eyck, *Bismarck*, III, 596–597; Hohenlohe, *Memoirs*, II, 424; K. A. Müller, "Die Entlassung," pp. 168, 170–173; *DDF*, 1 ser., VIII, 17; Lerchenfeld, *Denkwürdigkeiten*, p. 351; *The Times*, wkly. ed., March 21, 1890, p. 10; *Frankfurter Zeitung* article quoted by K. A. Müller, p. 176. Cf. *Pr. Jbb.*, 65:465; William II to Francis Joseph, *Österr. Rdsch.*, 58:104ff.

PART ONE
THE NEW COURSE

Chapter II
PERSONALITIES AND POLICIES

But where is the line between the independence and the obedience of a minister? With us a minister cannot support himself upon a parliamentary majority. . . . The minister must continually consider with himself whether, according to his own convictions, he is in a position to comply with the intentions and commands of the monarch, or whether the differences are so small that he can overlook them. . . . A thousand considerations of policies and personalities are perpetually in play. Who may say where steadfastness of character ends and simple obstinacy begins? . . . In our state, as paradoxical as it may sound, the relationship of the king to the minister is one of continual, inner conflict with each other.

Preussische Jahrbücher, January 1891

1

CAPRIVI: THE MAN AND THE SITUATION

To succeed Bismarck as chancellor of the German Reich and minister-president of Prussia William II appointed a Prussian general, Georg Leo von Caprivi, commander of the Tenth Army Corps in Hanover. Born on February 24, 1831, in Charlottenburg, near Berlin, von Caprivi was descended from a family of apparently Italian or Slavic origin, stemming from the old Austrian province of Carniola; the name appears originally to have been Kopriva.[1] In the seventeenth century his ancestors had become knights of the empire and Hungarian barons. They had also moved at that time into

[1] The supposed connection, much bruited about in 1890, with the famous Italian families of Caprarra and Montecuculi is not substantiated and was not taken seriously by Caprivi himself; cf. Alexander Meyer's article in *Biographisches Jahrbuch* (Berlin, 1897–1917), IV, 3; *Memoirs of Francesco Crispi* (London, 1912–1914), II, 432. For a thorough genealogy, see E. Schreck, *Reichskanzler Graf Leo von Caprivi* (Düsseldorf, 1891), pp. 7–12.

Silesia. In the following century, when Prussia took Silesia, the name had been changed to von Caprivi, and the family had since served the state with a long line of Prussian officers and officials. The most recent in the line, Caprivi's father, Julius, had been a judge and a member of the Prussian House of Lords. In the years of repression after the 1848 Revolution Julius von Caprivi had made himself particularly respected by his energy in trying political cases.

In 1848 young Leo Caprivi, seventeen and studying in a Berlin gymnasium, had taken very little interest in the local school clashes between "democrats" and "reactionaries." Politics, as such, apparently did not interest him. Faithful to old family and Prussian traditions he chose a military career and enlisted in the army in 1849. Commissioned a second lieutenant in 1850, he spent a few years in military school and began a process of steady advancement in position and rank. In the war of 1866 against Austria he served as major on the staff of the First Army under Prince Friedrich Karl. When the war against France broke out in 1870 he was a lieutenant-colonel and chief of staff of the Tenth Army Corps. In this position he particularly distinguished himself in the battle of Vionville before Metz and later at the battle of Beaune-la-Rolande, emerging from the war with the Iron Cross and Order of Merit. In the postwar period Caprivi continued his steady advancement, and, by 1882, had arrived at the rank of lieutenant-general, commanding a division at Metz. At this point he was unexpectedly made a vice-admiral and placed at the head of the navy, succeeding General von Stosch.

The German navy, then in its infancy and generally lacking in trained personnel, was still under the care of army men. For General von Caprivi personally, this precipitate transfer to a strange position which he did not desire was strikingly prophetic. He had neither knowledge of nor interest in naval affairs, did not even know the uniforms or the ranks of the officers. But, adhering faithfully to his duty, he threw himself into the work with great energy, and in a short time accomplished much. Caprivi found the navy with no over-all strategic idea and no tactical experience. He at once laid down the general concept of a two-front war with France and Russia, in which the navy's task would be to defend the coast. Since he considered this war to be imminent, there was no time for extensive building of large ships, and he hit upon the torpedo boat as the perfect instrument for coast defense. He pushed this torpedo-boat program so hard that Germany was soon supreme among the powers in this line. He also drew up a plan of mobilization and tried, with some success, to build a strong officers' corps, and to inspire it with greater discipline and morale.

Caprivi's naval career ended as abruptly as it had begun when, in 1888, the new Kaiser William II went over Caprivi's head and consulted directly with the chief of the shipbuilding section. The Kaiser's disregard of old Prussian traditions of protocol, along with Caprivi's general distrust of the special naval ambitions of the domineering new master caused Caprivi promptly to hand in his resignation. He was then, in July 1888, appointed general in command of the Tenth Army Corps in Hanover, his old outfit of 1870.[2]

Physically, Caprivi was a tall, strikingly military figure, "a typical Teuton of the hugest and most impressive type," wrote *The Times* of London. "He might very well pass for a brother or even a double, of Prince Bismarck himself. . . . In point, indeed, of stature and breadth of shoulders General von Caprivi even has the advantage of the man he is going to succeed. . . . A difference in the character of the two men might by some be discerned in their walk, for while Prince Bismarck treads sharply and heavily, like a trooper, the gait of General von Caprivi has something in it of deliberation and leisurely elegance, while not lacking either in verve or emphasis. He is a good enough speaker, but a brief one, and when at the head of the Admiralty he never failed, from his place on the Federal Council bench in the Reichstag, to put his case clearly and well." [3]

Caprivi at fifty-nine was white-haired, with a rather round head, short firm nose, widely spaced, clear, penetrating eyes, sweeping mustache, and strongly cleft chin. His hands were small and fine, his movements quiet and precise. In manner he was invariably friendly, frank, and open. He was a man of great self-discipline and devotion to duty, yet sociable, with a strong sense of humor usually running

---

[2]*Biographisches Jahrbuch*, IV, 3–14; *Allgemeine Deutsche Biographie* (Leipzig, 1875–1912), XLVII, 445–449, by B. von Poten; A. von Tirpitz, *My Memoirs* (New York, 1919), pp. 36–40, 54–55, 58–59; E. Kehr, "Schlachtflottenbau und Parteipolitik," *Historische Studien*, 197:257 (1930); William II, *The Kaiser's Memoirs*, pp. 51–53; Francis Joseph to William II, *Österr. Rdsch.*, 58:108; August Keim, *Erlebtes und Erstrebtes* (Hanover, 1925), p. 51; Waldersee, *Denkwürdigkeiten*, II, 4; Dr. von Schulte, "Erinnerungen an Graf Caprivi," *Deutsche Revue*, 24(II):230 (1899); Schreck, *Caprivi*, pp. 53–54, 59, 60.

There was also some court intrigue against Caprivi at this time: cf. Radolin to Holstein, February 12, 1888, A. v. Seckendorff to Prince Henry, December 25, 1887, Radolin to Holstein, March 2, 1888, Holstein to Radolin, March 5, 1888, *Holstein Papers, Correspondence*. The Kaiser's letter to Caprivi, July 5, 1888, is in Caprivi Papers, Hauptarchiv, Berlin; also letter of Prince Henry, February 25, 1892.

[3]Wkly. ed., March 21, 1890, p. 4.

to irony. He had no personal enemies, yet few close friends. He was unmarried, did not smoke, and generally lived a life of Spartan simplicity, dedicated to duty, a model of the old Prussian officer. He was very well read, especially in history, and spoke both English and French fluently. "With the sharp intellect, which was peculiar to the lawyer's son, and with his unusual industry he could quickly comprehend everything new and acquaint himself thoroughly with every problem." [4]

Caprivi had no independent income, and, as chancellor, insisted on spending all of his salary of 58,000 M for dinners and receptions. When, later, his enemies were propagating the rumor that he had lost 400,000 M through the fall of a banking firm, having received the money originally from a questionable source, Caprivi sent the following note to Hammann, chief of the Press Bureau of the Foreign Office:

B.[erlin] 17./6.

I should like

1. To establish publicly that this story of the 400,000 M. which is being systematically disseminated, is completely false; I have at no time had either wealth or any sort of connection with the banker Wolff. I am without property in the fullest sense of the word, having "stolen nothing and inherited nothing" [*niemand beraubt und niemand beerbt*].
2. To brand the perfidy of the editorial staff of the Farmers' League, who serve up lies to their readers to make me appear in a bad light and in bad company.

I believe it would be best to reply briefly and strongly in the *Norddeutsche*. Perhaps you would be so good as to draft a few words.

Moreover I authorize you to say, if you wish, that, since I was a captain, I have lived on my pay, have paid for all my horses out of my pay, and am proud to have managed as a poor officer decently to make ends meet.

v. C.[5]

There is a story that when Caprivi was walking by the brightly lighted Chancellor's Palace one evening, he turned to his companion and exclaimed, "What kind of a jackass will dare to be Bismarck's successor?!" One can, therefore, well imagine the general's frame of mind when, on February 1, 1890, he answered the Kaiser's summons

---

[4]Otto Hammann, *Der Neue Kurs* (Berlin, 1918), p. 105. See also Keim, *Erlebtes und Erstrebtes;* Hohenlohe, *Memoirs;* Lerchenfeld, *Erinnerungen, passim;* and the summary in Dr. Rudolf Stadelmann's thoughtful study, "Der neue Kurs in Deutschland," *Geschichte in Wissenschaft und Unterricht,* IV (September 1953), 538–564.

[5]Hammann, *Der Neue Kurs,* p. 106.

to Berlin only to have William II announce that he was considering him, Caprivi, to succeed Bismarck. Bismarck, said the Kaiser, was becoming old and infirm. To which Caprivi answered that Bismarck dead and borne before him like The Cid would be of more use to the Kaiser than he, Caprivi, alive.[6]

Caprivi then heard no more of the matter and had decided that the Kaiser had given up the idea, when, on March 18, the Kaiser announced to the commanding generals Caprivi's succession as chancellor and minister-president. One more evening with his soldiers in Hanover ended his military career. As he took leave of his officers he told them, as he later wrote, "with how heavy a heart I entered my new office and said to them — they remember it yet — that I knew that I should be smeared with mud, that I should fall ingloriously, but I wanted to try to satisfy the Kaiser's wish, and that I consoled myself that — whatever happened to me — they, my comrades, would never give up the belief that I was still a decent fellow." [7] Great men, when they pass, leave a vacuum. And next to their greatness, their majesty, the normal men who follow appear smaller still. For himself Caprivi knew what it would mean to follow Bismarck. He had no illusions. But he was a Prussian general and knew his duty to his king. "Right or wrong, Bismarck had to be followed by another chancellor," he wrote four years later; "how the latter felt about it did not matter." [8]

If William II had forced the great Bismarck out of office in order "to rule alone," as Bismarck said, why did he appoint as his successor Caprivi, a man noted for his independent spirit, even stubbornness, and one who had already reacted to the Kaiser's interference in the Admiralty with a prompt resignation from office? Perhaps it was the very opposition he had experienced from Caprivi that impressed the Kaiser. Caprivi had shown strength of character in 1888. In 1890 character was what was needed.[9] At any rate, during those critical days William II was inclined to be relatively cautious. There had been only one chancellor of the Reich, who was responsible for its creation; it had never stood without him. And he had not left the chancellorship voluntarily. It was possible that, like

[6] Keim, *Erlebtes und Erstrebtes,* p. 52; Caprivi to Dr. Max Schneidewin, December 28, 1894, in Schneidewin, ed., "Briefe des toten Reischskanzlers von Caprivi," *Deutsche Revue,* 47(II):142–143 (1922).

[7] Schneidewin, "Briefe," pp. 142–143.

[8] Schneidewin, "Briefe," p. 140.

[9] Cf. below, p. 88, Francis Joseph to William II, *Österr. Rdsch.,* 58:108. Caprivi had suffered from court intrigue in 1888 (see p. 31, n. 2) and had borne no grudge. The Kaiser may have become aware of this affair and been impressed by Caprivi's correct and loyal behavior.

Samson, he might try to bring the structure down with him out of revenge. At any rate, it was no time for overconfidence. It would be well, therefore, to try to construct as strong a government as possible, one that might command respect. This being the motive, there was hardly any choice. Bismarck's personality had left little room for other independent spirits. There was no one in the administrations of Prussia or the Reich who could manage the complexities of the position or command respect. In the monarchical Reich it would be impossible to give over the leadership of the government to a party man. Nor, with the multiplicity of parties, was there any politician of sufficiently broad public following. The next most powerful agency in the Reich was the army; the chancellor had to be a general. That being the case, Caprivi was the only general of note with any political experience, "a man belonging to Prince Bismarck's generation, who had held a leading position in the wars and had already filled a government position under him." He was, wrote the Kaiser to Emperor Francis Joseph of Austria-Hungary, "after Bismarck, the greatest German we possess, truly devoted to Me, and a rock-ribbed character!" [10] Caprivi was William II's personal choice. In the matter of the succession the advisers seem to have hung back. Their general attitude was well expressed by General von Waldersee, who noted in his diary on February 14 that he had no idea whom the Kaiser had in mind to succeed Bismarck, but that "In any case, I know quite well that I should be a fool to occupy myself with thoughts of the chancellorship [Kanzler-Ideen]. I shall stick to my old plan: first at least one successor to Bismarck must discredit himself [abgewirtschaftet]; then perhaps one could be persuaded." [11]

Caprivi was generally very well received. He was associated with no party and had been on good terms with the Reichstag when chief of the Admiralty. Above all, he was known to be moderate and conciliatory. The day of his dismissal Bismarck received Caprivi with the words, "If anything can lighten for me the oppressiveness of this moment, it is the fact that you are my successor." "He was received on all sides," commented Hans Delbrück in his "Political

[10]Cf. the interesting letter of Gen. v. Stosch in Waldersee, *Briefwechsel*, pp. 335ff.; William II, *The Kaiser's Memoirs*, p. 54; *Österr. Rdsch.*, 58:107.

[11]Waldersee, *Denkwürdigkeiten*, II, 102. Cf. II, 36. There is no present evidence that Holstein prompted Caprivi's appointment, but it is possible. A short time before he had written, "If only I knew how we could manage to keep Caprivi and Rado.[lin] in Berlin as Bismarck's allies in the struggles of the coming regime." (*Holstein Papers, Diaries*, pp. 373–374). See also Caprivi's letter to Holstein of July 5, 1885, headed "Dear Patron," *Holstein Papers, Correspondence*.

Survey" of the year 1890, "with approval and confidence because of his dependable, determined character." [12] Informed circles, however, did not expect him to remain long in office. Caprivi, said Bismarck, was more difficult and obstinate than he. It would be only a few weeks, stated his son, Count Herbert Bismarck, until the first friction arose between Caprivi and the Kaiser. "I question only whether he can manage well with the Kaiser," wrote Count Waldersee. "He has very much of a will of his own and is one of those people who can stand no opposition . . . Two such different natures and stubborn dispositions [*harte Köpfe*] cannot work together. It is not Caprivi's way gradually to achieve a position of dominance [*Übergewicht*] by cleverness and cunning, he is too open and direct for that. . . ." Even Caprivi himself did not think he would remain chancellor for long.[13]

The prospect before him certainly was not encouraging. "It must be confessed," wrote *The Times*, "that it is an experiment of the most extraordinary kind to call in a military man at once to take in hand the tangled skein of European diplomacy, to grapple at home with the social and economic problems of the Prussian Monarchy, to reconstitute a working majority in the Reichstag instead of that on which Prince Bismarck leaned, and, throughout it all, to give effect to the mind and purpose of the Emperor. This is a task from which even a brave and able man might recoil. . . ." [14] In foreign affairs, Germany in 1890, when Bismarck fell, was flanked on the east by a Russia which was still trying to recoup her losses in the Balkans, and on the west by a resurgent France, still nursing her resentment over the humiliation of 1870 and the loss of Alsace-Lorraine. When the smoke had cleared away from the crisis of 1886–1888 it had become painfully apparent that Bismarck's attack on Russian securities through the Reichsbank had merely transferred them to the French market. Russia desperately needed foreign loans, and France was quite willing to lend, especially to a potential ally. Also the Mediterranean agreements, aimed at Russia and France, would necessarily operate to bring these two powers together in self-defense. To add to the critical nature of the external situation,

[12] Thimme, "Bismarck und Kardorff," pt. I, p. 53; *Schulthess* (1890), p. 320; G. Gothein, *Reichskanzler Graf Caprivi* (Munich, 1918), p. 18; cf. also Hohenlohe, *Memoirs*, II, 423; Carl, Graf v. Wedel, *Zwischen Kaiser und Kanzler* (Leipzig, 1943), p. 125; Waldersee, *Denkwürdigkeiten*, II, 103; *Deutsche Rundschau*, 63:308 (1890); press comments in Schreck, *Caprivi*, pp. 76–80.
[13] Wedel, *Zwischen Kaiser und Kanzler*, pp. 49, 45; Waldersee, *Denkwürdigkeiten*, II, 103, 119, 121; cf. also K. A. Müller, "Die Entlassung," p. 169; Ponsonby, *Letters of Empress Frederick*, pp. 411–413; *Holstein Papers, Diaries*, pp. 159–160, 162–163.
[14] Wkly. ed., March 21, 1890, p. 10.

the heavy weight of Bismarck's personal prestige had suddenly been lifted from the lid of the Pandora's box of continental rivalries. A sense of expectancy pervaded the European capitals, tinged with dread in those of the Triple Alliance and joy in those of its enemies. France, especially, began immediately to take on new confidence.[15]

On the domestic scene reigned a kind of political chaos. Abroad there was still, at least, the Triple Alliance upholding the position of the Reich. Inside the Reich, however, Bismarck's Kartell had collapsed in the election, and nothing had taken its place. The resulting chaos, moreover, was twice confounded by the duality of German parliamentary life. In Berlin, throughout the winter there normally sat not only the deputies of the nation in the Reichstag on the Leipzigerstrasse but also those of Prussia — representing two thirds of the nation — in the House of Lords, also on the Leipzigerstrasse, and in the House of Deputies on the Dönhoffsplatz. Politically the Prussian Landtag was almost as important as the Reichstag, the same major parties being represented in both. They differed basically, however, in that the Reichstag was elected by universal and equal manhood suffrage, the Prussian House of Deputies by the complicated three-class indirect suffrage, which gave more weight to property owners; there were no Social Democrats as yet in the House of Deputies. The chief party leaders frequently held seats in both houses, making important speeches today on one measure in the House of Deputies, tomorrow on another in the Reichstag. Both Reichstag and House of Deputies were now elected for five years, but whereas the Reichstag had just experienced a new election, the present House of Deputies had been elected in 1888, in the heyday of the Kartell. The political complexion of the two was, therefore, quite in contrast, as the table shows. It was obvious enough that in the Prussian Landtag the Kartell still ruled, while in the Reichstag the preponderance of power now lay with the Catholic Center party.

Besides foreign dangers and domestic party conflicts there was also the difficult question of administration and personnel. Over the years Bismarck had built up a very effective team of ministers, secretaries, and diplomats. But all these had been mere tools for carrying out his own personal will. They had been subjected beneath the weight of his autocratic genius. The sudden removal of this oppression was, to be sure, a joy to many and a relief. But there were also

---

[15]Langer, *Franco-Russian Alliance*, pp. 98–99, 119–120; *DDF*, 1 ser., VIII, 8; Radowitz, *Aufzeichnungen*, II, 312.

POLITICAL COMPOSITION OF THE PRUSSIAN LANDTAG
AND THE REICHSTAG IN 1890[a]

	Prussian Landtag	Reichstag
Conservatives	130	73
Free Conservatives	68	20
National Liberals	89	42
Kartell total	287	135
Center party	99	106
Radicals	30	66
Social Democrats		35
Others (Poles, Guelfs, Danes, Alsatians, Anti-Semites, etc.)	17	55
Total	433	397

[a]Figures for the Landtag from A. L. Lowell, *Governments and Parties in Continental Europe* (Boston, 1896), I, 307 n.; for the Reichstag from F. Specht and P. Schwabe, eds., *Die Reichstagswahlen 1867–1897* . . . (Berlin, 1898), p. 104.

fears and uncertainties. "Individuals seem to have grown larger," noted Prince Hohenlohe, on a visit to Berlin in June. "Each separate personality is now conscious of his own value . . . They have all swelled out like sponges placed in water. This has its advantages but also its dangers. There is no unity of will." [16] These Bismarckian bureaucrats were all experienced and technically proficient in their respective departments. They, however, had never borne any independent responsibility. Could they do so now?

To Germany and to the outside world, however, in 1890 the most significant fact about the change of government was the clash between the two personalities of Bismarck and Kaiser William II. The young captain of the ship had dropped the pilot. For two years William II had reigned but not ruled; would he not now also rule, and rule alone? When Caprivi had had his first audience with the Kaiser on February 1, Bismarck was toying with the idea of resigning the minister-presidency of Prussia and retaining only the position of chancellor of the Reich. Doubtless influenced thereby, William II intimated to Caprivi in this first meeting that the government would eventually be reorganized, that Caprivi would become chancellor only temporarily. After the fateful days of March it was con-

[16]Hohenlohe, *Memoirs*, II, 429; cf. S. v. Kardorff, *Wilhelm v. Kardorff* (Berlin, 1936), p. 227; J. v. Eckardt, *Aus den Tagen von Bismarcks Kampf gegen Caprivi* (Leipzig, 1920), p. 1.

fidently assumed throughout Europe that the Kaiser intended to be
his own chancellor, that, indeed, he had appointed a general to the
position merely to carry out his commands. Had not Bismarck himself revealed in the press that he had been dismissed by the Kaiser
because he had refused to repeal the Cabinet Order of 1852, subordinating the separate ministers of Prussia to the minister-president? *The Times* interpreted the Kaiser's insistence on this point to
mean that "the Emperor, with his autocratic tendencies, desires to
gather into his hands the strings of public policy. . . . The Emperor
has determined to be his own chancellor." Rumors that the state
secretaries of the Reich were to be made responsible ministers and
the chancellor merely a kind of prime minister persisted. How could
Caprivi work into this situation? His was not a nature "that subordinates himself to the will of another against his better judgment." [17]

Perhaps the most important question of all was: what would
Bismarck do now? He had been forced from power; it would be
highly unlike him to yield either submissively or gracefully. He had,
in fact, on the day he received the official acceptance of his resignation, already revealed in the press his differences with the Kaiser as
set down in his letter of resignation, as well as the violent scene
between them on March 15. "He who has been accustomed to the
lasting possession of power never learns to renounce it." If Bismarck
continued his press attacks on the Kaiser he would inevitably involve the new government in the antagonisms of their personal
quarrel. It would be at the least a nuisance and an embarrassment;
it might well become much more.[18]

In the crisis after Bismarck's fall there were really only two possible attitudes for the German people as a whole or for Caprivi.
There was the attitude of the Bismarcks and their few faithful
adherents, expressed so well in those days by Count Herbert. "It
means the dissolution of the Reich," he told Baron von Reischach
on March 20. The Reich was a fine and delicate structure which
could not stand the shock of the removal of the craftsman who
created it. No one else knew how to run it. The treaties of alliance
would hold it together for twenty years, then it would collapse.

[17] *The Times,* wkly. ed., March 7, p. 15; March 21, pp. 4, 10; April 11, pp. 1, 14;
Waldersee, *Denkwürdigkeiten,* II, 110, 119; K. A. Müller, "Die Entlassung," pp. 140–
141 note, 169.
[18] Eyck, *Bismarck,* III, ch. XIV, p. 604; the articles mentioned appeared in the
Norddeutsche Allgemeine Zeitung, March 20, 23; cf. *Schulthess* (1890), pp. 43–44,
48.

War and revolution would result. "The Kaiser," declared Herbert passionately to Philipp Eulenburg, "knows not what he does." [19] The other attitude was well expressed by Reischach's answer to Herbert: "then your father's work was a utopia!" And this neither he nor other Germans — with the exception of the Social Democrats, who were busily constructing a utopia of their own — could then possibly believe. Their very veneration of Bismarck — even those who fought him — gave them the utmost faith in the strength and solidity of his Reich. The accusation that Bismarck had molded the institutions of the Reich to fit his own personality and that his departure would be followed by anarchy had now ignominiously collapsed, wrote Hans Delbrück in the April issue of the *Preussische Jahrbücher*. Rather, he wrote solemnly, quoting Ranke, it was the "fate and the greatness of the great man through his own achievements finally to make himself dispensable. . . . So, with pain and unextinguishable gratitude in our hearts for the departing chancellor, yet we look confidently to the future: full of new struggles, new work, but not without the hope of new victories and successes . . . firm and unshaken in the belief in its future, held together by its new but already strongly established institutions, the German nation takes leave of the great Bismarck Era in order to begin a new age." [20] This optimistic tone in the press and in the parties sprang partly from confidence in the Reich Bismarck had built, partly from confidence in the young and dynamic personality of William II. To him all the parties looked expectantly. To be sure they expected diverse and even contrary things, but this was not apparent at the moment. To foreign and informed German observers, however, the extent of this optimistic feeling seemed astonishing and rather frivolous. [21]

Caprivi might not share this optimism, but it never occurred to him to question the future of the Reich. As a soldier he had fought to bring the Reich into existence; his main purpose now must be faithfully to defend it — against all enemies both external and internal. The main thing was the danger of war — a war on two fronts. Admiral von Tirpitz later wrote that every year Caprivi expected this war the next spring. [22] Although, to Caprivi, the soldier, war against Russia and France was probably inevitable, he was equally

[19] Hugo, Freiherr von Reischach, *Unter drei Kaisern* (Berlin, 1925), pp. 167–168; Eulenburg, *Aus 50 Jahren*, pp. 237–238; cf. K. A. Müller, "Die Entlassung," p. 171. Reuss to Radowitz in Radowitz, *Aufzeichnungen*, II, 312.

[20] *Pr. Jbb.*, 65:461, 466 (1890).

[21] *The Times*, wkly. ed., March 21, p. 11; Lerchenfeld, *Denkwürdigkeiten*, p. 353.

[22] Tirpitz, *Memoirs*, I, 37, 40.

aware that it would be a much more difficult affair than anyone imagined and that therefore it must be postponed as long as possible. Against the external threat one would have to maintain the outer defenses: first the diplomatic breastwork of the Triple Alliance, then the army itself. But equally important were the spirit and morale of the inner bastion, without which the outer defenses would avail nothing. A unity of patriotic purpose could, however, only be achieved by abandoning the Bismarck system, that setting of one group against another, that perpetual seeking out of "enemies of the Reich": a system which, because it had hinged upon the personal genius of the great man, could not in any case be continued. The greatest internal danger threatening was socialism; against this threat the other factions in the state must be encouraged to unite. Support of the government would be made easier by a necessary abandonment of Bismarck's somewhat questionable and heavy-handed methods. Bismarck's removal was a great shock to the Reich; a period of calm and rallying of forces must necessarily follow. The appeal must be for conciliation, confidence in the government, and devotion to the nation. Both at home and abroad the government's policies, therefore, must be, above all, clear and simple.[23]

In December 1894, two months after his resignation as chancellor became effective, Caprivi wrote retrospectively regarding the tasks of his administration as follows:

I have often been astonished that, among political thinkers, especially among the National Liberals, the conviction does not make headway, that — with the fullest recognition of Bismarck's greatness and achievements — nevertheless one could not continue to rule in aeternum with his methods. That the one to whom it fell to accomplish the shift onto a different track would suffer for it was clear but did not detract from the necessity of undertaking it. I value Carlyle's "On Heroes and Hero Worship" [English in text] and fully agree with it, [and] also, as a soldier, have always acted in this sense: that one should not operate on heroes with critical shears; one should let them appear as great as possible for the advantage and benefit of the nation. Yet the mere circumstance that one thing does not suit everyone must lead to the realization, that even if in the government heroes followed upon heroes, a change in means and in methods would from time to time be unavoidable. And, indeed, it surely cannot be maintained that Prince Bismarck's manner of governing was completely unobjectionable. I believe, on the contrary, that a change had to come. By unscrupulously carrying over methods permissible in foreign affairs into domestic affairs, by training our old, good civil service,

[23]Caprivi's speech to the Bundesrat, March 27, K. A. Müller, "Die Entlassung," p. 170; also Lerchenfeld's report of March 30, ibid., pp. 173–174.

already injured by parliamentarism, to servility, by taking all opposition personally and humbling or removing the protagonists [*Charaktere*] he caused damage which could be outweighed by his greatness, but which will produce after-effects for a long time. The sober self-reliance of the nation, which looked to him for everything, was weakened by him to such an extent that finally it took such phrases as "it feared nothing but God," at their face value. . . . In my opinion the successor [to Bismarck] — even if his capabilities had been greater — had to strive to give the nation back its self-esteem [*Bewusstsein*]: one must get along, indeed, with average — or if you prefer, with normal people, and we must demand that the government present to the nation an example of faithful performance of duty, of veracity, of incorruptibility by influences of all kinds, of disinterestedness.

If, during about the first decade after Bismarck, this effort found recognition among the most vital part of the nation, then the attainable was attained; the government had not played a pleasant rôle, but would, I believe, have been entitled to gratitude.[24]

For Caprivi, having such concepts was one thing, putting them into practice another. Fundamentally, it all hinged upon his relationship with the Kaiser. This personal relationship, he felt certain, would be the most difficult part of his task. But, the confidence of the crown once gained, the rest could be worked out. He must try hard to get on with the Kaiser, to be indulgent, even compliant in small things, not to try to impose his will or to harass him with too frequent audiences, but to rest upon his dignity, give his advice calmly and simply, with the emphasis on facts and practicality, not emotions. As chancellor he was responsible to the Kaiser, but he was also, above all, responsible to his own conception of what would best serve the Reich and the crown. With his strong sense of duty, Caprivi took this responsibility very seriously. He doubted, however, that he could handle the Kaiser alone. Everywhere in the administration one felt the absence of Bismarck. No one person, as chancellor, could fill the gap left by his great personality. Perhaps a substitute might be found by trying to build up a spirit of responsibility within the Prussian Ministry. The minister-president was, constitutionally, only the chairman of the ministry, with no over-all responsibility. Under Bismarck, however, the ministers had actually been reduced to little more than secretaries. At the time of the crisis, they had handed in their resignations in a body to give the Kaiser a free hand; these, however, had been refused. The Kaiser and his new government needed all the help they could get to keep things going,

[24]Schneidewin, "Briefe," p. 142.

and the ministers, personally, had for the most part been loyal to the Kaiser during the crisis. Since Caprivi lacked Bismarck's prestige and experience, the ministers must now necessarily become more independent. By encouraging their independence and enhancing their dignity, however, Caprivi could try to produce a spirit of coöperation and solidarity which would be a "greater substitute for the *single* personality of Bismarck" and a heavier counterweight to "sudden decisions" of the Kaiser than Caprivi himself.[25]

Yet, in the final analysis, if there was to be any unity in the government at all, any solidarity, the minister-president — particularly since he was also chancellor of the Reich — must have some general, over-all authority of coördination and surveillance. For this reason King Frederick William IV had issued his Cabinet Order of 1852, and for this reason Bismarck had latterly felt it necessary to revive it. In the crucial days of mid-March, however, William II had demanded its repeal. On April 14, therefore, came a new Cabinet Order, countersigned by Caprivi, repealing the one of 1852 in the following manner:

Whereas the application of the decree of His late Majesty, King Frederick William IV of September 8, 1852, concerning the relationship of the president of My State Ministry to the members of the latter has given occasion for uncertainty, I, therefore, in repealing this decree, declare the following:

It is the duty of the president of My State Ministry to attend to the uniform and equal execution of the principles indicated by Me as decisive for the conduct of the entire state administration. To ensure the fulfillment of this task it is necessary that the heads of departments, concerning all measures which comprise a deviation from these principles or which are of fundamental importance, obtain My decision only after prior agreement with the president of My State Ministry.

In case of differences of opinion the report to be rendered to Me shall be presented jointly with the latter. . . .

The words of this new order were, indeed, different, but the content agreed almost exactly with the stipulations of the 1852 order and, furthermore, with Bismarck's well-reasoned defense of the

[25] K. A. Müller, "Die Entlassung," pp. 173–174; Wedel, *Zwischen Kaiser und Kanzler*, p. 78; Schneidewin, "Briefe," p. 146; Marie Radziwill, *Une grande dame d'avant guerre. Lettres de la Princesse Radziwill au Général de Robilant, 1889–1914* (Bologna, 1933–1934), I, 31; cf. also Caprivi's speech of April 15, for which see below, pp. 43–44; R. Freiherr Lucius von Ballhausen, *Bismarck Erinnerungen* (Stuttgart, 1921), pp. 523–524; T. Barth, "Caprivi," *Politische Porträts* (Berlin, 1904), p. 36. On Caprivi's relations with the Kaiser see below, Chapter VI, section 2, Chapter IX, sections 1 and 3.

latter in his letter of resignation. While soothing the royal feelings by repeal of the Order of 1852, Caprivi had, in effect, retained it. That this was done with the Kaiser's cheerful consent demonstrated anew of how little actual importance this issue had been in the previous crisis.[26]

In handling the Kaiser there was also the factor, for the moment favorable, that those influences around him which had worked successfully against Bismarck must now — particularly if Bismarck's press campaign were to continue — work for Caprivi, who was Bismarck's successor. And, given the impressionability of William II, the importance of this personal factor was not inconsiderable.

On April 15, 1890, General von Caprivi, accompanied by most of the State Ministry, made his first speech to the lower house of the Prussian Landtag. It was a short speech, concise, to the point, and "delivered with an easy precision and a deferential grace." [27] He had not, he said, appeared before them to unfold a new program. There had not been time enough yet to prepare one. "I have, however, considered it my duty and have had the wish to appear in order to take the first step toward the establishment of personal relations between you, gentlemen, and myself ('Bravo!'). You will understand that, as over against my great predecessor, I must strive vigorously to go at least as far in personal relations with you as such personal relations may further the practical dispatch of business ('Bravo!')."

The Reich, constructed "with the outstanding assistance" of Bismarck, had been built strong enough, declared Caprivi, "to withstand the wind and the weather . . ." It was also fortunate that "the character of our noble young monarch" was so admirably suited to fill the gap left by Bismarck's retirement. "I have," Caprivi continued, ". . . an indestructible belief in the future of Prussia ('Bravo!'); I believe that the continuation of the Prussian state and of the German Reich which leans on its shoulder is for a long time yet an historical necessity, and I believe that this state and this Reich face yet a hopeful future ('Bravo!')."

You will have read His Majesty's statement, that the course is to remain as of old, and already the circumstance that my colleagues continue firmly in their offices will have demonstrated to you that the state government does not have the intention of inaugurating a new era ("Bravo!" on the right). It is, however, in the nature of circumstances

[26]Published in Otto Gradenwitz, *Bismarcks letzter Kampf* (Berlin, 1924), pp. 114ff.; Zechlin, *Staatsstreichpläne*, p. 91; Lerchenfeld, *Erinnerungen*, p. 351.
[27]*The Times*, wkly. ed., April 18, p. 16.

and of personalities, that opposed to a force such as that of Prince Bismarck other forces could, with difficulty, find room, that under his purposeful, self-reliant manner of regarding and doing things, many other aims had to drop into the background, that many ideas, many wishes, even if justified, could not always be completely fulfilled. It will be the first result of the change in personalities that, in regard to the government itself, the individual departments will gain greater scope and will become more prominent than heretofore ("Bravo!" on the left). It will, then, be quite unavoidable that within the Prussian State Ministry the old collegiate system will make itself more felt than it could under its late powerful minister-president ("Bravo!" on the left). Without being formally authorized, I believe, indeed, that I can declare, in agreement with my colleagues, that the state government will be at all times prepared to take up such suppressed ideas and wishes, to examine them anew, and, insofar as it becomes convinced of their practicality, to realize them. We shall take the good from wherever and from whomever it may come (enthusiastic "Bravo" on the left) and we shall implement it if we are convinced that such implementation is consistent with the welfare of the state ("Bravo!"). . . . We shall gladly work together with all those — · and we hope for a close union in the face of the difficult domestic situation before which we presumably shall stand — with all those who have a heart for Prussia and who are resolved to carry on and to help promote the state as a monarchy, the Reich as a nation (repeated, enthusiastic "Bravo!").[28]

All sides of the house seemed enthusiastic. Several deputies went up to Caprivi and congratulated him personally. In the ensuing debate it was as if the lid had been taken off; the speeches were on anything but the budget.[29] "It must be said," commented *The Times,* "that if General von Caprivi can only succeed in retaining the good impression which he produced today on all parties without distinction in the Prussian Chamber he will be one of the most popular Ministers who ever addressed it." [30] Particularly approved was the passage in which he welcomed all ideas from whatever source, which could be interpreted not only as an appeal to the nation to rise above the level of factional disputes but also as a friendly nod to the parties of the opposition.[31] Although Caprivi

[28]*Stenographische Berichte über die Verhandlungen des* . . . *Landtages, Haus der Abgeordneten* (1889–1890), II, 1048–1049 (hereafter cited as *Landtag*); Schulthess (1890), pp. 55–56, with minor emendations; R. Arndt, ed., *Die Reden des Grafen von Caprivi im deutschen Reichstage, preussischen Landtage und bei besonderen Anlässen, 1883–93* (Berlin, 1894), pp. 369–371; Wippermann, 6(I):101ff.

[29]W. Müller, *Politische Geschichte der Gegenwart* (Berlin, 1890), pp. 51–53.

[30]Wkly. ed., April 18, 1890, p. 16.

[31]Cf. *Deutsche Rundschau,* 63:308 (1890); Karl Bachem, *Geschichte* . . . *der Zentrumspartei* (Cologne, 1927–1932), V, 123–124.

had announced a new attitude of coöperation instead of dictation, he, nevertheless, had reserved to the ministry the responsibility of deciding which of these future political proposals would be consistent with the good of the state. And he had thereby omitted any reference to an over-all standard for determining what would be good or bad. There was, in fact, as yet no program; and this, of course, Caprivi had admitted. He needed time to familiarize himself with affairs; he had documents and records to study, to which he applied himself with great diligence. The next few weeks until the opening of the Reichstag were a breathing spell, a period of general good feeling for the new government. Even Wilhelm von Kardorff, the leader of the Free Conservatives and a veteran Bismarck admirer, seemed satisfied with Caprivi.[32] Also, Caprivi's tactful reference to the character of "our noble young monarch" was well received. "The Kaiser," noted Waldersee on the following day, "is very much pleased with Caprivi." As in the case of the repeal of the Cabinet Order two days before, the general was quite willing to make a few gestures.[33]

During this period, however, one stand was taken by the government which was perhaps symptomatic of its general attitude. There had been, immediately after Bismarck's departure, a general demand for an abandonment of his "reptile" press system. Under it various "official" papers had submissively printed whatever news and views were handed to them by the government, and in return they had received subsidies secretly from the "Guelf fund," the income from the confiscated wealth of the Hanoverian royal house. Caprivi immediately put an end to these subsidies, ordered that no more information should be given out by departments, and privately expressed the desire to get rid of the secret "Guelf fund" entirely. This latter step, however, would be extremely difficult, because several governmental functions had hitherto been supported thereby. On April 16, in answer to an interpellation in the Prussian House of Deputies on the attitude of the government toward the press, Caprivi declared that in the future all official communications to the public would be made through the official *Reichsanzeiger*, that in foreign policy, however, from time to time articles might have to be inspired, but that this would be done more sparingly and with restraint. Thus, noted *The Times*, "the uses of Prince Bismarck's system are fully recognized, while its abuse is to be stopped.

[32]Thimme, "Bismarck und Kardorff," pt. I, p. 55.
[33]Waldersee, *Denkwürdigkeiten*, II, 123; cf. Gradenwitz, *Bismarcks letzter Kampf*, p. 118; Eulenburg to Holstein, April 25, 1890, *Holstein Papers, Correspondence*.

. . . It would seem . . . that the change is to be one of spirit rather than of method." [34]

2

FOREIGN MINISTER AND REINSURANCE TREATY

It appeared, at the time of the Bismarck crisis, that Kaiser William II's main concern was to present a calm, unruffled, and dignified façade to the outside world. The words in his official acceptance of Bismarck's resignation, mentioning "further attempts to persuade you to take back your offer," already implied, for public consumption, that the resignation was voluntary and for reasons of health. Foreign ambassadors were informed that it had been done out of a concern to spare the old man's health and tranquillity. It is even possible that William II believed this himself.[35] At any rate a bold, calm front must be maintained. It was doubtless in this mood that William II sent his famous telegram to Dr. Hinzpeter, which was then published with design on March 22 in the *Weimarer Zeitung* as if originally sent to the ruler of that state: "I am as miserable as if I had again lost my grandfather. But what God wills must be borne, even though one must perish for it. The position of officer of the watch on the ship of state has fallen to me. The course remains the same. Full steam ahead!" [36] It was this telegram to which Caprivi had referred in his speech as showing the lack of intention of the government to inaugurate a new era. One of its incidental effects was to pour oil on Bismarck's already hotly smoldering resentment. He had *not* retired voluntarily! [37]

It seemed to the Kaiser and to all concerned especially important not to give the impression that Bismarck's resignation meant a fundamental change in foreign policy. To this end extreme and prolonged efforts were made to retain the son, Count Herbert Bismarck, in the Foreign Office. He was his father's only real confidant in matters of foreign policy; Caprivi knew nothing of such matters. For the sake of continuity and, above all, to forestall the idea of a complete

[34]Hammann, *Der Neue Kurs*, pp. 72–73; Wedel, *Zwischen Kaiser und Kanzler*, pp. 79, 124; O. J. Hale, *Publicity and Diplomacy* (New York, 1940), pp. 63–66; *DDF*, 1 ser., VIII, 25; *Schulthess* (1890), p. 57; Wippermann, 6(I):129–130, 315–317; *The Times*, April 17, 1890.

[35]Cf. William II to Francis Joseph, *Österr. Rdsch.*, 58:102–103.

[36]*Schulthess* (1890), p. 47; Wedel, *Zwischen Kaiser und Kanzler*, pp. 62 and note, 98–100, 115–116. This sentiment was probably sincere: cf. William II to Francis Joseph, *Österr. Rdsch.*, 58:107.

[37]K. A. Müller, "Die Entlassung," p. 171.

break between "the Hohenzollern and the Bismarck dynasties" it was absolutely necessary to retain Herbert. Herbert, however, refused.

There is a special tragedy in the lives of great men's sons. Overshadowed by their fathers' reputations, they stand little chance of separate recognition of their own personal abilities, for the development of which the distorted environment to which they are subjected is not particularly conducive. Herbert's life had, in fact, long since been sacrificed to his father's career. He had no other ambition than to be his father's right hand, and perhaps one day to continue his work as his heir. He had, especially in his relations with others, taken on his father's domineering qualities, with much less justification. He made himself a caricature of the old man. He stamped through the embassies, wrote the French ambassador, with the tread of Field Marshal von Moltke. Such conduct had made him generally disliked.[38]

Now, the whole court and administration, from the Kaiser and Caprivi on down, pleaded with him to stay on, at least for a time. The Kaiser, on March 20, appointed him to his father's office of foreign minister of Prussia, Caprivi at that time receiving only the chancellorship and minister-presidency. The Kaiser, in addition, offered to decorate Herbert publicly to show his confidence in him and even hinted that "if Caprivi didn't work out" he would be next in line for chancellor.

It is interesting to speculate as to what situation might have resulted if Herbert had accepted the position of Prussian foreign minister and had remained state secretary for foreign affairs in the Reich. The latter position was subordinate to the chancellor, who was responsible for foreign affairs, as for everything else, in the Reich. The position of Prussian foreign minister, therefore, was confined entirely to the relations between Prussia and the other federal German states, to instructing the Prussian vote in the Bundesrat, which, for the most part, would be a matter of domestic, not foreign policy. Two things could result: either Herbert would achieve a position in foreign policy and in the Reich government independent of the chancellor, which would amount to the constitutional change everyone had been expecting, or his position under a new chancellor would be quite untenable. In any case, it is difficult to see how he

[38]For Herbert's character cf. Eyck, *Bismarck*, III, 445; Lerchenfeld, *Denkwürdigkeiten*, pp. 271–272; B. Bülow, *Memoirs*, IV, 607, 623, 631–632; *DDF*, 1 ser., VII, 641; *Holstein Papers, Diaries, passim.*

could have taken over the relations with the Bundesrat, since control of the latter by the chancellor was essential for support of his leadership in the Reichstag.[39]

Fortunately, however, Herbert continued adamant. To Philipp Eulenburg and to the Kaiser's adjutant, General von Wedel, he protested that he was in ill health, that he had had no experience with the Bundesrat, that he wouldn't be able to face the Reichstag, that he couldn't get along with Caprivi, that the Kaiser was unpredictable, that he couldn't work with anyone but his father, that with his father gone the tsar would no longer be able to restrain the Pan-Slavs, all Germany's foes would attack her, the Triple Alliance would fall, war would break out, and he, Herbert, would be held responsible. It was obviously a difficult time for the younger Bismarck. If he remained faithfully by William II, he might continue to hold an important position; if he left with his father, he would share his exile and his opposition, and, at forty, his career would be at an end. But for him there was no real choice; apart from his father he had not existed, he could not do so now. Without his father's backing he was obviously afraid — of foreign powers, of the Kaiser, of the Bundesrat, of the Reichstag, and even of his subordinates in the Foreign Office, whom he had thoroughly alienated by his rude ways. "I shall never separate from my father. Never! — You can hardly seriously believe that I would take upon myself the role of foreign minister under just anybody like . . . Caprivi?" [40] On March 21 Herbert handed in his resignation. His health, he wrote Bülow two weeks later, would not permit him "to take over the increased duties and responsibilities which my name causes to be thrust upon me." [41]

Although he had conscientiously tried to persuade him to stay, Caprivi was rather relieved at Herbert's refusal; but there now arose the problem of his successor. Caprivi wanted, if possible, a person with experience and a Prussian, and asked the two Bismarcks for a suggestion. They named Count Alvensleben, minister to Belgium. To this suggestion both Caprivi and the Kaiser agreed; the matter seemed settled. Alvensleben was sent for. Meanwhile all Berlin was speculating on possible successors, favoring the ambassadors to

[39]See Herbert's discussion of the constitutional difficulties in Gradenwitz, *Bismarcks letzter Kampf*, pp. 180–181, and Wedel, *Zwischen Kaiser und Kanzler*, p. 44.

[40]Eulenburg, *Aus 50 Jahren*, p. 249.

[41]Bülow, *Memoirs*, IV, 643. Text of Herbert's interesting letter of resignation with marginal comments of William II in Gradenwitz, *Bismarcks letzter Kampf*, pp. 178–182; for Herbert's general attitude cf. Wedel, *Zwischen Kaiser und Kanzler*, pp. 43–45; Eulenburg, *Aus 50 Jahren*, pp. 237–238.

England and Turkey, Hatzfeldt and Radowitz. On March 24, however, a new name suddenly began to circulate, that of the Baden ambassador and representative to the Bundesrat, Baron Adolf Marschall von Bieberstein.

What is known of the history of this last candidacy is worth recounting. It is closely connected with one of the most fascinating personalities in the history of the Second Reich, that of Baron Friedrich von Holstein. Holstein, now a *Vortragender Rat* (first counselor) in the Political Department of the Foreign Office, was a veteran in the German foreign service. He had served under Bismarck in the embassy in St. Petersburg, then in the embassies in Rio de Janeiro, Washington, Stuttgart, Florence, Copenhagen — the usual diplomatic apprenticeship. In 1871 he had served on the Foreign Office staff in Versailles and become attached to the Paris embassy as second secretary. There he had become involved in Bismarck's campaign against his presumed political rival, Count Harry von Arnim, the ambassador to France. In the trial brought against Arnim for removing state documents from the Paris embassy, Holstein was compelled by Arnim's defense to testify against his chief, a severe ordeal for his proud and sensitive nature. Holstein had cut quite a figure in the social worlds of Washington and Paris, had explored the jungles of Brazil, and had hunted buffalo on the Indian-infested plains of North America. After some further time in Paris under Prince Chlodwig zu Hohenlohe, he settled down quietly, in 1876, at a desk in the Political Department, Wilhelmstrasse 76.[42]

It is obvious from Holstein's rapid advancement in the diplomatic service that from the beginning he enjoyed the special favor of Bismarck, who was quite willing to allow him to satisfy his desire to be close to the scene of important action. In the Foreign Office Holstein quickly became one of the most significant figures, next to Bismarck himself. Quite aside from his formal duties, he was allowed by the chancellor to carry on an extensive private correspondence with special informants in all the principal embassies, London, Constantinople, St. Petersburg, Vienna, as well as in the south German states, at the court of the crown prince, and at other sources of political power. For the Bismarckian Juggernaut, which tended to roll majestically over persons as well as policies, Holstein became a sort of unofficial intercessor and trouble shooter. Through his letters — clever, masterful, pithy letters — he kept himself exceedingly well informed and carefully redistributed this information where it would do the most good. In the last days of Crown Prince (soon

[42]For Holstein see especially *The Holstein Papers;* Rogge, *Holstein.*

to be Kaiser) Friedrich, Prince Radolin wrote Holstein: "Tell me something new in politics that I can relate to the poor Master to keep him up with things. Two words from you give a clearer picture than a whole bundle of dispatches." [43]

Holstein was a brilliant but solitary man, a bachelor, who spent almost all of his time, seven days a week, in his office. Never did he invite anyone to his rooms; an enthusiastic gourmet, he would invite especially favored friends to elegant lunches at Borchardt's restaurant, or, indulging his second passion, would invite them to accompany him on long walks in the environs of Berlin. Society in the capital he shunned completely, consenting to appear only at the exclusive salon of Frau von Lebbin, where he himself was the central attraction. The chief and almost sole interest of his life was his work. He loved the hidden facets, the subtle intrigues, the concealed wire-pulling of diplomacy. He obviously savored the taste of power. Some of his loneliness was a defense against the Bismarcks. In the mid-eighties he strikingly described in a letter to his cousin Ida von Stülpnagel how Herbert Bismarck and his brother-in-law, Count Rantzau, had tested a small-bore rifle in the Chancellery garden by shooting at the windows of the Foreign Office.

I have described this scene, my dear Ize, because it explains to you a good deal about myself which you may not have understood until now. With rough types like Herbert and his family there is only *one* way of avoiding the alternative between degradation and conflict, namely to withdraw of one's own accord. That is what I have done, and at first it gave me rather a jolt. But when I see how others are treated I am glad I made a clean break. I hardly think they would shoot through *my* window.[44]

Holstein did not get along with Rantzau, the Bismarck son-in-law, and in the late eighties he gradually lost his close relations with the Bismarck family. He also began to disagree basically with what he took to be Bismarck's pro-Russian foreign policy. He even tried to conduct an opposing policy, with the collaboration of Count Hatzfeldt, through personal influence in Vienna and London. With everyone else, he foresaw the clash between Kaiser and chancellor and did his best for a while to soften it. But to the Bismarcks the German Reich was their personal possession, and no compromise was possible. Holstein could not go with them on this ultimate issue. Subtly but decisively he shifted to the winning side and encouraged various

[43] Radolin to Holstein, March 2, 1888, *Holstein Papers, Correspondence.*
[44] *Holstein Papers, Diaries,* pp. 271–272.

persons — Eulenburg, the grand duke of Baden, Miquel, and Waldersee — to encourage the Kaiser. Relations with the grand duke had been carried on through his representative in Berlin, Baron Marschall von Bieberstein. The latter was thus automatically associated with the anti-Bismarck faction. A man of considerable force of character, a lawyer, with experience in the Bundesrat, Marschall as foreign secretary could undoubtedly be very effective in the Reichstag. His complete inexperience in foreign affairs would leave Holstein in the position of chief adviser and policy maker.[45]

On March 24 Count Monts wrote to Count Wedel of concern in the embassy in Vienna about who was to be foreign secretary. He himself was afraid that a combination would not be found that would allow Holstein to remain as right-hand man — that he might leave the service. "And this man, in my opinion [*meo voto*], is the only one who is now capable of steering the diplomatic ship of the Reich." [46] Monts thereby greatly underestimated the old Geheimrat. As early as March 17 Philipp Eulenburg suggested Marschall to General von Waldersee as the best successor to Herbert — four days before Herbert's resignation. Immediately after the resignation Marschall was approached privately and persuaded to consider the appointment in spite of his personal misgivings about his lack of qualifications.[47]

On March 26 Count Alvensleben arrived in Berlin and absolutely refused to have any part of the position of foreign secretary. The Kaiser, Caprivi, Herbert Bismarck and others tried in vain to persuade him otherwise. To other obvious candidates there were various objections. The under-secretary, Count Berchem, a South German Catholic, apparently did not appeal to Caprivi or to the Kaiser. Count Radowitz was anathema to Holstein, and even Bismarck would not recommend him, nor would he have accepted if asked. Count Hatzfeldt was unacceptable for personal reasons. In addition, the Kaiser took the position that the ambassadors, in general, should not be considered but should remain at their posts to keep things

[45]Helmut Krausnick, *Holsteins Geheimpolitik in der Ära Bismarck, 1886–1890* (Hamburg, 1942); Lerchenfeld, *Denkwürdigkeiten,* p. 383; Waldersee, *Denkwürdigkeiten,* II, 85–91; Eisendecher to Holstein, April 4, 1890, *Holstein Papers, Correspondence.* Holstein's letter to Eisendecher of March 26, 1890, in which he says, "Who now will take Herbert's place I do not know," should not be taken too seriously. That at this tense moment Holstein should be uninformed is inconceivable. Cf. Arthur von Brauer, *Im Dienste Bismarcks* (Berlin, 1936), pp. 111, 114.

[46]Wedel, *Zwischen Kaiser und Kanzler,* p. 58; cf. Rogge, *Holstein,* p. 265.

[47]Waldersee, *Denkwürdigkeiten,* II, 118; K. A. Müller, "Die Entlassung," pp. 170–171, note.

going.[48] Under these circumstances, with the refusal of Alvensleben, Caprivi suddenly found people on all sides supporting Marschall. General von Waldersee, Under-Secretary von Berchem, and the Kaiser himself favored Marschall. Caprivi was not pleased; he still wanted a Prussian. But, a newcomer in foreign affairs, he could not very well oppose all these people. And he thought he sensed a special desire on the part of the Kaiser for Marschall, which he traced back to the grand duke of Baden.[49]

Consequently, on the 26th Caprivi asked and received the Kaiser's authorization to offer Marschall the appointment, which he did that evening, finding Marschall apparently completely prepared and willing to accept. The morning of the 27th William II went out for his usual ride with his adjutant, Count Wedel. In the course of their conversation he informed the count that Alvensleben had refused and that it looked as if it would have to be Marschall. Count Wedel worriedly warned the Kaiser of the danger of placing an inexperienced man in such a position. The Kaiser thereupon dropped in at Herbert Bismarck's to ask his advice. Herbert suggested that he try once more to persuade Alvensleben, and the Kaiser forthwith summoned the latter to appear at the palace at noon. So when Caprivi arrived at the palace with the ambassador to Russia, General von Schweinitz, to obtain the Kaiser's decision on the Reinsurance Treaty and to announce that Marschall had accepted the position of foreign secretary, he found that the Kaiser was again treating with Alvensleben. To the gentlemen assembled with him in the anteroom Caprivi declared that now that he had asked Marschall he was committed to him; if the Kaiser got Alvensleben to accept, he, Caprivi, must resign. This threatening crisis was most fortunately avoided, however, by Alvensleben's continued refusal. Herbert Bismarck had heard nothing about Marschall; the Kaiser had not mentioned it to him. "What a characteristic indication of the present way of doing things, and to what confusion must it lead!" wrote Count Wedel in his diary. Two days later the Kaiser was telling Wedel how glad he was he had parted on such good terms with Herbert Bismarck, he must really return and take over his old post of foreign secretary.[50]

---

[48]If one were suspicious, one could easily imagine that this somewhat unusual notion came to William II from Holstein, through Eulenburg. Radowitz, *Aufzeichnungen*, II, 322; Wedel, *Zwischen Kaiser und Kanzler*, pp. 60–64, 102; Hohenlohe, *Memoirs*, II, 423.

[49]Radowitz, *Aufzeichnungen*, II, 322; Hohenlohe, *Memoirs*, II, 425; Eisendecher to Holstein, April 4, 1890, *Holstein Papers*, *Correspondence*.

[50]Wedel, *Zwischen Kaiser und Kanzler*, pp. 65–66, 71, 91–92; Waldersee, *Denkwürdigkeiten*, I, 122. Waldersee has misplaced this entry under the wrong date.

The haste with which a person was sought to fill the foreign secretary's post was partly due to the very serious negotiations then in progress with Russia. The subject of these negotiations was Bismarck's secret "Reinsurance" Treaty of 1887, due to expire on June 18. Negotiations for its renewal had begun in February on the initiative of the Russians, who were well informed on the Bismarck crisis and wanted to act on the treaty while its author was still in office. By March negotiations had reached a crucial point, but when the Russian ambassador, Count Pavel Shuvalov, arrived in Berlin on March 17 to conduct the final phase, he found himself in the middle of the Bismarck crisis. Bismarck was then mobilizing his final attack on the issue of the Kaiser's belligerency toward Russia, and he immediately summoned Shuvalov and told him that he was being forced from office because of his pro-Russian attitude. Shuvalov then consulted with Count Herbert, and on the 20th Herbert sent two memoranda to the Kaiser announcing that Shuvalov had refused to go further with the negotiations, that under the changed circumstances the tsar would not want to renew the treaty, "since such a secret transaction could not be negotiated with a new chancellor." [51]

Late in the night of March 20 Count Shuvalov was awakened by a message from the Kaiser summoning him to an audience at the palace early the following morning. The whole Russian embassy became greatly excited — something terrible must have occurred in St. Petersburg. But the next morning it transpired that it was the memoranda of Herbert Bismarck on the Reinsurance Treaty that had caused William II to act in such haste. Shuvalov hastened to reassure the Kaiser; he had merely thought it proper, with the change in the German government, to request new instructions from his own government before proceeding further. The Kaiser assured the ambassador that nothing had changed in the relations between the two countries, that he had parted with Bismarck merely for reasons of health, that, as to the secret treaty, he was quite ready to renew it. "I beg you to tell His Majesty [the tsar] that on my part I am entirely disposed to renew our agreement, that my foreign

[51]Schweinitz, *Denkwürdigkeiten*, II, 396, 399–400; Sergei Goriainov, "End of the Alliance of the Emperors," *American Historical Review*, 23:342–343 (1917–1918); *Die Grosse Politik der europäischen Kabinette*, ed. J. Lepsius, A. Mendelssohn-Bartholdy, F. Thimme (Berlin, 1922–1927), VII, 3, 4 (hereafter cited as *G.P.*). Cf. Holstein's account, *Holstein Papers, Memoirs*, pp. 128ff. It is a fact that almost nobody in Berlin agreed with Bismarck's policy toward Russia. See especially Waldersee, *Briefwechsel; Holstein Papers, Diaries.* The Russians on their side did not approve of the Kaiser's liberal policies, Pourtalès to Holstein, February 22, March 19, 1890, *Holstein Papers, Correspondence.*

policy remains and will remain the same as it was in the time of my grandfather." The tsar noted on the margin of Shuvalov's report of this interview, "Nothing more satisfactory could be looked for. We shall see by the sequel whether deeds correspond to words. For the moment it is quite reassuring." [52]

In the meantime General von Caprivi, who had officially taken over the post of chancellor only on the 20th and who knew nothing of these developments, was faced with the necessity of immediately formulating the general guiding principles of his foreign policy. He had for this purpose at least one lengthy private discussion with Bismarck, during the course of which the old man expounded on a multitude of questions and even admitted some errors recently committed. But all Bismarck's careful exposition profited Caprivi little. He knew that he was a new man in a new situation; he could not possibly carry on as Bismarck had done. He could not juggle with five glass balls at once, Caprivi said plainly to both Bismarcks and to the ambassadors, but would do well to manage with only two.[53]

This, however, was a serious decision, and Caprivi was acutely aware of his own inadequacy in foreign affairs. He felt, he said, as if he had entered a dark room. Naturally he turned to his official advisers in the Foreign Office. Since Herbert's resignation the 21st, there was no foreign secretary with whom to consult. On the 23rd, therefore, Caprivi had a conference on the Reinsurance Treaty with Under-Secretary Berchem, Holstein, the head of the Political Department, and one other counselor, Raschdau. The sentiment of this conference was unanimously against the treaty. On March 25, Berchem submitted a memorandum summarizing the general opinion of the Foreign Office: (1) By supporting Russia in the Balkans Germany was encouraging a general war which it was in Russia's power to start; (2) that such an attitude if known would antagonize England, Austria, and Italy; (3) that the guaranty against support for a French attack was useless; (4) that the treaty was against the sense if not the words of the Triple Alliance; (5) that nevertheless it was to Germany's advantage to direct Russia toward the Balkans and the Straits; (6) Russia would not undertake a Bulgarian "adventure" lightly; (7) therefore Germany must continue to support Russia in

[52]Goriainov, "End of the Alliance," pp. 343–344; G.P., VII, 21; Schweinitz, Denkwürdigkeiten, II, 400.

[53]K. A. Müller, "Die Entlassung," p. 168; M. Busch, Bismarck, Some Secret Pages of His History (New York, 1898), p. 318; Schweinitz, Denkwürdigkeiten, II, 403–404; Eckardt, Aus den Tagen, pp. 52–53; Goriainov, "End of the Alliance," p. 344. Cf. Hammann, Der neue Kurs, pp. 34–35; Radowitz, Aufzeichnungen, II, 323.

Bulgaria, but (8) it would be better not to write a treaty on it; (9) at the same time Germany must keep alive the opposition of the other powers to Russia in southeast Europe; (10) because public support was necessary for war nowadays, as Prince Bismarck himself had recently said, Germany must not give the impression that she was leaving her allies in the lurch. Germany must, rather, conduct a "peaceful, clear, and loyal policy," which would preserve and promote the Reich, and not engage in dangerous diplomatic risk-taking.[54]

On the 27th Caprivi had further and extended discussions with the ambassadors to Russia and Turkey, Schweinitz and Radowitz. Both approved and supported his general attitude in foreign policy and, in particular, toward the secret treaty with Russia) Schweinitz was particularly impressed by the conflict between the Russian and Rumanian treaties. "If Bismarck were still at the helm I should have advised that the treaty be renewed without the protocol," [55] noted Schweinitz. Under the changed circumstances, however, it would be very dangerous to pursue such an ambiguous policy. Radowitz advised a "simple, peaceful policy," awakening trust in Germany's peaceful intentions, holding fast to the Triple Alliance, avoiding all misunderstandings in Vienna and concluding no more secret treaties with Russia. The new regime must "regard the epoch of ingenious acts as closed, secure what has been already achieved, defend our prestige, enter on no foreign enterprises, before the new government is established on all sides." Thus Caprivi found everywhere complete backing for his own inclinations. There was no dissenting voice. The general purpose of Bismarck's foreign policy was to be maintained; in the implementation of it, however, Germany would necessarily in the future be less self-assertive. "Prince Bismarck," Caprivi told Lerchenfeld, "in reality conducted the policy of all the states. Strong in the fear and the confidence which he at once inspired, he could pose problems for himself which would miscarry with a successor." [56]

Shortly after noon on March 27 Caprivi and Schweinitz arrived at the royal palace and, as has already been noted, found the Kaiser talking with Count Alvensleben. After Alvensleben had departed

[54] G.P., VII, 4–10.
[55] The separate assurance on the Straits.
[56] Schweinitz, Denkwürdigkeiten, II, 403–404; Radowitz, Aufzeichnungen, II, 322–323; K. A. Müller, "Die Entlassung," p. 173; B. Hutten-Czapski, Sechzig Jahre Politik und Gesellschaft (Berlin, 1936), I, 304, 306; C. Hohenlohe, Denkwürdigkeiten des Reichskanzlerzeit, ed. K. A. von Müller (Berlin, 1931), pp. 276ff.

they entered the royal presence and "took their places at the green table." Caprivi spoke first, explaining that he could not reconcile the existing treaties, that he, therefore, recommended that the Russian treaty not be renewed, especially because of the danger of its becoming known. William II listened silently, then asked, "Well, what does the ambassador say to this?" Schweinitz thereupon backed Caprivi's argument, saying that he would take upon himself the task of allaying Russian suspicions caused by this unexpected breaking off of negotiations. According to a later memorandum of Holstein's the Kaiser is supposed to have replied, "Well, then it can't be done whether I like it or not." [57]

The following day Schweinitz called on the Russian ambassador, Shuvalov. The latter joyfully informed the old general that St. Petersburg was very much pleased by the telegraphed report of his audience with the Kaiser on the 21st and the Kaiser's assurance that he was quite willing to renew the treaty. Bluntly, Schweinitz disillusioned him. The "new men" did not want to conclude such important matters immediately upon entering office. Poor Shuvalov was dumbfounded. To him it seemed that the German government was repudiating him personally. The Kaiser had said in so many words that he would renew the treaty; Shuvalov had reported it to his government; and now it was not to be done. He had instructions from St. Petersburg to see that Schweinitz returned with full authority to conclude the negotiations, and now nothing, nothing at all was to result. He talked of resigning his post. Schweinitz calmed Shuvalov as well as he could and hurried to inform Caprivi. This, apparently, was the first Caprivi had heard of the Kaiser's assurances to Shuvalov. It was a heavy blow. Immediately he drew up a summary of their decision of the day before and requested an audience with the Kaiser. The entry in Schweinitz's diary for the 28th reads: "With Shuvalov; very painful discussion; direct to Caprivi; serious situation; the noble and courageous man very distressed . . . restless sleep due to politics." [58]

The decision must have been a difficult one for William II. He had been free of Bismarck for only a week; must he now on the advice of his new chancellor contradict his own words? What would the Russians think of him? But it was equally impossible to dismiss Caprivi immediately after his appointment. On the following day

[57]*"Nun, dann geht es nicht, so leid es mir tut."* Schweinitz, *Denkwürdigkeiten,* II, 404–405; *G.P.,* VII, 49.

[58]Schweinitz, *Denkwürdigkeiten,* II, 405–407 and note; Caprivi's memorandum, *G.P.,* VII, 10–11; Schweinitz, *Briefwechsel* (Berlin, 1928), p. 266.

Caprivi informed Ambassador Schweinitz that the decision remained the same. Schweinitz left for St. Petersburg.[59]

And so the Reinsurance Treaty was not renewed. Schweinitz had some difficulty soothing the Russians. The pro-German foreign minister, Giers, was visibly shaken by the sudden change of front. Schweinitz, however, did his best; eventually Giers seemed satisfied, and the matter was dropped. But in May Giers came back to it. He did not like the prospect of the lack of a written guaranty after June 18. He would make certain concessions; he did not even ask for a formal treaty, merely an exchange of notes would suffice. Schweinitz was impressed. Some agreement, he thought, might now be reached which could stand publication and which would assure Russian neutrality for at least the first few weeks of a war instigated by France. It would not be wise to push back the hand that the tsar was again holding out to Germany.[60]

Berlin, however, remained unconvinced. Caprivi again consulted the Foreign Office and on May 30 received four memoranda from Marschall, Holstein, Kiderlen-Wächter, and Raschdau, all advising strongly against concluding any agreement whatsoever with Russia. Among these, Holstein's was the most important, Kiderlen's and Raschdau's confined to particular phases of the question. Secretary von Marschall's memorandum was supplementary to Holstein's. The main characteristics of these memoranda were distrust of Russian intentions, and distrust of Bismarck. Holstein especially called attention to Bismarck's recent revelations to a correspondent of the Russian *Novoye Vremya*. Holstein, who had worked so many years under Bismarck, was obviously afraid that the old man's rage against the Kaiser would lead him to reveal official secrets. And this fear was, indeed, justified. Bismarck did reveal the terms of the Russian treaty to an astonished public in 1896.[61]

This negative stand was accepted and elaborated by Caprivi in a final "sketch" drawn up on May 29, 1890, and sent to the ambassadors at London, Vienna, Rome, and Constantinople, as well as to St. Petersburg. Caprivi obviously distrusted Russia. Giers, he said, in all his proposals had never mentioned Italy; Russia was being too friendly to England at the Brussels Anti-Slavery Conference. Russia's real aim was doubtless to break up the Triple Alliance and to

---

[59]E. Eyck, *Das persönliche Regiment Wilhelms II* (Erlenbach-Zürich, 1948), p. 35; Schweinitz, *Briefwechsel,* p. 266.

[60]*G.P.,* VII, 11–20.

[61]*G.P.,* VII, 22–29; Eyck, *Wilhelm II,* p. 38; Hutten-Czapski, *Sechzig Jahre,* I, 301–307; Hohenlohe, *Denkwürdigkeiten des Reichskanzlerzeit,* pp. 270–278.

alienate England from Germany. If Russia wanted only peace she would not need an alliance; a disturbance of the peace could come only from Russia. There would be no "Bulgarian danger" if Russia did not desire it. Giers' urgent efforts to conclude a German alliance showed possible Russian aggressive intentions toward Constantinople. German support to close the Straits against England would in that case be very important. Germany had no interest, however, in supporting Russia against England and Italy. Any secret treaty would be a potential threat to the Triple Alliance; a *rapprochement* with Russia would alienate Germany's allies, wrong England, and mystify the German people, who were used to the idea of the Triple Alliance. Germany must one day choose between Russia and Austria; it would be better to choose Austria. Germany must continue good relations with Russia, but she must be loyal to her allies. Where she could not support their interests, whether in Bulgaria or Bizerte, she should at least not hinder them. No alliance was worth much unless founded upon public opinion. In an accompanying letter to Ambassador von Schweinitz Caprivi stressed the attitude of "the former Reich chancellor" which tended to promote indiscretions that would confuse public opinion and cause misunderstandings among Germany's allies. In this situation Germany must pursue a "simple and transparent policy." [62]

Even then Giers did not give up completely his attempt to obtain "something in writing." During August 1890, Kaiser William II and Chancellor von Caprivi paid a state visit to the Russian tsar, Alexander III, at the naval maneuvers at Narva. The occasion was used by both sides for conciliatory talks between the emperors and the ministers on their mutual relations. The visit went off very well, in spite of constant reports to the contrary in the German press. William II displayed all the charm of his winning personality before the tsar. Caprivi made an excellent personal impression upon the tsar and upon Giers. Subsequently Giers wrote up an account of his talk with Caprivi and had Count Muraviev, the Berlin chargé d'affaires, read it to Caprivi. The chancellor found it quite accurate, whereupon Muraviev suggested innocently that perhaps Caprivi would put that in writing. Caprivi, although admitting in a report of the incident that he could have signed the statement "with a good conscience," protested to Muraviev that such a step would be "entirely useless. I am completely resolved not to write down anything." Giers then hastily disavowed Muraviev's action. To the Germans,

[62]*G.P.*, VII, 30–36.

however, it was clear that once more the Russian foreign minister had tried to get "a piece of paper." They were apparently well satisfied with their thwarting of the attempt.[63]

It is fairly obvious from the series of developments sketched above that in the first months of 1890 the foreign policy of Germany retired basically from an offensive to a defensive position. There were to be no more risky "adventures"; the main preoccupation was stability and defense of the Triple Alliance. Two additional aspects of the situation may serve to round out the picture.

Bismarck in 1889 had begun a special attempt at a *rapprochement* with England which took the practical form of negotiations regarding their conflicting colonial interests in Africa. Broken off by Bismarck's retirement, these negotiations were taken up in May by the Caprivi administration and carried to a successful conclusion in the so-called Heligoland Agreement of July 1, 1890. By this agreement Germany rounded out her colony in East Africa, gained an adjustment of frontiers in Southwest Africa, including the narrow stretch of territory connecting with the Zambesi River known as "Caprivi's Finger" (*Caprivizipfel*), gave up her claims to Witu, Somaliland, and Uganda, and exchanged her rather dubious claim on Zanzibar for the island of Heligoland off her own North Sea coast. Although the cession of Heligoland was suggested by England, the driving force in the quick conclusion of the agreement seems to have come from Germany. Caprivi thus documented for the benefit of the English his disinterest in further German colonial expansion, and the Kaiser got Heligoland, which he had long desired. A rapprochement with England was apparently being sought by Germany to forestall any weakening of Italy (whose main interests were in the Mediterranean) and to encourage her continued enthusiasm for the Triple Alliance. The English, indeed, seem to have been aware of this motive and to have shared it, being especially friendly at this time to Bismarck's "League of Peace," which they regarded, rightly, as a strong support for the European *status quo*.[64]

[63]*G.P.*, VII, 347–348, 351–356, including the Kaiser's marginal comments on No. 1613, pp. 353–354; Kiderlen to Holstein, September 21, 30, 1890, *Holstein Papers, Correspondence;* W. Köhler, *Revanche-idee und Panslavismus,* v. I of *Amtliche Aktenstücke zur Geschichte der europäischen Politik 1885–1914* (Berlin, 1925), pp. 307–311; Goriainov, "End of the Alliance," p. 347; W. L. Langer, *Franco-Russian Alliance,* pp. 103, 105, notes; *Pr. Jbb.*, 66:298–300 (1890).

[64]Cf. Langer, *Franco-Russian Alliance,* pp. 72–73. For the negotiations leading up to the Heligoland Agreement see E. T. S. Dugdale, ed. and trans., *German Diplomatic Documents* (London, 1928), I and II; *G.P.*, VIII; Lady Gwendolen Cecil, *Life of Lord Salisbury* (London, 1921–1932), IV; Adolf Hasenclever, "Geschichte u. Bedeutung des Helgolandvertrages," *Archiv für Politik u. Geschichte,* 5:507–524

The second factor was Germany's relations with France. William II had since his accession been particularly gracious toward the French. Recently he had gone out of his way — with some success — to dazzle the French delegates to his International Labor Conference in Berlin, presenting the chief delegate M. Jules Simon with a handsomely bound volume of the musical works of Frederick the Great. On April 16 the Foreign Office counselor, Kiderlen-Wächter, sent a long private letter to Count Philipp Eulenburg, who was expected to be with the Kaiser on his visit to Hamburg and Bremen and accompanying cruise in the North Sea. With it he sent a report from Cairo on the subject of the Egyptian debt, which indicated a possible *rapprochement* there between England and France. There were also indications, wrote Kiderlen, that Italy was making advances toward France. These developments, he wrote, were the result of the apparent better relations between France and Germany, as reported in the press of both countries. If Germany flirted with France it would: (1) force Italy to make up with France — "a German *rapprochement* with France must operate much more intensively upon Italy than a German *rapprochement* with Russia would upon Austria"; (2) encourage England to be friendly with France; (3) be of no real advantage to Germany, which could give France nothing but "a friendly smile," while Germany's enemies could promise a great deal without costing themselves anything. "We must keep these friends who are impelled toward us by a common antagonism against France. By coquetting with France, we lose this antagonism without being able to hinder an understanding between her and our enemies. . . . His Majesty will now, in any case, discuss politics with you, as you go floating along with him again. You are therefore requested — not by me, I am authorized to write all this — to lay the points of view elaborated above before His Majesty . . . if he then ponders over these questions by himself on a lonely sea voyage his keen insight will surely find the right path. . . ."[65]

In both these instances the dominant note is defensive — to maintain the alliances with Austria and Italy.[66] It has been fashionable to blame Baron von Holstein for the nonrenewal of the

(1925); L. von Caprivi, *Die Ostafrikanische Frage u. der Helgoland-Sansibar-Vertrag* (Bonn, 1934); Wippermann, 6(II):14–27; Stadelmann, "Der neue Kurs," p. 542. See below, pp. 101–103.

[65]*G.P.*, VII, 266–270. For Eulenburg's report on his success with the Kaiser see Eulenburg to Holstein, April 25, 1890, *Holstein Papers, Correspondence.*

[66]Cf. Eckhardt, *Aus den Tagen,* p. 58.

secret treaty with Russia. There is no doubt that Holstein disagreed basically with Bismarck's Russian policy and that he was very suspicious of Russia. It is also obvious that, particularly in the later stages of the negotiations, after Count Berchem, who did not get along well with Holstein and Marschall, had resigned, Holstein's influence was predominant in the Foreign Office. Caprivi himself had, before his appointment, already been intimately acquainted with Holstein and told Radowitz in late March that he had the most complete trust in Holstein and would have often to rely upon his great experience. But this does not explain the attitude, taken at the beginning, of Berchem, Radowitz, and even Schweinitz, that there should be no more secret treaties. Nor does it change the fact that the determination to remain firmly loyal to Austria and not to make any secret agreements that could in any way embarrass that relationship was typical of General von Caprivi and the only possible attitude for him to take. "In spite of all criticism this decision remains the decision of an honorable man, whose character prevented him from betraying his allies behind their backs. Whoever recognizes in the politics that decide the fate of nations more than the art of taking away with the left hand what one has given with the right hand must approve Caprivi's attitude." [67]

The Berlin officials, however, seem to have overlooked the effect of all this upon the Russians. To them the change in attitude in Berlin seemed to bear out Bismarck's statement that William II was anti-Russian. The Kaiser had begun his reign with a visit to Constantinople, which Bismarck now revealed in the Russian press had been against his own advice; during the crucial days of March he had entertained his uncle, the prince of Wales, and his son George in Berlin with great pomp, decorated the latter with the Order of the Black Eagle, and, dressed in the British admiral's uniform given him by his grandmother the year before, had expressed the hope that the British fleet joined with the German army and fleet would keep the peace in the future. Then in May, at the very time Giers made his second treaty proposals, William II, speaking at Königsberg, and assuring the East Prussians that he would protect their province on the Russian frontier like a *"rocher de bronce,"* had gone on to say "and I have the feeling, that to those who dare to disturb the peace

[67]Eyck, *Wilhelm II*, p. 37; Krausnick, *Holsteins Geheimpolitik*, p. 73; also Radowitz, *Aufzeichnungen*, II, 326–327; Bülow, *Memoirs*, IV, 607, 638; Rogge, *Holstein*, pp. xxxvii, 150; Wedel, *Zwischen Kaiser und Kanzler*, p. 104; Tirpitz, *Memoirs*, I, 41.

a lesson will not be spared such as they will not forget in a hundred years!" [68]

Thus the Russians found it rather difficult to give much weight to Caprivi's peaceful assurances. As for Count Shuvalov, he could not forget, he told Schweinitz, "that one thing was said and another done." On a report of Shuvalov's the tsar commented, "No doubt a change has come over German policy, and we ought to be prepared for any event." [69] The fears and uncertainty of the new Berlin regime had induced corresponding fears and uncertainty in St. Petersburg. By releasing Russia from her German connection, the Berlin diplomats encouraged the Russians, who now found themselves isolated, to seek as a matter of self-defense a new connection — as Giers had plainly warned — which could only be with the other isolated power, France.

The breakdown of the treaty with Russia seems to demonstrate several things about the operation of the Caprivi regime, at least in its early days. There was no intention of breaking fundamentally with the policy of Bismarck. On May 16 Caprivi told the Reichstag,

In opposition to what the Deputy Liebknecht has said, I must recognize, and recognize thankfully, that the inheritance which I have taken over from my predecessor in office in respect to foreign policy is the most fortunate conceivable. I have met with relationships which for some time will require no action, no personal participation from me, because the relationships remain so clear and simple, that they can continue as they are. We support our foreign position, as you know, first upon our own strength, which, to maintain the alliances, we cannot increase enough; then, however, we depend upon our strong alliances, depend upon them all the more as they more and more enter also into the sentiment of the people. I can only let things go on as they went before and be thankful to my predecessor. [70]

It must be remembered that to the people of Germany and of other countries Bismarckian policy meant the Triple Alliance. Of other secret complications nothing was known. Caprivi was bound by this factor of public opinion. On a Foreign Office memorandum of July 1890 he wrote: "We must have much more regard for public opinion than in Prince Bismarck's time." This statement to the

[68]Langer, *Franco-Russian Alliance*, p. 67. For the visit of the Prince of Wales, *The Times*, wkly. ed., March 28, 1890, p. 5; Königsberg speech, *Schulthess* (1890), p. 86; Wippermann, 6(I):250–252; *The Times*, wkly. ed., May 23, 1890, p. 14.

[69]Schweinitz, *Denkwürdigkeiten*, II, 413; Goriainov, "End of the Alliance," pp. 345–346; *G.P.*, VII, 11–20.

[70]*Schulthess* (1890), p. 80.

Reichstag, therefore, represents the view of the situation which Caprivi wanted generally to establish, for the sake of the stability of his own new administration, of the prestige of the crown, and of the general stability of the country. Things were to go on as before; Bismarck's fall did not mean a crisis; the country was strong, the government was strong; threatening problems, whether the relations with France and Russia or the growing power of the Social Democrats, could be handled. Yet he was, of course, under no illusions as to the changes that had already taken place and must take place in the policies of an administration trying to carry on without Bismarck. He felt, he said, that he had entered office with a serious deficit. He could not dominate as Bismarck had done, he lacked his prestige. Nevertheless, he must carry on the affairs of Bismarck's Reich in a post-Bismarck world. All the great powers, for instance, had been trained to be suspicious of German diplomatic moves, yet had learned to have faith in and to depend upon the peaceful motives and ultimate wisdom of the great man. With Bismarck's departure this faith and this dependency were suddenly removed, while the habit of suspicion lingered on. The same situation existed domestically among the parties. Bismarck had never feared publicity for his Reinsurance Treaty. The respect and fear his personality inspired could perhaps, one way or another, have forced its acceptance upon a startled Reichstag and upon a startled world. But now, if the treaty had been kept in force, and if the old man spitefully had revealed its contents, Caprivi, not Bismarck, would have had to deal, not only with the cold suspicion of Austria, Italy, and England, but with the inevitable interpellation in the Reichstag. He was not Bismarck, he could not depend upon personal prestige and domination. He had to try to build up confidence in himself, in his government, and in Germany both at home and abroad. He could not make diplomatic agreements which he did not feel he could publicly defend. It is, however, apparent that in their concern to simplify and to legitimatize their diplomatic commitments Caprivi and the Foreign Office were too Berlin-centered in their attitude. Their handling of the Russians seems to have been unnecessarily tactless. The explanation probably lies in their sense of fright and helplessness after Bismarck's fall, and in the face of Bismarck's own continuing hostility. It is comparatively easy to criticize these fears, to complain from a vantage point in time that Caprivi and the Foreign Office overemphasized the importance of Bismarck the man and underestimated the natural strength of Germany's geographical, political, and military position in Europe, upon which Bismarck's policy was based. But to them Germany was Bismarck; and they themselves knew the difficulties of their situation best.[71]

It was plain that henceforward Holstein would be the dominating figure in the Foreign Office. He had long been on particularly friendly terms with Caprivi, having been of assistance to him in his Admiralty days. It is possible that in 1890 Caprivi offered him the position of foreign secretary; he preferred, however, to remain in the shadows, to act out his role of "gray eminence." Marschall, who had had a brilliant career in law and as Baden representative in the Bundesrat, but knew nothing of foreign policy, and who was well aware that he owed his position to Holstein, was necessarily completely dependent on him.[72] Besides chancellor and Foreign Office there was also the factor, as in the Shuvalov incident, of the sudden unpremeditated acts of William II. This called for tact and personal influence. It was a rôle not easily enacted by Caprivi, and very early in the game, as has been seen, recourse was had to William II's dear friend "Phili," the colorful Count Eulenburg.[73]

In 1890 Count Philipp zu Eulenburg-Hertefeld, twelve years older than William II, was in the prime of life, a striking personality, with his broad forehead, fine straight nose, and carefully trimmed beard. A writer of plays and children's stories, a singer and composer of songs and ballads, an amateur architect, above all a brilliant wit and charming conversationalist, Eulenburg's subtle sensitivity and keen understanding made him also a very able diplomat. An intimate friend of the Kaiser, he was to maintain himself in a position of great power and influence until his career ended tragically with his implication in the homosexuality scandals of 1908. In 1890 Eulenburg was Prussian minister to Oldenburg, but his real task from now on, as he said, was to be ambassador from the German government to the Kaiser, to act the rôle of mediator between "a hyper-temperamental Kaiser who would fall like lightning from heaven upon the assembly at the Foreign Office, and a brilliant, domineering Geheimrat of marked pathological tendencies, to say

[71]Cf. Langer, *Franco-Russian Alliance*, p. 67, *Diplomacy of Imperialism* (New York, 1935), pp. 5–6, *European Alliances and Alignments*, pp. 452, 459–460.

[72]Cf. Rogge, *Holstein*, p. 172; Radowitz, *Aufzeichnungen*, II, 327; Eyck, *Wilhelm II*, p. 25; Eulenburg to Holstein, August 1, October 16, November 28, 1890, Caprivi to Holstein, July 5, 1885, September 19, 1884, August 10, 1888, *Holstein Papers, Correspondence; Diaries*, pp. 163–164.

[73]Since Count Philipp zu Eulenburg-Hertefeld was usually called by his nickname, Phili, among his friends, including those at court, and the more familiar term seems best to indicate the intimacy and delicacy of his position, in the following pages he will usually be referred to as Phili Eulenburg.

nothing of an imperial chancellor who, always very sensitive about his dignity, regarded the said part as a necessary evil and, despite all his mumbled expressions of gratitude, never could really like me." [74]

From the Foreign Office Eulenburg received letters almost daily, mostly from Holstein. Sometimes he could sufficiently carry through his task with William II by letter, sometimes it called for a visit to Berlin. When the Kaiser traveled, to shoot in the spring at Prökelwitz and in the autumn at Rominten, to cruise on the *Hohenzollern* in Norwegian waters in July, Eulenburg or Kiderlen or both always went along, keeping the Foreign Office well posted from day to day. It was not an ideal system, but it was necessary.[75]

3

PROSPECTS AND PORTENTS

What were the auguries of the new regime? In a system of government that was only half parliamentary and that had been fitted to the domination of a single personality, where the position of the chancellor was poised between the independent and conflicting forces of Kaiser, Foreign Office, Prussian Junkerdom in army, bureaucracy, and Landtag, and the democratic parties in the Reichstag — in such a situation the pull and clash of personalities had more than a normal influence over policy. The personality of the chancellor especially would be basic to the fortunes of his government. Would, for example, his honesty, his intelligence, and his strength of will outbalance his political inexperience? Would he be able to control the forces that in the end had overpowered Bismarck?

In particular, what direction was government policy likely to take? In spite of all the disclaimers of "inaugurating a new era" it was quite obvious that the nation was in for something new. For the German Reich to exist without Bismarck was in itself radical enough. That Bismarck had been following a repressive policy in his last phase inexorably gave the new regime, intended or not intended, a push toward the left. And, in addition, Caprivi's honest desire to strengthen and preserve the Reich, to "take the good," as he said, "from wherever and from whomever it may come," would auto-

[74]Johannes Haller, *Philipp Eulenburg, The Kaiser's Friend,* trans. Ethel Colburn Mayne (New York, 1930), I, 302, 124. Cf. Bülow to Monts, K. F. Nowak and F. Thimme, *Erinnerungen u. Gedanken des Botschafters Anton Graf Monts* (Berlin, 1932), pp. 329–330.
[75]Haller, *Eulenburg,* I, 124, 133–134.

matically lead, if consistently followed, to some kind of conciliation, perhaps reform. To rally public opinion, to deal with a liberal Reichstag, and to build enough strength to withstand the attacks of Bismarck a new liberal program must be set forth. Had not the Caprivi government in foreign affairs, by dropping the Reinsurance Treaty and by concluding the Heligoland Agreement, turned somewhat symbolically from the authoritarian East to the democratic West? New forces seemed, indeed, to be in motion. How far they would be allowed to go or what precise forms they would take were questions that were as yet unanswered.

Chapter III

THE LEGISLATIVE PROGRAM

Why should not the monarchy succeed in roping in the fourth estate and making it a part of its organism since it managed, at the beginning of the century, to placate the third, under even more difficult circumstances.

Bernhard Bülow to Philipp Eulenburg, March 1890

The government can subjugate and suppress, but that is not the end of the matter; the injuries from which we suffer must be healed from within.

Caprivi in the Landtag, November 1890

He who wishes to have a parliament at all, who does not wish to have absolutism, has only the choice, either to let the parties rule alternately themselves or to make them alternately lesser or greater concessions.

Preussische Jahrbücher, February 1891

1

LABOR PROTECTION AND ARMY BILL

O<small>N</small> April 21, 1890, the Kaiser visited Bremen to lay the cornerstone for a monument to his grandfather, William I. The official reception included a tour of the city, the port, the stock exchange, and a banquet in the *Rathaus* with speeches. Late in the afternoon the royal party proceeded to Bremerhaven where the Kaiser was entertained by the North German Lloyd with dinner on board their steamer *Fulda*. At this point, in response to remarks of the managing director of the Lloyd, the Kaiser arose and spoke again. He spoke of the wonderful German ships which were transporting German goods and German skill all over the world, of commerce, for which peace was necessary. This peace might sometimes appear to be threatened, but things often were not as bad as they looked. By way of illustration, he was reminded of an incident in his own experience:

It was on my first voyage to the Baltic with the squadron; I had been proceeding since 3 in the morning in dense fog, and the only sounds were the sounding of the sirens and from time to time the firing of the guns to give the position of the ships. At 8 o'clock there was to be a change of course; the fog was so thick that one could not even see the chart house of the ship, to say nothing of seeing from one ship to another, and doubts arose as to how the change in course might take place. It did take place, and about an hour afterward suddenly we and the *Hohenzollern* came out of the fog bank and went forward with a fresh wind and a calm sea under a blue sky in the bright morning sun. We turned our eyes first of all back towards the fog bank, which lay like a great thick cloud upon the sea and from which only the tones of the sirens sounded across at us. All at once we saw high in the clouds, appearing as if borne by the hand of a cherubim, the German flag floating onward alone through the clouds; it was the admiral's flag, flying from the great mast of the *Kaiser*, which, proceeding still in the fog, had followed us as leader of the division. This was such a startling sight that all those with us on the bridge involuntarily clicked their heels and stared at this natural phenomenon [*Naturwunder betrachteten*]. Ten minutes later the entire squadron emerged out of the fog in perfect order upon the new course. Gentlemen, from this picture I draw the conclusion that whatever fogs and dark hours may be destined for our commerce, our navy, and our fatherland, that, nevertheless, we Germans shall succeed in conquering them and by strongly pressing onward shall reach our goal, according to that good maxim: "We Germans fear God and nobody else in the world!" [1]

Gone were the Kaiser's carefully repeated assurances that "the course would remain the same." Gone was Caprivi's disavowal of inaugurating a new era. This was what the people had been waiting for; this was what they expected from the era of William II. Somehow there was something very apt about it. The speech was widely quoted and warmly approved by the most diverse parties, perhaps because it so nobly implied progress and victory without disclosing any particular goal. For better or for worse, from now on the Caprivi era would be known as the "New Course." [2]

This frame of mind on the part of the German public was under the circumstances quite natural. The four and one-half million votes given in February against the old Bismarck system might be taken to

[1] *Schulthess* (1890), p. 59; W. Müller, *Politische Geschichte der Gegenwart*, pp. 135–136; Wippermann, 6(I):244–246. With less apparent justification the Kaiser changed Bismarck's *nichts* to *niemand*.
[2] Cf. Carroll, *Germany and the Great Powers*, p. 286.

indicate a demand for something new. A mood of expectancy prevailed. All of the protagonists of the Bismarck crisis were aware that the nation had reached a turning point; the core of the crisis was indeed contained in the disagreement between Bismarck and the Kaiser over the course to take. Bismarck had decided for more and severer repression; the Kaiser had demurred. This refusal to sanction a reactionary policy had seemed to imply — what with the Kaiser's startling edicts on the labor question — the adoption of a liberal one. Actually, however, beyond the Kaiser's project of regulating the hours and conditions of labor, there was no over-all policy, no program. The Kaiser had not been interested to go beyond the isolated measure of his labor bill. Furthermore, to carry on his government he had retained all of the ministers holding posts in the old regime and had headed them with a Prussian general.[3]

Although essentially a military man, Caprivi was not without imagination in other fields. He had not been in office three weeks when he was already concocting long-range schemes.[4] He was, however, determined to proceed with caution, but in a spirit of coöperation and flexibility. The ministries whose pet projects had been held back by Bismarck would be allowed to bring them out. But what was needed was some sort of general approach to coördinate diverse measures and to attract necessary support from the various parties.[5]

On May 6, 1890, the new German Reichstag was officially opened by the Kaiser with the customary ceremony in the White Room of the royal palace. A large number of deputies were present, excluding, as usual, the Radicals and Social Democrats, who were conspicuous by their absence. Preceded by a company of the picturesquely uniformed Palace Guard, the Kaiser, dressed in the showy uniform of the Gardes du Corps, entered and was received with "three resounding cheers." The Kaiser then ascended the dais in front of the throne, flanked by the male members of the House of Hohenzollern on the right and on the left by the members of the Bundesrat with Chancellor von Caprivi at their head. From Caprivi the Kaiser took his speech and read it to the assembly in "a very firm and deliberate tone of voice."

The speech from the throne was "a model of simplicity, directness, and clearness." It contained no great surprises, setting forth a program consisting of two bills for the protection of labor, a bill increasing the peace footing of the artillery, and a supplementary

---

[3]Waldersee, *Denkwürdigkeiten*, II, 49, 125, 138.
[4]See below, Chapter IV, section 3.
[5]Cf. Caprivi's speech of April 15, above, pp. 43–44.

appropriation bill for the administration of the colony in East Africa. It did not mention the anti-Socialist law, nor did it say anything concerning the change of chancellors. At the close, the Bavarian representative to the Bundesrat led the deputies in three more cheers for the Kaiser.[6]

On May 7 the Reichstag elected its officers: for president a Conservative, von Levetzow, president of the old Reichstag; for first vice-president a Centrist, Count Ballestrem; for second vice-president a Radical, Dr. Baumbach. The chair of the *Senioren-Convent*, the important control committee of party leaders, was also taken by Count Ballestrem, the representative of the Center. To the Center likewise fell the chairmanship of the important committee on the budget and the special committee for the new labor legislation. The National Liberals received nothing. In the new Reichstag, in fact, the Center, with its well-disciplined bloc of 106 votes, held a position controlling the life and death of the government's legislation. By joining with the right it could pass everything, by joining with the left defeat everything.[7] No one was as well aware of the potentialities of this situation as the leader of the Center party, the little, ugly, almost blind, but pleasant and urbane seventy-eight-year-old Hanoverian Catholic with the crooked spectacles, Bismarck's most tenacious enemy, the clever parliamentary tactician, Dr. Ludwig Windthorst.[8] The Center party, which Windthorst had created to oppose Bismarck's onslaught on the Catholic Church in the *Kulturkampf*, was a white raven among the other parties in the Reich. Whereas the Conservatives represented the social, economic, and religious interests of the aristocratic, agrarian, Protestant Junkers of Prussia; whereas the National Liberals represented in general the national, economic, and colonial interests of the upper industrial middle class; whereas the Radicals represented the doctrinaire laissez-faire and anglophile liberalism of the commercial and professional middle class; whereas the Social Democrats represented the economic, social, and political ambitions of the proletariat and lower middle class; the members of the Center — a conglomerate of aristocrats, middle-class citizens, and laborers — were welded to-

[6]*The Times*, wkly. ed., May 9, 1890, p. 2; text of speech in *Sten. Ber.* (1890–1891), 1st session, I, 1; also in *Schulthess* (1890), pp. 64–66. For the lack of reference to Bismarck, see below, section 4.

[7]Bachem, *Geschichte . . . der Zentrumspartei*, V, 132–134.

[8]On Windthorst as a political personality cf. August Stein, *Es war alles ganz anders* (Frankfurt a. M., 1922), pp. 15ff.; L. Bamberger, *Gesammelte Schriften*, II, 221ff.

gether only by Catholicism and by Windthorst's masterful parliamentary tactics.[9]

Not an ideological leader but a cautious, businesslike, political manager of his party's interests, Windthorst's chief concern was to throw his 100 Center votes as a bloc decisively into an issue. In contrast to the ways of the other parties, ideological consistency was secondary, and more often than not the outward show of discipline that could produce a solid front of 100 votes was the result of long and difficult negotiations and compromises among the party's diverse groups.[10]

Already in March Windthorst had outlined his tactics in the coming Reichstag to a correspondent of the New York *Herald:*

In the new Reichstag new groups must be formed. The Center party will enter no permanent coalition, only such temporary combinations as may be necessary from time to time. . . . There can be no question of a systematic opposition on our part against the government. . . . The main thing is that everyone, without regard for party viewpoints, should unite in support of society and the government and protect them against attack.

The Center was apparently willing to coöperate.[11]

In return, the government made conciliatory moves of its own. The bill repealing the law for the banishment of priests which had been passed by the Reichstag in January but not acted upon by the Bundesrat, was approved by the Bundesrat on April 25, the government thus moving to carry out the wishes of the Reichstag before that body met and had an opportunity to demand it.[12] On April 29 Minister of Public Worship and Education von Gossler introduced into the Prussian House of Deputies a bill to restore to the Catholic Church the yearly income from the accumulated funds (*Sperrgeld*) sequestered by the government during the *Kulturkampf,* a bill which had been previously prepared under the Bismarck administration. Toward this bill, however, Windthorst and his party took up a position of determined opposition, demanding that the government return to the church, instead of the income, the whole of the capital sum involved. In view of this opposition from the very group

[9]*Pr. Jbb.*, 65:236 (1890); Hammann, *Der Neue Kurs,* p. 142; W. Kremer, *Der soziale Aufbau der Parteien des deutschen Reichstages 1871–1918* (Emsdetten, 1934), *passim.*

[10]Stein, *Es war alles ganz anders,* p. 21; Barth, *Politische Porträts,* pp. 29–30.

[11]Bachem, *Zentrumspartei,* V, 122.

[12]Bachem, *Zentrumspartei,* V, 33–34.

the bill was designed to benefit, in the final reading the Conservatives and National Liberals dropped their support, and the bill was resoundingly defeated on June 7. Throughout the rather stormy course of the bill the State Ministry as a whole and Caprivi personally carefully refrained from taking any public position one way or another.[13]

In the final debate in the House of Deputies Windthorst summed up the situation with these words, "if today, we cannot agree, we at least leave this matter not without hope that what has not happened today will perhaps happen tomorrow. . . . You have need of us, and we have more need of you, because you have the majority." Windthorst, naturally, and his audience knew perfectly well that Conservatives and National Liberals might indeed have a majority in the Prussian Landtag, but that in the Reichstag the shoe was on the other foot. There they had greater need of him. The Center party was willing to coöperate — but at a price; and the price must be raised considerably higher.[14]

The program presented to the Reichstag by the government represented a deliberate attempt on the part of the Kaiser and Caprivi to avoid for the present all explosive issues in the interest of conciliation and stability. The anti-Socialist law would be quietly dropped; the army increases would be cut to a minimum; the bills for the protection of labor, it was hoped, would find general support among all parties.[15] The Kaiser's decree of February 4, 1890, on the labor question had included the following statement:

It is one of the tasks of the state administration [Staatsgewalt] to regulate the time, duration, and type of work in such a way that the preservation of health, the precepts of morality, the economic requirements of the workers and their claim to legal equality of rights are protected. For the fostering of peaceful relations between employer and employee statutory prescriptions [Bestimmungen] must be considered, which will enable the workers through trusted representatives to share in the regulation of common concerns [Angelegenheiten] and to protect their interests in negotiating with their employers and with the organs of My government.[16]

[13]Landtag (1889–1890), III, 1394–1423, 1839–1911, 1947–1971; Schulthess (1890), pp. 96–98.
[14]Bachem, Zentrumspartei, V, 137; Landtag, (1889–1890), III, 1968; Schulthess (1890), p. 98; Deutsche Rundschau, 64:152 (1890); Pr. Jbb., 65:588 (1890).
[15]Cf. K. A. Müller, "Die Entlassung," p. 173.
[16]Schulthess (1890), p. 20; Wippermann, 6(I):47; Das Staatsarchiv, ed. H. Delbrück (Leipzig, 1872–1919), LI, 211.

Now preservation of the workers' health and morality was one thing, but "equality of rights" (*Gleichberechtigung*), encouragement of the organization of the workers through a recognition of "workers' committees," a sharing of the workers in "the regulation of common concerns" — even the proposal to put a statutory limit on the working day — were, in 1890, proposals radical enough to shock not only German capitalists but the governing circles of Europe generally. Within Germany immediate opposition was voiced by the Central Association of German Manufacturers, whose general secretary declared that factory owners would never agree to deal on a basis of equality with representatives of organizations of their workers.[17] As part of his campaign against the initiative of the Kaiser in this question, Bismarck had prompted a calling of the State Council — an extraordinary advisory assembly of high dignitaries — apparently in the hope that the Kaiser's visionary schemes would get short shrift. The Kaiser, however, energetically took over the leadership of the Council sessions himself, and, in spite of the opposition of the big industrialists, Krupp and Stumm and Krupp's general manager, Jencke, the final recommendations in general — though somewhat vaguely — supported the Kaiser's program.[18]

Along with his decree on the protection of labor the Kaiser had simultaneously issued a second decree ordering the chancellor to invite the other European powers to an international conference on the labor question, the intention obviously being to prevent Germany's hampering her competitive position in the international market by getting too far out in front in the regulation and amelioration of the conditions of labor. When, on February 8, Bismarck sent out a circular to various west European nations suggesting such a conference, he included the question of a general limitation of the working day along with limitations on Sunday work and the work of women and children.[19] On February 11, in his opening speech to the State Council, the Kaiser again mentioned a limitation on the duration of work, as well as the organization of workers' committees. But the idea of regulating the hours of labor of "grown-up men" got such a negative reception in Great Britain and France that the conference agenda as finally sent out omitted any mention of it. The normal

[17] Martin Wenck, *Die Geschichte und Ziele der deutschen Sozialpolitik* (Leipzig, 1908), p. 172.

[18] The State Council met February 11–28, 1890. K. A. Müller, "Die Entlassung," p. 154; Herzfeld, *Miquel*, II, 180; Waldersee, *Denkwürdigkeiten*, II, 109; Hellwig, *Stumm*, pp. 400–401.

[19] *Staatsarchiv*, LI, 212.

working day was subsequently dropped also from the agenda of the State Council.[20]

Minister of Trade von Berlepsch, newly appointed by Bismarck, was thoroughly committed to the spirit of the Kaiser's program. His experience in handling the strike of 1889 in the Ruhr had convinced him that it was easier to deal reasonably and effectively — even in a conservative sense — with organized rather than unorganized labor. The Kaiser's emphasis on this point had probably originated with him. He set to work at once to elaborate the Kaiser's plans into specific legislation.[21] For under-secretary, Berlepsch chose Theodor von Lohmann, who had long served as *Geheimrat* in the Reich Office of the Interior, under von Bötticher, and who was a staunch advocate of reform. The point of view of Lohmann, who was largely responsible for the subsequent labor-protection bill, may be gained from a memorandum submitted by him in 1890 on the labor question.

The result of the present historical development will certainly be a new organization of production. It will tend towards granting a larger share of the fruits [*Ergebnissen*] of production and a definite influence on its organization [*Gestaltung*] to the laboring classes. A healthy social policy must tend towards lifting the laboring classes to that level of intellectual and moral cultivation [*Bildung*] which is conducive to enabling them to occupy the position probably devolving upon them without danger for the preservation or progress of civilization [*Kultur*], and, in addition, directing this development so that the transformation is completed by way of reform and not of revolution.[22]

This fundamentally liberal view of the minister of trade found support in the Prussian Ministry in the person of Vice-President von Bötticher, who, as secretary of the Reich Office of the Interior had long been active in the program of social reform. It was also supported, at least at the outset, by Caprivi. Most of the ministers, however, being Prussian conservatives and under the influence of industrialists like Stumm, were skeptical and fearful of possible bad effects of this sort of reform on the economic development of the Reich. Even those backing the reforms benefiting labor were not

[20]*Staatsarchiv*, LI, 213, 219–220, 223–225; *The Times*, wkly. ed., March 7, 1890, p. 12; A. Weber, "Die Entwicklung der Arbeiterschutzgesetzgebung seit 1890," [Schmoller's] *Jahrbuch für Gesetzgebung, Verwaltung und Volkswirtschaft im Deutschen Reich* (1897), p. 1152; K. A. Müller, "Die Entlassung," p. 154.
[21]Berlepsch, *Sozialpolitische Erfahrungen und Erinnerungen*, pp. 24–25.
[22]Berlepsch, *Sozialpolitische Erfahrungen*, pp. 29–30. On Lohmann see Hans Rothfels, "Theodor Lohmann u. die Kampfjahre der staatlichen Sozialpolitik," *Forschungen und Darstellungen aus dem Reichsarchiv*, VI (1927).

overly sanguine as to the possible effects of such reforms in discouraging the Social Democratic movement. Herrfurth, the minister of the interior, had agreed to drop the anti-Socialist law because he believed it was useless if not permanent, and the Reichstag would not pass a permanent law. Even Bötticher inclined toward the necessity of an exceptional law of some sort. Caprivi himself, while in favor of conciliating labor, believed that a law against the socialists might again become necessary, but that this would be possible realistically only when the middle classes became thoroughly frightened.[23]

During a debate in the Reichstag in late February 1891 Caprivi remarked:

When the Federated Governments refrained from reintroducing an anti-Socialist law, two things were clear to them: first, that the struggle against Social Democracy is the most serious question of our time . . . further, that, if, indeed, an anti-Socialist law in its entirety would not be reintroduced, all those measures must be put into effect which over a period of time had appeared suitable for opposing Social Democracy, whether by pulling the ground out from under it, or by entering upon an open struggle with it. . . . I am convinced that it is this question [of Social Democracy] which will be the dominating one for the end of this century and perhaps for decades in the next century ("Quite right!" on the right). I sincerely wish that it may be resolved in a peaceful way; whether this wish can be fulfilled, however, it is impossible for me to foresee, and I should think that the Federated Governments, if they did not take into account that a peaceful organic solution may be impossible, would not be doing their duty. I must also confess that when one finds it necessary to read socialist books and articles, especially those that have not appeared in Germany and in which the theory is completely developed, one is always left with the question whether after all anybody thinks that these things can be accomplished without overthrowing the state ("Quite right!" on the right)! I should think, therefore, that whoever advances such theories always envisages a struggle with the existing order [Verhältnissen], that, therefore, the government also is bound to prepare itself for such a struggle ("Bravo!" on the right). I am not fearful that if these matters are openly discussed, the danger inherent in them is thereby increased. The Deputy Richter maintains that if one speaks about this from the government table, then that produces the impression that Social Democracy is the one ruling power in the state or the Reich. That is not my opinion; but I do consider it at this time the greatest danger in the Reich, and because I so consider it, I believe that the means of fighting against it must be fully utilized at each new opportunity. So long as I have the honor to occupy this position [an dieser Stelle zu stehen]

[23]Herzfeld, *Miquel,* pp. 289–290.

no bill will be introduced here, no measure proposed that is not tested from the point of view: how will it affect the question of Social Democracy? . . . It has been sufficiently demonstrated through the measures taken over a period of years by the government — and not only this but the previous government — that we are also conscious of the duty to operate organically, and, where any kind of justified dissatisfaction could assist Social Democracy, to counteract it. We wish to have a clear conscience in this matter; we wish, however, on the other hand, if a serious situation should develop, which God forbid, also to have a strong hand (enthusiastic "Bravo!" on the right)! [24]

The old anti-Socialist law was to expire on September 30, 1890. During the summer, therefore, Herrfurth sent out instructions to the local officials to pay special attention to the activities of the Social Democrats, acting with decision against any "excesses," bearing in mind the changed legal status of the party after expiration of the exceptional law, but utilizing to the utmost all legal means at their disposal.[25]

At this time, the attitude of the Kaiser, the sponsor of the new progressive legislation, toward the problems of socialism and labor was somewhat more ambiguous. On April 1, 1890, an article appeared in the official *Reichsanzeiger* which stated among other things that "society is as a scale in the hand of the monarch; he must apply or withdraw his weight now on this side, now on that side to prevent fluctuations and to restore the harmony once it has been disturbed." [26] What might the implications of this be? Was the Kaiser supporting the Social Democrats? The Wilhelmstrasse became immediately concerned lest some new ill-considered move be in the making, and letters went off to Phili Eulenburg from Holstein, Kayser, and Dr. Fischer, the influential Berlin correspondent of the *Kölnische Zeitung* and close friend of Holstein. Eulenburg at once responded, sending Fischer's letter on to the Kaiser with a personal note warning him not to "envisage an extended program" at this time. After Bismarck's fall Germany was in a state of nervous tension and needed a quiet sleep. The Kaiser, however, bluntly informed Eulenburg that he had had nothing to do with the article, which had been printed without his authorization by two gentlemen on the *Reichsanzeiger* staff "for their private delectation." [27]

Three days previously, on March 27, a new strike having broken

[24] *Sten. Ber.* (1890–1891), III, 1767, 1792, 1794; *Schulthess* (1891), pp. 42, 51–54.
[25] *Deutsche Rundschau,* 64:470 (1890).
[26] *Schulthess* (1890), p. 53.
[27] Haller, *Eulenburg*, I, 125–126.

out in Gelsenkirchen, the Kaiser had himself ordered the assembled commanding generals to "use their repeating rifles at the first opportunity." Late in August a meeting of Social Democrats resulted in rioting with the Berlin police. The Kaiser, without consulting the chancellor, the minister of war, or even the chief of his own Military Cabinet, immediately withdrew a brigade of troops from the army maneuvers then in progress and nervously dispatched them to reinforce the Berlin garrison.[28]

With these conservative tendencies at work in the government it is not very surprising that certain conservative clauses crept into the labor-protection bill as presented in May by the Bundesrat to the Reichstag. These included provisions punishing breach of contract by a worker, encouraging greater discipline of younger workers, penalizing strikers' intimidation of nonstriking workers, as well as public incitement to an illegal strike (*widerrechtlichen*), but also penalizing the unjustified dismissal of a worker on the part of the employer. As a result of the insertion of the above provisions there were some in the Reichstag who irreverently referred to the workers' protection bill (*Arbeiterschutz*) as the workers' subjection bill (*Arbeitertrutz*).[29] Although loyally defended by Berlepsch himself, these sections dealing with punishments for illegal strikes and so on were defeated on the floor of the Reichstag after heated exchanges between Radicals and Social Democrats.[30]

On the other side of the issue the attempts of the Social Democrats and Center to limit the working day for adult male workers were successfully beaten off by the parties of the right. That the workers' protection bill passed at all was largely due to the efforts in the commission and on the floor of the influential Saar iron and steel industrialist, Baron Carl Ferdinand von Stumm-Halberg. A Free Conservative, Stumm, through the organization of his factories, had made himself a living example of paternalism in industry, and, while energetically opposing any suggestion of independent status for labor in his own works or elsewhere, he just as energetically supported protective legislation for the individual worker's welfare. On this score he came into conflict even with the majority of his fellow industrialists in the Central Association of German Manufacturers.

[28] Wedel, *Zwischen Kaiser und Kanzler*, p. 67; Waldersee, *Denkwürdigkeiten*, II, 142; *Schulthess* (1890), p. 149.

[29] Paragraph 153 of the bill, *Sten. Ber.* (1890–1891), 1st sess., *Anlageband* I, 10; Berlepsch, *Sozialpolitische Erfahrungen*, pp. 32–33; *The Times*, wkly. ed., May 9, 1890, p. 11; Hellwig, *Stumm*, p. 416; Werner Trappe, *Dr. Hans Freiherr v. Berlepsch als Sozialpolitiker* (Bochum-Langendreer, 1934), pp. 37–38, 42.

[30] Hellwig, *Stumm*, p. 417; *Sten. Ber.* (1890–1891), IV, 2469–2539.

In the Reichstag, however, he nevertheless managed to persuade the
two conservative parties to support the bill.[31]

Reported out of commission on January 17, 1891, the workers'
protection bill, or, formally, the Bill to Amend the Law Regulating
Industry and Crafts (*Gewerbeordnung*), passed the Reichstag on
May 8, 1891, with an overwhelming majority. Only the Social Democrats voted against it.[32] In its final form it provided for ensuring the
safety and health of factory workers, prohibited work on Sunday,
with certain exceptions, called for the formation and publication of
set rules and regulations for the conduct of work in the factories,
prohibited the labor of children under thirteen, and set maximum
working hours of six hours for children under fourteen excused from
school, ten hours for children from fourteen to sixteen years, and
eleven hours for women. There was no limitation of the working
hours of adult males, but a clause giving the Bundesrat power to set
maximum limits administratively in cases of possible injury to health
made it possible for the government in 1896 to order a limit of thirteen and a half hours a day for the baking industry.[33]

The first of the two labor bills, that creating industrial arbitration
courts, found little opposition and was approved in its third reading
by the Reichstag on June 28, 1890. Courts of this type were set up at
once in Prussia by Berlepsch.[34] As part of the new labor program,
Berlepsch, with the assistance of Lohmann, in 1892 also reorganized
and increased the scope of factory inspection in Prussia, and, the
same year, Caprivi created a Reich commission for labor statistics.
The 1896 regulation of hours of work in the baking industry was a
notable result of the activities of this commission.[35]

Whereas the labor-protection bill enjoyed a comparatively un-
eventful, albeit long and tortuous journey through the legislative
process, the bill to increase the field artillery produced the first real

[31]*Schulthess* (1890), p. 323; Hellwig, *Stumm*, pp. 418–419; Berlepsch, *Sozialpolitische Erfahrungen*, pp. 37f.

[32]*Schulthess* (1891), p. 84; text of the law in *Sten. Ber.* (1890–1892), 1st sess.,
Anlageband IV, 2764–2765.

[33] Paragraph 120e, *Sten. Ber.* (1890–1891), 1st sess., *Anlageband* I, 4; Ziekursch,
Geschichte, III, 55; Berlepsch, *Sozialpolitische Erfahrungen*, p. 43; Weber, "Die
Entwicklung," pp. 1156, 1160–1161. For a summary of the law amending the law
regulating industry and crafts see Wenck, *Sozialpolitik*, pp. 158–169; Trappe,
Berlepsch, pp. 21–38; for an illuminating discussion of the purposes and effects of
the law see Weber, *op. cit.*

[34]*Schulthess* (1890), p. 144; Hellwig, *Stumm*, p. 415; Ziekursch, *Geschichte*, III,
55; a summary of the law in Wenck, *Sozialpolitik*, pp. 169–170.

[35] Ziekursch, *Geschichte*, III, 55; Berlepsch, *Sozialpolitische Erfahrungen*, pp.
42–43; Weber, "Die Entwicklung," p. 1160; Rothfels, "Theodor Lohmann," pp.
110–113.

crisis for the new government, the first taking of positions on an issue by parties and government and by persons within the government, and the first testing of these positions. The large-scale army reorganization plans drawn up by Minister of War General Count von Verdy du Vernois, approved by Chief of Staff General Count von Waldersee, and used by Bismarck as a convenient weapon in his final struggle, had subsequently been laid aside. The bill now introduced called for increases in the artillery only, some 18,500 more men in peacetime, with the intent of matching recent increases in the French army. It was presented as a supplementary measure to the *septennat* of 1887, and would, therefore, cover only a four-year period, until the expiration of the *septennat* in 1894. The threat of the new French armaments had long been recognized in Germany. Consequently, it was expected that the reduced bill would find an easy passage, and, at first, it seemed indeed that such would be the case. Windthorst, at least, did not take up a strong position against it and ended his speech recommending it be handed over to a select committee with the assurance that in the face of her foreign foes Germany had no parties.[36]

A suggestion by Caprivi in his speech on the bill on May 16, that the *septennat* principle was "not a life-and-death question for the army" and might not be adhered to in the future, brought cheers from the left side of the Reichstag. Also, on May 14, the Reichstag was treated to a rare occurrence when the ninety-year-old Field Marshal von Moltke, the grand old man of German nationalism, arose and made a brief speech supporting the bill. The aged Moltke's warning that "the pacific assurances of both our neighbors in the east and the west, assurances for the rest which are tendered us simultaneously with the continuance of their warlike preparations ('very true!'), are no doubt very valuable, but security we can only find with and from ourselves," seemed to produce a deep and general impression.[37]

For a time it seemed that not only the Center but also a part, at least, of the Radicals might support the bill. Within the Radical party the more conservative wing of old National Liberal "secessionists" regarded the hopeful new era beginning under Caprivi as a time for the development of a more flexible, less negative program,

[36]Text of the bill in *Sten. Ber.* (1890–1891), *Anlageband* I, 51; *Schulthess* (1890), pp. 75–78; Ziekursch, *Geschichte*, III, 63; *Pr. Jbb.*, 65:237 (1890); *The Times*, wkly. ed., May 16, 1890, p. 14; Wedel, *Zwischen Kaiser und Kanzler*, p. 80; *Sten. Ber.* (1890–1891), I, 89.

[37]*Sten. Ber.* (1890–1891), I, 76–77, 115; *Schulthess* (1890), p. 85; *The Times*, wkly. ed., May 16, 1890, p. 15.

and in particular, as an opportunity to free themselves from the dogmatic dictatorial rule of the old Progressive leader Eugen Richter, who was, perhaps, also tending to coöperate too closely with the Social Democrats. The struggle for power between right and left wings within the party broke into the open between May 12 and 19, when Schrader, the right-winger, was elected by a small majority to displace Richter as leader of the party fraction in the Reichstag and Prussian Landtag.[38]

Since a vote of the larger part of the Radicals in favor of Caprivi's "little army bill" would, in effect, be equivalent to a decision on their part to swing into line and support the Caprivi administration, such a move might have seriously altered the political picture. To the degree that Caprivi received support from the Radicals he would be that much less dependent upon the Center. A wide, national legislative backing such as Caprivi desired might then be possible, rather than a narrow one based upon a particular party constellation. Certainly such an optimistic view was encouraged by the generally prevailing feeling of good will towards the new regime. Might not the election of a Conservative, a Centrist, and a Radical to preside over the Reichstag symbolize possible broad coöperation on a national basis between the parties? Such wide horizontal support would produce greater freedom and independence of action for the government on the one side as on the other it would, by bringing about internal, vertical stresses and strains, weaken the position of each party individually. Perhaps a new party line-up — already expected in some quarters — might result.[39]

This pleasant prospect, however, was abruptly obscured by the tactless statements of Minister von Verdy in the select commission of the Reichstag. In his speech during the first reading on May 14 Verdy had made vague allusions to larger plans which he would amplify later in the commission sessions. This general statement had immediately aroused suspicion and concern, which Caprivi in his own speech on the 16th had tried to allay by emphasizing that any such plans were a matter for the indefinite future, had not as yet been decided upon, and had no bearing upon the present bill. Verdy, however, persisted, in spite of a peremptory reprimand from the chancellor, and in the commission session of May 21 said flatly that

[38]L. Ullstein, *Eugen Richter als Publizist* (Leipzig, 1930), pp. 145–150; *Schulthess* (1890), p. 87; Wippermann, 6(I):307–309.

[39]*Pr. Jbb.*, 65:86–87 (1890); *Die Nation*, ed. Dr. T. Barth (Berlin), 10:647 (1893); see below, section 2.

this bill was only the first; more and greater increases in army strength would be required later.[40]

Like a sudden, jarring dissonance this statement of Verdy's immediately brought an end to the harmony of the political concert. Eugen Richter, seizing upon these undefined future plans for the army as welcome grist for his party propaganda mill, raised such a hue and cry against rampant militarism throughout the Radical press, which he dominated, that he thereby turned the threatened revolt within his party into a rout and was once more able to unite it under his own uncompromising leadership. Even Windthorst found himself in a most difficult position, as Center party members began to be concerned for the opinion in their constituencies and to move away from a position supporting the government.[41]

Caprivi, on June 9, appeared in the commission and did what he could to save the situation. Verdy's statement, he said, had given the wrong impression. Action on the present bill did not call for discussion of future expansion plans. Issues raised by such plans could just as easily be fought out later by the Reichstag as now.

The Reichstag loses nothing, whether it chooses to do battle sooner or later; the Federated Governments, however, have a very strong interest in seeing the bill passed now. The departure of Prince Bismarck from the service of the Reich has left behind conditions [Verhältnisse] which are not as secure as in the time when his fascinating personality still stood before the world. One has always had to reckon with the fact that sometime he would no longer be there, and that the transition period would be difficult was always clear; why then should one now wish to increase the difficulties without reason? Many things now will be handled, not as previously with an exclamation mark, but with a question mark.[42]

Although this speech of Caprivi's somewhat calmed the situation, a practical way out of the political impasse was achieved by the clever maneuvers of Windthorst. He continued to support the bill in commission on the ground that this was not the most favorable time for a knock-down battle, but, at the same time, he saved face for his party on the main issues and set the groundwork for the future struggle by introducing four resolutions, which demanded that the

---

[40]Sten. Ber. (1890–1891), I, 75, 113, Anlageband I, 594ff.; Schulthess (1890), pp. 79, 80–85, 87; Waldersee, Denkwürdigkeiten, II, 128.

[41]Schulthess (1890), pp. 87, 101, 321–323; Wedel, Zwischen Kaiser und Kanzler, p. 115; Bachem, Zentrumspartei, V, 141; Waldersee, Denkwürdigkeiten, II, 130, 132–133.

[42]Schulthess (1890), p. 99; cf. Thimme, "Bismarck und Kardorff," pt. I, pp. 55–56; Sten. Ber. (1890–1891), Anlageband I, 597.

government (1) should not impose in the future a plan for peacetime training of the army which would constitute an "unbearable
burden" on the Reich; (2) should abandon the *septennat* for a five-
year military appropriation; (3) should "effectively" decrease the
length of military service; (4) should seriously consider the introduction by law of two-year service for the infantry. He himself
based his own support of the bill upon some concession by the
government in the direction of two-year service.[43]

Windthorst's resolutions passed the commission by a large
majority, but no word came from the government as to possible
concessions. Violent dissatisfaction with Windthorst's tactics broke
out in the Center party. In the final vote on the bill in the commission half of the Center members voted against it, but the votes of
Windthorst and those remaining faithful to his leadership brought
a close majority of 16 to 12 for the bill. The fate of the bill began to
appear extremely dubious.[44]

Meanwhile Caprivi attempted to get imperial authorization for a
few concessions to pacify the Center. But the Kaiser would have
none of it. He would not even consent to include Windthorst —
upon whose tactical efforts in the Reichstag the entire fate of the bill
rested — among a group of parliamentary leaders to be invited to
a special party in their honor on June 21 on the *Pfaueninsel*. Windthorst, declared the Kaiser, was "an extremely dangerous, malicious
man, who has already terribly wronged my family." Caprivi pushed
the matter, and the first real clash between Kaiser and chancellor
resulted. Finally, the Kaiser declared that it was a matter of his
honor, to which Caprivi did not feel he could rightly reply. Windthorst was not invited.[45]

The situation threatened to become serious. Windthorst could
not risk supporting the bill without some concession which would
satisfy and hold together his party, and this the Kaiser refused to
authorize. Generals von Waldersee and von Verdy advocated a
strong line. Caprivi should threaten to dissolve the Reichstag. "What
are parliamentary tactical tricks to us; this is too serious a time for
such things." Again, only three months after Bismarck's departure,
rumors began to spread of a possible *coup d'état* — this time by the

---

[43]*Schulthess* (1890), p. 106; *Sten. Ber.* (1890–1891), *Anlageband* I, 598; Bachem,
Zentrumspartei, V, 141–142.

[44]Bachem, *Zentrumspartei*, V, 141–142; *Sten. Ber.* (1890–1891), *Anlageband* I,
598–599.

[45]Wedel, *Zwischen Kaiser und Kanzler*, pp. 111–112; Waldersee, *Denkwürdigkeiten*, II, 131.

Kaiser — resulting in a limiting of universal suffrage. In a session of the commission Windthorst replied to a remark of Richter's, "At this time I am better informed than others of the consequences of a rejection of this bill. It would bring about great danger. I am not thinking merely of a dissolution. That in itself could not frighten me. But if the Reichstag, once dissolved, should return with the same composition, it is what may happen then that concerns me." [46]

Caprivi, however, was determined not to provoke a quarrel with the Reichstag; if the Kaiser insisted on a dissolution he would resign. "Caprivi," wrote Count Wedel on June 6, "who was in the palace for an audience this noon, seemed very depressed. . . . God knew, he declared, that he had not wanted his present position; he would be happy if tomorrow he could go live as a pensioner in Wiesbaden." [47]

At length the Kaiser yielded; Caprivi agreed privately with the Center leaders, Windthorst, Ballestrem, and Baron von Huene, that 6,000 men a year should be added to the number "placed at disposition" at the end of two years. Since the over-all period of service was three years, this meant that a number equivalent to the total increase of 18,000 men provided for in the army bill would have their period of service reduced to two years. At this time some 49 per cent of the army were thus regularly placed on indefinite furlough at the end of 22 months of training. By this concession of Caprivi's the over-all number would now be raised to 53 per cent, so that more than half the army would be giving, in effect, only two years of service.[48]

With this concession, most of the wayward members of the Center came into line. In the debate on the second reading on June 24 Windthorst supported the bill with his resolutions before Caprivi spoke. Then Caprivi replied with a speech, more terse, more military than usual, asking for unity for the sake of Germany. He had been accused by the press of asking a closed hunting season for himself; he had wanted nothing of the sort. "Go ahead and shoot at me! I won't mind it! [*Mir soll es recht sein!*] I asked that the season be closed for Germany. . . ." At the end he announced his concession, which was most joyfully received. "A whisper of satisfaction ran

[46]Waldersee, *Denkwürdigkeiten*, II, 130–131; Bachem, *Zentrumspartei*, V, 141; cf. Zechlin, *Staatsstreichpläne*, p. 90.

[47]Wedel, *Zwischen Kaiser und Kanzler*, p. 109; Waldersee, *Denkwürdigkeiten*, II, 131.

[48]Bachem, *Zentrumspartei*, V, 142.

through the house, and in the Center faces brightened up again. . . ." [49]

On June 28 the "little army bill" passed the third reading in the Reichstag with a large majority, the Radicals and Social Democrats voting in opposition.[50] In effect, it was a dual victory for Windthorst and the Center. For the first time a concession had actually been wrung from the military! And, with the reuniting of the Radicals in opposition, the Center now fully commanded the political situation. Furthermore, Windthorst had placed the government greatly in his debt. It was essentially his tactics, his support which had saved the day. This service would have to be paid for.[51]

2

MIQUEL

At this juncture Caprivi's administration was greatly strengthened by the addition of a powerful personality, when Johannes Miquel succeeded Scholz as Prussian minister of finance. Of Spanish descent by way of France, as his name showed, Miquel had begun his political career in 1848, when as a twenty-year-old student at Heidelberg and Göttingen he had become acquainted with Hecker and Struve and become interested in the ideas of Karl Marx.[52] From this somewhat fruitless position on the extreme left, however, he had soon moved into the central stream of German liberalism and nationalism, becoming associated with Bennigsen in the formation of the National Liberal party in the 1860's and 1870's. He had in this capacity held seats in the parliaments of Prussia, the North German Confederation, and the Reich. From 1865 to 1870 and 1876 to 1886 he had been *Bürgermeister* of Osnabrück, from 1880 to 1890 *Oberbürgermeister* of Frankfurt am Main. As for so many other liberals, the year of 1866 had been for him a turning point. He had declared then at an election rally in Osnabrück, "The time of ideals is past. Today politicians must ask not so much as formerly what is desirable, but rather what is possible." [53] The National Liberals, and Miquel among them, had, in effect, given up immediate realization

[49]*Schulthess* (1890), pp. 139–140; Schreck, *Caprivi*, p. 108, text of speech, pp. 108–113; *Sten. Ber.* (1890–1891), I, 542–548.

[50]*Sten. Ber.* (1890–1891), I, 677; *Schulthess* (1890), p. 144.

[51]Bachem, *Zentrumspartei*, V, 142–143; *Pr. Jbb.*, 66:97–98 (1890).

[52]Miquel's letters to Marx in *Neue Zeit*, 32 Jahrg. (1914), II. For his early life see W. Mommsen, *Johannes von Miquel* (Stuttgart, 1928), also the convenient sketch in W. Geiger, *Miquel und die preussische Steuerreform, 1890–1893* (Göppingen, 1934).

[53]Geiger, *Miquel*, p. 6.

of their liberal, parliamentary aims for the sake of victorious nationalism. From then on, increasingly, they had tended to support
Bismarck's dictatorship and Bismarck's Reich. At the second critical
turning point of the party in the eighties, when the left wing had
seceded to form, with the Progressives, the new Radical party,
Miquel had led in the reorganization of the National Liberal party
to support Bismarck's tariff, colonial, and social policies. It was this
shift of the National Liberals further to the right that, in 1887, made
it possible for them to ally with the Conservatives in the Kartell.[54]
By then, national unity having been achieved in 1870, they had
really become a conservative party. Their support of Bismarck
meant, in terms of political actuality, support of the social and
political preponderance of the Junker aristocracy, the class which, in
Bismarck's Reich, continued to fill all the important administrative
posts in the civil service and the army. For this support middle-class
industrialists received economic assistance and encouragement from
the government. Thus in the tariff of 1879 both Junker agriculture
and middle-class industry were benefited. In addition, middle-class
professors, writers, and professional people received a certain
amount of professional and social recognition.

In 1890, at sixty-two, Miquel had changed considerably in personal appearance since the revolutionary days of 1848. The shock of
unruly black hair was now gray and in order, neatly brushed; on
either side of the prominent, high-bridged nose, the eyes had become less staring, softer, with a benign addition of crow's feet at the
corners. Only their flashing, restless mobility remained and constituted the dominant note in his face, an expression of the dramatic
intensity of his personality. The general air of tension, however, had
dissolved; the wild young revolutionary had been replaced by the
good-humored elder statesman with his patriarchal, closely trimmed
gray beard.[55] He was a man of brilliant intellect and fascinating
personality. "I have seldom met a man," wrote Phili Eulenburg,
"whose intellect, knowledge, and brilliant conversation fascinated
me so much." He had had much political and administrative experience. As befitted a political leader with years of experience in
the Reichstag, he combined an impressive amount of passionate
idealism with an equally astonishing degree of practical realism.[56]

[54]Hermann Oncken, *Rudolf von Bennigsen* (Stuttgart, 1910), pp. 512–514; O.
Stillich, *Die politische Parteien in Deutschland* (Leipzig, 1908–1911), II, 306–309.
On the middle class and the tariff see below, p. 142.

[55]See the striking series of photographs in Herzfeld, *Miquel*, I, 16, 416, 544, II,
153, 313, 391, 461, 510.

[56]Haller, *Eulenburg*, I, 303; Herzfeld, *Miquel*, II, 390; Geiger, *Miquel*, p. 6.

In 1889–1890 Miquel had led the group of National Liberals who, by insisting on a change in the anti-Socialist law, had contributed to the defeat and dissolution of the Kartell. He had felt, with Bismarck, that the hopes for the successful working together of the parties in a Reichstag based on universal suffrage had not borne fruit, that the constitutional life of Germany was standing before a severe crisis. The old parties, he felt, based on the old fight over a liberal, constitutional state, would have to be reconstructed to meet the challenge of the new epoch of social cleavages, of transformed economic and class relationships. In this interim of adjustment and confusion the monarchy was the natural center of gravity for German political life, the one remaining power which could lead the nation through a difficult period. This, as has already been noted, was a hope and a faith shared by all the parties — except the left opposition — and also by Bismarck. But Miquel parted company with Bismarck on the latter's pessimistic belief that only severe measures would work. Miquel optimistically hoped to achieve this essentially conservative goal, of rallying all classes of society around the monarchy and against revolution, through liberal reform. In the struggle for policy and power, then, it was only natural that Miquel should take the Kaiser's side. He allowed himself to become extremely enthusiastic over the Kaiser's potentialities as the leader of the nation. And here again he was not alone, as the story of the fall of Bismarck has already demonstrated. In return he succeeded in attracting the Kaiser's attention to himself. There was much in the older man's personality which the younger found exhilarating and delightful. In February the Kaiser had tried to appoint Miquel governor of the province of the Rhine, but Miquel had refused, preferring to retain his parliamentary position. That position, however, had been blasted by the disastrous election of February 20, and now Miquel accepted the powerful position of Prussian minister of finance.[57] Here he could operate to great advantage in promoting his own special kind of flexible conservatism as well as satisfying his personal ambition.

During the last phase of the Bismarck crisis — when Bismarck was making gestures toward dropping the Kartell and encouraging a coalition of the Conservatives with the Center — Miquel expressed his thoughts on the political situation in a letter to General von Waldersee, dated March 6. "We have," he wrote, "been too desirous of accomplishing everything with violence, while the German nation

[57]Herzfeld, *Miquel*, II, 157–161, 171–177; K. A. Müller, "Die Entlassung," pp. 155–156. Cf. Hans Leuss, *Wilhelm Freiherr v. Hammerstein* (Berlin, 1905), p. 85.

may be ruled much more easily with conciliation and good will, for which it always lavishes love and gratitude on its princes." A policy of conciliation emanating from the throne would win over the new Reichstag. Controversial issues such as the anti-Socialist law should be avoided, social legislation should be continued, long-desired reforms should be carried out in Prussia. In this manner the moderate elements in the Center and Radical parties would be appeased. "The great task at present is, without prejudice or embarrassment because of past battles, to gather together [*sammeln*] all the elements that support the state [*staatserhaltenden*] and thereby to prepare for the perhaps unavoidable battle against the Social Democratic movement, which is often misunderstood and still almost always underestimated." With such a program he hoped it would be possible "step by step to satisfy the justifiable demands of the working classes and in that way even to coöperate with them [*dabei selbst mitwirken zu lassen*]." This letter of Miquel's was shown by Waldersee to the grand duke of Baden on March 10, approved by him, and then on March 12 sent to the Kaiser upon whom it may have had a certain effect. The climactic scene with Bismarck came three days later.[58]

From the ideas of Miquel as expressed in this letter it is easy to see that in general they were not strictly liberal, but rather liberal-conservative. All essentially conservative groups were to be gathered together in support of property and order; by granting special favors to the working classes perhaps they too might be "won over." No fundamental change in the present paternalistic form of society and government, however, appeared to be envisaged. The "reform program" itself was to be carried out by the crown and in support of the crown. These ideas of Miquel's seemed in perfect accord with the ideas of Caprivi, for whose regime he would thus provide welcome support. This unprecedented step of appointing a middle-class National Liberal to a Prussian ministerial post might also allay suspicions that, after Windthorst's recent tactical triumph on the army bill, the government had been taken over completely by the Center party. "Nothing is more characteristic of our constitutional life," commented the *Preussische Jahrbücher*, "than that a party leader has become a minister, not after his party has won the majority [in the Reichstag] but after it has lost it." For the very important post of finance minister, therefore, Johannes Miquel seemed to be under the circumstances an obvious and a fortunate choice.[59]

[58] Herzfeld, *Miquel*, II, 183–184. See above, pp. 23–24.
[59] A. Wahl, *Deutsche Geschichte 1871–1914* (Stuttgart, 1926–1936), III, 521; *Pr. Jbb.*, 66:98–99 (1890).

It is consequently all the more interesting to note that Miquel was not the Kaiser's first choice for this position. On June 20 the Kaiser had visited the Krupp works in Essen and had been much impressed, so impressed that he had offered the general manager, Jencke, the vacant post of minister of finance. Herr Jencke — a man of courage — earlier in the year had distinguished himself in the State Council by openly and vigorously opposing the Kaiser's ideas on the labor question. Miquel on the other hand had, of course, supported them. What kind of influence Jencke might have exerted in the Caprivi ministry can only be imagined. Jencke, however, served the fates in this instance and refused to accept the position. Then, upon the recommendation of the retiring minister, the State Ministry unanimously nominated Miquel.[60]

3

THE REFORM PROGRAM IN PRUSSIA

When, in April, Caprivi had made his initial speech to the Landtag[61] the various party leaders, in responding enthusiastically, had requested action on a number of long-pending reforms in Prussia. With an impressive amount of agreement they had all demanded reform of the Prussian state taxes, reform of rural government in the eastern provinces, a reform and general regulation of the school system.[62]

In the speech from the throne opening the new session of the Landtag on November 12 and in his own speech to the Landtag two days later Caprivi introduced a series of bills containing all of these requested reforms, in taxes, rural government, and the school system. This sudden introduction of such a large package of important reform legislation created something of a sensation in the Landtag, which, as the Conservative leader, von Rauchhaupt, had remarked the previous April, had been in danger of going to sleep the last few years under Bismarck.[63] The "New Course" was beginning to live up to its name and to public expectations.

The bills, Caprivi stated in his speech on the 14th, formed a unified and related whole, with the aim of strengthening, not the government, but the state itself. By strengthening the financial system and shifting the tax burden from weaker to stronger shoul-

[60]Herzfeld, *Miquel*, II, 197, 200, note; Waldersee, *Denkwürdigkeiten*, II, 134–135; Wahl, *Deutsche Geschichte*, III, 521; *Pr. Jbb.*, 66:98 (1890).
[61] See above, pp. 43–44.
[62]*Landtag* (1889–1890), II, 1049–1074.
[63]*Landtag* (1889–1890), II, 1066; cf. Eyck, *Wilhelm II*, p. 49.

ders, by encouraging self-government in the rural districts, by creating a permanent system for the primary schools, increased loyalty to the state would be encouraged among the populace.

We must, it seems to me, become year by year more and more convinced that in opposition to the ever-spreading danger threatening the state [*staatsgefährdenden Tendenz*] a union of all elements supporting the state becomes ever more necessary ("Bravo!"). . . . The government can subjugate and suppress, but that is not the end of the matter ("Very true!" on the left); the injuries from which we suffer [*die Schäden, vor denen wir stehen*] must be healed from within ("Very good!" on the left), and this, in the judgment of the government, requires that love for the state, well being within the state, a feeling of belonging [*Sichheimischfühlen*], a participation with head and heart in the tasks of the state be carried over into a wider sphere ("Bravo!" on the left). . . .

Is it, then, not right to ask: what are all the questions which can produce conflicts and disagreements here among the parties as against the questions posed for us by Social Democracy? . . .

And so I should like to conclude with an appeal to the House, above and beyond the scope of these bills, to unite for the preservation of the state. We have experienced great wars, and one of the most gratifying and appealing aspects of these wars has been the fact that throughout their duration all the parties forgot their domestic quarrels and had only the one objective: the Fatherland ("Bravo!"). We are now also in a war, which in its effects is no less serious, no less dangerous ("Quite right!"). Why should it not be possible here also to say: here is the Fatherland, by it let us stand, for it let us work, for it let us forget all petty domestic disputes (enthusiastic "Bravo!").[64]

The individual bills comprising the new legislative program thus laid before the Landtag had in essentials been prepared long before by the respective ministries and held back only by Bismarck's negative attitude toward continued reforms at this time. The various ministers now were given free rein by Caprivi to sponsor and to defend their own measures before the Landtag; Minister of Finance Miquel for tax reform, Minister of the Interior Herrfurth for the reform of rural government in the eastern provinces, Minister for Education and Public Worship von Gossler for the bill regulating the school system.

Politically, this reform program of the "New Course" was not aimed at the two conservative parties or at the National Liberals, the parties which so easily controlled both houses of the Prussian

[64]*Landtag* (1890–1891), I, 12–15; summary and excerpts in *Schulthess* (1890), pp. 163–165; Wippermann, 6(II):210–215.

Landtag. The main concern, as ever, was with the effect on the Reichstag; it was hoped that popular reforms such as these might attract support from Center and Radicals, thereby bringing these oppositional parties into closer connection with the government. The opposition might be cajoled and encouraged to adopt a spirit of coöperation. Conservatives and National Liberals would support the government anyway, out of principle and from habit, and in the Reichstag they were in the minority.[65]

Tax Reform

The tax system of Prussia, as of other European states, had been based historically upon product or yield. The principal tax was the land and buildings tax, supplemented by a tax on factories and workshops. This sort of tax structure was most appropriate to the old, feudal, corporate society. But with the rise of the modern national state in Prussia, as elsewhere, and with the growth of commerce and manufacture, the emphasis changed from a society made up of variously producing groups or orders to one of individuals directly responsible to the state. In particular, the newer sources of wage income and income from investment were not touched by the old taxes. This development had led to the introduction in Prussia of various personal taxes, in addition to the old property taxes.[66]

The financial structure of the Reich had then been placed by Bismarck on a basis of indirect taxes, which rested most heavily on the lower classes. The groups, therefore, which in the 1880's were pressing hardest for tax reform in Prussia were, on the one hand, the landholders who bore the brunt of the continued emphasis on property, as opposed to income, and the lower classes and owners of small enterprises who suffered under both direct and indirect taxes. The answer was felt more and more to be a personal income tax. In 1878 Saxony put into effect an income tax which showed the way to the other German states. Saxe-Weimar followed suit in 1883, Baden in 1884, and Anhalt in 1886. The institution of these laws was accompanied by a lively and extensive discussion of the subject of tax reform and its basic principles by a host of experts, among whom Adolf Wagner and Gustav Schmoller were the most notable.[67]

[65]Cf. Thimme, "Bismarck und Kardorff," pt. I, p. 162.

[66]E. Seligman, *Essays in Taxation* (New York, 1919), p. 474, *The Income Tax* (New York, 1911), pp. 223–250; Geiger, *Miquel*, pp. 10–13; Herzfeld, *Miquel*, II, 204–224. For further technical articles see references in Seligman, *Essays*, p. 476 and note.

[67]Seligman, *Income Tax*, pp. 243–250; Geiger, *Miquel*, pp. 13–15; Herzfeld, *Miquel*, II, 210.

Given this favorable atmosphere, and with Bismarck gone, some sort of tax reform in Prussia was inevitable. Miquel had merely to follow the lead of his predecessors and of informed opinion. His principal service was in steering the reform successfully through the Landtag.[68] The over-all scheme for tax reform, as planned and set forth by Miquel, was to replace the basic state taxes on property with an expanded and reformed personal income tax, to be supplemented with an expanded inheritance tax. The old property taxes could then be dropped altogether by the state and handed over to the local communities. The local tax system in this way would also be reformed and would be given a sounder, more reliable basis, at the same time making it possible to dispense with the indirect taxation which local communities hitherto had used. Miquel's basic strategy was first to inaugurate the income and inheritance taxes, then, after these were established and if sufficient revenue resulted, to hand over the property taxes to the local communities.[69]

The salient features of the new income tax of 1890–1891, as finally enacted, were a progressive rate and the introduction of compulsory evaluation and declaration of income by the individual.[70] Incomes below 900 M were exempt. Incomes from 900–1,050 M paid a tax of 6 M (0.66–0.57 per cent), and so on through twenty-six separate stages until incomes of 9,500–10,500 M paid 300 M (3.15–2.85 per cent, or 3 per cent of the mean income), and then through further stages, until incomes of 100,000 M or over paid 4,000 M or more, at the top rate of 4 per cent. The compulsory self-declaration was meant to do away with the previous inadequate — particularly in the upper brackets — and even farcical system of assessment.[71]

The reform, as envisaged by Miquel, would carry out the principle of differentiating the source of local and state taxes, as between taxes on product (land, buildings, business) and on personal income, thus giving each administrative area a basic tax structure especially suited to it, and in addition, it would remove inequities and duplications and place the bulk of the tax burden on the higher incomes; that is, it would carry out the principle of taxation according to ability to pay.[72]

[68]Seligman, *Essays*, p. 476; Geiger, *Miquel*, p. 15; Herzfeld, *Miquel*, II, 151.
[69]Herzfeld, *Miquel*, II, 224–225.
[70]For a clear and thorough discussion of this tax, see Seligman, *Income Tax*, pp. 250–272; other references, *ibid.*, p. 250, note.
[71]Cf. *Schulthess* (1891), pp. 93–94.
[72]Geiger, *Miquel*, pp. 20–21, 23–27; Oncken, *Bennigsen*, II, 563–564; Miquel's speeches, *Landtag* (1890–1891), I, 19–30, 73–75, 103–110, 167–173, II, 876–880, 928–929, 938–939, 941–942, III, 1317–1319.

In order to put this admirably conceived and rational reform through the Landtag, Miquel, the experienced politician, was quite willing to resort to hard political trading and even to somewhat questionable tactics. In the Landtag the Conservatives, with a permanent grip on the House of Lords and more than one fourth of the seats in the House of Deputies, held the dominant position. Since Miquel held out the eventual promise of abolishing the land tax as a state tax, the agrarian Conservatives were favorably disposed toward the new income tax, especially because the progressive rate meant that the big industrial and commercial capitalists would thereby be taxed more heavily as compared with agriculture, where income had long been in decline. The Conservatives consequently demanded a top rate of 5 per cent rather than the 3 per cent advocated by the government. Miquel resisted this demand, but eventually yielded to an increase to a top rate of 4 per cent. The higher rate on large incomes alienated some of Miquel's old party, the National Liberals; but the exemption of low incomes and the mildness of the rate on small and middle incomes attracted votes from the Center party; public opinion and press generally favored the income tax; and the final vote in the House was 308 to 36 for the bill, an overwhelming endorsement.[73]

The fate of the supplementary inheritance tax was less happy. Intended to satisfy the demand that propertied income be taxed more than income merely from wages and to serve as a check on the self-evaluations for the income tax, the bill expanded the old inheritance tax to include direct as well as collateral heirs. Although the rate was limited to a maximum of 1 per cent, this inheritance tax met with general opposition in the Landtag. The Conservatives especially felt that it would be a hard burden on their landed estates. Miquel, accordingly, to save the income tax, dropped the inheritance tax, replacing it in the later stage of the reform, in 1892–1893, by a general personal property tax. The rejection of the inheritance tax, wrote the Preussische Jahrbücher, was a reminder that the Landtag represented primarily the propertied classes.[74]

In the first year of its operation the new income tax brought in so much revenue that with the comparatively slight addition of the personal property tax, it was possible for Miquel, in 1892–1893, to bring in bills abolishing the land, building, and business taxes alto-

---

[73]Geiger's account is limited to a summary of the Landtag debates. Herzfeld's *Miquel* is the best source for the political maneuvers, with a mild bias in favor of Miquel.

[74]*Pr. Jbb.*, 66:639 (1890); Geiger, *Miquel*, pp. 27–29; Herzfeld, *Miquel*, II, 229, 231–232, 237.

gether as sources of state revenue and turning them over to the local communities. This step, which carried out and completed his large scheme of tax reform, carried with it complex social and political implications quite peculiar to Prussia. First of all, the whole basis of the three-class system of voting[75] was the principle that property, and especially property in land, should carry more political weight. It was logical, therefore, to weight the voting according to the tax list as long as the chief state tax was a tax on land. But if the basis of state taxes was to be changed to personal income, this would give the bulk of political representation and political power merely to wealth per se, and, therefore, more and more into the hands of the prospering industrial and commercial capitalists and away from the ailing agricultural Junkers. It would tend to replace the aristocratic character of the state with a plutocratic character.[76]

Yet Miquel was able to get Conservative support for this second phase of his bill. He did it through another peculiar Prussian institution: the entailed Junker estate, which, in the East Elbian provinces, had all the official rights and duties of an independent administrative district, run by its owner.[77] Thus, when the land tax was handed over by Miquel to the local communities for their support, it was in a number of instances transferred to the jurisdiction of the owners of these independent estates, who were responsible for their own "districts." It amounted to a free gift from the state to the agrarian Junkers of some 12,000,000 M yearly.[78]

This special favor to the Junkers did not, however, pass unobserved. It aroused heated opposition, not only from Eugen Richter and the Radicals in the Landtag, but, even more seriously, from members of the Prussian State Ministry. Minister of the Interior Herrfurth was particularly critical of this gift to the Junker aristocrats and was backed in his opposition by Caprivi. But, owing to the general political situation in the summer of 1892,[79] Caprivi and Herrfurth could not effectively oppose Miquel, who also had the Kaiser on his side; and all of his critics, whether in ministry or Landtag, Miquel could overawe and silence by the sheer magnitude, inevitability, and logic of his reform scheme as a whole. And so the final measures were enacted in July 1893, thereby bestowing upon

---

[75] See above, p. 36.

[76] Ziekursch, *Geschichte*, III, 47–48; Herzfeld, *Miquel*, II, 269–270; see also below, pp. 221–222 and Chapter VII, section 4.

[77] *Rittergutsbezirk*.

[78] Cf. Herzfeld, *Miquel*, II, 269; Eyck, *Wilhelm II*, pp. 51–52; Ziekursch, *Geschichte*, III, 47.

[79] See below, pp. 220–223.

Miquel the unshakable reputation of being one of the most able of the Prussian ministers of finance. From the Kaiser he received a personal telegram comparing him to Stein and Hardenberg, followed in due course by the bestowal of the Grand Cross of the Order of the Red Eagle.[80]

Rural Government Reform

While Miquel was successfully wooing the Conservatives in the Landtag with his tax reform, Minister of the Interior Herrfurth was engaging them in a raging battle over his rural-government reform. The Rural Government Act (*Landgemeindeordnung*) was designed by Herrfurth to strengthen local rural government in the seven eastern provinces of East Prussia, West Prussia, Brandenburg, Pomerania, Posen, Silesia, and Saxony by trying to eradicate the last remaining traces there of the old feudal social and political relationships. Through the Stein-Hardenberg reforms at the beginning of the century and the county (*Kreis*) government reform of 1872, the manorial domains of the nobility had been separated legally and administratively from the villages to form independent districts (*Gutsbezirke*) of their own.[81] Some of the rural communities, many of less than 500 in population, thus left to their own devices, found it extremely difficult to maintain themselves financially, while the neighboring landlord, responsible merely for his own independent "district," could decide on his own initiative how much he cared to pay for roads or for poor relief. "This situation suited the interests of the Junkers to the same degree that it opposed the interests of the state."[82]

Herrfurth's bill, besides extending the suffrage within the rural communities to all residents (according to the three-class system) instead of merely landholders, proposed to reunite a sizable number of the 16,000 independent estates with their villages to strengthen the financial status of the village communities and to encourage a

[80]Herzfeld, *Miquel,* II, 269–273, 277, 285; cf. Baron von Zedlitz und Neukirch, "Miquel als Finanzminister," *Pr. Jbb.,* 105:1–18 (1901); Wippermann, 9(II):15. See below, Chapter VII, section 4.

[81] See above, p. 93.

[82]Eyck, *Wilhelm II,* p. 49; Ziekursch, *Geschichte,* III, 47, 51; Wahl, *Geschichte,* III, 525. Conrad Bornhak, "Local Government of Country Communities in Prussia," *Annals of the American Academy of Political and Social Science,* 3:393–408 (January 1893), presents a brief but interesting analysis of the reform. Dr. Friedrich Keil, "Die Landgemeinde in den östlichen Provinzen Preussens u. die Versuche, eine Landgemeindeordnung zu schaffen," *Schriften des Vereins für Sozialpolitik,* No. 43 (Leipzig, 1890), presents a thorough account of the historical background of the bill.

more healthy coöperation on a basis of equality between landlord and villager. In particular, such a reform measure would tend to remove sources of dissatisfaction and thereby render more difficult the possible organization of the "rural proletariat" by the Social Democrats.[83] As Caprivi said to the Landtag in his speech on November 14 in referring to this bill, "when the existence of the state is threatened with a life-or-death hostility, as an antidote one must, on the other side, seek to strengthen the devotion to the state ('Bravo!'). The way to this devotion to the state, however, for a large portion of our fellow citizens, proceeds through devotion to the community, and to increase, to awaken, to strengthen such devotion to the community is one of the purposes of this bill ('Very good!' on the left)." [84]

This reform in rural government had not, however, been held back all these years merely by chance, but because the ruling classes (and Bismarck) did not wish it; and the Conservatives did not approve of it now. At least they were not willing to tolerate the government plan to incorporate such a large number of the independent estates into the village communities. Such an idea, "to wish to weld together quite universally estates and communities into a clumsy hodge-podge without any compelling reason and in opposition to historical development," was dangerous, even revolutionary; it would mean a "weakening of the strongest bulwark of conservative traditions." It would also mean a considerable increase in their local taxes.[85]

In the commission the Conservatives attacked the government bill with a flood of weakening amendments. Against this attack Minister Herrfurth at first stood his ground, declaring boldly in the commission on December 17 that if the attitude of the Conservatives did not change in the debate on the floor of the House "then the State Ministry must give up trying to inaugurate a reform of the rural communities with this House of Deputies" — a clear threat of dissolution. The reform, declared Herrfurth, who was not a Junker, but, like Caprivi, a conservative Prussian official who put the interest of the state higher than that of any one class, would come about anyway, sooner or later.[86]

[83] Cf. *Deutsche Rundschau*, 66:300 (1891); *Schulthess* (1890), pp. 156–157.

[84] *Landtag* (1890–1891), I, 14; *Schulthess* (1890), p. 165.

[85] *Konservative Wochenblatt*, January 3, 1891, and Herman V. Petersdorff, *von Kleist-Retzow* (Stuttgart, 1907), p. 524, quoted in Karl H. Kröger, *Die Konservativen u. die Politik Caprivis* (Rostock, 1937), p. 30; Ziekursch, *Geschichte*, III, 51.

[86] *Schulthess* (1890), pp. 184–185; W. Müller, *Politische Geschichte* (1890), p. 199; Wippermann, 6(II):248; *Pr. Jbb.*, 67:103–105 (1891).

The largely Conservative Caprivi ministry thus faced the problem whether to carry through an all-out fight with the Conservatives over Herrfurth's bill or whether to try to achieve some sort of compromise. Herrfurth stood by his bill; Miquel, the National Liberal, however, who saw his own tax reform threatened by Herrfurth's stubbornness, demanded a compromise that would satisfy at least the moderate wing of the Conservative party, and most of the ministry also adopted this point of view. Such a compromise then followed in the House. Whereas Herrfurth's original bill provided for compulsory amalgamation of estates and communities where urgently necessary by order of the minister of the interior, the decision was now first to be made by the local county committees (*Kreisausschüsse*) — which were dominated by the Junker landlords — with final appeal, not to the minister of the interior, but to the whole State Ministry. It was, wrote Wilhelm von Kardorff, the leader of the Free Conservatives, to his wife, "a great defeat" for Herrfurth. "Before the whole State Ministry, with its clumsy business routine, can come to such a decision, three years or so will go by, while a ministerial order . . . could have accomplished the most radical changes in four weeks." [87]

The House then passed the compromise bill on April 24, 1891, with an overwhelming majority of 327 to 23, including the Center as well as the Radicals, who supported it because it was better than nothing at all. The 23 negative votes were mostly extreme right-wing Conservatives. But in the Lords Herrfurth made a few remarks which wounded the dignity of the Conservatives, so that when the bill (a few minor changes having been made in the upper house) came back to the House of Deputies, the Conservative party, led by von Rauchhaupt, voted against it almost en bloc, so that it finally passed the House over the Conservative vote, which was meant merely as a no-confidence vote against Herrfurth personally, since the party had every reason to be satisfied with the bill. [88]

Actually, in effect, the Junker aristocrats had largely succeeded in maintaining the *status quo*. Whereas Herrfurth had hoped to unite at least half of the 16,000 independent estates with the villages, only 641 were so united. Succeeding ministers of the interior,

[87] Herzfeld, *Miquel*, II, 291–292; Kardorff, *Kardorff*, pp. 234–235; Thimme, "Bismarck und Kardorff," pt. II, p. 168. On the effect of this conflict within the government see Eulenburg to Holstein, March 19, 1891, *Holstein Papers, Correspondence.*

[88] Cf. *Landtag* (1890–1891), IV, 1938–1940, 2477–2479, 2480–2482; *Schulthess* (1891), pp. 90–92; Kardorff, *Kardorff*, p. 240; Wahl, *Geschichte*, III, 528–531.

until 1918, had no interest in changing the situation. In January 1891, the *Preussische Jahrbücher* summed up the opposition of the Conservatives as follows:

The conflict over the Rural Government Act belongs in the great category of historical phenomena where a party in short-sighted blindness fails to recognize and opposes its own interest. . . . The purpose of our large eastern landholders must be to remain the ruling class in their part of the country. Under the constitution and with universal suffrage they can do this only if they give up every outward indication of privilege [*jede formell exceptionelle Stellung*]. As long as a remnant of feudal institutions and caste-like exclusiveness still endures, so long will also endure the conflict between the large landholders and the peasants, and so long as this conflict endures, so long will it at every election be exploited against the landholders and the ground shaken under their feet. As soon, however, as this breech is closed, historical experience teaches everywhere and again and again that the leadership of the country will devolve upon the old, settled, distinguished families. . . . It is not liberalism and conservatism that are in conflict here, but enlightened and unyielding [*verstockte*] conservatism.[89]

School Reform

The desire of the Caprivi ministry to attract support from the oppositional parties and to get coöperation from all parties in a program of national scope and moderate appeal seemed to have borne fruit: only the Radicals voted against the income tax, and both Radicals and Center voted for the rural-government bill. In the bill to reform the school system a further attempt was made to attract general support, especially from the Center, for a compromise solution.

The Prussian Constitution of 1850 had promised that a general law would be passed regulating the school system. In the forty years that had since gone by, however, no such law had been promulgated, the schools instead being regulated in a piecemeal fashion directly by the Ministry of Education and Public Worship. Schools in Prussia had historically been confessional; that is, they had included compulsory religious training in the curriculum, such training being under the general supervision of the Lutheran or Catholic churches, according to the individual case. To strongly religious Protestants, such as composed the right wing of the Conservative party, and to strongly religious Catholics, such as composed the

[89]*Pr. Jbb.*, 67:103–105 (1891); Wahl, *Geschichte*, III, 532.

Center party, however, it seemed that the lack of an over-all legal framework for the school system left religious influence in the schools open to attack and gradual subversion by the increasingly liberal, even antireligious tendencies of the time. Catholics were particularly eager for the protection of a general law, since in the recent Bismarckian *Kulturkampf* supervision of religious instruction in the schools had been completely taken away from the Catholic priests and put under state control by administrative order of Minister of Education and Public Worship Falk. Since the *Kulturkampf* the old confessional influence had been restored in the same way, by administrative order. Both Junker Protestants, who were interested in maintaining the influence of religion as a bulwark of the traditional social order, and Catholics, who were interested in protecting their minority rights in a Protestant state, therefore, wanted a firmer, more permanent guaranty than could be offered by the changing personalities and policies of succeeding ministers of education and public worship.[90]

In the rural-government bill, local communities had been strengthened, and the long-range tax reform plans included eventually handing over to these communities the state land, building, and business taxes to strengthen them further. Since one of the main concerns of the communities was the support and maintenance of primary schools, a general regulation of the apportionment of school costs and of the control of the administration and appointment of teachers could properly be brought forward at this time. These were the main purposes of von Gossler's bill as presented to the State Ministry. Because Caprivi was generally interested in making peace with the Center, further measures were included in the bill strengthening the confessional character of instruction, but retaining the final decision as to courses, textbooks, and control of instruction in the hands of the state. In regard to this control of religious instruction Caprivi declared in his speech to the Landtag on November 14 that "the state government has gone as far in this direction in favor of the religious societies as it believed it was possible to go in conformity with the protection of state interests."[91]

Favorably received by National Liberals and Free Conservatives, the Gossler school bill was denounced immediately by the Center. The Conservatives were divided. No matter how much consultation

[90]Bachem, *Zentrumspartei,* V, 135–137.
[91]Herzfeld, *Miquel,* II, 295–296; Schulthess (1890), p. 164; *Landtag* (1890–1891), I, 13.

with church authorities might be provided for, if final decisions as to what kind of religious instruction should be given were to be made by the state the Catholics could not accept the bill. In fact, in that it laid down the principle of final state authority for the first time by law, it was for them a step backward from the actual situation, a reversion to the *Kulturkampf* program, an attempt to bring religion under state control and to destroy the church. Windthorst immediately went into opposition on the bill and warned the majority that if it were passed by the House the battle would only have begun.[92]

In the middle of this difficult situation, the government brought in a new bill to restore the sequestered *Kulturkampf* funds (*Sperrgeld*) to the Catholic Church. This time not merely the income, as in the previous April,[93] but the entire capital sum was to be handed over to the church by the government. In short, the government had decided to comply completely with the Catholic demands. In introducing the bill on January 24 Caprivi stated that, inasmuch as the previous attempt had failed:

Then the state government had also failed in its purpose, for there still remained an issue [*es blieb dann ein Objekt stehen*] which, now as previously, could bring about attacks against the state government and disturb our Catholic fellow citizens.

After consulting with the bishops the present bill had, therefore, been prepared.

I have found in the press the observation that, inasmuch as the state government has recommended that the House accept this bill, it has apparently made a deal with one of the parties of this House. In the name of the state government I protest against such a supposition ("Bravo!"). As long as I have the honor to stand at the head of the State Ministry I believe I can guarantee that with affairs that affect the welfare of the state there will be no trading (enthusiastic "Bravo!"). Since the failure of the last *Sperrgelder* bill neither I nor the minister of public worship and education have ever at any time spoken about the *Sperrgelder* bill with any member of the interested party in this House.[94]

That there had been no specific horse-trading with the Center on the bill was undoubtedly true; Caprivi's statement must be

[92]Bachem, *Zentrumspartei*, V, 151–153; *Schulthess* (1890), p. 180; *Landtag* (1890–1891), I, 316; Thimme, "Bismarck und Kardorff," pt. II, pp. 177–178.
[93] See above, pp. 71–72.
[94]*Landtag* (1890–1891), I, 478; *Schulthess* (1891), p. 7.

accepted as honestly given. But the fact remains that the Caprivi ministry had made this big concession to the Center — at a time, not of crisis, but when they wanted and would receive nothing specific in return — "generally from the insight that with the dominating [*ausschlaggebenden*] party in the Reichstag one must necessarily establish a friendly relationship." This step, commented the astute *Preussische Jahrbücher*, which seemed like a great defeat, might well be an act of real statesmanship and the first original act of the Caprivi ministry.

All the great measures which were introduced to the House of Deputies in the fall, the rural government act, the school law, the tax reform, are really only the consequences of the Bismarck system, which Prince Bismarck himself obstructed only out of eccentricity . . . but in the manner, the sharpness and decisiveness of [this] shift, the spontaneity of this decision at a moment which presented no necessity for it, in this benevolence [*Entgegengehen*] there lies a touch of independent statesmanship, which is more than just letting things take their natural course, as one might otherwise characterize the achievements so far of the Caprivi ministry.[95]

If the government had hoped that this favor to the Catholic Church would make the Center more friendly to the school bill, it was grossly disappointed. The Center continued its opposition, and the government, although it could have mustered a majority of Protestant votes, finally withdrew the bill in May 1891. Nor was this the limit of the triumph of the Center party. On March 13 Minister von Gossler, who had made himself somewhat ridiculous by representing in the *Sperrgelder* affair a point of view diametrically opposed to the one he had so uncompromisingly defended the year before, and who had long been out of favor with the Kaiser and with Caprivi, resigned his office. In the school question new concessions would have to be made to the Center, and he did not want to make them. In a farewell speech to his subordinates in the Ministry of Public Worship and Education Gossler declared that he laid down the office he had held so many years (since 1881) "not because I long for rest, but because political conditions have recently so shaped themselves that, under the circumstances, I am afraid of being a burden and a hindrance to the transactions of the royal state government." [96]

[95]*Pr. Jbb.*, 67:218–219 (1891). Cf. Wippermann, 7(I):171–173.
[96]*Schulthess* (1891), pp. 60, 80; *Pr. Jbb.*, 67:396–399 (1891); Wedel, *Zwischen Kaiser und Kanzler,* p. 115 (June 21, 1890); Hohenlohe, *Memoirs,* II, 431; Stein, *Es war alles ganz anders,* p. 16; Bachem, *Zentrumspartei,* V, 155–156.

At the height of his triumph, on March 14, 1891, the elderly leader of the Center, Ludwig Windthorst, suddenly died. His funeral, attended by representatives of the Kaiser and other princes, by Caprivi and the Bundesrat, by the Center party Landtag and Reichstag deputies in a body, and by many other deputies from the two parliaments, was a most solemn and impressive affair. It was ironical that now the nation should shower honors upon the dead leader of the Center — the man whom Bismarck had called an "enemy of the Reich" — while Bismarck himself was in voluntary but rebellious exile at Friedrichsruh.[97]

4

THE BISMARCK FRONDE

Immediately after his fall from power Bismarck had begun giving interviews and articles to the press telling his own side of the story and strongly attacking the idea that he had retired voluntarily or for reasons of health.[98] He at first specifically denied that he had anything against the personality or policy of Caprivi. On April 1, 1890, when Caprivi sent him a birthday greeting, Bismarck replied by telegram: "Hearty thanks for friendly good wishes. My friendship and prayers are with you." [99] Since, however, he gave interviews to foreign papers, both French and Russian, and discoursed freely on foreign policy, while maintaining a tone sharply critical of the Kaiser, he began to be an embarrassment to the government.[100] It was, in fact, inevitable that sooner or later his attacks on the Kaiser personally must lead him into attacks on government policy. The first instance of the latter was an interview with a *Daily Telegraph* reporter which sharply criticized the principle of conciliating labor. The notion that labor could be satisfied through legislation, said Bismarck, was "an illusion." [101] With the publication of the Heligoland Agreement[102] with England, in June 1890, Bismarck again had

[97]*Schulthess* (1891), pp. 66–67, 310; Wippermann, 7(I):186–189; Bachem, *Zentrumspartei*, V, 154–162; E. Hüsgen, *Ludwig Windthorst* (Cologne, 1907), pp. 392–403.

[98] See above, p. 38.

[99]Cf. *Hamburger Nachrichten*, April 24, 1890, quoted in *Schulthess* (1890), p. 60; Hermann Hofmann, *Fürst Bismarck nach seiner Entlassung, 1890–1898* (Stuttgart, 1914), I, 254; Caprivi Papers, Hauptarchiv, Berlin.

[100]*The Times*, wkly. ed., May 23, 1890, p. 8; *Schulthess* (1890), pp. 68–69, 86–87, 89; Wippermann, 6(I):325ff.; Wedel, *Zwischen Kaiser und Kanzler*, pp. 97–98, 100–101.

[101]*Schulthess* (1890), p. 101; Wippermann, 6(I):337.

[102] See above, p. 59.

occasion to speak critically of government policy: England had the best of the bargain; he, Bismarck, would not have made such a treaty.[103] This time his criticism had a definite political effect.

Caprivi's first appearance in the Reichstag, on May 12, 1890, had been during a debate on the colonial question. In a clear, well-organized speech characterized by frankness, irony, and humor, he had admitted that he was no "colonial enthusiast" but had taken the line that now that the acquisition of colonies had been started one could not very well turn back. He recognized that colonies were a focal point for the expression of national spirit and idealism. But the approach to the matter had not been very realistic. "People believed that if we had colonies and bought an atlas and in it painted Africa blue, then we were somebody (laughter)." Later, in another speech on colonies in February 1891, he characterized the German colonies as "to a great degree children of sentiment and fantasy." And to his close collaborator Major Keim he subsequently said "the less Africa the better for us." Colonial expansion could only create new enemies for the Reich, would not be profitable economically, and would not increase Germany's potential strength for a continental war. These sentiments won Caprivi enthusiastic cheers from the Radicals in the Reichstag, but not from the colonial enthusiasts among the National Liberals and Free Conservatives.[104]

It was these colonial circles that reacted violently to the Heligoland Agreement, which, for the tiny island of Heligoland off the North Sea coast and some concessions in rounding out the colonies in East and Southwest Africa, had given up all German claims not only to Zanzibar but to Witu and Uganda. By this act, said the explorer Dr. Peters wrathfully, Germany had sacrificed "two kingdoms, Witu and Uganda, . . . for a bathtub in the North Sea." Hopes for further colonial expansion that had been raised previously by enthusiastic statements of the Kaiser were now dashed. Much excitement and opposition to the treaty and to the government was aroused, circulars were sent around, appeals published, and finally, in January 1891 a colonial society which was eventually to become the Pan-German League was founded and headed by Dr. Peters. Bismarck's opposition to the treaty gave special encouragement and

[103]June 22, July 11, 1890, *Schulthess* (1890), pp. 109, 145; Wippermann, 6(I):343.
[104]*Sten. Ber.* (1890–1891), I, 41; *Schulthess* (1890), pp. 70, 73; (1891), p. 14; Schreck, *Caprivi*, pp. 85ff.; *The Times*, wkly. ed., May 16, 1890, p. 14; Keim, *Erlebtes u. Erstrebtes*, p. 71; Stadelmann, "Der neue Kurs," p. 542.

backing to this movement, and he was immediately elected an honorary member of the new organization.[105]

It is difficult to explain Bismarck's ill-humored opposition to the Caprivi government. "Indeed, if the truth must be spoken," wrote *The Times* on June 25, "there have been statesmen of much smaller calibre, and incomparably smaller achievement, who have displayed greater dignity in retirement." The primary motive seemed to be rancor against the Kaiser mixed with a passion for self-justification. At first he may even have expected to return soon to his old position of power. But it was also evident that the old sorcerer who had for so long swayed the whole world found it difficult to refrain from mixing potions for the press and casting minor spells. "My father is completely disoriented," said Herbert Bismarck to the French ambassador in London; "after having been absorbed throughout nearly his whole life with the greatest affairs of state, he has suddenly found himself excluded from all that interested him in life." Writing startling articles for the *Hamburger Nachrichten* kept the old man occupied. It was a kind of sport.[106]

Whatever Bismarck's motives, the fact of his attacks on the Kaiser and on government policy posed a special problem for the Caprivi regime. At the beginning Caprivi characteristically drew up a sort of strategic plan, to which he strictly adhered. The Kaiser, argued Caprivi, had been exercising his recognized prerogative in dismissing Bismarck from office. There could, therefore, be no question of a conflict between the Kaiser and the former chancellor. If Bismarck insisted on creating one then he was in the wrong. As the Kaiser's highest official he, Caprivi, must necessarily protect the Kaiser against Bismarck's attacks, always within the limits imposed by Bismarck's great services to the Reich.

At the very beginning, when preparing the Kaiser's speech from the throne to be delivered at the formal opening of the Reichstag May 6, 1890, Caprivi had included a paragraph recognizing and honoring the great achievements of his predecessor. He intended thus to establish a dignified line of patriotic respect and gratitude for Bismarck's work which could be followed and elaborated upon

---

[105]Mary E. Townsend, *Rise and Fall of Germany's Colonial Empire 1884–1918* (New York, 1930), pp. 163, 164–165; Waldersee, *Denkwürdigkeiten*, II, 131–132; Manfred Sell, *Die deutsche öffentliche Meinung u. die Helgoland-Sansibarvertrag* (Berlin, 1926), *passim;* Mildred Wertheimer, "The Pan-German League," *Columbia Studies in History, Economics, and Public Law*, No. 251 (1924), pp. 25–38.

[106]*The Times*, wkly. ed., June 27, 1890, p. 12; Eyck, *Bismarck*, III, 603–613; *DDF*, 1 ser., VIII, 88; Bülow to Eulenburg, Haller, *Eulenburg*, I, 159.

by the party leaders in the Reichstag. But three days before the ceremony Bismarck published an ill-tempered attack on the Kaiser and Bötticher, and Caprivi cut all reference to Bismarck out of the speech. He could not, he felt, try to establish an atmosphere of national respect for a man who was currently attacking the Kaiser and his officials in such an irresponsible and unjustified manner.[107] To make use even of Bismarck's experience and advice was impossible as long as he carried on his campaign against the government. In any case, it would be inadvisable to do so; Caprivi as responsible head of the state could not share his authority; he must carry on his own administration in his own way.[108]

There was danger to the Reich, Caprivi felt, in Bismarck's attacks. Already, in the summer of 1890, Bismarck had begun to gather around him elements in opposition to government measures, industrialists dissatisfied over the labor bills and colonialists offended by the Heligoland Agreement. Something had to be done.[109] To negate the interviews with the foreign press Caprivi sent a memorandum to the German ambassadors instructing them to make it known privately abroad that Bismarck's statements had nothing to do with government policy. On June 4, 1890, a report of this action was allowed to seep out into the press. But Caprivi had no desire to engage in a general press battle with the practiced old master of propaganda. He decided, rather, to defend the policy of the government in a dignified manner in the Reichstag, where, in his speech on February 5, 1891, in reference to the Heligoland treaty, he quoted passages from official documents in which Bismarck himself had said that "England is more important to us than Zanzibar and East Africa." Bismarck, indeed, had himself begun the negotiations which led to the African settlement, but this sally of Caprivi's, aside from the "hear! hear!" it attracted from the Radicals in the Reichstag, merely brought forth a further barrage from Bismarck. Caprivi, wrote Bismarck, was so unsure of his own policy that he was trying to push the responsibility for it off onto him.[110]

On the same day that Caprivi made his statements in the Reichstag the *Hamburger Nachrichten* published a general attack by Bismarck on the domestic reform program of the New Course. The

[107]K. A. Müller, "Die Entlassung," p. 174; Hofmann, *Bismarck*, I, 261–262.

[108]Hammann, *Der neue Kurs*, pp. 25–27.

[109]Kardorff, *Kardorff*, p. 231; Waldersee, *Denkwürdigkeiten*, II, 135.

[110]*Schulthess* (1890), pp. 93–94; *The Times*, wkly. ed., June 13, 1890, p. 14; Wedel, *Zwischen Kaiser und Kanzler*, pp. 141–142; *Sten. Ber.* (1890–1891), II, 1332; *Schulthess* (1891), pp. 23, 35–36; Hofmann, *Bismarck*, I, 315–319.

Sperrgelder law had only increased the general impression that "the responsible ministers in the attempt to please everybody and to achieve popularity are going too far. Doubtless 'successes' have been obtained, but many that were worth only a nickel have been paid for with a 20 M piece." This kind of conciliation was not difficult. Wide circles of the German people, however, were wishing for something to happen to restore the "old feeling of strength and trust." [111]

Bismarck, in fact, keeping in touch with his old followers in the parties of the Kartell, was taking advantage of the opposition among the National Liberal industrialists to the Reich labor-protection bills, among the National Liberals and Free Conservatives to Caprivi's attitude on colonies, and among the extreme Conservatives to the rural-government bill, to rally all discontented groups around himself. This attempt was all the more promising in that old Kartell leaders such as the extreme Bismarck follower, von Kardorff, were anxious and uneasy over the increasingly powerful position of the Center party.[112]

Bismarck, however, did not stop with attacking government policies. He had long been nursing a grudge against Vice-Chancellor and Reich Secretary of State for the Interior von Bötticher, his old chief assistant. In March he let out into the press a revelation of a secret transaction in 1886 by which Bötticher at Bismarck's initiative had been saved from an embarrassing financial crisis by money from the secret Guelf fund — that is, by the use of state money. The revelation of this transaction, which threw as unfavorable a light upon Bismarck as it did upon Bötticher, did not radically disturb Bötticher's political position. It did contribute, however, to the final regulation and abolition of the Guelf fund.[113]

The growth of the Bismarck Fronde[114] reached a climax in April 1891 with the election of Bismarck to a former National Liberal seat in the Reichstag. It was not exactly a brilliant victory. In the first

[111]*Schulthess* (1891), p. 35.

[112]Wedel, *Zwischen Kaiser und Kanzler,* pp. 135, 141; Leuss, *Hammerstein,* pp. 102–103; Hofmann, *Bismarck,* I, 333–335, 339–340, 354–355; Kardorff, *Kardorff, passim;* cf. *Schulthess* (1891), pp. 70–71; Wippermann, 6(II):312–314; 7(I):208–212; 8(I):212ff.

[113]Hammann, *Der neue Kurs,* pp. 11–12; Wedel, *Zwischen Kaiser und Kanzler,* pp. 162–166; Eyck, *Bismarck,* III, 609.

[114]The possible comparison of the fallen Bismarck to Condé or Turenne and the general spirit of frivolity characteristic of the Fronde make this analogy fairly apt; William II may, in certain ways, have resembled Anne of Austria; but Caprivi, unfortunately, was no Mazarin.

balloting Bismarck failed to obtain an absolute majority over his
principal opponent, a Social Democratic cigar-maker, and in the
run-off he was elected with the aid of Radical and Centrist votes.
But the prospect of having the formidable old man appear at the
head of the opposition in the Reichstag weighed heavily upon the
minds of the government and the Kaiser.[115]

5

THE KAISER

William II had, of course, not remained passive under the attacks
of Bismarck. On the contrary, each new blast from Friedrichsruh
heightened his anger and his excitement. Frequently he talked of
bringing Bismarck to court martial under his military titles. Given
this mood of the Kaiser, Caprivi was apprehensive lest new attacks
by Bismarck — which were to be expected — would one day provoke the Kaiser to a precipitate and unpremeditated action against
the old man. To head off this possibility he tried privately to enlist
the help of the Kaiser's entourage. And he did succeed in preventing
rash acts; it was practically impossible, however, for Caprivi to
prevent rash speeches. Thus on February 21, 1891, in speaking at
a banquet of the Brandenburg Provincial Assembly, the Kaiser
declared:

A spirit of insubordination is abroad in the land; veiled in iridescent
and alluring garb it seeks to confuse the minds of My people and of
those who are devoted to Me; it presses into its service oceans of printer's
ink and paper to conceal the path which does and must lie clearly mani-
fest to every one who knows Me and My principles. . . . Now, Brandenburgers! Your margrave speaks to you, follow him through thick and thin,
upon all the paths where he will lead you! You may be sure, it is for
the prosperity and greatness of our Fatherland. . . .[116]

Again, on May 4 at the end of a routine speech at Düsseldorf,
during the course of which the Kaiser praised the Rhineland industry, he concluded with these seemingly irrelevant words:

I am convinced, now as ever, that prosperity lies only in unity. There
is only one ruler in the Reich, and I am he. I tolerate no other.

[115]*Schulthess* (1891), pp. 71–72, 74–75; Wippermann, 7(I):243–248; Thimme,
"Bismarck und Kardorff," pt. I, pp. 48–49, 58 and note, 171–172; *Pr. Jbb.*, 67:548
(1891).
[116]Wedel, *Zwischen Kaiser und Kanzler*, pp. 91, 98, 100–102, 106–107, 135, 165;
Hutten-Czapski, *Sechzig Jahre*, I, 158; *Schulthess* (1891), pp. 40–41; Wippermann,
7(I):121–123, 189–191; Haller, *Eulenburg*, I, 200–202.

To the informed, the association of the big industrialists with Bismarck explained the timing and the content of this statement. By the general public, however, who were not closely acquainted with the Kaiser's thought processes and might take his statements at face value, these words could easily be misunderstood.[117]

On June 6 the Kaiser declared to an assembly of the commanding generals that Bismarck was systematically opposing him. He was trying to stir up the South Germans against him, he had tried to force Bötticher out of office, he recently had tried to take over the leadership of the National Liberal party, he had mentioned secret treaties in the *Hamburger Nachrichten*, which verged upon high treason. "All of these phenomena aroused in him the conviction that one of these days the prince would end up in Spandau prison." He wanted to prepare the generals so that in that case they might explain it to the army. "My God! . . ." wrote Count Wedel, "Bismarck in Spandau, that would be a whiplash in the face of the German people, that would be the death blow for the Kaiser's popularity!" [118]

To try to counteract such statements by the Kaiser recourse was had again to Phili Eulenburg. On February 26, after the Brandenburg speech, Eulenburg wrote the Kaiser, advising economy in further speech-making and sending along a sheaf of clippings of comments by the press. But this seemed to produce very little effect.[119]

The problem of the Kaiser's speech-making covered, of course, other topics besides the Bismarck Fronde. As head of the state he took an active interest in everything; he was determined to be helpful. His "insubordination" speech, for example, had been directed as much against the opposition of the Junker Conservatives to Herrfurth's rural-government reform as against Bismarck.[120] He had even agreed, after the opening of the fall session of the Landtag, to change his uncompromising position on Windthorst and went out of his way thereafter to flatter and to charm the old Center leader. And, although Windthorst was rather embarrassed when the Kaiser asked him point-blank before a dozen people if he would support two warships in the Reichstag, he was, on the whole, pleased with this attention.[121]

[117]*Schulthess* (1891), pp. 80–82; Wippermann, 7(I):128–131, 193–196; Wedel, *Zwischen Kaiser und Kanzler*, pp. 191–192.
[118]Wedel, *Zwischen Kaiser und Kanzler*, pp. 191–192.
[119]Haller, *Eulenburg*, I, 201–202.
[120]See text of speech, *Schulthess* (1891), pp. 40–41.
[121]Waldersee, *Denkwürdigkeiten*, II, 161–162; Wedel, *Zwischen Kaiser und Kanzler*, pp. 152–153; Stein, *Es war alles ganz anders*, p. 16; Bachem, *Zentrumspartei*, V, 158–159.

The Kaiser's most striking action during the year had been his sponsoring of reform in the Gymnasia, the secondary schools. While Gossler's bill regulating the primary schools was under fire in the Landtag, the Kaiser, on December 4, 1890, opened a conference in Berlin on the curriculum of the secondary schools. Influenced by his old tutor, Professor Hinzpeter, and a Professor Schottmüller, who was a subordinate official in Gossler's ministry and a friend of Count Waldersee, the Kaiser in his opening address launched an all-out attack on the "classical" education of the Gymnasia. "We must train national young Germans and not young Greeks and Romans." One of the more noteworthy aspects of this strongly worded speech (which Waldersee said had been written by Professor Schottmüller) was that its content was diametrically opposed to the ideas of Minister of Education von Gossler, whom, nevertheless, the Kaiser praised very highly and in whom he seemed by all indications to have the greatest confidence. So great was the discrepancy in basic attitude and policy between the Kaiser and his minister that the *Preussische Jahrbücher* printed their public statements in parallel columns to reveal the contrast and followed that with an essay on ministerial responsibility under the Prussian constitution. This anomalous situation was, of course, resolved by the resignation of Gossler in March, but the impression left upon the public (and upon the school system) was not a happy one.[122]

Even less happy was the impression left by a speech made shortly before, on November 20, 1890, to the new army recruits in Berlin who were being sworn in according to the new ceremonious manner. Obviously referring to the possible effect of Social Democratic propaganda, the Kaiser declared "briskly and impressively" to the young men assembled that there was a spirit of rebellion abroad, but that now as soldiers they belonged to him and must be ready to shoot even their fathers and brothers if he so commanded them.[123]

6

AT THE END OF THE FIRST PHASE

In the spring of 1891, at the end of its first year, the Caprivi regime found itself in an extremely paradoxical position. It had lived

---

[122]*Schulthess* (1890), pp. 174–179, 181–184; Wippermann, 6(II):289–301; Waldersee, *Denkwürdigkeiten*, II, 139, 162, 164–165; K. v. Schlözer, *Letzte römische Briefe* (Stuttgart, 1924), pp. 162–163, 164–165; *Pr. Jbb.*, 67:106–109 (1891).

[123]Waldersee, *Denkwürdigkeiten*, II, 162–163; Wedel, *Zwischen Kaiser und Kanzler*, p. 131. On the Kaiser's speeches see also press comment in Wippermann, 7(I):201–205.

up to its name of "New Course" by taking a definite turn away from both the spirit and the practice of the latter days of the Bismarckian system. Specifically, it had introduced a series of important measures in both Reichstag and Landtag — labor protection, industrial courts, army increases in the Reichstag; tax reform, rural-government reform, *Sperrgelder* bill in the Landtag. And it had brought all of these through successfully to final adoption in every case by large, unprecedented majorities.[124] Underlying this program of legislation the Caprivi administration had formulated a basic political strategy of conciliating the Radical and Center parties — which dominated the Reichstag — and bringing them together with the old Kartell parties — which dominated the Landtag — in a national program of coöperation to strengthen the state, and, specifically, to defend it against the threat of Social Democratic revolution. On the face of it, a great part of this intention had been realized. Caprivi, inclined perhaps from the first to put his faith in the Center party, had reached an understanding with Windthorst and that party, in a spirit of mutual confidence and respect, so that the Center party had voted for all the important bills and had begun to be regarded as a "government party" (*Regierungspartei*).[125] In turn, no bill had been put through by the government against the wish of the Center. Even the Radicals had been at least partially won over. With the growth of the Bismarck Fronde they found that their preference for Caprivi as against Bismarck conflicted with their traditional opposition. Indeed, Caprivi's attitude on the colonial question and his apparent gestures at this time in the direction of free trade[126] coincided completely with their most cherished political traditions; yet he was a conservative and a representative of Prussian militarism. And so a sort of lovers' quarrel broke out in late February, during a debate in the Reichstag, between Eugen Richter and Caprivi. Caprivi, with understandable impatience, suggested that a vote in support of government measures would mean more to him than all the favorable comment in the Radical press. The Progressives[127] had opposed 45 bills since 1870. "So long, therefore, as the Progressive party maintains this negative attitude," declared Caprivi, "it will be impossible for any government, even one from the Progressive party,

[124]*Schulthess*, "Politische Übersicht" (1891), p. 314.

[125]Waldersee, *Denkwürdigkeiten*, II, 121, 152, 161; Stein, *Es war alles ganz anders*, pp. 15–16; *Schulthess*, "Politische Übersicht" (1891), p. 312.

[126]See Chapter IV.

[127]The Radical party was made up of old Progressives and National Liberal "Secessionists"; by limiting his criticism to the former Progressives (Richter) Caprivi thus showed special favor to the "Secessionist" right wing of the party (Rickert and Barth).

to enter into a close alliance with it (lively applause on the right)."
In retaliation, Richter denounced this statement as a personal attack
worthy of Bismarck himself.[128] Rather than alienating the Radicals
as a whole, Caprivi's reprimand seemed to make it easier for the
moderate wing of the party to break away from Richter and to support the government. In the months that followed, the Rickert ("Secessionist") group voted for the compromise navy budget in the
Reichstag, against Richter, and the whole party voted for the rural-
government bill in the Landtag. Thus the solid phalanx of the opposition of the Center and Radicals had been shattered during this
first year and a general coöperation of all parties on a national program in large measure achieved.

Yet these achievements brought with them no feeling of victory,
of pride, or of confidence in the future. Rather, in the press and in
the parliaments a general feeling of dissatisfaction and uncertainty
prevailed. Generally, the major cause of the discontent seems to
have been a misunderstanding or a lack of appreciation of the motives of the government on the part of press and parties. The lapse
of the anti-Socialist law, the mild and reasonable attitude eventually
taken by the government toward Social Democratic meetings and
publications caused uneasiness and misgivings among Conservatives and National Liberals who were desperately afraid of socialist
revolution. And coupled with these misgivings was a general resentment of the new liaison between the government and their old
enemy, the Center party. Apart from general principles, many of
the government measures — Herrfurth's rural-government bill, the
current negotiations for foreign-trade treaties, the sugar tax passed
in the Reichstag — all seemed not only to be a trend to the left but
also opposed to the agricultural, economic, and aristocratic social interests of the Conservatives and Free Conservatives. Likewise, the
cautious, even negative attitude of the government toward colonies
and also its labor-protection measures conflicted with the industrial
interests dominant among the National Liberals. Thus, although the
government program had not yet completely destroyed opposition
within the Center and Radical parties, the same program had already begun to awaken opposition among the former "government
parties." Bismarck had won support for his social legislation from
agrarian aristocracy and capitalist middle class by paying them off
with protective tariffs, by catering to their economic interests. The

[128]*Sten. Ber.* (1890–1891), III, 1793, 1809–1810; *Schulthess* (1891), pp. 45, 50–
51, 54. Cf. Wippermann, 7(I):176–177.

"New Course" continued the social legislation but also infringed upon the economic interests.[129]

All of these isolated grievances would perhaps have remained rather unimportant if they had not been illuminated and electrified by the lightning flashes from Friedrichsruh. Bismarck's prestige, his connections in parliament and press made him a natural rallying point for all elements which were becoming disillusioned with the New Course. At the same time, further experience with the personality and rule of William II, his arrogant tone, his restless and disconcerting activity, increased the disillusionment.[130]

In the center of this threatening storm the Caprivi administration itself was beginning to show the strain. Basic differences between Ministers Herrfurth and Miquel had openly appeared, the former coming into conflict with the Junkers, the latter catering to their interests. Miquel, concerned lest Herrfurth's stubborn demands on the Conservatives would ruin the prospects of his tax reform, intimated to von Kardorff, Free Conservative leader and prominent member of the Bismarck Fronde, that he would willingly throw Herrfurth to the wolves. There were even indications that Miquel, the only member of the government with parliamentary experience, was ingratiating himself with the Kartell parties in the Landtag at the expense, not only of Herrfurth, but also of Caprivi, with the apparent ambition of replacing Caprivi — not as chancellor, which could not be done on a Kartell basis — but as minister-president of Prussia. Such a move, of course, if successful, would split the government in two, would separate Prussia from the Reich.[131] With all these intrigues and possibilities in the air the fate of the government itself seemed uncertain. "I am curious," wrote Holstein on June 20, 1891, "as to how long the present regime will last. I await it in philosophical calm. For the present Caprivi is probably reasonably safe, so long as Bismarck threatens on the horizon. Aside from that, however, I don't put very much on the steadfastness of the Kaiser. . . . Let us hope that he will yet mature somewhat without serious tests. In any case, if we don't want a republic we must take the princes as Providence sends them to us." [132]

The bright hopes for the new era which had flowered so profusely when Bismarck fell had, within a year, suffered an early frost.

[129]*Pr. Jbb.*, 67:308–309 (1891). Cf. Wippermann, 7(I):4, 213–215.
[130]*Schulthess* (1891), p. 314; cf. Schweinitz, *Briefwechsel*, p. 278.
[131]Kardorff, *Kardorff*, pp. 235, 238; Hutten-Czapski, *Sechzig Jahre*, I, 158.
[132]Rogge, *Holstein*, p. 154.

Both inside and outside the government, all its achievements to the contrary notwithstanding, disillusion, dissatisfaction reigned. It was as if the Germans, used for so many years to a tight dependency on a strong single will, had now found a certain discomfort in the uncertainties of their freedom. They thought they knew their constitution, their Reich; actually they were only now beginning to discover it. In April 1891 Phili Eulenburg wrote to an old university friend:

Our present state is that of transition from Prussian ministerial centralization to a decentralization. At the same time we are in a phase of parliamentary reform which we never expected to see before the death of the German Jupiter, Bismarck, but which we are now experiencing, with the addition of a jar of mixed pickles from Friedrichsruh. It is curious that even international newspapers like the *Kölnische Zeitung* can't understand this, but keep plaintively whimpering for a "steady course," into which it is to be hoped we may steer after we have got over the difficulties of the transition period.

Our Bismarck was too great for us to be able to start at once without convulsions on a new regime . . .[133]

[133]Herzfeld, *Miquel*, II, 287–291; Haller, *Eulenburg*, I, 161.

Chapter IV

TRIPLE ALLIANCE
AND TRADE TREATIES

General von Caprivi has exhibited the foremost quality of statesmanship in knowing both when to follow and when to relinquish the policy of the past. From Prince Bismarck's hands he took up the strings of the frame of the Triple Alliance, and, working on broader lines, has made it more tenacious than ever. He has given it a capacity, practically boundless, for absorbing every healthy element in Europe tending to the confirmation of peace.

The Times, December 21, 1891

We make great sacrifices to bind Austria and Italy to us, whereas previously we were in a position to let them beg us to protect them. Herein lies the great difference between the policies of Bismarck and of Caprivi.

General von Waldersee, December 19, 1891

1

RENEWAL OF THE TRIPLE ALLIANCE

W HILE the Caprivi administration had been strengthening the internal condition of the state through its reform program and had reinforced the first line of defense through its increase in the size of the army, it had not ceased to try to maintain and to strengthen the outer defenses, the diplomatic alliances. It was not enough to retire cautiously from the exposed and dangerous position on the left flank by dropping the Reinsurance Treaty with Russia;[1] the main bastion, the Triple Alliance, must be reinforced. The new freedom in international affairs following Bismarck's fall must not

[1] See above, pp. 53ff.

be allowed to corrupt Austria or Italy and to entice them away from the League of Peace!

In August 1890 the Bulgarian minister, Stambulov, achieved a minor international coup and insulted Russia by persuading the sultan of Turkey to appoint two Bulgarians to Orthodox bishoprics in Macedonia. As the incident developed it became apparent, much to everyone's astonishment, that at Constantinople Bulgaria enjoyed the support not only of the Austrians and the English but of the German government as well.[2]

In late August the Kaiser and Caprivi had paid their visit to the tsar.[3] Almost immediately afterward, however, from September 17 to 19, they entertained the Austrian emperor, Francis Joseph, and his foreign minister, Count Kálnoky, at the German army maneuvers in Silesia. At the little town of Rohnstock the emperors and ministers met and discussed foreign policy. With the apparent intention of counteracting Russian advances to Austria and of demonstrating the good intentions of the new German government, the Kaiser informed the Austrians at this time of the recently expired Reinsurance Treaty with Russia. The two parties then thoroughly discussed the eastern question and came to a verbal agreement. The Germans conceded that a Russian solution of the Straits problem was impossible,[4] that any change in existing treaties or any concessions to Russia in the Near East would be made by Germany only with the consent of Austria.

It is to be noted that the Kaiser and Caprivi at Rohnstock did not depart so far from Bismarckian traditions as to adopt a pro-Austrian policy in the Near East. Their attitude was no more pro-Austrian than Bismarck's had been out-and-out pro-Russian. They shifted merely the emphasis of their official disinterest: from support of Russia without injuring Austria to support of Austria without injuring Russia. It must be stressed that this was not merely a diplomatic move, but a real change in attitude, and that this change, although only a shift in emphasis, would continue to make itself apparent, as in the case of the Bulgarian bishops. The Russian ballast having been dropped overboard, the ship of imperial Ger-

---

[2]Langer, *Franco-Russian Alliance,* p. 101 and note; cf. H. L. v. Schweinitz, *Denkwürdigkeiten,* II, 413–414; Dugdale, *German Diplomatic Documents,* II, 257–258.

[3]See above, p. 58.

[4]See especially Kiderlen to Holstein, September 21, 1890, *Holstein Papers, Correspondence;* also the retrospective account of Baron Marschall, *G.P.,* XXX[1], 223, No. 10987, with William II's marginal comment: "those were the Kaiser's very words"; also Waldersee, *Denkwürdigkeiten,* II, 146; Langer, *Franco-Russian Alliance,* p. 108 and note.

man policy had begun to show a decided list to starboard. As far as Austria was concerned, this new support from Berlin might tend to give her more freedom of action in Balkan and Near Eastern affairs and to encourage her to engage in further "flirtations" with Russia, in order to procure still more German support in the east.[5]

Italy, on the other hand, had always been the weakest sector of the Triple Alliance fortifications. Her dominant interests were Mediterranean, whereas this area interested Austria only secondarily, Germany hardly at all. But, for one reason or another, the position of Italy at this time was largely decisive for the course of European diplomacy. For one thing, there was always the possibility that France might shatter the Triple Alliance by sapping the position of Italy. There were various means for France to accomplish this aim, including her support and influence at the Vatican and her encouragement of Italian republican agitation. The most important, however, was the use of economic pressure. From 1887 to 1889 Italian exports dropped 40 per cent, the shipment of cheap wines stopping almost completely. In one year French bankers withdrew approximately 700,000,000 francs of capital from Italy. By the end of 1889 the economic situation was almost intolerable.[6] On April 21, 1890, King Humbert received the new French ambassador, Billot, and insisted on the necessity of a settlement between France and Italy. At the end of the month negotiations were opened to settle the disputes between the two nations in East Africa. These negotiations broke down, however, in July over Italy's refusal to give up her claims to Tunis. With the announcement of the Heligoland Treaty, giving England a protectorate over Zanzibar, France demanded compensation. Francesco Crispi, the Italian premier, immediately became extremely excited, fearing that England, in the subsequent Anglo-French negotiations, would allow France a complete protectorate over Tunis as well as Madagascar. Forthwith he appealed to Berlin to exert Germany's influence to prevent England from making concessions in Tunis. Although Caprivi thought a war with France over Tunis would be "a much more doubtful perspective than the breakup of our alliance with Italy," Berlin complied with the Italian request, and Lord Salisbury rejected the French demands. The French then boldly took the initiative, offering Italy the partition of Tripoli in return for abandonment of the Italian claims in Tunis.[7]

---

[5]*G.P.*, XXX[1], 223; Langer, *Franco-Russian Alliance,* pp. 99–100, *Diplomacy of Imperialism,* I, 10.

[6]Langer, *Franco-Russian Alliance,* p. 117.

[7]Langer, *Franco-Russian Alliance,* pp. 122–126; Dugdale, *German Diplomatic Documents,* II, 122, 126.

Berlin now became seriously alarmed. France and Russia were currently pressing the British position in Egypt; if Italy were to be wooed away by the lure of Tripoli, the whole Mediterranean question, and with it the alignment of the Powers, would undergo a profound crisis and perhaps lead to war. Holstein wrote:

If Italy and France start partitioning the Province of Tripoli, it will not be easy to hold the Balkan Peninsula quiet, for the Porte may then at the eleventh hour conclude the alliance with Russia. . . . This would be a bad look-out for England and Austria. On the other hand, we cannot prevent Italy from doing so for fear of her breaking away. A middle course might be for England, Austria and ourselves to promise Italy that no other European Power shall acquire Tripoli. For England and Austria this promise would be a lesser evil than a flare-up in the Balkans and the loss of Italy . . . France's present offer is the beginning of a world crisis whereby Italy will be brought into a false position, isolated, and finally left at the mercy of Russo-French domination and caprice in the Mediterranean.

England was urged by Germany to recognize this threat to her own position in the Mediterranean and to reassure Italy in order to retain the *status quo*. In accordance with this line of policy, Lord Salisbury thereupon promised Crispi support in Tripoli in the future, and the Italian statesman refused the French offer. The French had failed again in their diplomatic efforts to split the Triple Alliance.[8]

In October 1890 Caprivi was still concerned enough about the position of Italy to meet with Crispi in Milan at his request, although Caprivi was quite aware that the conference, which had little diplomatic significance, had been arranged by the Italian premier primarily to enhance his own position in the Italian elections.[9] In November the Triple Alliance met with a diplomatic setback as Cardinal Lavigerie toasted the French Republic before a group of French officers. The Vatican, heretofore true to monarchical tradition and to the Triple Alliance, was now — with an eye on a restoration of the temporal power in Rome — swinging over to a policy of friendship with republican France.[10]

Thus, at the end of 1890, although the diplomatic scene appeared tranquil, it had been basically altered. To be sure, the Triple

[8]Holstein to Hatzfeldt, August 2, 1890, in Dugdale, II, 126–127, 127–129; Langer, *Franco-Russian Alliance,* p. 127.

[9]*G.P.,* VII, 53–56, 58–61; Crispi, *Memoirs,* III, 406, 6–16; Solms to Holstein, June 13, 1890, Kiderlen to Holstein, September 21, 30, 1890, *Holstein Papers, Correspondence;* Waldersee, *Denkwürdigkeiten,* II, 155; Langer, *Franco-Russian Alliance,* pp. 129–130; *DDF,* 1 ser., VIII, 288.

[10]Langer, *Franco-Russian Alliance,* pp. 131–136.

Alliance had remained triumphantly intact, the Russians had not attacked Constantinople, the Triple Alliance, with English aid, had maintained the Mediterranean *status quo* against the French. But France, strong and prosperous under the moderate government of Freycinet, had turned from a passive to a dynamic foreign policy, and, clothed in the light of the new benevolence streaming from the Vatican, could only seem the more attractive to the Russian tsar — and, thereby, a greater threat to Germany. In January 1891 the ambassador to France, Count Münster, reported that the New Year's speech of the president of the Republic showed "a certain assurance," that the French nation was more arrogant than a year ago, that it would be more inclined to attack in case of complications in the east.[11]

On January 31, 1891 Francesco Crispi fell from power in Italy and was succeeded by the Marchese di Rudini. The hot-headed Crispi "was not much regretted anywhere in Europe," but "his fall was an event of the greatest moment for it placed the whole political future in the balance." The Triple Alliance expired in 1892, and Rudini, who was known to favor a policy of retrenchment, might make some kind of deal with the French. In addition to the dangerous situation in Italy, Russia and Austria were exchanging, it seemed to the Germans, suspiciously friendly gestures. In November 1890 Tsarevich Nicholas had been received warmly in Vienna on his way to the Far East. Now, in February 1891, Archduke Franz Ferdinand was sent by the Austrians on a visit to Russia. Caprivi, who had staked everything on the Triple Alliance, was greatly worried. Bismarck, watching the drama from Friedrichsruh, wrote articles warning of the danger of a Russian-Austrian-French alliance against Germany.[12]

In this tense atmosphere Caprivi and the Foreign Office decided to make use of a projected visit to Paris of the Kaiser's mother, Empress Frederick, to sound out French opinion.[13] In some ways the empress was a good choice for this mission. Since 1870 she had made several visits to Paris, incognito; she was much interested in art, and it was hoped that she might encourage various French painters to contribute to the coming art exhibition in Berlin. The

---

[11]Langer, *Franco-Russian Alliance*, pp. 130–131, 137–138; *G.P.*, VII, 270–271.

[12]Langer, *Franco-Russian Alliance*, pp. 138, 106–107, *Diplomacy of Imperialism*, p. 17; Waldersee, *Denkwürdigkeiten*, II, 206; Köhler, *Revanche-idee u. Panslavismus*, pp. 276–279; Reuss to Holstein, February 11, 1890, *Holstein Papers, Correspondence*; Hofmann, *Fürst Bismarck*, I, 314, 363.

[13]Count Münster told the French foreign minister that the visit was supported especially by Caprivi. *DDF*, 1 ser., VIII, 386.

German passport restrictions in Alsace-Lorraine had recently been somewhat relaxed; the Kaiser had sent condolences to the French Academy upon the death of the painter Meissonier; on February 12 the Kaiser had been entertained at the French embassy. The empress's unofficial visit to Paris, it was hoped, would contribute, with these other gestures, toward generally improving the atmosphere.[14] But the visit was not well conceived nor tactfully carried out. The empress's incognito was not strictly observed; she included in her itinerary not only Versailles but also St. Cloud, "the ruins of which were a monument to the German invasion of 1870." The result was a storm of indignation in Paris. The artists, frightened, withdrew from the Berlin exhibition. The press of both countries flared into violent language. When, on February 27, the empress finally left Paris for England, six hundred secret service men were stationed along the route to the railroad station, and she was hurried away an hour before her scheduled departure.[15]

The Kaiser, who had had some misgivings about his mother's French expedition in the first place, now became greatly enraged and excited. He suspected the French and Russians of deliberately stirring up the trouble. He was disgusted with Count Münster, who continued to send in optimistic reports from Paris. His own friendliness toward France evaporated with sudden rapidity. After talking, in the course of a trip through the Rhineland, with a Major von Huene, who had formerly been military attaché to the Paris embassy, the Kaiser telegraphed to Caprivi that he agreed with Huene's view that the French were planning to attack in the fall. Huene, he wrote, knew more about the situation than the whole Paris embassy put together. Count Münster was to be notified forthwith of his dismissal and was to be replaced by General von Wedel.[16]

Confronted with an excited public opinion both at home and abroad and with an angry Kaiser, Caprivi and the Foreign Office tried to get out of the situation as best they could. The Alsace-Lorraine passes were restored immediately with full rigor. It was, Caprivi told the French ambassador, "a satisfaction rendered to the national pride of Germany." At the same time, the Foreign Office

[14]G.P., VII, 271–274; DDF, 1 ser., VIII, 375; cf. DDF, VIII, 289; Waldersee, Denkwürdigkeiten, II, 197.

[15]Langer, Franco-Russian Alliance, pp. 140–141, 142 and note; Ponsonby, Letters of Empress Frederick, pp. 423–425; G.P., VII, 263–275; Münster to Holstein, March 5, 9, 1891, Radolin to Holstein, August 13, 1891, Holstein Papers, Correspondence.

[16]G.P., VII, 293–296, especially the marginal comments on pp. 293, 295; Langer, Franco-Russian Alliance, p. 143; Waldersee, Denkwürdigkeiten, II, 197; DDF, 1 ser., VIII, 379–381, 385–386, 390–400, 405–408, 410–411; Wedel, Zwischen Kaiser und Kanzler, pp. 181–183, 186–189.

(Holstein and Raschdau) prepared cogently argued memoranda to lay before the Kaiser, setting forth, among other things, the danger at this tense moment of replacing the ambassador in Paris with a general. It was suggested that Major von Huene present his viewpoint in writing, along with his sources of information, which was done. It turned out that the major, who was obviously trying to get his old job back, had secured his information from two American munitions salesmen and an Italian with connections with the French stock exchange. Count Münster was not removed.[17]

Throughout the crisis the French government maintained an attitude of strict correctness; it was polite but firm. The Russians, who had been watching the German advances toward France with suspicion, were, of course, delighted. They proceeded to back the French. On March 26 Baron Mohrenheim, Russian ambassador to France, presented President Carnot with the Order of St. Andrew, "the highest Russian decoration," and it was then decided to send a French naval squadron to visit the Russian port of Cronstadt the following summer. Instead of advancing the cause of Franco-German amity, the visit of the empress to Paris had given "a new impulse to the Franco-Russian *rapprochement.*" [18]

German-Russian relations became more tense. The tsar had neglected to send the customary New Year's greetings to the Kaiser. During the excitement over Empress Frederick's visit Ambassador Shuvalov suddenly visited Bismarck at Friedrichsruh, causing speculation and anger at Berlin. In this atmosphere the Kaiser, on April 18, 1891, addressed a military gathering at a large dinner in the White Room of the Schloss. After remarking upon great events in German history which had also occurred on April 18, including the defense of "that valiant Wittenberger monk" (Luther) and a battle in 1864 against "a valiant enemy" (Denmark), the Kaiser continued:

The soldier and the army, not parliamentary majorities and decisions, have welded together the German Reich. My faith rests in the army. These are serious times in which we live and evil times may perhaps await us in the next few years. . . . But whatever may come, let us hold high our flag and our traditions, mindful of the words and deeds of Albrecht Achilles,[19] who said: "I know no more reputable place to die than in the midst of my enemies." This is also My innermost thought, upon which rests My unshakable confidence in the fidelity, the courage,

[17]*G.P.*, VII, 296–302; Wedel, *Zwischen Kaiser und Kanzler*, pp. 182–183; *DDF*, 1 ser., VIII, 410–411, 413.
[18]Langer, *Franco-Russian Alliance*, p. 145.
[19]Elector of Brandenburg, 1470–1486.

and the devotion of My army, and especially all those comrades who stand on the frontiers.

Some unofficial and overzealous confidant had apparently given the Kaiser erroneous information on Russian troop movements. The government saw to it that the speech was carefully edited before it was given to the Berlin papers, but nevertheless the real version leaked out in the foreign press. It was apparently thought wise to have Bötticher deliver a speech a few weeks later, emphasizing that "the political horizon is clear and fair, don't let yourselves be disturbed by French or Russian exaggerations! In my opinion there is no reasonable ground for starting anything with us, and we shall never start anything!" But the impression, once made, was difficult to counteract. The Russians expected an imminent German declaration of war either on themselves or on the French.[20]

This situation seemed made to order for French diplomatic ambitions, and they proceeded at once to make the most of it. Some time in late March or early April the French ambassador asked the tsar what Russia would do in case of war between France and Germany. The attempt was premature. The tsar did not give an encouraging answer, nor was he at all pleased. The Russians knew they could count on French support in case of war with Germany; they were not yet willing to engage themselves formally to France. In spite of all the "alarums and excursions," the shift in the policy of the New Course had as yet produced no tangible alteration of the political scene.[21]

Meanwhile, the advent of the Rudini ministry had given France another opportunity to try to detach Italy from the Triple Alliance. During the period of German-French tension, following the visit of Empress Frederick, the French foreign minister, Ribot, asked the Italian chargé d'affaires for assurance that the Triple Alliance was not a menace to France; given such an assurance, France would then engage not to attack Italy nor to disturb the *status quo* in the Mediterranean. Confronted with this demand on the part of the French for information on the terms of the Triple Alliance, the Italian minister could make his decisions and shape his policy, in the last analysis, only on the basis of friendship with England, still the controlling Mediterranean power. England at this point was associated with the Triple Alliance. On March 7, 1891 the Italian ambas-

[20]*Schulthess* (1891), pp. 72–73, 85; Wippermann, 7(I):127–128, 191–192; Waldersee, *Denkwürdigkeiten*, II, 198; Wedel, *Zwischen Kaiser und Kanzler*, pp. 174–176, 180; cf. Langer, *Franco-Russian Alliance*, p. 146, note.
[21]Langer, *Franco-Russian Alliance*, p. 148.

sador read the Italian answer to the French demand to Baron Marschall, the German foreign secretary, who approved it and sug- bested it be communicated to London as well as to Vienna. It stated, in effect, that Italy could not accept the French proposals unless they also included Germany and Austria. Rudini was staying in the Triple Alliance camp. Not daunted by this rebuff, however, the French next tried to bring further financial pressure on Italy through the Rothschilds. Indignant, Rudini refused any further talk of an arrangement with France. The aggressive French diplomatic campaign had merely pushed Italy further into the arms of Germany and Austria.[22]

To cut short the intrigues of the French and put an end to in- ternal Italian agitation against the Triple Alliance, Rudini decided to negotiate in favor of an immediate renewal of the treaties. He found a favorable reaction to this proposal in both Berlin and Vienna. Caprivi was now as anxious as Rudini to settle the matter of renewal and clear up the diplomatic situation. "Rudini's position was not very secure, and there was no knowing what attitude his successor might take." In the new treaty, signed May 6 and ratified May 17, 1891, Germany extended her support of Italy in North Africa from a recognition, in 1887, of the *casus foederis* only in the event that an actual extension of French spheres of influence in Tripoli or Morocco obliged Italy to take action, to an engagement to work diplomatically for the "territorial" *status quo* in Cyrenaica, Tripoli, and Tunis, and, in case the *status quo* could not be upheld and this situation were recognized by both parties after examination and agreed to in a formal accord, to back any action there that Italy might decide to take in the interest of equilibrium or legitimate compensation. The "escape clause" here for Germany was, of course, that stipulating prior agreement, inserted on the insistence of Berlin. But, neverthe- less, the new German engagements went further than those of 1887.[23]

In a protocol to the renewed Triple Alliance treaty between Italy, Germany, and Austria, the Powers agreed to "exert them- selves at the opportune moment" to extend the agreement of 1887 with England to provide more specific guaranties for the western as well as the eastern Mediterranean. The Germans felt that, "in view of the increasing development of the French navy, it might be easier than it was formerly to justify before British public opinion an Anglo-Italian understanding regarding the defense of the coasts of Italy against the menace of hostile fleets." Negotiations were immediately started between Germany and England to try to work out a more specific British guaranty for Italy. The Germans at this time were very suspicious of Russia, expecting an imminent thrust on her part at Constantinople. They were, therefore, interested in strengthening the anti-Russian coalition in the Mediterranean and were also trying simultaneously to bring about an alliance of England and Turkey through an understanding on Egypt.[24]

The course of these negotiations, however, was overtaken and effectively submerged in an increasing tide of publicity and rumor. Certain statements in the Italian press and Chamber of Deputies emphasizing the closeness of England to the Triple Alliance and a similar statement in the newspaper *Figaro* were picked up by a pro-French member of the British Parliament, Labouchere, and made the basis of interpellations in the House on June 2 and 4, questioning British policy in regard to Italy. In answering for the government, Fergusson, the under-secretary, made clear that England had no military or naval engagements beyond those known to the House, but that England would naturally be found on the side of the Powers favoring a defense of the *status quo*. On June 4 an inspired article in the *Standard* emphasized that the natural interests of England would bring her to the defense of Italy even without any previous agreement. Because of the extensive publicity, Lord Salisbury requested Count Hatzfeldt, on June 8, "to hold up the whole matter for a little." It was never mentioned again. The Triple Alliance had failed to gain for Italy the further guaranties in the Mediterranean that she desired. But Fergusson's statement in the House provided a public assurance to Italy on the part of Great Britain which was undoubtedly fully as valuable as a private agreement.[25]

During a stormy session of the Italian Chamber on June 28 and before the Senate on June 29, Rudini made statements which, in effect, announced the renewal of the Triple Alliance. "Long before the old treaties lapse the new agreements will be in force, because in foreign policy there should be no break in continuity. Our alliances, firmly and sincerely maintained, will assure the peace of Europe for a long time to come." At the same time the Kaiser, en

[24]Dugdale, II, 56–57, 96–97, 102–105; Langer, *Franco-Russian Alliance,* pp. 163–165. These Anglo-Italian negotiations were carried on by the German Ambassador because of Lord Salisbury's distrust of the Italian ambassador, Count Tornielli; see Dugdale, II, 98, 99, 103, 206, 209. For Egypt and the Straits, *ibid.,* II, 73ff.

[25]Dugdale, II, 105–108, 139; Hale, *Publicity and Diplomacy,* pp. 90–91; Langer, *Franco-Russian Alliance,* pp. 166–169.

route from Hamburg to Heligoland, announced the renewal, "in rather grotesque fashion," by personally informing the president of the steamship company.[26]

Apparently to calm the Italian fears and to give them further assurance of British support, a British squadron visited the Adriatic port of Fiume on June 23 and was "honored" by Austrian Emperor Francis Joseph. From Fiume the British naval force went to Venice to attend the launching of the Italian battleship *Sicilia* and was visited by King Humbert. As if further to celebrate the solidarity of interest of England and the Triple Alliance, the Kaiser visited England, from July 4 to 13. This was no "family affair"; for the first time he was officially received in London "with all the attendant pomp and circumstance." During the visit Baron Marschall held a "long and confidential conversation" with Lord Salisbury on the general European situation and especially on the Straits. Marschall explained that German policy was hampered there by the well-known attitude of Prince Bismarck — "The 'bones of the Pomeranian Grenadier' has become a household expression with us" — which had exerted a great influence on public opinion. That fact, however, "would not prevent England's being able to count on our constant sympathy and support, when it was a matter of maintaining and strengthening her influence in the East — always on the assumption that England was prepared to guard her own interests at the decisive moment." Lord Salisbury interrupted at this point and surprised the German minister by declaring emphatically, "You can count on us, as long as the present government is in power; we shall be there in time." Both diplomats felt satisfied with the situation in Italy and the unskillful diplomacy of the French. Although Salisbury showed great interest in the relations of Russia and the tsar's attitude towards France, he concurred in Marschall's confident opinion that the tsar's "lethargy," his championing of the Orthodox faith, and his "feeling for monarchy" constituted a guaranty of peace.[27]

The visit of the Italian crown prince to England, during the last week of July 1891, was "simply the finale of a large-scale demonstration of solidarity and good feeling." By these demonstrations and the attendant publicity England had been openly drawn to the support of Italian allegiance to the Triple Alliance. No wonder that Marschall was pleased with the result of the Kaiser's visit and of his own talk with Salisbury. All over the continent the press was speculating

[26]Langer, *Franco-Russian Alliance*, p. 169; *Schulthess* (1891), p. 101.
[27]Langer, *Franco-Russian Alliance*, p. 172; Dugdale, II, 132–136.

and circulating rumors on what the four allied Powers would do next, what secret conferences had been held, what secret protocols had been signed, and so on.[28]

Some of the speculating was being done at St. Petersburg. Since the tsar's feelings had been affronted by the French bluntness in April, relations between the two countries had deteriorated rapidly. In May the Rothschilds had refused a Russian loan. The same month a serious dispute had broken out between the Franciscan and Greek monks at Bethlehem, causing tension between Catholic France and Orthodox Russia. It was this worsening of relations that accounted for the confident attitude of Marschall and Salisbury on July 6. But now the "noisy" renewal of the Triple Alliance, the English naval demonstrations in the Adriatic, the enthusiastic reception of the Kaiser in London, the visit of the crown prince of Italy, all combined to convince the tsar of his worst fears. "The Russians," wrote Schweinitz on August 22, "had gradually, though unwillingly, grown accustomed to the Triple Alliance. After the fall of Crispi they thought that it would break up, so that when it was renewed after all they were annoyed. But when it appeared that the British government intended to join it, and the British people gave a demonstration of their satisfaction they were upset and felt themselves threatened." [29]

On July 17 Giers summoned the French ambassador, Laboulaye, and confided to him that the new situation might make further steps in the direction of an entente advisable. Then on July 23, 1891, a French squadron visited Cronstadt and was welcomed by the Russians with two weeks of festivities and with a delirious enthusiasm which astounded the European world; the autocrat of all the Russias actually stood and uncovered while his own band played the revolutionary "Marseillaise"! The first step toward the formation of the Franco-Russian Alliance had been taken. The fears of the Germans and their preoccupation with defending their position and with maintaining the alliance with Italy had, in turn, increased the fears of the Russians and had pushed Russia closer to the eager arms of France.[30]

The Cronstadt delirium was at first a great shock to Berlin. It was difficult to believe that reactionary Tsar Alexander III had actually

---

[28]Langer, *Franco-Russian Alliance*, pp. 175, 176–178.

[29]Langer, *Diplomacy of Imperialism*, pp. 22–23, *Franco-Russian Alliance*, pp. 181–183 and note; Dugdale, II, 134–135.

[30]Langer, *Franco-Russian Alliance*, p. 184, *Diplomacy of Imperialism*, pp. 22–23; cf. Bernadotte Schmitt, *Triple Alliance and Triple Entente* (New York, 1934), pp. 39–40; *G.P.*, VII, 227; Köhler, *Revanche-idee*, pp. 82, 86–88, 344–345.

taken his hat off to the "Marseillaise." They had gambled heavily until now upon the tsar's "feeling for monarchy," his repugnance for the French republic. Now they realized they could no longer depend so confidently upon this personal factor. Russia had consistently, since the days of Metternich and Alexander I, placed herself in support of the conservative monarchies of Europe as over against the radical republicanism of France. But now — perhaps partly because of a desperate financial condition — she was apparently departing from this essentially conservative standpoint. "I have now the painful conviction," wrote old General von Schweinitz in his diary on August 12, "that the dynastic policy, the union of the monarchies against revolution, has finally been scrapped. For thirty years . . . I have collaborated in this three-emperor policy, and now I ride out for review [*reite ich . . . zur Parade*] with the orders of the Black Eagle, St. Stephen, and St. Andrew on my chest, as a living anachronism; my thirty-year political career is soon to end with the collapse of all the principles for which I have worked. . . ." [31]

The test, however, of whether the Franco-Russian *rapprochement* was of aggressive intent would be discerned in the subsequent attitude of France. Consequently, when the French government continued to display a mild and peaceful front, the Berlin Foreign Office began to regain its confidence. He did not believe, Caprivi told the Austrian ambassador, that the French and the Russians had concluded any kind of written agreement. Caprivi, indeed, seemed to take the whole development resignedly and rather fatalistically. [32]

It was decided, after these sudden squalls, to try to pour oil upon the troubled diplomatic waters. In early September the Kaiser and Caprivi agreed with the Austrians at Schwarzenau to follow a course of calm and conciliation. On September 21 the compulsory passport restrictions in Alsace-Lorraine were effectively repealed. On September 27 Caprivi delivered a speech on the world situation at Osnabrück, at the twenty-fifth anniversary banquet of the 78th East Frisian Infantry Regiment, of which he was honorary colonel. It was the first time a German chancellor had deigned to speak on matters of public importance outside of the Reichstag. Speaking in the historic "Hall of Peace" in the Town Hall of Osnabrück, scene of the negotiation of the Treaty of Westphalia in 1648, Caprivi declared that the recent *rapprochements* of certain states gave no ground for

[31]*G.P.*, VII, 210, 212; cf. *G.P.*, VII, 204; Köhler, *Revanche-idee*, pp. 328–331, 344–345; V. P. Potëmkin, *Istoria Diplomatii* (Moscow, 1945), II, 104ff.; Schweinitz, *Denkwürdigkeiten*, II, 427–428.

[32]Köhler, *Revanche-idee*, p. 343; Langer, *Franco-Russian Alliance*, p. 195 and note; Schweinitz, *Denkwürdigkeiten*, II, 424; Rogge, *Holstein*, p. 155.

anxiety. They were only the outward expression of already existing relations and were perhaps nothing but the establishment of a balance of power in Europe such as formerly existed. No government, as far as he could judge, desired to bring about a war that would probably exceed all former wars in suffering and in its effects. As for Germany, "the thoughts and aspirations of His Majesty have for their aim the well-being of the Fatherland and the maintenance of peace. At the present moment there is not the slightest ground for doubting that peace will be maintained. No cloud darkens the political horizon." [33]

By an interesting coincidence the French foreign minister, Ribot, had anticipated Caprivi by giving, the day before, at Bapaume, a speech which was remarkably similar to Caprivi's in its peaceful emphasis. France was now recognized by Europe once more as an important power; her interest could only be to maintain the peace. These two speeches had a somewhat soothing effect upon the nerves of Europe. England, wrote *The Times,* had never considered the Triple Alliance as an "engine of aggression"; but now any aggression on its part was "a practical impossibility." [34]

2

DOMESTIC DIFFICULTIES

The Polish Question

One of the less obvious effects of the slowly developing *rapprochement* between France and Russia was the resulting change in the orientation of the nationalist aspirations of the Poles. Divided between the three conservative eastern empires, but with the bulk of their nationality enclosed in Russian territory, the Poles had traditionally pinned their hopes on liberal, republican France. But by 1890 France was obviously flirting with Russia. In the future war, then, which was to reconstitute Poland as a nation, they could not count on France. As the New Course, in 1890–1891, turned more away from Russia, the Poles turned their hopes more and more toward Germany and Austria. Already, in June 1890, the Poles in the Reichstag, under the leadership of Josef Koscielski, had voted for Caprivi's "little army bill." Again, in March 1891, the Poles had

[33]Langer, *Franco-Russian Alliance,* p. 197; *G.P.,* VII, 309–310, note; Hohenlohe, *Memoirs,* II, 439–440; Eulenburg to Holstein, October 3, 1891, *Holstein Papers, Correspondence; The Times,* wkly. ed., October 2, 1891, p. 5; *Schulthess* (1891), pp. 111–112; Wippermann, 7(II):21–25.
[34]October 2, 1891, pp. 4, 10.

helped pass the naval appropriations. For this service Koscielski received from the Kaiser a picture of the fleet of the Great Elector and an expression of the royal gratitude. He was also dubbed "Admiralski" by his political critics.[35]

In the Prussian Landtag in May 1891 Caprivi had recognized this new attitude of the Polish deputies, but had expressed a certain caution and skepticism on the part of the government. "We have heard about this milder tone, but here and there we still lack complete faith in it; but — (Deputy Dr. von Jazdzewski: 'That will follow!') — After you! That's the way we want it! (laughter) Then we shall come with you . . . You look at us in a friendly way; that pleases us, but you cannot expect us to kiss you (laughter)." As yet, Caprivi refused to consider repealing the Colonization Act.[36]

The great growth in Polish national feeling in recent years had been part of the general heightening of nationalism and racism common during this period to all of Europe. Associated with the new imperialism, it found expression in such disparate phenomena as Home Rule for Ireland, Russification under Tsar Alexander III, the Dreyfus Case in France, the Pan-German League, the Primrose League in England, and the League of Patriots in France. It was natural, then, that tension should also develop between Poles and Germans in eastern Prussia, especially since the Poles formed one tenth of the Prussian population and in general were increasing their numbers faster than the Germans.[37]

But within Prussian Poland certain special factors had contributed to the growth of a spirit of solidarity among the Poles. Bismarck's attack on the Catholic Church had drawn Poles of all classes together to defend their religion. Then Bismarck's Colonization Act of 1886, under which the state subsidized the purchase of Polish farms by Germans, had brought about a strong counteroffensive among the Poles. Poles of all classes worked together financially to buy up land from Germans, and in the end succeeded in transferring more land from Germans to Poles than the state with its subsidies could manage to transfer from Poles to Germans.[38]

Gradually a small group of influential Germans became con-

[35]*Cambridge History of Poland* (Cambridge, 1950), II, 424, and for general background; R. W. Tims, *Germanizing Prussian Poland* (New York, 1941), pp. 17, 19; Kehr, "Schlachtflottenbau und Parteipolitik," pp. 23–24; Wedel, *Zwischen Kaiser und Kanzler,* pp. 113–114; *Schulthess* (1891), p. 56; cf. "Die preussische Polen," *Deutsche Revue,* 16(III):309–318 (September 1891).

[36]*Landtag* (1890–1891), IV, 2106–2107; *Schulthess* (1891), pp. 77–79.

[37]Tims, *Germanizing Prussian Poland,* pp. 48–49, 11.

[38]Tims, *Germanizing Prussian Poland,* pp. 14–16.

vinced of the disadvantages of Bismarck's repressive policy. Notable among these was the new minister of education and public worship, Count Robert von Zedlitz-Trütschler, former governor of the province of Posen.[39] Directly upon the appointment of Count Zedlitz to the Ministry of Education in March 1891 to succeed Gossler, certain significant concessions were made to the Poles in Prussia. In April 1891 permission was granted for the use of the Polish language, where necessary, for religious instruction in the schools and also for the use of state teachers and school buildings for private instruction in Polish. In a limited way the government had decided to reciprocate.[40]

With the public display of Franco-Russian enthusiasm at Cronstadt, leading Poles came out even more strongly for loyalty to Germany. At an assembly of Polish Catholics at Thorn, Father Florian von Stablewski, a former opponent of the Prussian government during the *Kulturkampf*, declared that Poles could not remain neutral in the present situation. "Upon which side we should station ourselves is determined for us by our history, our education, our culture. We are the sons of a people which has never denied its attachment to the West. . . ." They wanted politically to be Prussians, said Stablewski, culturally to remain Poles.[41]

To Caprivi's general policy of conciliation and acceptance of support for the government from whatever source, and to the fact that since 1890 the Poles commanded 16 seats in the Reichstag, there was now added since Cronstadt the increased danger of a war on two fronts, in which the sympathies of the Poles on the eastern front might be a decisive factor. In November Chief of the General Staff Count von Schlieffen requested the German-Polish Count von Hutten-Czapski to travel around Russian "Congress" Poland and to make a thorough report on the conditions there. On November 2, 1891, the state government nominated Dr. von Stablewski for the archbishopric of Posen and Gnesen, a position previously held by a German.[42] Favors to Poles and to Alsatians might seem wise and constructive policy to the government but, like Caprivi's caution in colonial matters, such moves frustrated and disgruntled extreme

---

[39]Hutten-Czapski, *Sechzig Jahre*, I, 191; Tims, *Germanizing Prussian Poland*, p. 16.

[40]*Schulthess* (1891), pp. 69, 70; Hutten-Czapski, *Sechzig Jahre*, I, 192.

[41]*Schulthess* (1891), p. 130; Hutten-Czapski, *Sechzig Jahre*, I, 193–194; Wahl, *Geschichte*, III, 549–550; Ziekursch, *Geschichte*, III, 70.

[42]Waldersee, *Denkwürdigkeiten*, II, 196, 221; *Schulthess* (1891), p. 130; Wippermann, 7(II):226–231; Tims, *Germanizing Prussian Poland*, pp. 18–19; Hutten-Czapski, *Sechzig Jahre*, I, 192–194.

nationalists, especially those from the Conservative and National Liberal parties.[43]

"Regis Voluntas"

Indeed, the discontent apparent in the spring of 1891 had been increased and deepened by the events during the summer and fall. As if to add to the uneasiness caused by the new uncertainties of the international situation and by the dissatisfaction in nationalist circles with the apparent "weakness" of the government, in mid-October the Social Democrats met in party congress at Erfurt and drew up a new and more radical program. Hounded and persecuted by Bismarck since the passage of the exceptional anti-Socialist law in 1878, they had, nevertheless, emerged victorious from the struggle. In the election of February 1890, in spite of the ban on socialist assemblies, they had polled a million and a half votes, and had placed thirty-five deputies of their party in the Reichstag. In the face of this challenge the Reich government had not taken a strong stand, but had yielded. The great Bismarck himself had fallen, the anti-Socialist law had been dropped from the books, and the New Course government had started to carry into effect some of the conciliatory gestures toward the working class made by the Kaiser in his February proclamations. The Erfurt Congress was the Social Democratic Party's first full-scale public appearance since it had become legitimate again in September 1890. The old Lassallean Gotha Program of 1875 was now, at Erfurt, brought more into line with the more radical and revolutionary theories of Karl Marx, which had proved so effective in sustaining the party during its underground existence. The party was in a defiant and triumphant mood. Bebel declared confidently, "Bourgeois society is working so hard at its own destruction that we need only await the moment when we take up the power which has fallen from their hands. Yes, I am convinced that the realization of our ultimate goal is so near that there are few in this room who will not live to see it." [44]

Into this volatile atmosphere were tossed certain new statements of the Kaiser. In early September at Erfurt the Kaiser referred to Napoleon as a "Corsican parvenu" who had "ravished us most abominably, but from here went forth that flame of vengeance that dashed him to the ground." This speech had been one more reason

[43]*Schulthess* (1891), p. 133.
[44]See above, pp. 8, 14ff., 18ff.; below, pp. 331ff. K. Kautsky, *The Class Struggle* (*Erfurt Program*) (Chicago, 1910); Hammann, *Der Neue Kurs*, pp. 131–139; Ziekursch, *Geschichte*, III, 55–56.

for Caprivi's own peaceful reassurances in his speech later in September at Osnabrück.[45] On October 27 the *Reichsanzeiger* published a long discourse by the Kaiser, directed to the attention of the State Ministry, but without a ministerial countersignature, on the subject of pandering in the city of Berlin.[46] Then on November 23 came a new speech to the recruits at Potsdam, very similar to that of the year before, but with much more publicity.

Recruits! You have sworn Me allegiance; that — children of my Guard — means that you are now My soldiers, you have given yourselves over to Me body and soul; there is only one enemy for you, and that is My enemy. With the present socialist agitation it may be that I shall order you to shoot down your own families, your brothers, yes, your parents — which may God forbid — but then too you must follow My orders without a murmur.[47]

The press, reported the French ambassador, in this case tried "to lead the public astray by publishing several versions of the imperial words." "Here in Berlin," Empress Frederick wrote to Queen Victoria, "the people are becoming accustomed to these very strange utterances and think it a peculiar style to which it is well not to attach too great importance — it is put down to ignorance and childish impetuosity, and some of the best newspapers mildly criticise, remonstrate and advise. . . . I fear, however, it does not make the slightest effect." [48]

Ephemeral speeches, indeed, could be contradicted, variously reported, and forgotten, but not words written down on paper. In mid-November it began to be reported that when the Kaiser had visited Munich in September he had written in the city's visitors' book: "*Suprema lex regis voluntas esto* [let the king's will be the highest law]." This was not mere tactlessness but a political challenge which could not be overlooked.[49] It offended not only the very

[45]*Schulthess* (1891), p. 110; *DDF*, 1 ser., IX, 88; Ponsonby, *Letters of Empress Frederick*, p. 427.

[46]*Schulthess* (1891), pp. 127–128; Wippermann, 7(II):38–46; cf. *DDF*, 1 ser., IX, 88.

[47]*Schulthess* (1891), p. 141; Wippermann, 7(II):55–59. The *National Zeitung* suggested that probably a speech similar to that so variously reported in the press had indeed been delivered, but that the reported versions originated in the speech of the previous year. *Ibid.*, 7(II):57.

[48]*DDF*, 1 ser., IX, 155–156; Ponsonby, *Letters of Empress Frederick*, p. 431.

[49]Sir J. Rennell Rodd in his *Social and Diplomatic Memories, 1884–1893* (London, 1922), I, 267–268, reports an explanation of the incident current in Berlin at the time: Munich had two visitors' books and by mistake the wrong one had been presented to the Kaiser for his signature. The Bavarian prince regent then insisted that the Kaiser should not be further importuned by repeating his signature in the Golden Book; in spite of this wish, however, the book was brought, and then the

sensitive Bavarian state pride but every political party without exception. "A Tsar, an infallible Pope — the Bourbons — and our poor Charles I — might have written such a sentence," wrote Empress Frederick to Queen Victoria, "but a constitutional Monarch in the 19th century!!! So young a man — the son of his father — and your grandson — not to speak of a child of mine — should neither have nor express such a maxim." [50] In the December issue of the *Preussische Jahrbücher* Hans Delbrück, who had been tutor to the Kaiser's brother and whose political orientation was independent conservative, courageously and frankly summed up the situation.

The press invokes the constitution, asks where are the constitutional ministers and storms against Byzantinism. The officials whisper biting comments to each other with dark looks. The professors interlard their lectures with historical and legal opinions that from the beginning the Teutons have had a monarchy, but never an absolute one. The clergy have made use of the opportunity to preach last Sunday on the text that the will of God is the highest law.

This storm, not over an actual policy, but over a mere phrase, Delbrück went on, had arisen because public opinion felt insulted. Here lay the danger for the future: that this anger of the public was turning against monarchy itself. This could only lend support to Radicals and Social Democrats and would end by bringing on a constitutional crisis. Opposition among the parties to social legislation, tax reform, or even army bills or colonial policy was a mere matter of tactics and could easily be overcome by the government. "But the appearance of a spirit of personal opposition to the monarch must poison the very vitals of our political life."

The actual tradition, as all constitutional doctrines agree, is that opposition should direct itself, not against the monarch, but against the ministers. At this moment the exact opposite is the case. The ministers are recognized as first rate men, who scarcely suffer from a little opposition here and there, and the course of legislation as of the administration is marked by irresistible progress. The course is clear and definite for anyone whose eyes are not blinded by party passions. The bills presented to the parliaments by the government are passed by majorities which border on unanimity. It is the Kaiser and king who chose these

Kaiser, intending to show his obedience to the prince regent, wrote the famous motto instead of his name. The explanation is plausible enough but, if true, merely emphasizes further the political irresponsibility of William II. Cf. Wippermann, 7(II):185.

[50]*Schulthess* (1891), p. 136; Wippermann, 7(II):176–189; Ponsonby, *Letters of Empress Frederick,* p. 429.

ministers, and it is his policy which they are carrying out. Every important thing, every positive thing is good — yet the attitude of the Nation
is not only one of discontent but of excited opposition, the Conservatives because the Kaiser is too liberal, the Liberals because they want
constitutional not personal rule. What the Kaiser wants and what really
constitutes the core of the present government one may perhaps designate
as enlightened conservatism. What the people mistrust and against which
they are in the act of placing themselves one may call, by that expression
of the previous century, enlightened despotism. Which of the two concepts wins the upper hand, on this will depend fundamentally the fate
of Germany in the immediate future [*der nächsten Epoche*].[51]

All over Germany papers of every party reproduced the article
without comment. Phili Eulenburg, now minister to Bavaria, wrote
the Kaiser a serious letter on the subject and especially on the bad
effect in Bavaria. "To say that Your Majesty, by such an inscription,
has very greatly added to the difficulties and destroyed many of the
hard-won victories of those who are earnest in Your Majesty's service
alone, is to say something which goes very much against the grain
with me. . . . That is serious at a time when we need loyal imperial
feeling." Eulenburg's letter, as usual, went by way of the Foreign
Office and elicited this comment from Holstein: "Your letter to
H. M. is an *heroic deed!* Marschall thinks so too, and the Imperial
Chancellor, to whom it was submitted. . . . Your Sermon on the
Mount about *suprema lex* is impressive." But the Kaiser, apparently,
was less impressed. He replied to Eulenburg by open telegram:

Sincere thanks for letters. Entirely agree with contents, which reflect
my own ideas. Am surprised and completely in the dark about the reason
for both; unless it derives from the sphere of poetic imagination and
dream existence; you must have been most impudently taken in by
somebody. The premises are absolutely and completely false. I am steady
as the Northern Star! Philipp, don't you fall into every fool's trap.

William[52]

The Bismarck Fronde

The decline in the Kaiser's personal popularity was all the more
serious because of the continuing attacks of Bismarck and his supporters. In the fall of 1891 the campaign of the Bismarckians to
cripple the Caprivi administration and to restore Bismarck to some

[51]*Pr. Jbb.*, 68:902–903, 904 (1891).
[52]*DDF*, 1 ser., IX, 156; Waldersee, *Denkwürdigkeiten*, II, 225; Haller, *Eulenburg*,
I, 203–205.

degree of influence shifted from the open method of press attacks to the more obscure, subtle, and dangerous method of personal intrigue. Headed by Wilhelm von Kardorff, various political friends of Bismarck had been trying actively since the spring of 1891 to bring about a reconciliation between Bismarck and the Kaiser. Their attempts so far had been frustrated by the fact that both parties insisted that the other make the first move. After the dismissal of General von Waldersee from his post of chief of the General Staff in early February, a common enmity against the Kaiser and the government brought even this old enemy of Bismarck's over onto Bismarck's side.[53] Taking advantage of the crisis in Caprivi's standing with the Kaiser caused by differences over new army increases,[54] which had begun in June and continued throughout the fall of 1891, the various individuals working for Bismarck increased their efforts to effect a reconciliation.[55]

In October Waldersee tried to sound out Phili Eulenburg on the matter of effecting a reconciliation. In early December the Empress Frederick wrote to Queen Victoria that "the party that wish a reconciliation with Prince Bismarck are working very hard. . . . They want his influence to be all-powerful again, even if he does not take office. First they want to obtain a complete reconciliation with W. [sic] I have even been spoken to. . . . You may imagine how I laughed. . . ." [56]

Eulenburg was not sure but that there might be certain psychological advantages in achieving a superficial reconciliation between the old chancellor and the Kaiser, but he ran into a solid front of opposition in Holstein and Caprivi, as is indicated by the following passages from a letter of Holstein's of December 1891. Caprivi, wrote Holstein, had declared:

"If the Kaiser really does do anything which will show the world that Bismarck has regained influence over him, then I go, and go for the simple reason that the Triple Alliance can no longer exist. The Kaiser himself told Count Kálnoky that Bismarck had even at the last moment tried to force upon him a treaty with Russia by which the obligations we have undertaken towards Austria would have been neutralized — and

[53]See below, pp. 317–319.
[54]See below, pp. 207ff.
[55]Thimme, "Bismarck und Kardorff," pt. I, pp. 285, 173; Waldersee, *Denkwürdig-keiten*, II, 223, 225–226; Haller, *Eulenburg*, I, 157–160. Cf. Wippermann, 7(II):156.
[56]Haller, *Eulenburg*, I, 163; Ponsonby, *Letters of Empress Frederick*, pp. 430–431.

that it was a cardinal reason for the rupture between him and the Prince."[57]

"Since his dismissal," wrote Holstein, "Bismarck has let the Russian cat out of the bag much more flagrantly. There is no possible doubt of his policy."

The Kaiser is in two minds, for the moment he takes the first step towards Bismarck he ceases to be the first man in the Reich — Bismarck again becomes *that*. The Kaiser will be his slave, and that to the delight of the many who don't relish *regis voluntas*.

Caprivi has gained in prestige by recent events. If he goes *whom* will the Kaiser take? H. M. should not forget how desperate his position was in March 1890. And yet he had not then destroyed his position in the country. Then he was an unwritten page. Today the page shows: "*Sic volo, sic jubeo, regis voluntas*"; "you must shoot down your own brothers" — and so forth. Bismarck would stand better now than in March 1890 — considerably better . . .

Holstein then asked Eulenburg to come and warn the Kaiser. Caprivi intended to talk with the Kaiser about the danger to the Triple Alliance of a public reconciliation, but Eulenburg would be more tactful.[58]

Eulenburg then wrote a letter to the Kaiser following Holstein's arguments, but in a milder, more elaborately reasoned and respectful way:

A reconciliation with Prince Bismarck, effected by Your Majesty, would at this moment annihilate Caprivi's undeniable achievements, and either cause him to be unsatisfactorily replaced or reintroduce the Bismarckian system, which is nearly eighty years old, and would itself have to be no less unsatisfactorily replaced in a short space of time.

[Caprivi], as leading statesman, has the *right* to assert himself on the question of whether a reconciliation is, or is not, at this moment desirable.[59]

[57]This statement, taken with the Kaiser's remark to Wedel on March 17, 1890, that Bismarck was dickering with Shuvalov to let the Russians go into Bulgaria and to desert Austria (Wedel, *Zwischen Kaiser und Kanzler*, pp. 36–37), and with allusions in Hutten-Czapski, *Sechzig Jahre*, I, 304, and in Hohenlohe, *Denkwürdigkeiten des Reichskanzlerzeit*, p. 276, to incriminating conversations with the Russians in March 1890 which were never recorded, gives the distinct impression that Bismarck, before his fall from power, was indeed exploring the eastern question with the Russians with a view to a pro-Russian shift in foreign policy, above and beyond the scope of the Reinsurance Treaty.

[58]Haller, *Eulenburg*, I, 166–168.
[59]Haller, *Eulenburg*, I, 169–172.

Over the combination of Caprivi and the New Course program, Holstein and Eulenburg, and the Kaiser's own reluctance the Bismarckian forces did not, for the moment, prevail. The reconciliation did not take place.

Caprivi's Counterattack

Against the condition of public unrest and uneasiness caused by all these disturbing factors on both the foreign and domestic fronts, General von Caprivi at length decided to take the offensive. On November 27 he delivered a speech in the Reichstag in which, taking as his text an article by a member of the Free Conservative Party in the *Deutsches Wochenblatt* suggesting that he was becoming tired of office (*amtsmüde*), he launched a strong attack on all criticisms being currently leveled against the government. It was a speech characterized by confidence, reasonableness, and good humor.

He had read the article in question, said Caprivi; it had been printed in several papers. It was not the first attempt to represent him as being weary of office. "I can assure the gentlemen who may have been inclined to think that I was tired of office that after the most careful observation I have found no trace in myself of any such feeling ('Bravo!' laughter)."

In taking as the subject of the first part of my discussion the unrest which pervades or is said to be pervading the country, I shall remark beforehand that newspaper writers do not disturb me; I only wish that they also did not disturb themselves about me (laughter). It cannot be denied: the country is pervaded by a pessimism which is, to me, extremely serious. As long as only German philosophers occupied themselves with pessimism it might be for many even an attractive occupation; when this mental tendency, however, spreads into wider circles which are concerned with trade and industry then pessimism becomes dangerous. . . . It is . . . as if an uneasiness bacillus were in the air, which has become epidemic, and even many distinguished newspapers, which otherwise consider themselves standard-bearers of national feeling, seem to me to be cultures of this bacillus ("Bravo!" and laughter). "The government is no good, it's doing things badly, the result is that it won't work, and Germany is going more and more downhill" — I read this every day . . . everybody complains, but a useful bit of advice, the directions for a practicable course of action I have as yet received from no one.

There were complaints that the administration had destroyed the Kartell. "This is a reproach which astonishes me. The last elections took place before this government had come upon the scene ('Very true!')." His administration was ready to coöperate with any political group. "This Kartell, however, was no longer in operation; and if it continues now to go to pieces that is due to internal causes, not to the malevolence or clumsiness of the government."

The same writer, however, had also accused the government of not aligning itself with any party, and had predicted that it would thus fall between two stools. He had no intention, said Caprivi, of sitting upon any party's stool, but had rather remain standing between the parties. "[I] have wished to follow that policy which, after mature consideration, the Federated Governments have considered right; whether or not it pleases a particular party is for me at most a tactical consideration — the essential thing is: is the measure good in itself?"

There had also been concern over foreign policy, which, however, was very straightforward and simple. "I am of the opinion that in foreign policy also truthfulness and openness are the most effective means. It is not necessary continually to carry one's ultimate purposes around on a platter; but it is also not necessary continually to try to deceive other people: in the majority of cases one gets further by a direct route." This honesty combined with a favorable international situation had meant that very little had happened in the last year and a half. "The modern newspaper reader has a certain need for the sensational; he desires that something should be doing (laughter), and if nothing is doing, then he is dissatisfied — then naturally the government is to blame because nothing has happened (laughter)." Contrary to press reports, the Kaiser's visit with the tsar the year before had been very successful.

Certainly the German government could not be blamed for the Franco-Russian display at Cronstadt: "Now actually I do not know what we should do to hinder it, if two other people want to clasp hands. . . ." Perhaps too many drums and trumpets were sounded in the press at the time of the renewal of the Triple Alliance, but this renewal had not changed relations with Russia and France in any way. "Through the Cronstadt meeting a situation has become perceptible to the eyes of the general public and to their minds which has already been in effect for a long time." Cronstadt had not increased the danger of a war on two fronts. He was convinced of the peaceful intentions of the tsar. "No power has so pronounced a preponderance in the world situation that it may say lightheartedly: let us now start a war."

The Heligoland Agreement had also caused dissatisfaction, but the excitement had largely died down. They were having trouble enough with the territories they already had in Africa. As he had said before, "the worst that could happen to us would be for someone to give us the whole of Africa (laughter). . . ."

As for Poland and Alsace-Lorraine, since these peoples on the frontiers who spoke different languages could not very well be eliminated they must be conciliated. "We — the Prussian and Federated Governments — are striving vigorously to hold together the forces which contribute to the preservation and, even if it should not be necessary, the defense of the state, and not to allow them to diverge from each other ('Very true!' on the right), and in line with this tendency to gather together our forces are the repeal of the [Alsace-Lorraine] passports and what has occurred in the Province of Posen . . ."

There was also a regrettable feeling of military insecurity in the air. The present government, however, had, the past year, already increased the army by 18,000 men; "and I can perhaps say that I do not believe it likely that we therewith consider the development and completion of our organization as finally accomplished (murmurs)." It might be convenient for the newspapers to compare the over-all strength of the French and German armies in round numbers, but, uninterpreted, these numbers meant very little. It was easy to increase armies on paper, but often these "increases" were drawn from groups of people "who have already lost their strength in various types of exacting employment, and who through a sedentary mode of life have been rendered incapable of exercise, many of whom are not only fathers, but grandfathers (laughter)."

The public had also been disturbed over Russian troop movements. "Generally such a division marches around in the newspapers for weeks. First it is reported in the place from which it is to come, then to which it is to go, then the individual regiments are brought to our attention . . ." Actually, within a comparable distance from the border, there were more troops on the German and Austrian than on the Russian side.

I am, therefore, of the opinion that in all these areas there is no ground for uneasiness . . . Pessimism is weak . . . If, however, one wishes to accuse us of weakness . . . let him talk about what we have really done, what we could have done better, where the mistakes are. Of what use is it to me to speak with a question mark of mysterious dangers, of measures which the government is not in a position to carry out. Enlighten us — we have no objection; but leave this kind of — shall I say — underground political tactic against a government that, as far as I can see, is in a position to defend what it has done. There exists, moreover, between the government and the Nation a certain reciprocal relationship, and I believe no nation on its own account has an interest in unnecessarily representing its government as weak; and though I do not wish to plead in my own cause, nevertheless I am of the opinion that if a nation esteems itself, it ought to be somewhat more chary of such attacks against the government ("Bravo!"). We are sincerely endeavoring abroad to live at peace with all other nations. We have so far succeeded; I do not know why we should not succeed further. In my opinion the policy of Germany is in a very favorable situation, in that it can support itself upon a good army and upon a nation which with all its peoples finally, if necessary, stands behind the army ("Bravo!"), and I do not know why this policy should not be able under all circumstances to uphold the dignity and the authority of Germany (enthusiastic "Bravo!").[60]

This speech accomplished its purpose and served, at least for a time, to silence the various oppositional elements. Three days later Eugen Richter felt it necessary to explain in the Reichstag, that, although, except for the military passages, his party heartily supported Caprivi's speech and considered that he had knocked down the criticisms of the Bismarck Fronde one by one, nevertheless they must not be mistaken for "Caprivi men." Differences still remained, which he then carefully enumerated.[61]

But speeches were not enough; actual measures were more important. Early the previous summer plans for the further reorganization and strengthening of the army had already been taken up, leading, as has been indicated, to an internal crisis. Now on December 10 Caprivi introduced into the Reichstag for ratification a series of important trade treaties with Austria-Hungary, Italy, Belgium, and Switzerland.

3

TRADE TREATIES (I)

Led by France in the Cobden Treaty of 1860 with England, Europe had generally from 1860 to 1879 followed a policy of relatively free trade. This free-trade atmosphere had at that time suited agrarian Prussia, which could thus export her surplus grain in exchange for English manufactures. But Prussian soil was light, and

---

[60]*Sten. Ber.* (1890–1892), V, 3107–3114; *Schulthess* (1891), pp. 145–158. For a critical viewpoint see Kardorff, *Kardorff*, p. 242; also Waldersee, *Denkwürdigkeiten*, II, 224–225.

[61]Cf. *DDF*, 1 ser., IX, 128–132, 148; *Sten. Ber.* (1890–1892), V, 3162.

more intensive cultivation steadily raised production costs. Furthermore, in the 1870's the new railroads and steamships began to open up huge, distant tracts of virgin soil to the world market. The German Reich with its growing population, its developing young industry, its accumulating hordes of wage earners, turned from the export to the importation of grain. The old feudal estates of East Prussia faced ruinous competition in the influx of grain from America with her vast areas of virgin soil. In 1879 Bismarck, to fortify his Reich, turned from free trade to protection; in an economic move that reflected his political philosophy he took advantage of the French network of trade treaties by concluding a host of most-favored-nation agreements, but at the same time set up a new autonomous tariff around Germany. This tariff of 1879 was double-edged, protecting both the infant industry of middle-class Liberals and the agricultural products of the Junker Conservatives. It was the positive side of the Bismarckian attempt to solidify the propertied classes behind his Reich, the policy of a national economy under state control for the benefit of agriculture and industry which had split off the laissez-faire, free-trading "Secessionists" from the National Liberal party. Its later expression was the Kartell, and the negative side of it was the exceptional anti-Socialist law. The result had been that, in a society of economies still clinging to relatively free trade, protectionist Germany had forged ahead. Her agriculture had survived, her industry had steadily developed. An autocratic, self-assertive policy, with its autonomous tariff, it was centered in Berlin and was characteristically Bismarckian.[62]

Impressed by the German example, however, other European nations were now turning towards protection. The French network of treaties would lapse in February 1892, and there was every indication that France would then adopt a protectionist policy of her own, thus minimizing the value of the German most-favored-nation agreements. To Caprivi, entering office in Germany in the spring of 1890, it seemed clear that unless some new solution were quickly found, Europe, as he later told the Reichstag, would soon find itself engaged in a tariff "war of all against all." And over across the Atlantic in the United States the McKinley tariff was introduced to

[62]W. Lotz, "Die Handelspolitik des deutschen Reiches unter Graf Caprivi u. Fürst Hohenlohe, 1890–1900," *Schriften des Vereins für Sozialpolitik,* 92(II):51–66 (1901); Ziekursch, *Geschichte,* II, 342–343; J. H. Clapham, *Economic Development of France and Germany 1815–1914* (Cambridge, 1936), pp. 210–211; G. Stolper, *German Economy 1870–1940* (New York, 1940), p. 64; T. v. d. Goltz, *Geschichte der deutschen Landwirtschaft* (Stuttgart, 1903), II, 390ff.

Congress in April 1890. With its high duties on textiles it was to have a disastrous effect on German industry.[63]

Bismarck would probably have raised his tariffs further and fought it out. Germany was in as favorable an economic position for such a struggle as any other nation, and probably in an even more favorable one. But in 1890 the whole attitude of the New Course, as has been seen, in foreign policy, in domestic affairs, was one of cautious consolidation rather than aggressive risk-taking. As early as April 7, 1890, Caprivi informed Count Wedel that he was intensely occupied with a plan for bringing about a customs union for central Europe, when the trade treaties ran out in 1892. Political and diplomatic consolidation must be bolstered by economic consolidation. Throughout the spring and summer of 1890 he busied himself with elaborating this idea, with the assistance especially of Count Berchem and the economic division of the Foreign Office. At a decisive session of the State Ministry in September Caprivi declared, "An alliance and a tariff war with Austria are incompatible . . . the object is to consolidate central Europe economically into a trading area for German industrial exports against the brutal tariff barriers of Russia and of North America." [64]

When in the same month the German and Austrian emperors and ministers met at Rohnstock, Caprivi suggested to Count Kálnoky that the Triple Alliance could be consolidated with a trade treaty. The possibility of such a treaty with Italy was discussed by Caprivi in his meeting in November with Crispi in Milan. Crispi was very much in favor of a commercial "monarchical league" to defend the Triple Alliance, and Italy in particular, against the French economic offensive.[65]

Combined with the concern in foreign policy to defend and bolster up the Triple Alliance by all possible means, there were also motives of domestic economic, social, and political policy. The comparatively favorable economic climate which had accompanied the general relaxation after the war scare of 1888 had not lasted long.

---

[63]Lotz, "Handelspolitik," p. 65; *Sten. Ber.* (1890–1892), V, 3302; P. Ashley, *Modern Tariff History* (London, 1910), pp. 86, 275–281. On the McKinley tariff see E. Stanwood, *American Tariff Controversies in the Nineteenth Century* (Boston, 1903), II, 243ff.; F. W. Taussig, *Tariff History of the United States* (New York, 1910), pp. 251ff.; I. M. Tarbell, *The Tariff in Our Times* (New York, 1911), pp. 181ff.

[64]A. Sartorius v. Waltershausen, *Deutsche Wirtschaftsgeschichte. 1815–1914* (Jena, 1923), pp. 385–386; Lotz, "Handelspolitik," p. 66; Wedel, *Zwischen Kaiser und Kanzler*, pp. 83, 108; Herzfeld, *Miquel*, II, 321.

[65]See above, pp. 114–116; *G.P.*, VII, 53–56, 58–61; Langer, *Franco-Russian Alliance*, pp. 108–109.

The year 1890 brought a slump which, especially after the collapse of the English banking house of Baring Brothers in the fall of that year, had deepened by 1891 into a severe economic depression. At the same time, the rise in the cost of living, which had so strongly contributed to the victory of Center, Radicals, and Social Democrats in the 1890 Reichstag election, had continued and, as the result of bad harvests, had taken an especially sharp upturn in 1891. Rye, the basic ingredient for German bread, had risen from 129.9 M per 1000 kg. in 1887 (Leipzig) to 179.7 M in 1890, and to 215.2 M in 1891. Wheat had jumped from 190.1 M per 1000 kg. in 1887 (Munich) to 213.3 M in 1890, and to 239.5 M in 1891. In Berlin 1 kg. of rye bread cost on the average in 1888 21.22 Pfennigs, in 1890 27.18 Pfg., in 1891 31.62 Pfg., with a high in September 1891 of 40.65 Pfg. To add to the distress, Russia, the chief source of supply of rye outside of Germany, facing famine conditions at home, placed a ban in July 1891 upon all export of the grain, followed in November by a similar ban on the export of wheat. The Caprivi government began to encourage the use for bread of a mixture of wheat flour and corn meal.[66]

Under these circumstances the effect of the tariff on grain began to be keenly felt; wide circles of people were impressed by the knowledge that bread was cheaper outside of Germany. All this was natural political capital for the free-trade Radicals and working-class Social Democrats. Bills to lower the tariffs on grain drastically were introduced into the Reichstag early in 1890 by both parties, but were not debated until later. By December of 1890, however, the government was sufficiently swayed by pressure of public opinion to repeal the prohibition on the import of pigs, pork, and sausage from Sweden, Norway, and Denmark. When in January 1891 Richter's bill to lower the grain tariff came up for debate, Caprivi spoke neither for nor against it but suggested that debate on such a proposition might embarrass the trade treaty negotiations then in progress with Austria. The bill, consequently, failed to pass. But a bill introduced the same month by the Radical Dr. Barth to repeal the 1883 ban on importing American pork was supported not only by Radicals and Social Democrats but by a number of protectionist National Liberals. Even Windthorst, who gave the decisive Center vote against the bill, declared that he might be in favor of repeal if the necessary sanitary regulations were set up. In August the government signed the Saratoga Convention with the United States,

[66]Lotz, "Handelspolitik," pp. 71–72, 77–78 and notes. Sartorius v. Waltershausen, *Wirtschaftsgeschichte*, p. 383.

which promised to set up sanitary controls, and, as a result, in September finally repealed the ban on American pork.[67]

German industry, grown by 1890 to a more independent maturity, was becoming restive within its protective framework and was feeling the need more and more for expansion into foreign markets. The push towards free trade started by the Radicals and based on popular resentment of high grain prices thus struck a responsive chord among the industrialists. Caprivi's cryptic remarks about pending trade treaties merely heightened the swelling tide of comment and argument in the press between free traders and protectionists. In June 1891 a party convention of the National Liberals took an evasive stand. The official resolution proclaimed that economic questions should not be allowed basically to influence political parties, that, therefore, the party would allow its members to follow their own personal judgments on the tariff question. Within the Free Conservative party a severe quarrel broke out between the agrarian leader, von Kardorff, and the party newspaper, *Die Post*, which in March 1891 led to Kardorff's resignation from the supervisory board.[68]

But German industry did not want to go too far in opposing the interests of agriculture. The agricultural interest, after all, was embodied in the Prussian Junkers, the ruling class of Prussia and the dominant class in German society. The economic benefits for middle-class capital from allowing and supporting the Junker political preponderance had been too great to give it all up too hastily and rashly. On February 6 the directors of the Central Association of German Manufacturers issued a statement declaring that "German industry does not desire any advantages achieved only at the cost of agriculture." The statement provoked a sharp retort from the government *Reichsanzeiger* that the Central Association did not represent all German industry. The strained situation resulting from the exchange was eventually smoothed over by a long interview between the general secretary and Caprivi and the explanation that the Central Association had only been trying to strengthen the hand of the government in the trade treaty negotiations.[69]

By spring 1891 the food shortage had become so acute and prices had already climbed so high that a strong movement developed for

---

[67]Lotz, "Handelspolitik," pp. 69, 72–73, 77–78; *Sten. Ber.* (1890–1892), II, 920, 1116–1118, *Anlageband* V, No. 571; Sarah Tirrell, *German Agrarian Politics after Bismarck's Fall* (New York, 1951), pp. 100ff.

[68]Hellwig, *Stumm*, pp. 453–454; *Schulthess* (1891), p. 93.

[69]Hellwig, *Stumm*, p. 455; *Schulthess* (1891), p. 13.

immediate reduction or repeal of the grain tariff, leading in late May to demands in the Prussian House of Deputies for some action on the part of the government. Caprivi, who was then negotiating the Austrian trade treaty, felt it necessary to appear before the House on June 1 to explain the government position. "On the Monday morning when he went before the House . . . ," wrote Holstein, "I asked him: 'Which of the ministers, then, does Your Excellency have with you?' He answered: 'I stand alone. Even those like Heyden and Zedlitz who share my opinion shirk the responsibility.' It is remarkable how few people there are who will take responsibility of any sort upon themselves." [70]

To stormy acclaim from the right side of the House Caprivi declared that the government would not temporarily lower or suspend the grain tariff. A real state of emergency, he said, did not exist. Short-range fluctuations in the tariff would be unsettling, a long-range moderation would be of more use to the working classes. Once lowered or suspended temporarily, the tariff would be much more difficult to reëstablish. "('Very true!') The Prussian government and, as far as I know, also the Federated Governments have no intention whatsoever and have had no intention of going over to a system of free trade in grain ('Hear! hear! Very good!' on the right and in the center)." [71]

Nevertheless, Rickert of the Radicals introduced a resolution to request the government for data on the grain supply and the prospects for the next harvest. Caprivi then reappeared in the House on June 11 and asked it to reject this bill. "The state government is conscious of the responsibility it bears; it wishes, however, that those who speak publicly about these things and whose opinion is spread far and wide may also be conscious of what great damage may result from too far-reaching a discussion (enthusiastic 'Bravo!' on the right)." On August 14 the *Reichsanzeiger* published a further government statement explaining its reasons for maintaining its previous decision not to suspend the grain tariff. [72]

Throughout the summer government offices worked furiously to complete the trade treaties. On June 20 Holstein wrote, "Here now we are studying weather and crop prospects. If we come through without a great famine and the trade treaties are ready in the fall, then Caprivi is a great man. . . . If we conclude trade treaties with Austria, Switzerland, Belgium, Italy, Rumania, and Serbia, then that

[70]Rogge, *Holstein*, p. 154.
[71]*Landtag* (1890–1891), V, 2447–2450.
[72]*Landtag* (1890–1891), V, 2699–2700; *Schulthess* (1891), pp. 106–107.

will be a means of economic and also political pressure on France."
On August 14 Holstein wrote that soon he would be going on leave

with all kinds of worries. The worst is the crop failure and the resulting
discontent. I certainly hope that the government will not give in to the
pressure to lower the tariff . . . the opposition will try to lay hold of
Caprivi in every kind of way, also through his good-heartedness, by
telling him that he is getting the trade treaties at the cost of the suffering
of millions, who for months now have had to pay exorbitant prices. I
understand now the correctness of the statement made by the very gifted
Bavarian finance minister, Riedel, who said already last winter: "I am a
protectionist, but I consider the projected lowering of the tariff in the
trade treaties as a security measure. At its present height the tariff would
suddenly be blown away in a storm." [73]

Trade treaties with Austria-Hungary, Italy, and Belgium were
signed in Berlin on December 6, 1891, and presented to the Reichstag for ratification by Caprivi on the 10th. Their main features were a
reduction of wheat and rye duties from 5 M to 3½ M per 1000 kg. in
exchange for favorable rates for German manufactured products. All
rates for a detailed list of articles were fixed on both sides for a
term of twelve years, to expire in 1903.[74]

As the system of unilateral autonomous tariffs was a natural expression of the Bismarckian regime, so the conclusion of a series of
conventional tariff agreements, not imposed on Europe from Berlin,
but quietly negotiated on the basis of mutual interests and mutual
concessions, was a natural expression of the New Course. Just as at
home the state was to be strengthened by a program of adjustment
and conciliation of outstanding grievances, so the Triple Alliance
was to be stabilized by a long-range adjustment of economic interests. Caprivi had, naturally, not been able to achieve his original
concept of a European customs union, although he may still have
envisaged it for the future;[75] a reduction from 5 to 3½ M was not
exactly free trade. The latter rate was still higher than that of 1885.
Caprivi had, in fact, retained the protectionist principle; he especially realized the importance of continuing to encourage agriculture. Thus, again, as against free-trading Radicals and high-tariff
agrarian Conservatives, the treaties were a typical New Course
compromise.

In December 1891 Bismarck complained to Waldersee that the

[73] Rogge, *Holstein,* pp. 154, 162. Cf. Wippermann, 7(II):49–53.
[74] For the text of the treaties see *Sten. Ber.* (1890–1892), *Anlageband* V, 3215ff.,
Staatsarchiv, LII, 309ff.; for an analysis of them see Lotz, "Handelspolitik," pp.
80–84.
[75] See below, p. 149.

trade treaties had originated with an obscure free-trading Geheimrat Huber in the Reich Office of the Interior, who had influenced Caprivi through Geheimrat Göring, an old school friend whom Caprivi called from his place in the legal section of the Foreign Office to head the staff of the Reich Chancellery.[76] Others have since borne witness to this influence, and, at the time, the idea gained considerable currency among the extreme agrarians.[77] But to the suggestion of Count von Kanitz in the Reichstag on December 10 that the treaties had originated with some free-trading Geheimrat who had advised Caprivi badly, Caprivi replied, "The insinuation that things are transacted within the Reich departments and emanate from these departments which do not conform to my views, for which I do not accept the responsibility, is one which I most definitely and emphatically reject ('Bravo!' on the left)."[78] This is a statement that, in combination with his rather visionary schemes as elaborated to Count Wedel so early in 1890 and to the Reichstag in December 1891, and with the fact that his friend Göring was not transferred to the Chancellery until February 1891, seems rather to lend support to the reminiscence of Count Lerchenfeld, a close observer, that Caprivi "collected all the statistical data on his desk and with impressive industry established the fact himself that the welfare of the Reich demanded such a step." "Seldom in my life," declared Caprivi to the Reichstag in the course of his speech on November 27, 1891, "have I been so close to the joy of creating as in this moment when the treaties are approaching completion . . ."[79]

No matter where the trade treaty idea originated, it was, as has been noted, a natural, even a necessary policy for the New Course to adopt. Caution and a defensive attitude in foreign policy meant avoidance of the threatening general tariff war and the substitution of trade treaties centering about the Triple Alliance and negotiated on a basis of mutual concessions. Attention to the need of industry for foreign markets, combined with the general idea of conciliating the laboring classes, and therefore, of heeding the demand for cheaper bread, meant that concessions were made in agricultural imports to gain advantages for industrial exports. Yet grain duties

[76]Waldersee, *Denkwürdigkeiten*, II, 226.

[77]Cf. letters of Holstein, in 1901 and 1902, Rogge, *Holstein*, pp. 199, 207; especially A. Wermuth, *Ein Beamtenleben* (Berlin, 1922), pp. 193–197.

[78]*Sten. Ber.* (1890–1892), V, 3318.

[79]Lerchenfeld, *Denkwürdigkeiten*, p. 370; *Sten. Ber.* (1890–1892), V, 3108. On Göring, see Hammann, *Der Neue Kurs*, p. 73; *Schulthess* (1891), p. 13; Keim, *Erlebtes und Erstrebtes*, p. 53.

were not completely abolished; rather, they were saved and protected from attack on a semipermanent basis. Contrary to the Bismarckian tariff, it was not a "class" but a "national" system, for the
good, not only of agriculture and industry, but of all classes. It was
directed, above all, at increasing the economic — hence political
and military — power of the state.[80]

Chancellor von Caprivi introduced the trade treaties into the
Reichstag on December 10, 1891, with a long and detailed speech.
Briefly he sketched the background of German tariff legislation,
showing himself, for a general of infantry, to be remarkably conversant with economics. The autonomous tariff had greatly benefited
industry but had tended to restrict it to the home market. As industry developed further, overproduction and a flooding of the
market resulted. Foreign markets became at the same time less
accessible because of the trend towards protection abroad. In recent
years imports had exceeded exports by more than 800 million marks.
Since imports were for the most part absolutely necessary foodstuffs
and raw materials, with a rising population the problem was growing
from year to year. "We have more people at home to feed, and we
must create work for more hands." The only way to make up this
unfavorable trade balance was to increase the export of manufactures. "It very soon appeared unquestionable that to continue in the
previous way would be the ruin not only of our industry and of our
laboring class, but perhaps of the state as well." Climate, soil, and
economic development made foreign trade necessary for Germany.
The only practical way out was through trade treaties to secure
abroad the new markets for industry which could not be provided at
home. To obtain these treaties concessions naturally had to be made
on both sides. At home, also, various economic groups would have
to make concessions; this must be done out of patriotism, for the
good of the whole. "I am, however, of the opinion that even the
agrarians have no ground for the belief that the Federated Governments have any intention of injuring them (murmurs on the right)."
If, in the spring, when the agitation was at its height to suspend the
grain tariff, the government had so much as lifted a finger, the House
of Deputies would have approved the suspension. But the government had held out stubbornly against all opposition. "I should like
to see the agrarian who can claim that he has done more to maintain
the tariff than this government! If we had given in at that time, and
if for the second time we had had an insufficient harvest, then the

---

[80]Cf. Caprivi's speech on December 10 as reported in the following pages; Alexander Gerschenkron, *Bread and Democracy in Germany* (Berkeley, 1943), pp. 44–51.

agricultural tariff would have gone a-glimmering ('Very true!' on the left). All provocation, therefore, from this side I decidedly reject (enthusiastic 'Bravo!' in the center and on the left. Murmurs on the right)." The government, however, fully realized the increasing difficulties facing agriculture, and, whereas the tariff had not been as beneficial as had been envisaged, nevertheless it was absolutely necessary to retain it.

I do not underestimate . . . the value of agriculture. I have already often expressed the idea that it is necessary to strengthen and to increase the forces supporting the state, and, without wishing to offend any one class, it is my opinion that there exists in the conditions of agricultural life a strong motivating factor which under all circumstances makes of the farmer — let him belong to whatever political party he likes — a person who supports the state. . . . The final and ultimate motive, however, for the preservation of agriculture is completely and exclusively political. I am convinced that we absolutely cannot dispense with a production of cereals which, with, to be sure, some restrictions, can suffice to feed even a growing population in time of war ("Very true!"). The existence of the state is put in question if it is not in a position to live from its own resources ("Very true!").

There might, of course, be special emergencies, years of bad harvests, but the government had provided somewhat for that by forming a close economic tie with an important grain-producing state (Austria). In wartime there would of course be the prospect of supply from neutral states overseas, but this was uncertain. "What, in the event of a world conflagration, the states controlling the sea will declare as contrabrand, as an effective blockade, that we have yet to learn, and I believe it to be more correct for Germany to depend upon, to maintain her own agriculture, even if it can be done only by making sacrifices, than to depend upon such an uncertain factor as the support of a third party in wartime." Then, in a famous and prophetic passage: "I am unshakably convinced that in a future war the feeding of the army and of the country can play an absolutely decisive rôle." He did not, however, believe that lowering the grain tariff from 5 to 3½ M would ruin agriculture. This was, indeed, not a sacrifice demanded by the nation from agriculture, but rather, the remaining 3½ M tariff on grain was a sacrifice made for agriculture by the whole nation.

The rates on certain types of wine had been lowered to encourage the use of Italian as against French wines. As for industry, "The value of industry for the state grows from year to year. . . . It has been said that Germany has become an industrial state, and I am not disinclined to accept this statement, inasmuch as industry continues to grow and to increase in importance for the state." Unlike agriculture, industry was not held down to a fixed and limited capital but could grow and increase without limit. It was, however, dependent upon markets. The trade treaties would expand the markets, and an unlimited expansion of industry would result. "Trade and industry are and remain the most fundamental sources for prosperity, and thereby of political power and cultural significance . . ."

The treaties were also intended to help the working class. First, by lowering the price of bread. "I regard it, however, as much more fundamental to the support and prosperity of the working class to provide it with work ('Quite right!' on the right) . . . If, however, these treaties are ratified and come into full operation, profitable employment will be found. We shall find it through exporting; we must export: either we export goods or we export people."

For the rest, Caprivi had not given up hope of eventually winning over the working class. In spite of his natural distaste for the sort of thing said and done at Erfurt, he agreed with Stöcker (a right-wing Conservative, formerly court chaplain, and a leader in the Christian Socialist and anti-Semitic movements) that one must not merely oppose (*entgegentreten*) the workers but must also conciliate them (*entgegenkommen*). This sentiment brought approval on the right side of the House but silence on the left.

As far as motives of foreign policy went, Caprivi declared, he expected nothing from Belgium or Switzerland, which were neutral states. With the Triple Alliance, however, it was a different matter. The purpose of this alliance being to maintain peace, it was impossible to live indefinitely with one's allies in a state of economic warfare. "When I impose an economic war upon someone, I want to weaken him; our interest, however, is precisely that of strengthening our allies ('Very true!')." In Frederick the Great's day alliances could be made, armies raised, and wars fought without much concerning the population at large. "This has completely changed. Since the end of the previous century wars have been national, and there is not the slightest question but that the next war will require the coöperation of the people [*des Volkes*], not only with their hands but with their hearts . . . If an alliance today is to be guaranteed to remain strong at the decisive moment, it must enter into the souls of the people."

The purpose of the treaties, however, went beyond the interests merely of the Triple Alliance. He hoped, Caprivi continued, that in time other nations would join in this treaty system. In recent times a very significant historical development had been taking place in the rise of great self-sufficient empires, such as Russia and the United States — also possibly China, which was "at the beginning of a great revolution."

The stage of world history has broadened: and thereby the proportions have altered, so that a state which has played an historical rôle as a great European power can, as far as its material strength is concerned, within a reasonable space of time be reduced to the level of a small state. If, however, the states of Europe wish to maintain their world position, they, in my opinion, cannot do so as long as they follow their former inclinations and shut themselves up tightly against each other. It is not impossible that the time will come when they will realize that there is a wiser course than that of impoverishing each other ("Very good!"), because then it will be necessary for them to stake all their strength on an economic struggle for existence.[81]

Taken all in all, this interesting speech was national in concept, and what it recommended was a national policy. Between the lines lurked the Cronstadt demonstration and the two-front war. To meet this ever-present threat, the power of the nation, actual and potential, must be increased. At the same time, and particularly at the end, the hope was expressed of working for a European world of peaceful and fruitful consolidation. No doubt there was implicit here a deep and fundamental contradiction; but it was a contradiction common to the time.

There was little real opposition to the treaties. Free-traders were jubilant over the step away from extreme protectionism, and protectionists were relieved that so much of their program had been salvaged. Industry generally favored the treaties, especially the fixing of rates for such a long period. After only one week of discussion on the floor the treaties were accepted by the Reichstag on December 18 by the overwhelming vote of 243 to 48. The majority vote in favor included votes from every party group: all of the Radicals, the Center, the Guelfs, the Poles, and wonder of wonders, the Social Democrats; most of the National Liberals and the Free Conservatives; plus even one third of the Conservatives.[82]

[81]*Sten. Ber.* (1890–1892), V, 3301–3309; for evidence that Caprivi envisaged the ultimate inclusion in his system of France, see *DDF*, 1 ser., VIII, 289, IX, 149.
[82]Lotz, "Handelspolitik," pp. 89–95; cf. Haller, *Eulenburg*, I, 173; *The Times*, wkly. ed., December 11, 1891, p. 4; *Deutsche Revue*, 17(III):82–89; *Pr. Jbb.*, 69:117ff. (1892); Bachem, *Zentrumspartei*, V, 253–254.

The opposition was no less vocal or heated for being confined to the most extreme agrarians. Deputy Count von Kanitz declared in answer to Caprivi's speech that the agrarians had lost faith in the government. Wilhelm von Kardorff of the Free Conservatives led the opposition, speaking daily and trying to stall for time. He arranged with Bismarck, who had long been waging war against the Austrian treaty in the *Hamburger Nachrichten,* to come and speak in the Reichstag against the treaties. A special train was kept with its steam up to fetch the Iron Chancellor from Friedrichsruh at the proper time. Reports of the imminent appearance of Bismarck circulated in the press. The old man apparently really wanted to come this time, but his doctor and family prevented him. As Kardorff's attacks became more bitter, he and Caprivi came to a personal clash in the Reichstag. Kardorff disparaged Caprivi's patriotism in contrast to that of his predecessor, Caprivi lost his temper, and Kardorff was later able to reprove him in a condescending tone. "I am very glad," wrote Count Udo von Stolberg to Count Hermann von Arnim-Muskau, "that I was not in Berlin yesterday; my nerves can't stand it when, to the sport of the Center and all the other enemies of the Reich people like Caprivi and Kardorff, who really belong on the same side, get in each other's hair. Caprivi . . . becomes angry, as he said when I tried to calm him, when 'people from good old families say rude things.' " [83]

It is difficult to judge dispassionately what exact effect the Caprivi trade-treaty policy had upon the German economy. Opinions differ greatly still, according to one's theoretical orientation in economics. Certainly from about 1895 to beyond 1903 Germany enjoyed an unprecedented expansion of her foreign trade and a correspondingly great industrial development. Whether or not this would have occurred without the treaties is impossible to say. It is true that the rest of the Caprivi era, from 1891 to 1894, continued to languish in an economic depression, which hit agriculture particularly hard,[84] yet this depression was not confined to Germany. Oddly enough the lower tariff actually benefited agriculture in the long run by forcing more attention to production methods. Production, therefore, increased more from 1890 to 1900 than it had from 1880 to 1890 under the higher tariff. The increase in cattle and hogs

---

[83]*Sten. Ber.* (1890–1892), V, 3533–3537, 3560–3561; *Schulthess* (1891), pp. 178–180; Busch, *Bismarck,* III, 378–379; Hofmann, *Bismarck,* I, 305, 313, 314, 363–364; Thimme, "Bismarck und Kardorff," pt. II, pp. 174–177; Kardorff, *Kardorff,* pp. 243–247, 248.

[84]See below, Chapter VIII, section 2.

was especially great.[85] Also, by the end of the century, although population increased at an unprecedented rate, the number of Germans emigrating overseas had markedly decreased.

Yet, as the Caprivi-Kardorff clash in the Reichstag revealed, the commercial policy of the New Course was a most radical departure from the Bismarckian system. To be sure, Kardorff, with his bimetallist theories, and the few other fanatical agrarians who voted with him were, indeed, a small and insignificant number.[86] But they belonged to the ruling class of Prussia, and, through Prussia, of Bismarck's Reich. For the first time since 1879 the agrarian interest had been defeated. It had been sacrificed for the benefit of industry. For the first time the government, through this unequal distribution of favor, had broken the solid front of middle-class industry and Junker agriculture. No wonder important industrialists were lukewarm and showed distinct signs of uneasiness. No wonder Radicals and Social Democrats — in the latter's first step of coöperation with the government — voted enthusiastically for the treaties. For the Conservatives this was only the most recent of a long series of governmental measures which offended them politically: dropping of the anti-Socialist law, easy treatment of Social Democrats, rural-government reform, sugar tax, and now a reduction of the tariff on grain. And all this from a government headed by one of their own class! Caprivi did not carry the "von" in front of his name for nothing. He and Kardorff did, indeed, belong to the same class. And his government had hit this group, this ruling agrarian aristocracy, where it hurt worst, in their material, economic interests. For the moment prices were high; most of them could be glad it had been no worse; when prices inevitably dropped, things would be different.[87]

At present, however, the administration was in a powerful position. On December 18, the Kaiser officiated at the dedication of a new assembly hall for the *Kreis* of Teltow in Berlin. He had just finished his after-dinner speech when he received a message from Caprivi announcing the passage of the trade treaties by the Reichstag with an overwhelming majority. He arose and read the message, then continued:

[85]Cf. Sartorius v. Waltershausen, *Wirtschaftsgeschichte,* pp. 386–389; Ziekursch, *Geschichte,* III, 58; Wahl, *Geschichte,* III, 554–555; Lotz, "Handelspolitik," pp. 194ff.; Kehr, "Schlachtflottenbau und Parteipolitik," pp. 252–253.

[86]On the agrarians, see below, especially pp. 217, 238–239, 246ff., Chapter VIII, section 2; on bimetallism, Chapter VIII, section 2.

[87]Eyck, *Wilhelm II,* pp. 52–55; cf. the statement of the chairman of the Rhine-Westphalian Industrial Association, Lotz, "Handelspolitik," p. 96; also *DDF,* 1 ser., IX, 172; Oechelhäuser to Bennigsen on National Liberals, Oncken, *Bennigsen,* II, 569–570; T. Veblen, *Imperial Germany* (New York, 1915), p. 214.

Gentlemen! We owe this result to the work of the Reich Chancellor von Caprivi. This simple, homely Prussian general has, in two years, known how to acquaint himself thoroughly with matters which, even for the initiated, are extraordinarily difficult to master.

With far-seeing political insight he has known how to preserve our Fatherland, at the right moment, from grievous dangers. It goes without saying that individual interests must make sacrifices in order that the general welfare may be advanced; I believe, however, that this achievement, which in the negotiation and conclusion of the trade treaties will constitute for our own age and for all posterity one of the most important events in history, this achievement is a real deliverance [*geradezu eine rettende zu nennen ist*]. . . .

In spite of the accusations and difficulties which are being created for the Reich chancellor and for My advisors by the most diverse elements, we have succeeded in leading the Fatherland into these new paths. . . .

I call upon you to empty your glasses with Me to the health of the Reich chancellor: His Excellency General of Infantry von Caprivi: General Count von Caprivi, hurrah! hurrah! hurrah! [*er lebe hoch! und nochmals hoch! und zum drittenmal hoch!*][88]

And so Caprivi became a count. A bitter comment of the Kaiser's towards the close of the speech, apparently aimed at Bismarck, was deleted by the local officials before publication.[89]

The successful conclusion and passage of the trade treaties had been a great personal success for Caprivi, wrote the French ambassador. His position with the Kaiser was again secure. "The Kaiser escapes him in his speeches, but not in his acts. He yields, without too much resistance, to his advice, just as in the Alsace-Lorraine passport affair. But, since he is changeable, violent, and capricious, persons who approach him too often find themselves brutally treated on the day after they have been shown special favor. General von Caprivi does not expose himself to this danger: he appears before His Majesty only when he is summoned; he does not at all attempt familiarity with the Kaiser, and, by his dignified and reserved attitude he holds his respect." [90]

Caprivi's achievements in these first two years were indeed impressive. In the spring of 1890 the overwhelming rejection by the electorate of the Bismarck system had led the Iron Chancellor to

[88]*Schulthess* (1891), p. 182; Wippermann, 7(II):18; *The Times,* wkly. ed., December 25, 1891, p. 12. For a critical opinion cf. Waldersee, *Denkwürdigkeiten,* II, 227–228.

[89]Hammann, *Der Neue Kurs,* p. 8. The Kaiser's graceful letter bestowing his new rank upon Caprivi is in Caprivi Papers, Hauptarchiv, Berlin.

[90]*DDF,* 1 ser., IX, 171 (December 21, 1891), 150 (December 7, 1891); cf. Kardorff, *Kardorff,* p. 247.

advocate a crisis policy of *coup d'état* and repression. Caprivi had then agreed to step into the breach, to replace Bismarck and to put himself at the head of a policy of optimism and reform. This meant conciliating the parties at home, holding up Germany's position abroad, demonstrating that Germany could exist without Bismarck, while fighting off the attacks of Bismarck himself. It was a tall order, but the general had largely succeeded. Through reforms and friendly tactics he had attracted the Center party, the Radicals, Poles, and Alsatians; through the trade treaties he had begun to appeal to National Liberal and Free Conservative industrialists. He had thus apparently to a large degree reconciled the government with the public; the morale of the inner bastion seemed secure. The first line of defense, the army, had also been strengthened. The outer diplomatic breastworks — the Triple Alliance — had been maintained. And in the trade treaties new economic and political support had been created for the state at home and for its allies abroad. Caprivi had tried to bring all the parties together in a national program. The massively favorable endorsement of the first trade treaties by the Reichstag, including sizable blocs of votes from every party — even the Social Democrats — seemed a clear indication of his success. In commenting upon the adoption of the treaties and Caprivi's new title, *The Times* of London editorialized on December 21: "Two years of office have seldom been crowned by a more remarkable achievement; and never has the bold experiment of converting at a moment's notice a good Commander of a Division into a supreme Minister been more amply justified." [91] The passage of the trade treaties marked, in fact, the high point of the Caprivi Era.

[91] Wkly. ed., December 25, 1891, p. 13.

PART TWO
THE INTERNAL CRISIS

Chapter V

THE SCHOOL BILL

Do the moderate parties, then, . . . have a constitutional right
not to be overruled by majorities? . . . We have not threatened;
we have been threatened.

Caprivi

By such a method of taking a majority now here, now there,
one bankrupts either the parties, or one bankrupts oneself.

Deputy Friedberg (National Liberal)

If the condition which Deputy Dr. Friedberg desires is to be a
lasting one, only three situations are possible. Either there must be
a permanent understanding between the government and the
party, — which in Prussia is unlikely, since happily we have no
parliamentary ministers, but ministers whom His Majesty the King
chooses according to his judgment — or . . . the party gets control over the royal state government, a situation which I have
already repeatedly guarded myself against. . . . Or, the party lets
the government get control over it and goes with it through thick
and thin — a demand which I should not dare to make of the
gentlemen of the National Liberals.

Caprivi, from the School Bill debate, January 30, 1892

1

BACKGROUND AND MOTIVES

THE decision taken in the early days of the administration, in
the spring of 1890, to postpone the large-scale reform of the army
until the new government was more firmly established had doubtless been a wise one. Yet, in politics, problems postponed are thereby
rarely rendered more easy of solution. At any rate, the reform could
not continue to be put off much longer. With the rapidly growing
military power of Russia on the one hand and of France upon the

other, the Prussian War Ministry, under General von Verdy, as well as competent outside opinion,[1] had long since reached the conclusion that something must be done to provide for the more extensive and efficient use of the available German manpower. An extensive reform bill had been drawn up by Generals von Verdy and von Waldersee early in 1890 and had been accepted by Bismarck for his own private reasons.[2] But then with the coming of the Caprivi administration it had been laid aside, and only the absolute minimum expansion in the field artillery had been with difficulty put through the Reichstag.[3] The tactless references to future plans which von Verdy had then made in the Reichstag commission, and which had threatened the passage of the bill, had, therefore, been in complete good faith. These plans had not been given up, only postponed. After Cronstadt, however, it was felt that they could not with safety be postponed much longer. In his speech in November 1891 Caprivi had hinted, to the distress of the Reichstag, that further army reforms would presently be forthcoming. It had, in fact, been determined to introduce such a large-scale army reform in the fall of the following year.[4]

The "little army bill" of 1890, however, had been put through the Reichstag by means of a concession to secure the votes of the Center and accompanied by a series of threatening resolutions. For the more drastic army bill envisaged for 1892, Caprivi must also depend finally upon the votes of the Center party. In questions of national defense one could always count upon the votes of the old Kartell: Conservatives, 73; Free Conservatives, 20; National Liberals, 42: or a total of 135 votes. A majority in the Reichstag was 199. The Radicals, with 66 votes, were antimilitarist by principle. They had ultimately united in opposition against the little 1890 bill. The Center, therefore, with its 106 votes was absolutely necessary. Even Bismarck had not been able to shake this solid Center bloc with all the tumultuous propaganda of the dissolution and election in 1887. His gains then had been at the expense of the Radicals, and that feat, anyway, could not now be repeated. A dissolution under present conditions could not help. For the coming army bill Caprivi

[1] Cf. *Pr. Jbb.*, 65:679ff. (June 1890).
[2] See above. p. 21.
[3] See above, pp. 79ff.
[4] See below, Chapter VI, section 2; J. Werdermann, *Die Heeresreform unter Caprivi* (Greifswald, 1928), p. 34; cf. Eugen Richter's reaction to Caprivi's allusion, *Sten. Ber.* (1890–1892), V, 3160.

had to have most of the votes of the Center.[5] And to corral and to control those votes he was now without the clever assistance of the dead master tactician, Windthorst.

The traditional and eminently successful tactic of the Center party had consistently been a policy of barter, to remove the last government restrictions on the Catholic Church left over from the Kulturkampf by offering support for important government bills in exchange. The important concessions now put up for sale in this manner included the return of the Jesuit Order to Germany and a general regulation for the schools in Prussia which would guarantee to the churches full control over religious instruction. The return of the Jesuits would be too extreme and inflammatory a gesture and would offend all the other parties and all Protestants. But it might very well be possible to discover a formula for the schools which would draw the support of at least the strongly religious Protestants in the Conservative party. At the time of the withdrawal by the government of the Gossler school bill and the resignation of Gossler himself the previous year, it was evident that further concessions would have to be made to the Center point of view on this issue.[6]

Since the Center had the dominating position in the Reichstag and the Conservatives had the dominating position in the Prussian Landtag, a government that had to deal constantly with both parliaments, that was supposed to represent a union of Prussia and the Reich, could not very well avoid some sort of connection with these two parties. A fundamental part of the policy of the New Course from the beginning had been to try to replace the fierce enmities of German party relations with a milder and more constructive spirit. A basic understanding with the Center party, however, which would fundamentally reconcile them to the existing order and clinch their position as a "government party" could be achieved only in the sphere of religion.

A basic *rapprochement* between government and Center party on the religious issue, moreover, had been rendered much easier by the many pronouncements of various Catholic bodies during the past two years, holding up religion in general — and the Catholic Church in particular — as the only real defense against socialist revolution. The new double-edged policy adopted by the church

[5]Kurt Richter, *Der Kampf um den Schulgesetzentwurf des Grafen Zedlitz-Trützschler vom Jahre 1892* (Halle, 1934), p. 12; *Schulthess*, "Politische Übersicht" (1892), p. 351; Ziekursch, *Geschichte*, III, 53; Waldersee, *Denkwürdigkeiten*, II, 237; Kardorff, *Kardorff*, p. 255. Cf. Wippermann, 7(II):121.

[6]See above, p. 100 Cf. Wippermann, 8(I):57.

precisely at this time and made known to the world by Pope Leo XIII's famous encyclical *Rerum novarum*, issued on May 15, 1891 — just one week after the Reichstag finally passed Berlepsch's labor-protection bill — this new policy of supporting the rights of labor and at the same time opposing socialism as a doctrine of unbelief and a threat to the church could very easily fit into the New Course program of combining reform with a union of all parties against the socialist threat.[7] Also, a strengthening of religious influence in the schools, by attracting the right-wing Conservatives, would please the very group of Junker aristocrats who had been so violently antagonized by the trade treaties.

2

THE ZEDLITZ BILL

It may well have been for these reasons that Caprivi supported the new school bill which the new minister of public worship and education, Count Robert von Zedlitz-Trützschler, introduced in October 1891 to the Prussian State Ministry, and which basically supported the Catholic point of view. Count von Zedlitz-Trützschler, a member of the old Silesian nobility, was a man of great strength and independence of character, of no special party affiliation, whose rise in government service to be in 1886 governor of Posen and in 1891 Prussian minister of education had been due to recognition of his personal merits. There was no doubt that he believed wholeheartedly in the bill which he was now sponsoring before the ministry. He had even drawn up some of the provisions of the bill over the protests of judicious and cautious Catholic leaders, including Archbishop Kopp of Breslau, who thought they went too far for public acceptance.[8]

The bill, as presented by Zedlitz, comprised a detailed and complete regulation of the primary schools (*Volksschule*), touching on a number of important points, such as an increase in local as over against state control and participation in the local supervision of the

[7] W. Müller, *Geschichte*, pp. 186–191; Bachem, *Zentrumspartei*, V, 144–147, 246. Cf. L. Bamberger's interesting discussion of this alignment in "Der staatserhaltende Beruf der Hölle," *Die Nation*, 9:313ff., *Gesammelte Schriften*, I, 361ff.

[8] Archbishop Kopp was, nevertheless, blamed at first by the liberals as the real originator of the bill, as expressed in the pun which was circulated about Zedlitz: "*Sein Korpus ist hier aber der Kopp ist in Breslau*," Thimme, "Bismarck und Kardorff," pt. I, p. 180; Richter, *Kampf um den Schulgesetzentwurf*, pp. 24–26; Wahl, *Geschichte*, III, 533.

schools by the teachers. But the sections which later became a subject of such controversy were those dealing with religious instruction. Here the intent was faithfully to carry out in specific legislation the confessional provisions of the Constitution of 1850.[9] The bill, as Zedlitz maintained later before the Landtag, was an attempt merely "to codify existing practice." [10] It provided, first, that all new schools must be confessional; if a school contained a minority of thirty children who belonged to a different religious confession recognized by the state, a separate school could be provided for them; when the number reached sixty such action became mandatory. Less than thirty children belonging to different religious confessions recognized by the state could be excused by the district president if they could show that they would be given adequate religious instruction by their own sect. Children not meeting this requirement, belonging to confessions not recognized by the state, or belonging to no religious sect at all, had to receive the religious instruction as given in their school. Religious instruction was to be supervised by church officials (the local pastors), and if it were not carried on to their satisfaction, it could be taken over directly by them. The confessional character of the schools was to be further carried out in that all teachers in a given school were to belong to the confession of that school, and also in the strictly confessional composition of the local governing school committee. The church was also given a large voice in judging the qualifications of teachers giving instruction in religion. Since religion was traditionally one of the most important subjects in the primary schools, and since a great many of these schools had only one class and one teacher, who taught a number of subjects, it may readily be seen that the general supervision of the church bodies over religious instruction thus provided for in the bill must have resulted in a strong clerical influence on the primary schools as a whole.[11]

3

IN THE MINISTRY

The Zedlitz bill was not received by the State Ministry without opposition. The strongest, naturally enough, came from the former

[9] See above, pp. 97ff.

[10] *Landtag* (1892), I, 18. Text of the bill in *Anlageband* II, 879ff.; list of the most important paragraphs in Richter, *Kampf um den Schulgesetzentwurf*, "Anhang I," pp. 114–115; *Schulthess* (1892), pp. 8–11.

[11] See the discussion of the clerical portions of the bill in Richter, *Kampf um den Schulgesetzentwurf*, pp. 29–30, 53; *Deutsche Rundschau*, 70:306.

National Liberal party leader, Miquel. Although never a rabid *Kulturkampf* anticlerical, Miquel was afraid that this bill, by yielding too much to the Center, would call up the old *Kulturkampf* spirit in the liberals and ruin any prospect of a real political compromise between Center and Kartell.[12]

Miquel, in fact, was in a very difficult position. With only half of his tax reform accomplished, he did not want any such explosive issue as this matter of church and state to disrupt the party constellation in the Landtag. As a National Liberal he could not look with confidence at the possibility of a Conservative-clerical alignment. As a Prussian minister his duty was to support royal policy or resign. Through the shoals of these conflicting motivations he steered a tortuous course. In the meetings of the State Ministry in December 1891, he sharply attacked the Zedlitz bill. He warned that the bill could never be accepted by the Free Conservatives and the National Liberals, the "middle parties," that they would certainly oppose it. But to these objections Caprivi returned the characteristically blunt answer that the bill was not to be put through in a form unacceptable to the Center. In fact, Caprivi's need of the Center for the Reichstag played directly into Zedlitz's hands. The less independent ministers allowed themselves to be persuaded, and at the decisive vote in the ministry Miquel found himself alone in his opposition.[13]

At this point he might very properly have resigned. The necessity for the completion of the tax reform, the possible effect of his resignation on the Kaiser, the sympathy of some of the moderate Conservatives were all cards in his favor. But this potential backing apparently did not seem powerful enough. He knew as an experienced politician how little chance a school bill of any kind, and particularly this one, had in the Prussian Landtag. There was bound to be a storm of opposition; he could wait until it developed before he took any positive personal action against the bill. If Caprivi and Zedlitz were foolish enough to tempt the political fates with this school bill, let them take the consequences. After a lifetime of political activity this dynamic and ambitious personality had finally at the end of his career arrived at a position where he could really make some sort of impress upon the state. In his revolutionary youth he might have been willing to give up everything for principle. But now, a royal minister and on the threshold of his sixty-fifth year, he

[12]Herzfeld, *Miquel*, II, 290, 294–295; Richter, *Kampf um den Schulgesetzentwurf*, pp. 27–28.

[13]Herzfeld, *Miquel*, II, 297–298; Richter, *Kampf um den Schulgesetzentwurf*, p. 28; Oncken, *Bennigsen*, II, 557; Bamberger, *Gesammelte Schriften*, V, 431–433.

could not sacrifice the possibility of further concrete achievements for mere doctrinaire idealism. Along with the other ministers, he signed the bill. On January 2, 1892, the bill was presented to the Kaiser and accepted and signed by him on the 14th.[14]

4

THE LIBERAL ATTACK

On January 15 Count Zedlitz introduced the School Bill into the Landtag with an explanatory speech, which called forth cheers from the right and the center. The party line-up for and against the bill began immediately to form. The Center and the right-wing Conservatives were jubilant, while the Radical, National Liberal, and Free Conservative press attacked and scored the bill unmercifully. Old Kulturkampf slogans concerning the clerical threat and the supremacy of the state over the church as well as protests in favor of freedom of conscience once more became current.[15] In the House of Deputies on January 21 the first reading of the budget turned into a general and heated debate on the School Bill. Speakers for the Radicals, National Liberals, and Free Conservatives attacked the bill, while the Center, Zedlitz, and Caprivi defended it. Radical Deputy Rickert professed astonishment and chagrin that the same ministry which last year had specifically declared that the Gossler bill was the furthest limit to which it could go in meeting the wishes of the religious bodies had now brought in a bill which acceded to practically all of the clerical demands. He called for a general rallying of Germans against this attempt to hand over control of the schools to the churches and expressed the wish — as an old National Liberal "secessionist" — that the Radicals and National Liberals might come back together again through common opposition to this bill.[16] Free Conservative Baron von Zedlitz-Neukirch stressed in a more moderate fashion that the question was not whether there should be Christian schools, but the extent of Christian influence upon the schools. The National Liberal speakers pointed out the basic similarity of the confessional provisions of Zedlitz's bill to Windthorst's school bill of 1888–1889. Furthermore, they attacked the clauses in the bill which — following the constitution — allowed

[14]Herzfeld, *Miquel,* II, 299–300; Richter, *Kampf um den Schulgesetzentwurf,* p. 28; Eyck, *Wilhelm II,* p. 48; cf. Wedel, *Zwischen Kaiser und Kanzler,* p. 131.

[15]For a résumé of initial press opinion see Richter, *Kampf um den Schulgesetzentwurf,* pp. 31–37; Wippermann, 8(I):57–61. Zedlitz's speech on January 15, *Landtag* (1892), I, 17ff.

[16]*Landtag* (1892), I, 35f.

the free erection of private schools as an invitation to the Catholics to set up an independent, ultramontane school system in Prussia.[17]

Zedlitz's expressed intention, in fact, of merely carrying out the provisions for confessional schools as specified in the constitution and of codifying the existing administrative practice was in itself fundamentally unacceptable to the liberal view. The constitution had been granted in 1850; since then many significant developments had occurred in the question of the relation of church and state. In 1870 the pope had lost his temporal control over the holy city of Rome to the Kingdom of Italy and had been impelled thereby to launch a long and stubborn diplomatic offensive to get it back. Also in 1870 had come the declaration of papal infallibility, followed shortly by the Kulturkampf in Germany. And with the Kulturkampf there had arisen in Germany a powerful political party united on the basis of the Catholic religion and with the purpose of pursuing in German politics the religious aims of the Catholic Church. For anticlerical liberals and liberal Protestants, therefore, any law carrying out the provisions of the constitution was retrogressive, while a legal codification of existing practice was dangerous for the future.[18]

At this first stage of the debate Zedlitz and Caprivi confined themselves to a general defense of the bill. To the accusation of the Radicals that the introduction of the School Bill represented a government swing to the right, Caprivi replied that he still believed the government should not line itself up with any particular party. This was especially true since parties increasingly represented economic or sectional interests.

I believe, also, that in a fundamentally monarchical state, such as ours, a government never can nor should pledge itself to work permanently with a particular party, and today I still adhere to the point of view that one should take the good where one finds it. The gentlemen of the Radical party have held this statement up to me upon every occasion where they believed that the good lay more on their side. Now, when, according to the view of the Deputy Rickert, the pendulum is swinging a bit more towards the other side . . . now we should no longer adhere to this principle . . .

The government was trying to create a situation in the schools that would "make peace" with the Catholics.

[17]*Landtag* (1892), I, 45, 62f., 73.
[18]Cf. Richter, *Kampf um den Schulgesetzentwurf*, pp. 41–42. *Landtag* (1892), I, 169.

The present government did not conduct the Kulturkampf. We are aware that we are living in a very serious time. We face the development of forces within the state, as I have already repeatedly elaborated, against which we must bring together every means at our disposal ("Quite right!" on the right and in the center).

That the schools are one of the most important means of opposing this movement, there is no question. That, however, precisely from this special point of view, if they are to fulfill their task, the schools cannot get along without religion, is just as certain ("Bravo!" on the right and in the center).

If the schools were to teach religion, however, they could not do this without the coöperation of the churches.

This seems to me to be a logical deduction which is not open to challenge. The matter of degree can, indeed, be disputed. Do that in the commission, familiarize yourselves with the bill, examine the individual details; but in my opinion these basic principles cannot be set aside ("Very true!" in the center).

If the liberal parties, Caprivi went on, carried their opposition to coöperation with the churches to its logical conclusion, they would end by demanding that religion be taken out of the schools altogether.

If that is what you want, then I understand the general attacks which have been directed against the bill from this side. If, however, that is not what you want, then you place yourselves with us upon the ground of the confessional school; there is no other way out for you ("Quite right!" on the right).

To the accusation that the government was shifting its program and flouting the popular will, Caprivi replied that all basic government measures had so far been passed through the Landtag and the Reichstag by majority vote. "That it has not always been the same majority or one desired by this or that party is a situation which can by no means be altered." [19]

In the battle over the bill, the lines of which already were beginning to form, the Conservative party would hold the decisive position. The 84 National Liberals in the House of Deputies added to 66 Free Conservatives and 27 Radicals (plus 4 independents) would total 181 votes against the bill; if to the 98 votes of the Center and the 14 Poles were added all of the 125 Conservative votes (plus 10 independents) there would be a total of 247 votes for the bill, a safe

[19]From speeches on January 21 and 22, 1892, *Landtag* (1892), I, 40, 65f.; Arndt, *Reden,* pp. 399–402.

majority.[20] In the budget debate on January 21 and 22 the Conservative speaker, alone among the party spokesmen, made no mention of the bill. Free Conservatives and National Liberals could still hope to draw the support of enough moderate Conservatives seriously to endanger the passage of the bill in its initial form. But on the 21st, in the Reichstag, the Center party cast the decisive vote to validate the seat of a Conservative. The position to be taken by the moderate Conservatives in the first reading was, therefore, awaited with great suspense.[21]

By the multiplicity of German parties the central position was the most strategic; that party which could throw its weight now to the left, now to the right, and thus pass or defeat legislation would hold the real power. Until 1890 the National Liberal and Free Conservative moderate "middle parties" had, in effect, held this position but had in practice drifted too far over into the rightist camp, so that with their disastrous defeat in the 1890 election the left had been strengthened, the right had remained the same, and the powerful middle position had been seized by the Center party, which because of its own special inner contradictions could all the more easily straddle the fence.

Now, in 1892, National Liberals and Free Conservatives could not look blandly on while a political formation threatened in Prussia which would relegate their parties in the Landtag to the same unimportant position they held in the Reich. On January 22 the elderly and highly respected leader of the National Liberals, Rudolf von Bennigsen, observed in the Reichstag, in the course of remarks on the Swiss trade treaty, that the modified protectionism of the new trade-treaty policy had made it possible for Radicals and National Liberals to act together in a matter which had so far been basic to their separation.

Conditions could occur in the development of our domestic life which would make it desirable, indeed, perhaps necessary, for the liberal groups and persons now fighting each other to join together again ("Hear! hear!") in common battle, not on the ground of material interests, but in other fields concerned with idealistic, not material things. . . . That would be, in my opinion, who have always been and will remain a liberal, only beneficial for the further development of Germany. The liberal mid-

<hr>

[20]These figures taken from Richter, *Kampf um den Schulgesetzentwurf*, p. 38. For the political composition of the House of Deputies in the Prussian Landtag, as of the 1888 election, see table on p. 37, above.

[21]Richter, *Kampf um den Schulgesetzentwurf*, p. 44; Thimme, "Bismarck und Kardorff," pt. I, p. 178 and note; Kardorff, *Kardorff*, p. 252.

dle class [*Bürgertum*] in city and country, the liberal point of view has a claim to greater consideration than it at present possesses ("Quite right!" Catcall — laughter).

Thus the leader of the National Liberals had answered favorably Rickert's suggestion for a closer union on the left. The challenge thereby thrown down to the Conservatives and to the government was all the more startling because of Bennigsen's official position as governor of Hanover. In Prussia officials were not supposed to criticize the policies of the royal government.[22]

The day before, the 21st, the other leader of the National Liberals, Johannes Miquel, sent in his resignation as finance minister. He had already aired his misgivings in a talk with Caprivi on January 7 or 8, but that conversation had ended on a friendly note, and since then he had made no further move. Perhaps some sort of compromise between Center and Kartell could yet be worked out. But now, with his own party taking an all-out stand against the bill, he could wait no longer. Perhaps his old friend and colleague, Bennigsen, helped to persuade him to be loyal to the party and strike a blow for the liberal cause. Caprivi, naturally, was not pleased. The more critical the situation became, the more necessity, in his eyes, for the ministry to hold together. A public break in the ministry at this decisive point would seriously endanger the government's position. In his characteristically terse military manner he declared, "I am of the opinion that Miquel has absolutely no grounds for regarding his position as altered by supporting the School Bill. He is the king's minister and has nothing more to do with party considerations." Caprivi also needed Miquel for the completion of the tax reform. He refused to push acceptance of his resignation, and on January 23 the Kaiser issued a cabinet order rejecting it. On January 25, however, the incident was reported in detail in the *Kölnische Zeitung*. Miquel — who immediately denied any connection with the article — was apparently making sure of his position in his party and with liberal public opinion and also, incidentally, thereby strengthening his influence on the Kaiser and his personal position in the ministry.[23]

[22]Oncken, *Bennigsen*, II, 556–557, 559; *Sten. Ber.* (1890–1892), VI, 3822.
[23]Herzfeld, *Miquel*, II, 300–301; Richter, *Kampf um den Schulgesetzentwurf*, pp. 65–67.

5

DEBATE IN THE LANDTAG

At this point, on the 25th, there began the first formal debate on the bill in the Landtag. It was a furious battle of words, philosophies, and political motives. The opening gun was fired by Deputy von Buch, who stunned the "middle parties" by announcing that the Conservative party *as a whole* was in favor of the entire bill, including the most extreme sections.[24] This announcement effectively decided the issue in advance, since all the Conservatives with the Center could muster a majority of the House. But the middle parties were not inclined to give in without a fight. The Conservatives' apparent acceptance of the political alignment with the Center, which they had so denounced when Bismarck had made moves in that direction in 1890, only made the middle parties more fanatical, more heated in their attacks — and all the more so because now their only recourse lay outside of the House, with public opinion, and perhaps — judging by the Miquel crisis — also within the higher echelons of the government itself. For five whole days the battle raged in the House, arousing extraordinary interest, excitement, even passion in the press and among the educated public.

Save for some extremists among the Radicals, the liberal opposition had no thought of removing religious instruction from the schools. They wanted the schools to be religious but not under the influence of the churches (having in mind, of course, the Catholic Church in particular). On the other hand, the government, backed by Center and Conservatives, maintained that religion could not be made a part of the curriculum without granting the churches supervision and control over it. Between these views — perhaps because of the general tenseness of the political situation — no compromise seemed possible.

The Centrist deputy, Dr. Porsch, declared:

There are basic antitheses here that must be placed over against each other . . . My political friends believe that Christianity is not a poison, but a food for the soul . . . that Christianity is not merely a sum of positive knowledge which is introduced into the heads of children, but rather that it must penetrate the heart of the child in every way and . . . , therefore, in every place where the instruction offers the opportunity for it . . . An evangelical child has the right to demand that the history of the age of the Reformation be stated clearly and concisely from the

[24]*Landtag* (1892), I, 100; Richter, *Kampf um den Schulgesetzentwurf*, p. 45.

evangelical point of view; a Catholic child has the same right to demand that his teacher present the same period to him from the Catholic point of view. When a teacher in an undenominational school has to deliver a lecture which shall suit *both* denominations (laughter), then one child is not being educated as a Protestant nor the other child as a Catholic ("Quite right!" in the center).[25]

Count Zedlitz replied to the objections to forcing religious instruction on unaffiliated children,

I do not in the least want to exert any compulsion, but rather only to give, as it were, a favor, which I myself have received, to these unfortunate children, whose hands no pious mother has folded, and who have never heard in their family life a word of religious truth (enthusiastic "Bravo!" on the right and in the center).[26]

As over against this positive religious philosophy, with its declared opposition to socialist materialism, the liberals of all the other parties had only the negative defense of freedom of the individual conscience, which some of them — not wanting, above all, to appear irreligious or un-Christian — seemed, in this question of the schools, to confuse with the supremacy of the state. The *Deutsche Rundschau* summed up the situation in its March number as follows:

Today in Germany there are only two parties with wide mass support which possess an ideology common to both leaders and followers. One represents the Catholic, the other the Social Democratic ideology . . . Between these two masses, each one of which is held firmly united by the single tie of a great ideology, stands the independent, educated middle class, until a short time ago still the leading element of the German nation, but now torn apart and disunited.[27]

There were implications, however, in this clerical-conservative line-up which might encourage and support a general liberal opposition. They were expressed most crudely and openly in the Landtag by the eighty-two-year-old Centrist deputy Peter Reichensperger, who argued for the School Bill on the grounds that the more religious instruction there was in the schools, with its emphasis on the other world, the less time there would be for instruction in things of this world, and, therefore, the less opportunity there would be for new and dangerous ideas to make the lower classes discontented with their lot. He recommended that the number of hours of instruction

[25]*Landtag* (1892), I, 162.
[26]*Landtag* (1892), I, 140.
[27]70:455.

per day and the over-all extent of compulsory schooling be reduced.[28]

Although Zedlitz disavowed this statement of Reichensperger's,
and no other member of the Center or of the Conservatives went
that far, it is probable that there were many in those two parties who
inclined in that direction. There was, therefore, an anti-intellectual,
feudal, reactionary cast to their support of the School Bill. And this
reactionary spirit was expressed, in the School Bill debate, precisely
in the field most open to general liberal opposition. Freedom of
thought and of scientific inquiry were long since firmly entrenched
in the German way of life. Since 1866 the liberal middle class had,
indeed, put up with the political domination of the Junker conservative aristocrats. It could not now, however, at this late date, give
up its treasured intellectual freedom too. Not that any great threat
really existed. The Ferry laws which excluded religion completely
from French public schools had been put through ten years before.
To the later observer the Zedlitz School Bill seems more like a rear-
guard action against a scientific, materialistic, liberalizing tendency
which at the time — as the rapid growth of the Social Democrats
showed — was clearly in the ascendant.[29]

But, hopelessly divided and uncertain over the important political and economic problems of the day — parliamentary democracy
versus monarchical absolutism, free trade versus protection, *laissez
faire* versus state paternalistic control of industry and provision of
compulsory benefits for the worker — liberals of all sizes and vari-
eties could cheerfully unite on this issue of freedom of thought and
inquiry, already well over a hundred years of age. Against their old
clerical enemy they could bring out their grand old battle flags and
march off enthusiastically, shoulder to shoulder. Divided on every
other issue, the educated German middle class had only this one
issue of anticlericalism left to provide the basis for common political
action. If they were ever going to reunite politically, it would have
to be on this issue. The Zedlitz bill, therefore, presented the liberals
not only with a challenge, but with a political opportunity, and one
which, if necessary, they were willing to utilize.[30]

During the first two years of the Caprivi regime the National
Liberals had found little to please them in government policy. They
had been dissatisfied with the new colonial policy, with the labor-

[28]*Landtag* (1892), I, 108; Richter, *Kampf um den Schulgesetzentwurf*, pp. 50–
51.

[29]Cf. Wahl's handling of the School Bill issue, *Geschichte*, III, 538ff.; C. J. H.
Hayes, *A Generation of Materialism* (New York, 1941), pp. 131ff.

[30]Stillich, *Politischen Parteien*, II, 313.

protection bill; they had given only reluctant and grudging support to the trade treaties;[31] some of them had developed more and more nostalgia for the good old days and had fallen in with the Bismarck Fronde. Recently this dissatisfaction had been increased by forebodings over the expected Zedlitz School Bill. Already on January 1 the *Kölnische Zeitung* wrote:

Not a few among us were originally freedom-intoxicated idealists and were transformed inwardly into rational monarchists only by Bismarck and by the great and good Kaiser [William I]. It consequently makes us thoughtful and anxious to notice that many of these persons have begun in recent years quietly to subject their basic political principles, with respect to recent experiences, to a thorough-going revision. The results of this quietly continuing thought-process could one day reveal themselves in an astounding manner.[32]

Then had come the introduction of the School Bill and the violent attack on it by the middle parties at the earliest occasion, during the budget debate. In his speech at this time the "Secessionist" Rickert had suggested an alliance of all liberals against the bill. The following day Bennigsen had replied with his proclamation in the Reichstag. At the same time Miquel had handed in his resignation, and his action was revealed in the *Kölnische Zeitung*. In the first reading the middle-party spokesmen seemed as excited over the fact that the government had made the bill acceptable to the Center as over the bill itself. They also repeatedly reminded the Conservatives of their support of the Gossler bill the previous year. Kardorff warned the government that it must not ignore the middle parties, "upon which the whole development of Germany since 1866 has rested." [33] By dividing the "state-supporting" elements into clerical-Conservatives on the one side and anticlerical liberals on the other, the bill would weaken the state and encourage, not deter, the Social Democrats. "Out of the black present," wrote the Free Conservative *Post*, "must necessarily grow the red future." [34] The bill, declared National Liberal deputy von Eynern, was "a declaration of war against all, even the most moderate, liberals." [35]

To the ideological excitement over the bill itself, then, was added the sharp animosity of clashing political interests. The result was an exchange between the speakers of exaggerated statements and ac-

---

[31]Cf. Oncken, *Bennigsen*, II, 569–570.
[32]Printed in Bachem, *Zentrumspartei*, V, 255.
[33]*Landtag* (1892), I, 148; Thimme, "Bismarck und Kardorff," pt. I, p. 179.
[34]Richter, *Kampf um den Schulgesetzentwurf*, pp. 60–61.
[35]*Landtag* (1892), I, 168.

cusations which served only to heighten the tension and to make any possibility of compromise even more remote. Whereas the Centrist Dr. Porsch had accused the opposition of being un-Christian, Deputy von Eynern declared that the bill gave the schools over to the domination of the Catholic Church.

Gentlemen, the debate on the educational system of our nation which has been taking place here these last few days is an event of epoch-making [*weltgeschichtliches*] importance . . . it is a question of the realization of the dictum of a Roman prelate that the battle between Protestantism and Catholicism will take place upon the soil of Brandenburg [*auf märkischem Sande*] . . . It was the plan of Deputy Windthorst to divide the nation in two halves in order to take up the battle against the Protestant half and to achieve the victory for the Roman Catholic half, and I maintain that in this bill the first and most important concessions have been made to the Roman Catholic Church in line with this wish of the Center party . . .

Gentlemen, there is no question that, if this bill is put through, with its emphasis on confessionalism, instruction in all fields will become saturated with it, especially in the field of history. . . . I do not desire that in Prussian primary schools, under the authority of the Prussian state, it should be possible to teach that Luther was a scoundrel and a suicide tortured by qualms of conscience ("Hear! hear!" from the National Liberals) and that Protestant doctrine is the foster-mother of the monstrous doctrine of the Social Democrats.

As for the children of dissenters, they did not come from evil, irreligious families, but rather from families that, for the most part, were "very serious and pious people . . . whose children often learn better how to pray than the children of those who adhere to strict dogmas." If the bill merely carried out the provisions of the constitution, then the constitution should be changed.[36]

Von Eynern's speech came on January 28. The climax of the debate came the following day, the 29th, when Caprivi entered strongly, and somewhat rashly, into the fray. At this tense moment his directness in thought and expression played him false. The fact, he declared, that the Prussian state included two great religious confessions was not, as had been said, a condition pregnant with the danger of clerical theocratic rule; rather the presence of two priesthoods itself made such a theocratic state impossible. As for the statements in the House and in the press, he did not believe it would be possible to make such statements if one person out of a thousand had actually read and studied the bill. If the opposition were not so

[36] *Landtag* (1892), I, 167ff.; Wahl, *Geschichte*, III, 541–542.

swayed by echoes from the past they could probably come to an agreement on it.

Deputy von Eynern, said Caprivi, had accused the government of declaring war on the National Liberal party and even upon all liberals. But if they were indeed at war, then it had been declared by the opposition.

To my sincere regret, I have for a long time now had to read in the press of the party to which Herr von Eynern belongs repeated attacks against the present government, attacks which were not instructive, but from which I was forced to conclude that a more or less hostile attitude existed . . . I have long since asked myself, and was especially concerned with the question after a certain great paper printed a New Year's article, which was read with astonishment by wide circles: what does this party want? . . . Now, since recently the great liberal party has been proclaimed . . . many things become clear to me . . . I do not at all want to say, if the National Liberal party strengthens itself by attracting a part of the deputies from the other side, that this in itself is unwelcome to me; only the way in which the speakers of the National Liberal party have come forward, from the provocative speech of Herr Hobrecht to the fighting speech of Herr von Eynern, this has convinced me that it is a fight which is wanted, that there is to be a declaration of war . . .

As for the fear that the government would align itself permanently with the Center party, with consequent additional concessions, it had had the courage to make a break with the National Liberals and would not always necessarily agree with the Center. He, for instance, was sure that the Prussian government would not vote in the Bundesrat for the return of the Jesuit Order.

The National Liberal party has always been characterized by a certain idealism, and that has been one of its most attractive features. Through the establishing of the German Reich this idealism has become, I will not say pointless, but it cannot be deepened further. If you want to give special expression to your nationalism, then you must now become a National Conservative party. But that you are endeavoring to maintain idealism on German soil, with that I thoroughly sympathize, there I can agree with you. We are sick, I think, from the loss of our idealism. And if as a result of your present inner development you end by laying a stronger emphasis on idealism, then that will be most gratifying to the present government and especially to myself.

If, however, in this present bill differences have appeared, I believe, indeed, that the basis and the roots of these differences lie deeper than is generally accepted, and on this point I find myself in complete agreement with Deputy Dr. Porsch. I believe it is a question here, in the last instance, not of Protestant and Catholic but of Christian and atheist (applause on the right and in the center — great disturbance on the left).

The House broke into an uproar. In vain Caprivi tried to explain that he had not meant to refer to the parties in opposition by the word "atheist," that he had meant to refer to "an ideology coming more and more to the fore which stands in opposition to every religion." His explanations were not heeded; the close of his speech was greeted by stormy applause on the right and by loud continued hissing on the left. With the words "Christian and atheist" Caprivi had poured oil into the fire, and the flames of popular passion leaped up higher.[37]

It is difficult to interpret the motives for Caprivi's obvious concern over the threat of a new united liberalism. It is possible that, along with the *Kreuzzeitung,* he suspected the Bismarck-oriented middle parties — led by von Kardorff and Bennigsen — which heretofore had not been very warm in their support of the government, of taking the School Bill as a pretext for building up a party of broad and fundamental opposition, incarnating the Bismarck Fronde in a political party basically opposing the Kaiser and the New Course at all points. If so, his fears were doubtless exaggerated. As for the reference to "atheism," which has been quoted here in its full context, it is possible that Caprivi, in emphasizing the idealistic basis of a liberal party, intended to suggest that, as against materialism and essential atheism (read: Social Democrats), religion and liberal idealism (read: Center and National Liberals) really had much in common. If this was his thought, then it demonstrates with incisive clarity how far removed his whole attitude was from the contending parties and the political arena in which he stood. In the midst of the clash of party passions and political interests he thought in terms of political philosophy. And what he thought he spoke. Certainly this incident demonstrates Caprivi's limitations as a politician.[38]

<hr>

[37]*Landtag* (1892), I, 193–195; Richter, *Kampf um den Schulgesetzentwurf,* p. 63; Wippermann, 8(I):65ff.

[38]Richter, *Kampf um den Schulgesetzentwurf,* p. 70; cf. Wahl, *Geschichte,* III, 543; *Schulthess,* "Politische Übersicht" (1892), pp. 333–334. The *Preussische Jahrbücher* pointed out in its February issue that the possible *rapprochement* between National Liberals and Radicals was itself a product of the Caprivi policy. Only a "suspicion that . . . something greater is afoot" explained Caprivi's otherwise unreasonable anger (69:289). Cf. M. Schneidewin, *Ein wenig mehr Licht über Bismarck, Caprivi, u. die jüngst erlebte Mobilmachung des Liberalismus* (Berlin, 1892), pp. 22–24. Cf. also Richter's speech on January 30, *Landtag* (1892), I, 238.

6

IMPACT OF THE OPPOSITION

Caprivi's strong attack on the National Liberals on the 29th looked as if the government were determined to crush all opposition. Bennigsen, whom Caprivi had mentioned in his speech practically by name, was roundly denounced by Conservative leaders in the Landtag. His dismissal from his post as governor of Hanover — given to him by the Kaiser in 1888 — was imminently expected. From an official ball given by Bennigsen on January 30 most of the important guests excused themselves at the last minute.[39]

But already the wind had begun to change and to blow from a new quarter. On the 29th Miquel sent Bennigsen a cryptic note: "I urgently beg you to take no step before you have spoken with me. I have important things to tell you." The next day Bennigsen returned to Berlin and found the atmosphere quite friendly. The government, he wrote to his wife, was now "blowing the pipe of peace [*Friedenschalmei*] in every key." In a private talk Bennigsen assured Caprivi that there was no intention of shaping a policy of fundamental liberal opposition to the government, and Caprivi assured Bennigsen that there was no thought on the part of the Kaiser of removing him from his position. At a dinner at the Chancellery the Kaiser spoke with Bennigsen in a very friendly manner and did not mention his speech in the Reichstag. He was very effusive and talked with Bennigsen about the School Bill for a considerable time, in spite of Caprivi's efforts to disengage him. The Kaiser, who had inherited the Kartell policy from Bismarck, had begun to be worried by the extent of the liberal opposition to the bill.[40]

On January 30 the School Bill was sent to committee. But the excitement did not die down; on the contrary. The battle in the press raged even more violently. And, as the Conservative-Center majority in the committee (16 to 12) gave no indication of yielding on any important point, the liberals began actively organizing public opinion against the bill. The committee did adopt an amendment sponsored by the Center, which remembered its experience as a minority during the Kulturkampf, removing the clause forcing children of dissenters to participate in the religious instruction of their school. In the general hue and cry this concession was hardly no-

[39] Oncken, *Bennigsen*, II, 560; Richter, *Kampf um den Schulgesetzentwurf*, p. 70.
[40] Oncken, *Bennigsen*, II, 561–563.

ticed.[41] During February a veritable flood of petitions and resolutions poured into the House of Deputies: from liberal party organizations, from teachers' organizations, from special committees organized to fight the bill, from city governments, most of which in Prussia were Radical in make-up. The most impressive petitions came from the faculties of the great universities. The sixty-nine names signed to the petition from the University of Berlin included those of such distinguished persons as Wilhelm Dilthey, Hermann von Helmholtz, Theodor Mommsen, Gustav Schmoller, Heinrich von Treitschke, and Rudolf Virchow. Treitschke declared, in a statement prepared for the *Münchner Allgemeine Zeitung*, that the School Bill "sacrifices inalienable rights of government [*Staatsgewalt*]." There can be no doubt that at least a sizable part of the public agitation was spontaneous, and that, in general, it showed that the bill, as it stood at the first reading, gave too much influence over the educational process to the churches to be accepted by educated and enlightened Germans. When, during a performance of Schiller's *Don Carlos* in the Court Theater in Stuttgart, an actor spoke the line: "*Sire, geben Sie Gedankenfreiheit!*" ("Sire, grant us freedom of thought!"), the audience broke into a storm of applause.[42]

Under the mounting pressure of public protest the ranks of the bill's defenders began to waver. Various moderate Conservatives, such as von Rauchhaupt and von Helldorff, declared privately against the bill in its present state. Even more important, within the government itself the divergence in views between Caprivi and Zedlitz and Miquel became more and more apparent. And, buffeted by the various winds of opinion, the Kaiser changed his mind almost daily. To the silently working and ever present influence of Miquel was added that of the influential Free Conservative Stumm, who spoke to the Kaiser very sharply against the bill. Von Helldorff also seems to have advised the Kaiser against it. Also, on January 28 Phili Eulenburg — now acting on his own responsibility — wrote to the Kaiser from Munich, warning that the liberals were the only ally of the Reich against separatism in Bavaria, that the School Bill, by encouraging the ultramontane party, was endangering the Reich in South Germany. "I think, too," he wrote, "that if, after an interview with Zedlitz, it came to people's ears that Your Majesty's

[41]Richter, *Kampf um den Schulgesetzentwurf*, pp. 85–86.
[42]Richter, *Kampf um den Schulgesetzentwurf*, pp. 76ff., 82–83, 80, note; text of the University of Berlin petition, *ibid.*, "Anhang III," p. 117; *Schulthess* (1892), pp. 68–70.

attitude is a very moderate one, the best effect would be produced in *all quarters,* and that would help to smoothe things down." Eulenburg wrote in the same sense also to Caprivi. Holstein agreed with Eulenburg. Various ministers, such as Herrfurth, Thielen, and Bötticher, began to waver. The chief of the Kaiser's Civil Cabinet, von Lucanus, one-time under-secretary in the Falk Kulturkampf ministry, seems to have worked against the bill.[43] And to this list one should probably also add the liberal grand duke of Baden.

In the *Hamburger Nachrichten* Bismarck contributed his personal criticism. The bill, he said, was clearly part of a political deal with the Center and an "apple of discord unnecessarily thrown among the parties." It would bring about a new Kulturkampf. The bill was a political mistake, which the Conservatives supported out of servility: "One wants a promotion, the other is considering a career for his son, the third desires to be decorated, the fourth is working for invitations to court for his family. . . ."

The basic error lies in the belief of the government that with concessions it could reconcile irreconcilable enemies such as the Center, the Poles, and the Guelfs and base government policy upon the support of elements which had already for decades proved themselves deadly enemies of Prussia or the Reich and against which one of the chief tasks of the previous government was an unrelenting struggle.[44]

Kardorff was positive that if the bill eventually passed the House unchanged he could get Bismarck to appear against it in the House of Lords. "M. de Bismarck," wrote the French chargé d'affaires on February 6 from Munich, "has become really the leader of the opposition. He is the real bond between all the parties that compose it, with the exception, however, of the Social Democrats. All those who don't approve of the Kaiser are with him, and Germany is thus divided into two camps." [45]

On February 15, to show its strength, the new Radical–National Liberal–Free Conservative coalition mustered a majority in the Reichstag for its own version of an innocuous resolution over the

[43]Thimme, "Bismarck und Kardorff," pt. I, pp. 179–180, 182–183; Kardorff, *Kardorff,* pp. 253–255; Hellwig, *Stumm,* pp. 424–425; Haller, *Eulenburg,* I, 110–113; Eulenburg to Holstein, January 28, 29, 30, February 14, 22, March 5, 1892, *Holstein Papers, Correspondence;* Richter, *Kampf um den Schulgesetzentwurf,* pp. 74, 87f., 92; Rogge, *Holstein,* p. 163; Hohenlohe, *Memoirs,* II, 443; *DDF,* 1 ser., IX, 344; Waldersee, *Denkwürdigkeiten,* II, 236. Cf. the *Kolnische Zeitung* articles reproduced in Wippermann, 8(I):66–67, 76–77, 82–83; also *ibid.,* 85, 87.

[44]Hofmann, *Bismarck,* pp. 13ff., 27; Richter, *Kampf um den Schulgesetzentwurf,* pp. 77–78, notes.

[45]Thimme, "Bismarck und Kardorff," pt. I, pp. 182–183; *DDF,* 1 ser., IX, 275.

reform of army court-martial procedure.[46] Already rumors began to circulate that Caprivi would resign and be replaced by General von Waldersee, now friendly with both the Miquel and Bismarck factions.[47] On February 21 Waldersee, who had ears at court, noted: "A deplorable game of intrigue is going on, in which Caprivi, Boetticher, Miquel, Zedlitz, Lucanus are all trying to go their own ways, none trusts the other, none really knows what the Kaiser wants, especially how far he wants to go, and all suspect other influences which they don't quite know about."[48]

On February 24 the Kaiser spoke at the yearly banquet of the Brandenburg Provincial Diet. The year before on this occasion he had wielded a verbal lance against the "spirit of insubordination . . . abroad in the land."[49] Now, in a speech prepared without the knowledge of the ministry, he sallied forth once more.[50] It had become the fashion, said the Kaiser, to grumble at everything done by the government. If Germany was such a bad place, perhaps these grumblers would be happier if they left it. It would be a great favor to the rest. Germany was going through a difficult period of transition, but calmer days would follow. This thought he illustrated with a story about Sir Francis Drake [sic], who was searching in Central America for a great new ocean, which he was sure existed. He had been led in a long, arduous climb to the top of a mountain.

The [Indian] chief pointed to the sheet of water behind them, and Drake beheld the wildly agitated waves of the sea which he had just navigated. Then the chief turned and led the admiral around a small projecting rock, and suddenly there opened before his enraptured gaze the wide expanse of the Pacific Ocean, spread out in majestic calm, its surface lit with the golden rays of the rising sun. — So let it be with us! The firm conviction of your sympathy constantly renews My strength to persist in My work and to press forward on the path which Heaven has laid out for Me. I am helped thereto by My feeling of responsibility to the Ruler of all, and the firm conviction that He, our old ally of Rossbach[51] and Dennewitz[52] will not now leave Me in the lurch. He has given Himself such endless trouble with our old Mark and with our House that

[46]*Schulthess* (1892), pp. 70–71; Thimme, "Bismarck und Kardorff," pt. I, pp. 181–182.

[47]Herzfeld, *Miquel,* II, 302; cf. Waldersee, *Denkwürdigkeiten,* II, 233, 236.

[48]Waldersee, *Denkwürdigkeiten,* II, 232–233.

[49]See above, p. 106.

[50]Cf. *DDF,* 1 ser., IX, 313; but see also Waldersee, *Denkwürdigkeiten,* II, 239.

[51]A famous victory of Frederick the Great in the Seven Years' War over imperial German as well as French troops, since, at the time, France was allied with Austria and the Holy Roman Empire against Prussia.

[52]A Prussian victory over a Napoleonic army in 1813.

we can assume that He has not done this for nothing. No, Brandenburgers, on the contrary, we are called to greatness, and to glorious days will I lead you. Do not let grumblings and the party speeches of discontented persons darken your vision of the future, or lessen your pleasure in coöperating with Me. With slogans alone nothing can be done, and to the unending complaints about the new course and the men who direct it I answer confidently and decidedly, "My course is the right one, and I shall continue to steer it." That my brave men of the Mark will assist Me I confidently expect.[53]

If the Kaiser had expected to shatter all opposition and restore peace and tranquillity by this forensic foray, he must have been sadly disappointed. The press, both at home and abroad, broke into the strongest criticism of this further evidence of reactionary absolutism. The *Vossische Zeitung* remarked tartly that so many Germans were "dissatisfied" that if they all emigrated Germany would be reduced to the status of a third-rate power. The speech, said the *Kölnische Zeitung*, throwing all caution to the winds, had made of the School Bill controversy a fight for freedom of thought and the progressive development of institutions against what was now seen to be a general reaction. "If any doubt existed," wrote the *Preussische Jahrbücher,* "in the circles of the moderate parties that they must again tend more to liberalism, the Kaiser's speech . . . has removed that doubt . . . It is not believed that the passionate feeling aroused by the speech will pass away. The speech itself may again be forgotten, but the body of sentimental attachment that has thereby been washed away anew is permanently lost." The foreign press joined the chorus. The head of the Reich, commented *The Times* of London, seemed to be more theologian than statesman. The *Standard* deplored the Kaiser's "fatal gift" of eloquence. "The time has come," screamed the liberal Vienna *Neue Freie Presse,* "to draw all our swords!" [54] "Everyone is asking with one derisive accord," wrote Phili Eulenburg in his diary, " 'What may these days of glory be to which he is *now* going to lead us?' The dismissal of Bismarck has not yet proved a day of glory." [55]

The speech, added *The Times* correspondent, demonstrating small knowledge of the real character either of German politics or of William II, "proves that the measures of the government will be forced through, *coûte que coûte* [cost what it will]." The Kaiser's

[53]*Schulthess* (1892), pp. 71–72; Wippermann, 8(I):253:254; *The Times,* wkly. ed., February 26, 1892, p. 5.

[54]*DDF,* 1 ser., IX, 314–316; *The Times,* wkly. ed., February 26, p. 9; *Pr. Jbb.,* 69:433; Wippermann, 8(I):200–209.

[55]Haller, *Eulenburg,* I, 205.

mother, Empress Frederick, had a clearer view. "I wish I could put a padlock on his mouth for all occasions where speeches are made in public," she wrote to Queen Victoria. "It is no use to say anything — the Bismarckian education and the school of the Emperor William's entourage have made him what he is . . . Some of his Aides-de-Camp were beside themselves with enthusiasm about this speech, which quite brought the perspiration to my forehead when I read it . . . I assure you I tremble for him — with all his rashness and obstinacy, etc., he is a big baby." [56]

In the weeks following, the Kaiser was somewhat indisposed. To a letter from Phili Eulenburg on March 10 describing the bad effect of the speech in Bavaria he replied by open telegram,

Best thanks for letters, which told me nothing essentially new. Am very wretched, though, and must abstain from work. Condition caused by strain and overexertion. Fever abated. But still great lassitude. Shall perhaps, when better, have to get away and take a change of air. Therefore all politics, home and foreign, are for the moment out of my thoughts so long as they keep the usual course. Best regards from yours,

William[57]

7

THE MINISTERIAL CRISIS

Under the circumstances the School Bill controversy reached its denouement sooner than expected. On March 17, exactly two years after Bismarck had composed his letter of resignation, a routine Crown Council meeting took place, with the Kaiser attending. The discussion was over a building program of the Kaiser's for the royal palace, which he wanted to finance with a lottery. When one of the ministers[58] remarked that public opinion was against this scheme, the Kaiser replied that now they were opposing him with public opinion, whereas with the School Bill they told him not to pay any attention to it. He understood that the bill was acceptable only to the Conservatives and the Center, whereas he had never intended this. The opposition was very great. Defense of the bill in the Landtag and in committee had been too uncompromising. Such a law, however, must be put through only with the assistance of the moderate parties. Miquel then supported this speech of the Kaiser's

[56]*The Times*, wkly. ed., February 26, 1892, p. 6; Ponsonby, *Letters of Empress Frederick*, pp. 434–435.
[57]Haller, *Eulenburg*, I, 206–207; cf. Waldersee, *Denkwürdigkeiten*, II, 234–235.
[58]One source ascribes this comment to Zedlitz.

by declaring that future policy must be based on the Kartell idea, which had been the political basis of all the great legislative achievements since 1866, not only in Prussia but in the Reich. One could still conciliate the Center, but one should not let things go to extremes and cause a new Kulturkampf. To gain time and to mollify opinions, the question should be postponed.

In opposition to the Kaiser and Miquel, Caprivi then remarked that in his opinion the government should continue to defend the bill as drawn up and signed by the ministry and by the Kaiser. Furthermore, the Center would not be willing to make any great concessions on the bill. The support of the Center, however, was absolutely necessary for the Reichstag. If the Center was not to be satisfied by the bill, then it had no further importance for him.

Between these two points of view an argument ensued. Caprivi indicated that if the Kaiser should decide to withdraw the bill, then he must resign. The Kaiser countered by suggesting the question be postponed until the next session, thus again following Miquel's line. Caprivi, who was quite aware of the working of Miquel's influence in the whole episode, attacked the practicality of the Kartell policy and suggested that his views and those of the finance minister might not be permanently reconcilable. Against this the Kaiser continued to maintain that the moderate parties must approve of the bill, and that he did not care whether or not it were put through in the present session. Caprivi suggested that a compromise might still be worked out in the committee sessions, to which the Kaiser agreed but added that, in any case, there must be a change of tactics and a fundamental agreement on the matter with the moderate parties.[59]

Throughout the discussion Count Zedlitz said nothing, but afterwards quietly went home and sent in his resignation. As far as he was concerned, no satisfactory compromise with the National Liberals was possible. In the evening of the same day Miquel, quite correctly, offered his resignation to Caprivi. After a long talk with Zedlitz the next afternoon, the 18th, Caprivi also sent in his resignation as Prussian minister-president and foreign minister and also as chancellor of the Reich. The same day the Kaiser left Berlin for his hunting lodge, Hubertusstock in the Schorfheide.

[59]Richter, *Kampf um den Schulgesetzentwurf*, pp. 88–90; Herzfeld, *Miquel*, II, 303–305. On March 25, 1892, M. Herbette, the French ambassador, reported: "William II had read and discussed the projected school law article by article. It was he who had instigated M. de Caprivi to intervene in the debate; he had held, here and there, veritable parliamentary assizes to push the adoption of the new system." *DDF*, 1 ser., IX, 360. Cf. Kardorff, *Kardorff*, p. 258; Waldersee, *Denkwürdigkeiten*, II, 236.

With three ministers, including the chancellor, resigned from the government and with the Kaiser gone from Berlin, a state of complete confusion set in and lasted for a week. Who should go and who should stay? The Kaiser seemed completely taken by surprise by the whole development. He saw no necessity for Zedlitz's resignation and even had the empress write a note pleading with Zedlitz not to desert him. On the margin of Caprivi's resignation he wrote: "Wouldn't dream of doing this. First to drive the cart into the mud and then to leave the Kaiser sitting there is not nice. Caprivi made a mistake, everybody sees that. His leaving now would be a national misfortune and is impossible." [60]

Zedlitz, however, who had believed sincerely in his School Bill, would not be moved and persisted in his resignation. Constitutionally Zedlitz was not resigning because of a defeat of his policy in the Landtag. On the contrary, the very character of the crisis, of the attitude of Miquel, shows that there still was a very good chance of a Conservative-clerical majority. Nor would a parliamentary defeat in any case have necessitated the resignation of a Prussian minister. It was rather the confidence of the crown which had suddenly been withdrawn in the Crown Council of March 17 and which logically demanded his resignation, all the Kaiser's protestations to the contrary. The victory of Miquel within the ministry had automatically necessitated the withdrawal of Zedlitz, who was an upright and independent man, not a bureaucrat.[61]

The same reasoning holds for Caprivi's extreme action in resigning all his offices over a mere regulation of the primary schools in Prussia. With the resignation of Zedlitz, Caprivi declared in his resignation, the situation had basically altered. He had formerly expected that a continued strong stand of the government would eventually bring the National Liberals and Free Conservatives to support some kind of compromise. But now this was no longer possible. With the dropping of the bill he could not expect to continue to hold the confidence of the necessary parties in the Reichstag. And finally he saw that the Kaiser, by his sudden reversal, had withdrawn his confidence from him. "With deep sorrow," he wrote, "I must recognize that I have not succeeded in winning Your Majesty's [Allerhöchst] inestimable confidence to such a degree as to be able personally to rely upon it [dass ich daran in mir selbst hätte einen

[60]Richter, Kampf um den Schulgesetzentwurf, pp. 90–92; Herzfeld, Miquel, II, 306; cf. DDF, 1 ser., IX, 387; Waldersee, Denkwürdigkeiten, II, 235–236.
[61]Cf. Wahl, Geschichte, III, 533, 545–546; Pr. Jbb., 69:563 (April 1892).

Halt finden können]." [62] Caprivi was especially angry with Miquel. He had tried from the beginning to hold the government together through a united working together of the State Ministry, to offset just such precipitate actions of the crown through the solidarity of the ministers. For this reason he had been willing to support Zedlitz so strongly under the heavy attack in the Landtag. And this was one of his strongest motives in seconding Zedlitz's resignation with his own. Secretary Marschall later told Prince Hohenlohe privately that Caprivi should have left Zedlitz to fight the battle alone; "chivalry here was out of place." [63] But with Caprivi the general principle of ministerial solidarity was more than a matter of mere chivalry. During the past year, particularly with the preparation of the new budget the previous January, Miquel had shown a tendency to push his influence beyond his own department, to try to influence or to dominate the work of other departments not only in Prussia but in the Reich.[64] Ministerial solidarity, wrote Caprivi in 1895 after his retirement, "Herr Miquel destroyed for me by the way in which he first agreed to the School Bill and then intrigued against it, and I have him to thank for the surrender of the minister-presidency. But even if the latter had not become necessary, a minister-president would never have been fully effective [*vollwerthig*] when the Miquel vote and the Miquel influence on the Kaiser could daily threaten anew the stability of the ministry. In spite of his skill I believe that he has so far been of more harm than of service to the state." [65]

As rumors of the ministerial crisis filtered out into the press and the parliaments, the initial reaction of shocked incredulity changed to anger on the one side, joy on the other, and a general clamor of speculation as to the outcome. The wildest rumors flew about as to who would be the new minister of education, the new chancellor. Some parliamentary-minded Germans expected Miquel to succeed Caprivi, with Bennigsen replacing Marschall as foreign secretary.[66] Others were inclined towards Waldersee. There was even some talk of the return of Bismarck, while a whole string of names, from

[62]Letter in Caprivi Papers, Hauptarchiv, Berlin; Richter, *Kampf um den Schulgesetzentwurf*, p. 91; Herzfeld, *Miquel*, II, 306.

[63]Hohenlohe, *Memoirs*, II, 444.

[64]H. Goldschmidt, *Das Reich u. Preussen im Kampf um die Führung* (Berlin, 1931), pp. 319–321; DDF, 1 ser., IX, 233–235. Cf. Ponsonby, *Letters of Empress Frederick*, p. 430.

[65]Schneidewin, "Briefe," p. 146.

[66]Cf. *Die Nation*, 19:389–390 (March 26, 1892).

Lucanus to Rauchhaupt, were suggested as possible successors to Zedlitz. The prolongation of the crisis, caused in large measure by the Kaiser's absence from the scene, further encouraged speculation and rumor: for example, that four doctors had been summoned to attend the Kaiser at Hubertusstock. On the Kaiser's absence, Holstein wrote to Eulenburg, "I think it positively shocking that at this terribly important moment the Kaiser should be sitting at Hubertusstock with a couple of aides-de-camp. It really is something like Louis XVI. And who knows what will be decided there, without a reasonable creature to consult! You alone can break the magic circle; reflect upon that!" [67]

The crisis was not one to be easily solved. In the first place, there was no available supply of suitable statesmen to form a new government. "In no country of the world are personalities suited to top leading positions so rare as in Germany," wrote Delbrück in his "Politische Übersicht" for 1892. Germany possessed no training ground for statesmen, only for bureaucrats.[68] It also seemed somewhat scandalous, especially abroad, that the chancellor of the German Reich should lose his position in a fight over the Prussian primary schools. The other federal states immediately protested this intrusion of Prussian affairs into Reich politics, and Count Kálnoky of Austria-Hungary sent a telegram to the Kaiser expressing the hope that Caprivi, who possessed the confidence of Germany's allies, would remain in office.[69] As for the Kaiser, there was still the army bill to be put through the Reichstag; Caprivi could not desert him now.

Under pressure from these quarters and especially from his own close collaborators in Chancellery and Foreign Office, Caprivi finally let himself be persuaded to remain chancellor of the Reich. He was helped to this decision, he told the Bavarian ambassador, Count Lerchenfeld, by the thought of the bad effect which would be produced abroad if he were succeeded in the Chancellery by the ambitious and warmongering Waldersee.[70] But Caprivi absolutely would not remain minister-president of Prussia. He would not collaborate further with Miquel. He was willing to remain as chancellor

[67]*DDF*, 1 ser., IX, 344; Kardorff, *Kardorff*, p. 257; Richter, *Kampf um den Schulgesetzentwurf*, p. 92; Haller, *Eulenburg*, I, 112. As to the Kaiser's state of health, cf. *Letters of Queen Victoria*, 3rd ser., II, 106 and note.

[68]*Schulthess* (1892), p. 336.

[69]*The Times*, March 24, 1892, p. 11; *DDF*, 1 ser., IX, 419; Schweinitz, *Briefwechsel*, p. 288.

[70]Goldschmidt, *Reich u. Preussen*, "Akten u. Aufzeichnungen," no. 99, pp. 321–322.

only if he could avoid any further dealings with the Prussian minister of finance. And all the pleadings of Kaiser, staff, ministers, and advisers could not budge him from this decision.[71] Consequently, the crisis was resolved — to nobody's satisfaction — in that Caprivi stayed on as chancellor and that the minister-presidency of Prussia was given to Count Botho Eulenburg, former minister of the interior under Bismarck, a cousin of Phili Eulenburg, and Caprivi's personal choice.[72]

This solution was submitted to the Kaiser in writing on March 22, and followed up by Caprivi in a personal conference in Hubertusstock on the 23rd. The appointments followed on the 24th. To the vacant post of minister of education and public worship the state secretary of the Reich Department of Justice, Dr. Robert Bosse, was appointed upon the nomination of Count Botho Eulenburg, the new minister-president. On the 25th the Kaiser told the Saxon and Baden ambassadors in Hubertusstock that "he valued Caprivi most highly for his ability and for his loyal, honorable character. Caprivi, however, was a stubborn mule [*eigensinniger Dickkopf*] who would not let himself be influenced by him in any way and who handed in his resignation at every opportunity." He, the Kaiser, knew perfectly well that the separation of the offices could not work out permanently, but he could do nothing with Caprivi. He hoped that later Caprivi himself would come and ask to take back the minister-presidency.[73]

And so, in this manner, the government was divided into two parts: Prussia was separated from the Reich.[74] In the Reichstag on March 26 Eugen Richter commented that the chancellor had indeed finally reappeared in the house but that he had been cut in half. In replying, Caprivi tried to put on as bold and confident a front as possible. The separation of the offices of Prussian minister-president and chancellor of the Reich, Caprivi declared, was not a misfortune but an advantage for the Reich. He quoted two speeches of Bis-

[71]Major v. Ebmeyer, "Caprivis Entlassung," *Deutsche Revue,* 47(IV):207 (1922); *DDF,* 1 ser., IX, 346.

[72]Holstein, who had backed the elderly president of the Landtag, von Köller, for minister-president, was not happy over the appointment of Eulenburg and wrote gloomily of resigning. Rogge, *Holstein,* pp. 163–164. See also P. Eulenburg to Holstein, March 22, 1892, *Holstein Papers, Correspondence.*

[73]*DDF,* 1 ser., IX, 346; *Schulthess* (1892), p. 76; Goldschmidt, *Reich u. Preussen,* p. 99.

[74]Bötticher, who as vice-president of the Prussian ministry had represented the chancellor there and occasionally in the Landtag, now lost this function through the separation of the offices of chancellor and minister-president and was personally passed over in the appointment of Eulenburg. He therefore submitted his resignation, which was graciously refused. Goldschmidt, *Reich u. Preussen,* p. 99, note.

marck's on the impotence of the Prussian minister-president, who had no legal authority over the Prussian ministers. Personal influence in the ministry could be brought to bear by the chancellor just as well in his capacity of foreign minister as of minister-president of Prussia. There would be, on the other hand, the positive advantage that now the chancellor would be free of the problems of domestic Prussian politics. Bismarck had often complained of this added responsibility, and he, Caprivi, could say that this responsibility for Prussian affairs, about which he knew very little, had been heretofore the heaviest part of his burden.

I am, however, of the opinion that out of this separation proceeds a direct advantage for the Reich inasmuch as in the future the Reich chancellor will not of necessity be involved in every Prussian crisis. Now one can say, indeed: you don't need to be involved; as minister-president keep yourself aloof, so that when one or another of your colleagues falls you don't need to fall with him. That, however, from my conception of the duties of the minister-president, would not always be possible. I should like to say at the beginning that these duties and positions are not at all to be strictly and generally delimited; in such important positions everything must be cut to the individual person. My conception of my duties as minister-president, however, was that, if a minister introduced a bill which was agreed to by the State Ministry, it was my duty to support the minister ("Bravo!" on the right and in the center). I believed that if the minister-president deserted a minister in such a situation he would then count for nothing in the State Ministry; at least my own in itself not very considerable influence would have become as nothing if my colleagues had not been able to assure themselves that the minister-president, as much as lies within his weak powers, will back us up ("Bravo!" on the right).

Richter, noted Caprivi, had suggested parliamentary government as a way out. He did not believe he was serious about it for Prussia, and thank God they were still a long way from that. Richter had also suggested the expedient of independent ministries for the Reich. "There may be many here who believe this to be desirable — the Federated Governments do not believe it to be desirable — ; but whether there is anyone here who believes it to be practicable now, without doing away with the Bundesrat, without standing our whole Reich constitution on its head, I am extremely doubtful ('Quite right!' on the right and in the center)."

I believe, however, that we shall do well to wait and see how things develop, and I believe that Germany is still too strong to be shaken by such a question as whether the chancellor shall or shall not give up a part of his Prussian offices, which he himself considers unimportant. I am convinced that Germany will survive this question and will not lose, but will profit thereby (enthusiastic "Bravo!" on the right and in the center).[75]

Opinion generally at home and abroad might be satisfied with this optimistic view of the split in the government. Party leaders and informed observers, however, continued to regard it with foreboding. The whole basis of the Reich constitution was the principle of identity of interest between Prussia and the Reich. The king of Prussia, wrote the *Preussische Jahrbücher* in April, could not very well oppose the German Kaiser.[76] There was also no doubt that loss of the presidency of the Prussian government, along with the Kaiser's repudiation of him on the School Bill, had severely weakened Caprivi's political prestige. "And whither are we drifting," wrote Heinrich von Treitzschke, "under this half of a chancellor, who already was no statesman whole?" The day after Caprivi's speech Kardorff wrote caustically to his wife, "Caprivi completely dead, talked nonsense yesterday . . . People believe generally that Eulenburg is already really chancellor . . ."[77]

The effect of the sudden denouement upon the parties was profound. Count Botho Eulenburg was strongly hissed upon his first appearance in the Landtag when he announced the withdrawal of the School Bill on March 28. The Conservative and clerical press raged and stormed and tried to find someone on whom to fasten the guilt for the fiasco. The right-wing Conservative press compared sarcastically the dead Kaiser William I who "did not speak much, but acted" with the "strong *speeches* of His Majesty" and compared the government unfavorably with Bismarck.[78] The Conservatives, with some justification, felt especially piqued, since the crown had not only deserted them but had done so prematurely, before the bill had reached the floor for its second reading. Whereas, so far, the Conservatives had taken an uncompromising position along with the Center, their tactic obviously was to shift their stand towards a more moderate position at a later stage. This they had not been able to do before the crisis broke, so that now many moderately inclined members of the party were placed in a false position towards their old friends among the Free Conservatives and National Liberals. Un-

[75]*Sten. Ber.* (1890–1892), VII, 5015ff.
[76]69:565. Cf. Wippermann, 8(I):91–92.
[77]*DDF*, 1 ser., IX, 359–360, 362, 374; Goldschmidt, *Reich u. Preussen*, p. 100; Richter, *Kampf um den Schulgesetzentwurf*, p. 97; Kardorff, *Kardorff*, p. 257.
[78]*Landtag* (1892), II, 1162; Kardorff, *Kardorff*, p. 257; Richter, *Kampf um den Schulgesetzentwurf*, p. 93.

able to vent their frustrated anger upon the Kaiser, the Conservatives took it out on their own party leaders. A battle broke out between the right-wing Baron von Hammerstein's *Kreuzzeitung* and the moderate von Helldorff's *Konservatives Wochenblatt*. Helldorff was accused of bearing the chief responsibility for the Kaiser's action against the bill. Since Helldorff had hitherto been titular leader of the party, the quarrel threatened a serious split. Finally Helldorff himself called for a "clean break" between the factions. The break came, but left Helldorff standing alone. To prevent a serious split in the party, all his moderate friends, such as Rauchhaupt and Limburg-Stirum, followed the lead of the triumphant Hammerstein and Stöcker. Helldorff was deposed from his position as chairman of the executive committee and was excluded from the party fraction in the House of Lords. The crisis had carried the Conservatives even further to the right. On March 31 the *Kreuzzeitung* declared that the party from now on would not support the Free Conservatives in elections. The only victor in the School Bill question, remarked the *Preussische Jahrbücher* in May, seemed to be Hammerstein.[79] As for the Center party, Count Ballestrem declared in the Reichstag, in the general debate following Caprivi's speech, that the Center still had the greatest confidence in Caprivi personally, and hoped he would soon take over the minister-presidency again. Nevertheless, the Center took the opportunity to show its strength and its disappointment by voting a corvette out of the naval budget on the 29th.[80]

8

CONCLUSION

What the ultimate fate of the School Bill would have been if the Kaiser had not interfered is rather difficult to say. Caprivi agreed emphatically with the Conservative leaders that a satisfactory compromise would have been worked out and was, in fact, already being quietly negotiated.[81] In view of the extreme public agitation already aroused, however, it is difficult to believe that the moderate parties could have agreed to a compromise bill even if they had wanted to. Also, in view of the bitterness of feeling, it is likely that any compromise which would have satisfied the moderates would thereby

[79]Richter, *Kampf um den Schulgesetzentwurf*, pp. 93–96; *Pr. Jbb.*, 69:289, 563, 705; Thimme, "Bismarck und Kardorff," pt. I, p. 183; Hellwig, *Stumm*, pp. 425ff.

[80]*Sten. Ber.* (1890–1892), VII, 5018; *Schulthess* (1892), pp. 79, 82; Richter, *Kampf um den Schulgesetzentwurf*, p. 97; Waldersee, *Denkwürdigkeiten*, II, 237.

[81]Hohenlohe, *Memoirs*, II, 444. Helldorff seems also to have shared this opinion; cf. Wippermann, 8(I):107.

have been unacceptable to the Center. The wavering attitude of some of the moderate Conservatives also makes it doubtful whether the unmodified bill could have successfully passed the third reading. It therefore seems probable that the bill eventually would have been defeated. But how much better a parliamentary defeat would have been for all concerned than what actually occurred! The government would have been in the position of having done all it could for the Center party, thus leaving this party in its debt, and could have continued to maintain its general prestige in Prussia and Reich on the basis of an honest attempt at conciliation. The Center, defeated in spite of a most favorable line-up in the Landtag, would have had to recognize certain limits to its clerical ambitions, whereas now it could continue to believe that the victory already in its grasp had been snatched away by the purely arbitrary personal act of the crown. Instead of drawing the Center into a position of general support for the government, the actual denouement of the School Bill crisis was to repulse the Center and drive it back into its old position of tactical opposition. Nor, with such a normal development of events, would the Conservatives have been so alienated or their internal shift to the right have been so extreme. And, finally, the government itself would have been unimpaired; it would not even have been necessary for Zedlitz to resign, since he would still have retained the confidence of the crown.[82] But to suppose all of this is already to suppose too much.

It would, indeed, be superficial to interpret the scene in the Crown Council of March 17 as a purely personal drama and to place the responsibility for the resulting crisis entirely on the arbitrary, impulsive, and autocratic will of William II. That the Kaiser was not capable of pushing through a fixed, determined course of action, that he was extremely susceptible to all influences, sometimes even when contradictory, has been illustrated amply enough to require no further demonstration here. His action throughout the course of the School Bill crisis clearly illustrates his basic weakness and his indecision. There was a whole host of influences at work upon the Kaiser during this crisis; it is not surprising that he responded to them, and in a typically unconsidered, unprepared, impulsive manner. He had, however, had such impulses before. He had promised Shuvalov to renew the Reinsurance Treaty; he had refused to make concessions to the Center on the "little army bill"; he had refused to have anything to do with Windthorst; he had ordered the dismissal of Count Münster, and so on. Each time he had successfully

[82]*Pr. Jbb.*, 69:561–566; Richter, *Kampf um den Schulgesetzentwurf*, pp. 98ff.

been persuaded to change his mind. It seems clear enough that if, this time, William II had continued to be confronted with a united and determined ministry, he could not have acted as he did against the bill, no matter what outside influences, including Phili Eulenburg, were brought to bear. The ministers, however, who were not politicians nor independent statesmen but, for the most part, loyal, hard-working bureaucrats reared in the Bismarck school, were neither united nor determined. And they included in their midst Miquel: Miquel, the exception to the bureaucratic rule, the experienced politician, the former leader of the anticlerical National Liberal party, the dynamic, brilliant personality who so successfully charmed and impressed the Kaiser. One would not leave the superficial plane, however, if one were merely to push responsibility for the crisis from the Kaiser to Miquel, from king to minister. Miquel might have been ever so ambitious, so brilliantly clever, and yet would have had no chance of success, no opportunity to act, if the clash of political forces in the nation had not invited the action which he took. At the crucial point he spoke out for the Kartell; Caprivi for the Center. He was not speaking for the Reich; the Kartell alignment was impossible there for sheer lack of votes. But it was still possible in Prussia; and Prussia was the Reich. Or was it? The political foundation, the practical justification for the great anticlerical demonstration staged by National Liberals, Free Conservatives, and Radicals against the School Bill lay in the numerical composition of the parties in the Landtag, just as the practical basis for Caprivi's friendly gesture to the Center lay in the numerical composition of the Reichstag. And the resulting crisis and split between the offices of minister-president and chancellor openly expressed, therefore, this difference in the political composition of the houses. In so expressing it the crisis merely brought out into the open the concealed duality of the interests of Prussia and of the Reich. It was, no doubt, significant and symbolic that this catastrophe, this split, should have been brought upon the conscientious Caprivi government by an attempt to coöperate with a German political party that was neither conservative nor liberal and whose political purposes were religious.

What, after all, had happened to Caprivi's "national" program? The School Bill debacle had alienated everybody — Left, Right, and Center. But could one divine the "will of the nation" in any better, more practical way than by trying to satisfy a majority of the representatives of the Nation in the Reichstag? Here was a party, however, with 106 deputies, which represented ideas and loyalties that were more parochial than national, more ideological than political. After the failure of the School Bill, the Center party might still respect Caprivi's personal integrity, but they now lacked the *quid pro quo* that would make it possible for them to support his program. And what of the coming big army reform? This piece of materialistic military planning had been the real basis, after all, for the intended concessions to religion. Now, with no tactical political advantage from which to operate, how could the Caprivi government possibly carry this bill? And what would be the future of the Reich if the government actually failed to put through a measure that it considered essential to the security of the nation? The Reich itself seemed in danger of dissolution. The deep cleavages and basic contradictions revealed by the story of the School Bill conflict might even be seen to pose the question, whether, in fact, there was a German nation.

One feels compelled to say a few more words for William II. No doubt the break within the ministry was decisive in influencing his action. This break itself has been shown to have proceeded from practical political realities. But, in addition, one must not overlook the strong influence of public opinion. The floods of petitions, the protests on all sides made their impression. There is no doubt that in acting impulsively against the bill the Kaiser carried out to the letter the national, the liberal wish. With his keen, sensitively facile mind, "William II was not a ruler; he was a medium. He reflected the political mind of Germany and expressed it with genius." [83] The old smoldering anticlericalism of the Kulturkampf was still too hot to stand this type of bill. The liberal German public grew excited; it wanted action. It got it.

[83]*The Times Literary Supplement,* December 11, 1948, "The Ruler in Berlin," p. 690.

Chapter VI

THE BIG ARMY BILL

Who, then, are you who dare to question the patriotism of a
Bismarck?

Preussische Jahrbücher, July 1892

1

THE BISMARCK FRONDE

Reconciliation?

WOEFULLY weakened and shaken by the School Bill crisis,
the Caprivi government lay helplessly open to attack. But it was not
the radical left nor the moderate liberals who now pressed home
their advantage; rather it was the group of reactionary elements and
political intriguers clustered around the rebellious Bismarck which
now tried to take advantage of the critical weakness of the government. Coming directly after the Kaiser's contradictory and unfortunate actions in the School Bill affair, Bismarck's birthday on April
1, 1892, became the occasion for more and greater celebrations and
congratulations for the old chancellor than heretofore. In the following weeks rumors began to spread in the press of a revival of the
Kartell and of a personal reconciliation between Bismarck and the
Kaiser. Many persons, noted General von Waldersee on April 16,
who formerly were for Caprivi were now working against him. On
April 25 the sixty-one-year-old Caprivi wearily left Berlin for a
month's rest at Carlsbad. On the same day Ambassador Herbette
reported that his personal position was "severely shaken." [1]

[1] *The Times,* wkly. ed., April 8, 1892, p. 5, April 15, p. 5; *Schulthess* (1892),
p. 86; Waldersee, *Denkwürdigkeiten,* II, 238–239; *DDF,* 1 ser., IX, 419. Cf. Schneidewin, *Bismarck, Caprivi u. die jüngst erlebte Mobilmachung des Liberalismus,* pp.
10–12, 25–31; Wippermann, 8(1):212ff.

On April 24 the Kaiser visited Baron Carl von Stumm at Halberg Castle and inspected the measures in force protecting the workers' welfare in Stumm's factories at Neunkirchen. Stumm took this opportunity to urge the Kaiser to a personal reconciliation with Bismarck. Unlike his party colleague, Kardorff, Stumm's flirting with reconciliation schemes was not motivated by a fundamental antipathy to the Caprivi regime. He seems to have been one of the many Germans whose patriotic sentiment was suffering at this time over the fact that the personal breach between Kaiser and ex-chancellor was preventing the government from profiting by the "incomparable experience and wise advice" of the great German hero. Stumm, also, as an industrialist and an arch-enemy of the Social Democrats, probably hoped that Bismarck's influence might restrain the New Course from going too far in a liberal direction.[2] Especially because of the effect on the social question, Stumm told the Kaiser, a reconciliation with Bismarck would be highly esteemed by industry. To this proposal the Kaiser replied that he was quite ready for a reconciliation, but that Bismarck must make the first move. Stumm received his permission to continue to negotiate with Bismarck toward this end.[3]

Shortly thereafter Stumm left for Madrid to visit his brother, Ambassador Baron Ferdinand von Stumm, and consequently was not able immediately to carry out his commission in Friedrichsruh. In the meantime Deputy Vopelius, who had been present, informed von Kardorff of this conversation with Stumm and of the Kaiser's favorable attitude, but was too discreet to report the specific details. On April 30 Kardorff went down to Friedrichsruh and reported to Bismarck on the Kaiser's favorable disposition. Bismarck did not seem displeased with the idea of reinstatement in the royal favor. It could not, however, be more than a formal social relationship. After two years' absence from the councils of the government he could not give advice, and if he did give advice he would subsequently be held responsible for all the failures of the government. An aloof position would make it more possible for him to exert his influence on the Kaiser on his own initiative if some crisis in foreign policy should demand it. In general he was more worried by the estrangement from Russia than by any developments in domestic politics.[4]

During his visit Kardorff was able to persuade Count Herbert

[2] Cf. his letter to Caprivi on May 13, 1891, Hellwig, *Stumm*, 429–430, also letter of July 1, 1892, *ibid.*, pp. 440–441.

[3] Hellwig, *Stumm*, p. 430.

[4] Hellwig, *Stumm*, pp. 430–432; Thimme, "Bismarck und Kardorff," pt. I, pp. 285–287; Kardorff, *Kardorff*, pp. 259ff.

Bismarck not to oppose a reconciliation of his father and the Kaiser. "Before God, his father, and Germany," declared Kardorff, Herbert could not be responsible for excluding his father from the possibility of once more, through his counsel, warding off disasters from Germany. Herbert himself, however, in Kardorff's opinion, had now too many enemies to be able to count on an ambassadorship; he would do well to have himself elected to the House of Deputies.[5]

On May 4 the Bismarck forces were encouraged in these attempts by a gesture of the Kaiser's. In 1890 the Kaiser had been careful to send birthday greetings and gifts to the old man, and had repeated these at Christmas in that year. April 1891 and 1892, however, had brought only silence. Now, on May 4, 1892, the announcement of the engagement of Herbert Bismarck to Countess Hoyos produced a telegram of warm congratulations from the Kaiser. The press immediately broke out into a new flood of reconciliation rumors.[6]

In Berlin Waldersee and Kardorff went the rounds of court and government circles and sounded out sentiment for a reconciliation move. Generally the situation seemed favorable. Among the ministers both Miquel and Botho Eulenburg seemed favorably inclined. Miquel confided to Waldersee that he had always known Caprivi was incompetent and false; now there were ministers but no ministry; everything was falling apart. Eulenburg, wrote Kardorff, already regarded himself as chancellor. Rumors circulated that Ambassador Ferdinand von Stumm was to succeed Baron Marschall in the Foreign Office.[7]

On May 26 Carl von Stumm, who had recently returned from Spain, visited Bismarck at Friedrichsruh. From Stumm Bismarck was shocked to discover that the Kaiser's condition for a reconciliation was that he make the first move. The strong-minded old ex-chancellor had no such intention. "He came to ask me to debase myself," Bismarck told Countess Hoyos after Stumm had left.[8] The Bismarck press had already been very skeptical of the reconciliation rumors. It now denounced such attempts outright.[9]

[5]Thimme, "Bismarck und Kardorff," pt. I, p. 285; cf. DDF, 1 ser., IX, 519.

[6]O. Gradenwitz, "Akten über Bismarcks grossdeutsche Rundfahrt vom Jahre 1892," Sitzungsberichte der Heidelberger Akademie der Wissenschaften (Heidelberg), 12:7* (1921).

[7]Waldersee, Denkwürdigkeiten, II, 240–241; Thimme, "Bismarck und Kardorff," pt. I, p. 286.

[8]Kardorff, Kardorff, p. 267; Hellwig, Stumm, p. 433.

[9]Thimme, "Bismarck und Kardorff," pt. I, pp. 282–283; Gradenwitz, "Akten," p. 7*.

Meanwhile General von Waldersee was hoping to clinch the reconciliation matter with the help of the Eulenburgs while the Kaiser was at Count Dohna's hunting lodge in Prökelwitz the end of May. But on May 28 Waldersee found, to his astonishment, that Botho Eulenburg (influenced, perhaps, by his cousin Phili?) was now quite cool towards the idea. If the Eulenburgs did any influencing at Prökelwitz, it was probably in a negative direction as far as reconciliation with Bismarck was concerned.[10]

Another opportunity, however, quickly presented itself when on June 7 the Kaiser met Tsar Alexander III of Russia at Kiel. The railroad line from Kiel to Berlin passed through Friedrichsruh; beginning on June 3 rumors appeared in the press suggesting that the Kaiser would take this opportunity to stop at Friedrichsruh and effect the long-awaited reconciliation.[11] At Kiel Waldersee found the opportunity to approach the Kaiser and to broach the subject of reconciliation. The Kaiser apparently reacted favorably enough to give Waldersee some hope of success. Nevertheless, the imperial train did not stop at Friedrichsruh on the return to Berlin on June 8.[12]

On June 7 Caprivi wrote in a private letter to Ambassador Schweinitz that the much talked-of reconciliation with Bismarck "is intrinsically impossible. The mere belief that the prince is giving advice would produce insupportable [*unannehmbare*] consequences in both domestic and foreign policy." [13] On the 9th, after the Kaiser's return from Kiel, Caprivi requested an audience and reminded the Kaiser that in the matter of reconciliation with Bismarck it was important that the initiative should come from Bismarck. On the 10th the Kaiser wrote to Waldersee that he would not take the idea of reconciliation seriously until he received a written statement directly from Bismarck requesting it.[14]

The Vienna Journey

Herbert Bismarck's engagement to the Hungarian Countess Hoyos had been celebrated at the home of her parents in Fiume. Originally it was planned that the wedding should also take place

[10]Waldersee, *Denkwürdigkeiten*, II, 241, 243, note; Gradenwitz, *Bismarcks letzter Kampf*, p. 234; Wippermann, 8(I):259.

[11]Thimme, "Bismarck und Kardorff," pt. I, pp. 281–282; *The Times*, wkly. ed., June 3, 1892, pp. 4–5; June 17, p. 5; *Schulthess* (1892), p. 101; Wippermann, 8(I):229ff.

[12]Waldersee, *Denkwürdigkeiten*, II, 243.

[13]Schweinitz, *Briefwechsel*, p. 292.

[14]Kaiser's letter and Waldersee's answer in Waldersee, *Denkwürdigkeiten*, II, 243–246; Gradenwitz, "Akten," pp. 1–2, 56.

there, as is customary. But simultaneously with the new wave and counterwave of reconciliation rumors, the locale of the ceremony was suddenly changed from the provincial city of Fiume to the Austrian capital and German city of Vienna, and the elder Bismarck decided to attend. He would travel by way of Dresden to Vienna, then through Munich to his seat at Kissingen. From Friedrichsruh he sent letters to the king of Saxony and prince regent of Bavaria excusing himself from seeking an audience with Their Majesties because of the shortness of his stay in those cities. But before the end of May he had already made soundings as to the possibility of an audience with Emperor Francis Joseph of Austria-Hungary, through the good offices of the wife of Prince Henry VII of Reuss, the German ambassador in Vienna; the answer, unofficially, was favorable.[15]

On June 1 Prince Reuss reported to Caprivi that it had been decided to hold the Bismarck wedding in Vienna on June 21. He then added cryptically that Emperor Francis Joseph was expected to return to Vienna from Budapest on the 11th or 12th and to remain in the city until the 25th. Thus the experienced, elderly diplomat, who had served more than twenty years under Bismarck and was a close friend of the old ex-chancellor, neglected to inform his present chief that Bismarck had already asked for an audience with Francis Joseph and been answered favorably, but contented himself with hinting at the possibility.[16]

In Berlin the Kaiser, Caprivi, and the Foreign Office regarded Bismarck's projected journey through Germany to Vienna and return as an attempt, through popular demonstrations of his personal popularity, to bring pressure to bear upon the Kaiser in connection with the reconciliation campaign and especially to rally and to encourage opposition to the Caprivi government. The well-informed *Kölnische Zeitung* correspondent, Dr. Franz Fischer, reported from Berlin that

A number of silly sentimentalists [*Gefühlsduselanten*], like Stumm, Hammacher, have been taken in by the idea that it will suffice to bring about a purely personal reconciliation between the Kaiser and Prince B[ismarck]; that there, of course, can be no question of a return of the prince to power. Today this phase has been long since passed by. The prince naturally cares nothing for such a personal reconciliation; he would regard it . . . as an empty comedy; he wants to conquer the

---

[15]Eyck, *Bismarck*, III, 615–617; Gradenwitz, "Akten," p. 10*; Hofmann, *Bismarck*, I, 78; *DDF*, 1 ser., IX, 525–526.

[16]Gradenwitz, "Akten," pp. 10*, 4–5; Eyck, *Bismarck*, III, 617. Gradenwitz, *op. cit.*, has collected and published all the official documents relative to the Vienna incident.

Kaiser completely, and to this end now the greatest demonstrations will be staged, to make clear to the Kaiser how universally the people desire this reconciliation and with it the Kaiser's submission.

Without danger to the government such a reconciliation could take place, not now after the weakening School Bill defeat, but only after a political victory, perhaps after the coming Army Bill had been successfully disposed of.[17]

On June 9 Caprivi, as has been seen, conferred with the Kaiser on the Waldersee reconciliation attempt and also obtained the Kaiser's approval of a telegraphic instruction to Prince Reuss. Strongly backed by the Foreign Office[18] Caprivi ordered Reuss and the embassy personnel to restrict their relations with Bismarck to the conventional forms and to "avoid" an invitation to the wedding (*"einer etwaigen Einladung zur Hochzeit aber auszuweichen"*).[19] Caprivi's attitude may best be perceived from a further telegram to Reuss on June 12. Bismarck, he stated, had attacked government foreign and domestic policy and the Kaiser personally in the worst manner in the press.

With great patience we, however, have ignored the invective of Prince Bismarck, always mindful of his past, and without attempting to defend ourselves. Nor can there be any question of his being out of favor. His Majesty's government bears the consequences of a situation brought about, not by it, but by Prince Bismarck. A purely outward, formal alteration of this situation would be desirable to us also. That, however, the first step in this direction must be taken by Prince Bismarck and that until then any contact with him must remain unofficial has been for more than two years laid down and adhered to as the leading principle for the conduct of our domestic officials. Why there should now be a departure from this conduct on the part of officials such as those of the royal embassy, who so directly represent abroad the person of His Majesty I cannot conceive. . . . We have not doubted for an instant that ovations will be prepared for the prince in Vienna. We cannot prevent that, but we must avoid the participation of the German embassy in festivities that will be accompanied by demonstrations where one cannot tell whether they are meant as more pro Bismarck or contra Kaiser William.[20]

[17]Fischer's interesting letters to Dr. J. Neven du Mont, publisher of the *Kölnische Zeitung*, dated June 8, 12, 13, 17, and 29, are published in Hellwig, *Stumm*, pp. 436–440.

[18]Gradenwitz, "Akten," pp. 13°–14°, 23°, Waldersee, to Dr. Arendt, Kardorff, *Kardorff*, p. 270, and Haller, *Eulenburg*, I, 175, blame Holstein for this decision; Lerchenfeld, *Denkwürdigkeiten*, p. 370, and Hammann, *Der Neue Kurs*, p. 26, blame Caprivi; cf. Keim, *Erlebtes*, p. 53.

[19]Gradenwitz, "Akten," p. 5.

[20]Gradenwitz, "Akten," pp. 10–11.

Reuss was also requested to inform Count Kálnoky of these instructions.

Obviously Berlin expected coöperation from the Austrian government in its attempt to ignore the Bismarck Vienna festival. Since, however, Emperor Francis Joseph had already agreed unofficially to receive Bismarck, the emperor, Kálnoky, and Reuss now found themselves in an embarrassing position. Reuss informed Berlin that the Austrian emperor was inclined to grant Bismarck an audience, thus causing a condition of strain and suspicion between Caprivi and himself and between the two governments. He still did not inform Caprivi of Bismarck's private inquiry or of the emperor's favorable reply. Nor did he inform Caprivi of his action in immediately forwarding to Count Kálnoky Bismarck's official request for an audience, which arrived in Vienna on June 14.[21]

Also on the 14th there arrived in Vienna a private letter from the Kaiser to Emperor Francis Joseph. Since his retirement Bismarck, wrote the Kaiser, "has waged war in his press and in that of foreign countries against me, Caprivi, my ministers, etc., in the most perfidious manner." Bismarck, wrote the Kaiser, had attacked the Triple Alliance and especially Austria. The recent "reconciliation" campaign was a new "swindle."

He is trying with all his craft and skill to twist things so it will appear before the world as if I am the one who is making the advances. He has planned an audience with you as the main event on his program. While most insolently ignoring my court and the empress he takes himself to Dresden and Vienna in order immediately to parade himself there in the rôle of the grand old man [den alten, treuen Mann herauszubeissen] . . . In the interest of myself and of my government, therefore, I should like to beg you as a true friend not to render the situation in the country more difficult for me by receiving this rebellious subject before he has approached me and said his peccavi . . .[22]

Although this letter undoubtedly reflected accurately the mood in Berlin, it is not likely that Caprivi or the Foreign Office wished to put pressure on the Austrians to this extent. It appears that they were at first not aware of the exact content of the Kaiser's letter.[23]

[21]Eyck, Bismarck, III, 617–618; Gradenwitz, "Akten," Bismarck to Reuss, p. 4, Reuss to Caprivi, pp. 6–10, 12–14, 16, 17–18, Caprivi to Reuss, pp. 10–11, 16, 19.

[22]Published in Österreichische Rundschau, 59:109–110 (1919), and in Gradenwitz, Bismarcks letzter Kampf, pp. 240–242.

[23]Cf. Marschall to Eulenburg, Gradenwitz, "Akten," p. 34; Wedel, Zwischen Kaiser und Kanzler, p. 194; Keim, Erlebtes, p. 53; Lerchenfeld, Denkwürdigkeiten, p. 370; E. v. Wertheimer, "Ein kaiser- und königlicher Militärattaché über das politische Leben in Berlin, 1886–95," Pr. Jbb., 201:270 (1925).

The letter, of course, made it impossible for Francis Joseph to receive Bismarck, and Count Kálnoky informed Prince Reuss to this effect.[24] Kálnoky also sent a copy of his refusal of Bismarck's official request directly to Caprivi, which was the first news to reach Caprivi from Vienna that Bismarck had actually asked for an audience with the Austrian emperor.[25]

Bismarck's request for an audience had thus initially been graciously accepted, then later peremptorily refused. During his stay in Vienna he was boycotted by the inner circle of Viennese society, which took its cue from the imperial court; only the Hungarian nobility took him in.[26] No representatives of the court or of the diplomatic corps attended the wedding. It was, of course, obvious to Bismarck that this change of atmosphere must have been induced from Berlin. In a rage the old magician sent for an editor of the *Neue Freie Presse* and hurled a handful of his most powerful thunderbolts. It was an open declaration of war against the Kaiser and the Caprivi government.

I no longer have any personal obligations to the persons now in power [*jetzigen Persönlichkeiten*] or to my successor. All connections are severed [*Alle Brücken sind abgebrochen*]. There has been talk of making me president of the State Council. Why not rather an adjutant general, since then I would wear a uniform. Then I could support the ministers against the Kaiser or the Kaiser against the ministers, and the camarilla would be complete.[27]

He reiterated his charge that Austria had made the better bargain in the trade treaties, but put the weight of his criticism on foreign policy. The previous January, during the height of the School Bill debate, he had published an article in the *Hamburger Nachrichten* which argued that an understanding with Russia had never been considered incompatible with the alliance with Austria. Rather, the possibility of an understanding with Russia had acted as a brake upon Austria in the Balkans. To the initiated these statements came very close to a revelation of the secret Reinsurance Treaty which had been dropped by Caprivi: "This advantageous situation, the maintenance of which certainly demanded considerable diplomatic skill, was later considered to be too complicated." [28]

[24]Gradenwitz, "Akten," p. 15.
[25]Cf. Caprivi to Reuss, Gradenwitz, "Akten," p. 19.
[26]Eyck, *Bismarck*, III, 618; *DDF*, 1 ser., IX, 525–528.
[27]*Schulthess* (1892), p. 232; Wippermann, 8(I):242; Eyck, *Bismarck*, III, 618–619.
[28]Hofmann, *Bismarck*, II, 4.

When, in early June, the tsar of Russia had visited Kiel, the reconciliation rumors had been in the air, and the tsar had been careful
not only to send word to Caprivi that he was glad he had remained
in office after the March crisis, but also to send greetings to Bismarck
via Waldersee. It is possible that Bismarck's personal rancor against
the Kaiser and the New Course was mixed with a measure of sincere
concern over present developments in German foreign policy, as
opposed to his natural confidence in his own diplomatic strength
and sagacity.[29] Now, to the *Neue Freie Presse*, he spoke even more
plainly. The tsar, he said, had trusted him and been influenced by
him. "So far my successor has possessed neither this personal
authority nor this trust. . . . The wire which connected us with
Russia has been cut." [30]

To the general public, who were quite in the dark, this mysterious allusion to a "wire to St. Petersburg" was confusing and alarming.
Did it mean there was really imminent danger of war with Russia?
Many Germans were shocked by the unpatriotic spectacle of Bismarck's attacking the German government so crudely from a foreign
capital.[31] Even Stumm saw the error of his ways and decided definitely to throw in his lot with the Kaiser and Caprivi. On July 1 he
sent Caprivi a long, carefully worded explanation of his past conduct
and his future resolves. "As things are now, I give up all connection
with Friedrichsruh and do not doubt for a moment that I must stand
firmly by Your Excellency and His Majesty's government . . . I
. . . only thought through my attempts at pacification to be of
service to Your Excellency. This illusion is now past . . ." Stumm
managed to influence the Free Conservative *Post* to revise its pro-
Bismarck position, but his shift was the beginning of a cleavage in
the party between himself and Kardorff, which other issues later
served to strengthen. His newspaper articles in support of the government were highly gratifying to the Kaiser as well as to Caprivi.
Thus this turning point already foreshadowed the "Stumm Era." [32]
To friendly foreign observers Bismarck's revelations seemed the
height of irresponsibility. His statements, editorialized *The Times*
of London, revealed "something like a moral degeneracy." "It is
melancholy," commented Emperor Francis Joseph to Prince Hohenlohe, "to think such a man can sink so low." [33]

---

[29]Hammann, *Der Neue Kurs,* p. 16; Waldersee, *Denkwürdigkeiten,* II, 241–242,
246; Hellwig, *Stumm,* p. 432.
[30]*Schulthess* (1892), p. 231; Wippermann, 8(I):241–242.
[31]Hohenlohe, *Memoirs,* II, 446; *The Times,* wkly. ed., July 1, 1892, p. 5.
[32]Hellwig, *Stumm,* pp. 440ff.
[33]*The Times,* June 29, 1892, p. 11; Hohenlohe, *Memoirs,* II, 447.

As for the government, Caprivi's soldierly instincts were all in favor of a strong counterattack; but against the magic power of the Bismarck name and the Bismarck fame he knew any action would be useless. To take no action at all would be interpreted as weakness, to take extreme action against Bismarck, the German hero, was impossible. On June 28 the "official" *Norddeutsche Allgemeine Zeitung* strongly attacked Bismarck's statements on relations with Russia, which it declared were contrary to fact. "No one," it concluded, "can measure the extent of injury which the prince may be willing to inflict on his own Fatherland. No one knows the weapons which he may believe he has ready; but the duty to defend the highest interests of the German Nation even against the man who once most advanced these interests may neither be ignored nor denied by the leaders of the state." Along with this statement was published an 1883 decree of Bismarck's to the heads of all departments requesting information on the political and economic background of all candidates for appointments to subordinate government positions. This decree had been repealed after Bismarck's retirement. It was obviously a silent allusion to the probable treatment which Bismarck himself would have meted out to anyone attacking the government as he was now doing.[34] "What can be the motive for his violent action against the new government?" Caprivi earnestly asked Hammann, as they sat in the garden of the Chancellery. "He neither can nor wishes to again take over his old position. The only explanation remaining is a passionate bitterness and the desire to bring the Kaiser to Canossa. The underlying motive for the most extreme acts is hate." [35]

To the admonition of the *Norddeutsche Allgemeine Zeitung* the *Hamburger Nachrichten* replied in a series of articles that a legal action by the government against Bismarck would be very interesting; the prince had no objection to a dramatic ending to his career.[36] Caprivi, it declared, had been made chancellor by the Center party, with which he had once conspired against Bismarck. The *Norddeutsche* had questioned whether Bismarck's attitude was patriotic: "We reply with a counter question, whether it was really patriotic to accompany the appearance in Vienna of a man of the prince's position and past achievements with a 'Uriah-letter' that made it impossible for him to be received by a monarch with whom the

[34]Hellwig, *Stumm*, pp. 439–440; Hofmann, *Bismarck*, II, 82, note; *Schulthess* (1892), pp. 112–113.
[35]Hammann, *Der Neue Kurs*, pp. 16–17; cf. *Pr. Jbb.*, 70:119–124 (1892).
[36]Hofmann, *Bismarck*, II, 82ff.

prince had been officially and personally associated for forty years . . ."[37] Two days later Caprivi telegraphed to the Kaiser, who, with Phili Eulenburg and Kiderlen, was on his usual Norwegian cruise, that immediate action was necessary against Bismarck's latest statement. He was publishing his instruction of 1890 to the ambassadors disavowing Bismarck's statements and influence and also his instruction to Prince Reuss in connection with the Vienna affair.[38] "The prince talks of a Uriah-letter which prevented his reception in Vienna . . . Apparently the prince knows of Y. M.'s letter to the emperor of Austria."

While the battle raged in the press, nationalist feeling combined with dissatisfaction with the New Course to make Bismarck's return journey a triumphal procession. En route through Bavaria to Kissingen the old man stopped and made public speeches at Munich and Augsburg. At every way-station, even along the overpasses, crowds stood to cheer the founder of German greatness. At Kissingen there were deputations, more speeches, and more newspaper interviews in the same vein. From Kissingen, at the end of July, he continued his triumphal march to his estate at Schönhausen, stopping off for a grand reception by the city and University of Jena. Everywhere he reminded his hearers of the great events of the past — of his own incomparable accomplishments. With the greatest skill he took advantage of the Vienna incident to play the powerful rôle of aggrieved hero, the wounded Siegfried.[39] "In my heart," he declared, "lives the same love for the Fatherland as ten years ago, when I had a decisive influence in politics. My views on the appropriateness and correctness of those things which we must do are still the same today. I do not see why I should not express them." To the crowds gathered in the Jena market place the man of "blood and iron" actually preached the virtues of a strong Reichstag. He who had split and broken the parties to suit his convenience now called for a strong, stable majority which could give the Reichstag its necessary authority. He had always been against absolutism, he said. And now he could not be accused of fighting against the monarchy, but only against the responsible ministers, according to the constitution. He compared himself, to the great appreciation of

[37]Hofmann, *Bismarck*, II, 89. Uriah, it will be remembered, was the captain in the army of Israel who at the order of King David was so exposed in battle as to be killed, so that David might have Uriah's wife, Bathsheba.

[38]See above, p. 104. Noted on the margin of this telegram: "Request notification as soon as the telegram is delivered to the telegraph bureau." Gradenwitz, "Akten," pp. 26–27, note. Cf. Wippermann, 8(II):26ff.

[39]Cf. Gradenwitz, "Akten," p. 4*.

the students and professors, to Goethe's Götz von Berlichingen. "One can be a true supporter of one's dynasty, of the Kaiser and king, without being convinced — as it says in *Götz* — of the wisdom of the measures of his agents. I am not so convinced, nor will I conceal my convictions (stormy applause and enthusiastic cheers for the prince)." [40]

If there was to be a politically effective opposition to absolutism, if the Reichstag was to be strengthened and developed along parliamentary lines, Otto von Bismarck was hardly the man to head the movement. He himself had greatly encouraged German subservience to the government; it was he who had accustomed them to the strong hand. His spectacular rallying of the opposition in this journey and by these speeches could have no practical effect. But the great public demonstrations did create the psychological impression which it was obviously intended that they should create upon the mind of the Kaiser. He had yielded the School Bill to an aroused public opinion; it would not be long before he would give in, at least outwardly, to Bismarck. [41]

Temporarily, Bismarck's all-out attack strengthened Caprivi's personal resolve to remain in office as well as his position with the Kaiser and with the anti-Bismarck parties, the Radicals and the Center. Bismarck, wrote the Radical *Die Nation,* was another Napoleon; there could be no reconciliation with him other than the complete submission of the Kaiser. The reconciliation campaign was really a struggle over future policy.

There has been a sentimental outcry over the opposition of Count Caprivi to a reconciliation between the Kaiser and Prince Bismarck. Could one make a more childish reproach? The present Reich chancellor would be naïveté personified if he were to encourage such a reconciliation. As things stand reconciliation can mean nothing other than the removal of the present chancellor and the substitution of a government which by means of a secret connection would be permanently allied with Friedrichsruh. The whole reconciliation campaign, therefore, has been nothing other than an attempt to place the sentimentality of the German people at the service of political intrigue. . . . We Radicals have no cause to be especially satisfied with the present government, but in its fight against Bismarckianism it will always find us on its side, even at the risk of thereby forfeiting forever the respect of the iron men of the National Liberals [*eisernen nationalliberalen Charaktere*]. [42]

[40]*Schulthess* (1892), pp. 122–129; Wippermann, 8(II):48–53, cf. 56–57; Eyck, *Bismarck,* III, 620–621; Stillich, *Politischen Parteien,* II, 311.
[41]Ziekursch, *Geschichte,* III, 71–72.
[42]9:671–672 (August 6, 1892).

Things had slowly progressed since Bismarck's day:

Let us compare the two periods! During the regime of the first German Reich chancellor a former ministerial colleague, after similar exploits in Vienna, would unfailingly have been arrested on the frontier. If under Count von Caprivi such brutal police methods have been renounced then this shows that today in Germany a freer and more humane spirit rules, which, however, as the articles in the *Norddeutsche Allgemeine Zeitung* prove, does not at all for that reason need to be weak.[43]

In the long run, however, the whole Bismarck incident could only further weaken the government's political position. By publishing his telegram to Prince Reuss, Caprivi had meant to shift the center of the Bismarck storm from the Kaiser to himself, and in this he was successful; the Kaiser's letter to Emperor Francis Joseph did not become public property until long after Bismarck's death and after his own abdication. But by this act of self-sacrificing loyalty Caprivi ruined his own standing with the German public. Henceforward he would be known to Germans only as the author of the "Uriah-letter." [44]

2

CAPRIVI'S ARMY BILL

The Kaiser and Two-Year Service

It was thus after the ignominious confusion of the School Bill crisis in the spring and the subsequent Bismarck demonstration in the summer of 1892 that Chancellor von Caprivi, on November 23, introduced his big Army Bill to the Reichstag. In February 1890 the *Preussische Jahrbücher* had pointed out that by its recent army reorganization France was much closer to actual universal service than was Germany; with a population of only 38 million France was now training 220,000 recruits per year, whereas Germany, with a population of 48 million, was training only 191,000 per year. In his original plan for the reorganization of the German army General von Verdy laid down the goal of a complete practical implementation of the old Scharnhorst idea of universal service; every German physically capable of service was to receive army training. To achieve this goal Verdy called for an increase in the peacetime

---

[43] 9:599 (July 2, 1892).
[44] Eyck, *Wilhelm II*, p. 63; Hohenlohe, *Memoirs*, II, 448. Cf. *Pr. Jbb.*, 70:124–126.

strength of the army of 115,000 men at an additional cost of approximately 100,000,000 M.[45]

This plan was based on the continuation of the three-year period of service. Verdy himself was doubtful whether such a large increase could be put through the Reichstag, and in the fall of 1890, as a result of his handling of the "little army bill" in the Reichstag and the resulting differences with the Kaiser and with Caprivi, Verdy was replaced as minister of war by General von Kaltenborn-Stachau. Caprivi, experiencing difficulties enough with the 18,000-men increase in 1890, quickly came to the conclusion that the essential reorganization could successfully be put through the Reichstag only by reducing the term of service to two years. This reduction, in Caprivi's opinion, would not necessarily be harmful to the efficiency of the army and would in some respects even be distinctly advantageous. In actual practice almost half the number of recruits were furloughed indefinitely after two years. The 1890 bill had been accepted by the Center party and passed only after the government had, in effect, conceded that the additional number of recruits would serve only two years. It would, therefore, be better to divide and weaken the opposition by accepting the principle of two-year service in advance than to be forced to concede it later by a triumphant Reichstag. Above all, Caprivi wanted to avoid a conflict with the Reichstag. The monarchy could not come out of such a conflict unscathed.[46]

On the question of two-year service, however, Caprivi immediately ran into difficulty with the Kaiser and the army. Since 1848 the army had been the conservative bulwark of the monarchy against the ever-recurring onslaughts of liberal democracy. Although based on the principle of "the nation in arms," the Prussian army had managed to retain its status of a special, separate caste, officered by the aristocracy and taking its oath of allegiance, not to the constitution, but to the person of its supreme commander, the king. The core of the crisis of 1862, which Bismarck had resolved, had centered around the liberal desire to make the army represent the nation and be responsible to the Landtag. To minimize the class-consciousness of the army, the liberal Landtag had insisted that the

[45]J. Werdermann, *Die Heeresreform unter Caprivi*, pp. 55, 116, 89, note. Werdermann has based his account on an intensive study of the archives of the War Ministry, the value of which is somewhat lessened by his narrow, technical approach and his concern over placing responsibility for the defeat of 1918.

[46]Caprivi's memorandum of August 27, 1891, Werdermann, *Heeresreform*, p. 23.

term of service be kept at two years, while King William I and Albrecht von Roon, the war minister, had demanded the introduction of a three-year term. With Bismarck's help the king and army had won this fight, and the army's independence of the Landtag — symbolizing by inference the king's independence of the constitution — had been maintained. Under Bismarck the Reich army, led and dominated by Prussia, occupied an even more separate and privileged position in the nation. As in Prussia, it took its oath, not to the Reich constitution, but to the Kaiser and king; but, unlike the Prussian army, it was not controlled by a responsible ministry. There was no Reich ministry of war; rather, Reich army affairs were managed through the Prussian War Ministry. The only measure of control over the army possessed by the Reichstag was in its right to refuse military budgets, and this control had been greatly attenuated by Bismarck by the so-called "compromise" of the semipermanent, long-term *septennat* budget. As the monarchy's independence from the Reichstag was symbolized by the Kaiser's independent, personal control over the army, so that control was in turn symbolized by the upholding of the unpopular three-year term of service.[47]

At least, this three-year tradition was very strong in the mind of the Kaiser, who was impressed with the duty of carrying on the Hohenzollern traditions as inherited from his grandfather. "When I entered office," wrote Caprivi in 1895, "I was confronted with the big Verdy bill, which was based on three-year service, although Verdy himself seemed to realize that that could not be achieved. The Kaiser, mindful of his grandfather, had expressed himself, to generals too, so decidedly in favor of three years that when for the first time I remarked to an officer from the War Ministry that the thing could be done only with two-year service the gentleman replied, 'Keep still, if the Kaiser hears that he'll send for the guard and have you arrested!' " [48]

In 1890 the larger issue of reorganization had been postponed, only to come up again in the spring of 1891, primarily as a result of the Kaiser's excitement over the international situation. On April 3, 1891, Caprivi notified Minister of War von Kaltenborn that the Kaiser was going to broach the question of an increase in the army. On the 7th Caprivi and Kaltenborn came to an agreement in sup-

---

[47]Gordon A. Craig, *The Politics of the Prussian Army, 1640–1945* (Oxford, 1955), pp. 138–179, 217–245; E. R. Huber, *Heer u. Staat* (Hamburg, 1943), pp. 197–219, 269–272.

[48]Schneidewin, "Briefe," p. 145.

port of the principle of two-year service, the new system to go into effect at the end of the *septennat* in 1894.[49] On April 28 the Kaiser instructed von Kaltenborn that legislatively the three-year service was not to be given up, but that there might be an increase in the furloughs "at disposition." The reorganization bill was to be quickly prepared and presented at the next session of the Reichstag in the fall. A few days later, however, the Kaiser admitted to Caprivi that he had no practical objections to two-year service but that its adoption must be carried out so that there would be "no noticeable break with the past." The Kaiser agreed to order an actual experiment with two-year service with a special contingent of troops in the fall.[50]

The influence of the army, however, including that of the new chief of staff, General Count von Schlieffen, was on the side of the traditional three-year service, and on June 15 the Kaiser sent letters to Caprivi and von Kaltenborn in which he announced that he would never give up the three-year period of service, by means of which his grandfather and Bismarck had founded the German Reich.[51]

Through and since the Conflict of 60–66 two-year service has been singled out as a power question, which the legislative [*Volksvertretung*] — especially the radical democrats — have always tried to use to bully and compel the kings. . . . before God and my ancestors . . . I declare plainly that I shall never agree to two-year service nor allow it further opportunity for official discussion; I write this to you as a holy resolve this day. . . . I do not doubt for an instant that we must fight just like Grandpapa . . . The occasion is good, a strong discussion will clear the air, like a storm may cleanse the overloaded atmosphere. At that time Grandpapa found Bismarck to help him in the fight and in victory, today I have Caprivi . . .

To this Caprivi replied courteously but coolly that he saw little chance of success for the Kaiser's reorganization program on the basis of three-year service. There would most certainly have to be a dissolution and new elections.

Such new elections, in my most humble [*allerunterthänigsten*] opinion, on the basis of increases in the military budget and without any intended concession toward the implementation of two-year service, would not produce a more docile Reichstag. Having once entered upon this course of action, in further pursuit of it Your Majesty would be faced with the question whether or not and in what way to achieve your pur-

[49]Werdermann, *Heeresreform*, pp. 19–20.
[50]Werdermann, *Heeresreform*, pp. 33, 20–21.
[51]Werdermann, *Heeresreform*, p. 22 and note.

pose through some means similar to a *coup d'état* — such as a change in the election law.

I should act irresponsibly were I to withhold from Your Majesty my conviction that in the loosely constructed German Reich and under present circumstances such a *coup d'état* would threaten the disintegration of this Reich. The political situation is a completely different one from that in Prussia in the sixties. I doubt that the Federated Governments would agree completely with the increases planned by Your Majesty, but I have no doubt whatever that at present they would not be inclined to put through any kind of *coup d'état*. . . . A hazardous undertaking such as the above can succeed only if the one whose duty it is to carry it out believes in it. Aside from other qualities necessary for carrying out so difficult a task, I, however, lack this belief. Finally I cannot deny that the fact that your Majesty has been pleased to make important decisions in such an extremely important political question without previously granting me a hearing has convinced me that I do not possess your most gracious [*allerhöchstderen*] confidence to that degree without which I should be hindered at every step by the apprehension that I might stumble.

Your Royal and Imperial Majesty I therefore beg, with repeated assurances of my respectful thanks for all the favor that has been granted me, most humbly, to graciously approve my discharge with the prescribed pension.

von Caprivi[52]

At once the Kaiser backed down, declared that his letter had been meant only as the basis for discussion, asked for a full report on the subject by Caprivi, agreed all over again to two-year service, and withdrew his demand that the bill be introduced in the fall. It was now to be presented some time in the next three years.[53]

On June 24, 1891, the Kaiser departed on his Norwegian cruise and visit to England, accompanied by Phili Eulenburg and Kiderlen. In spite of his assurances to Caprivi, he had not by any means given up the idea of sticking to his grandfather's three-year service. He was determined to retain both the three-year service *and* Caprivi. "He can't go, I simply won't let him go," the Kaiser told Kiderlen. "I shall ask the ministers, and when the whole Cabinet Council agrees with me then Caprivi will have to give in." In reporting all this to Holstein Kiderlen continued:

As I judge H. M., he wants to do as he did in H. E.'s [Bismarck's] time: by argument, threats, and flattery to win over the ministers *sep-*

[52]Caprivi Papers, Hauptarchiv, Berlin; Schneidewin, "Briefe," p. 145; Rogge, *Holstein*, p. 160; Werdermann, *Heeresreform*, p. 22 and note; Eulenburg to Holstein, June 17, 1891, *Holstein Papers, Correspondence*.

[53]Haller, *Eulenburg*, I, 148; Werdermann, *Heeresreform*, p. 33.

arately to his plans, then suddenly bring the latter out in a Crown Council and let the minister-president be outvoted by the other ministers. The affair is still a long way off, but, in my humble opinion, it would nevertheless be good meanwhile to put a crimp in such tricks as that [*solchen Wippschen . . . einen Riegel vorzuschieben*]. . . . I am, I believe, acting with your agreement and according to the R. C[hancellor]'s intentions if I do not, as Phili E. has done and, indeed, could do, artfully steer the conversation with the Kaiser onto this subject, but rather await H. M.'s initiative and limit myself to observation, but then when H. M. brings it up express myself as directed? R.S.V.P. if I am *mistaken*.[54]

Eulenburg also talked at length with the Kaiser on the subject and sent off reports to Caprivi and Holstein. The Kaiser, wrote Eulenburg, was determined to retain both Caprivi and the three-year service. If it meant a serious conflict with the Reichstag, well and good, they must get used to the idea of such a conflict sometime in the next three years. If worst came to worst he would put the reform through the Prussian Landtag. The federal princes would certainly agree to that. The Kaiser's feelings had been hurt by the tone of Caprivi's letter. Since Caprivi had left the army, he had let himself be too much influenced by government officials and parliamentary personages and against the army's interests. But to let Caprivi go would be impossible. A way out of the impasse, wrote Eulenburg, could be found if Caprivi would be conciliatory.

This unfortunate question, in my opinion, originated in H. M. solely in connection with some sort of precise information on French armaments. H. M. will then have asked the Military Cabinet for an opinion — and in these questions [General von] Hahnke agrees with H. M.'s point of view . . . I am as good as certain that neither Waldersee nor the military attachés are behind this.[55]

Kiderlen did not regard the impasse as darkly or as seriously as did Eulenburg. In his own letter to Holstein he wrote:

Try to see to it that the R. C. does not assume from what Eulenburg writes that the question must necessarily lead to a conflict. Two things especially must be borne in mind: (1) that H. M. constantly recurs to the three year interim; within this period many things can happen; (2) that H. M. is holding onto the R. C. absolutely, and will, therefore, in any event, seek a basis for understanding with him. The R. C. will surely find a formula for coming to an understanding with H. M. according to his

[54]Rogge, *Holstein,* pp. 158–159.
[55]Rogge, *Holstein,* p. 161; see below, pp. 316ff., for the Military Cabinet.

own ideas but without formally deciding against him. *Mais rien ne presse.*[56]

The fact was that Phili Eulenburg was himself in favor of three-year service ("from the standpoint of national discipline") and already in this crisis in 1891 tended to lean toward the Kaiser in his liaison activities, whereas Kiderlen and Holstein were much more inclined to support the chancellor.[57] Eulenburg's letter, wrote Holstein a few days later, had been written "evidently with the Kaiser's knowledge and according to his ideas to work through me on Caprivi to make him give in, which I *have not done*. I submitted Kiderlen's letters to the R. C., but not Eulenburg's." About the Army Bill crisis Holstein wrote:

The Kaiser dreams of an ideal Reichstag, which will appropriate unlimited sums for army, navy, and magnificent building enterprises. Unfortunately, in his last days, when, without worrying much about *après moi le déluge*, Prince Bismarck was ruling from hand to mouth, he imparted this idea of conflict with the Reichstag to the Kaiser, and now Caprivi has it to deal with!

A conflict with the Reichstag is impossible. The other German princes would graciously refuse to take part in it, and if the Kaiser proceeds against them with force Russia and France will merely intervene as they have done often enough before in internal German affairs. Where will we be then? [58]

From August 8 to 21 the Kaiser attended the naval maneuvers in the Baltic. Here, when General von Waldersee spoke to him in favor of three-year service, reminding him of his grandfather's courageous stand on the question, the Kaiser declared that under no circumstances would he give it up.[59] Back in Berlin, on the 24th he attended a picnic on the Pfaueninsel in Potsdam, to which, at a rather late hour, he suddenly summoned Minister of War General von Kaltenborn. There, in the presence of Chief of Staff Count von Schlieffen, the Kaiser informed Kaltenborn that his decree ordering an experimental trial of two-year service was to be rescinded; the full three-year period was to be retained; the reorganization project, however, was not only to proceed but the bill must be ready by the spring of 1892.[60]

Again Caprivi and Kaltenborn took counsel together and ar-

[56]Rogge, *Holstein*, p. 159.
[57]Haller, *Eulenburg*, I, 149.
[58]Rogge, *Holstein*, p. 157.
[59]*Schulthess* (1891), p. 103; Waldersee, *Denkwürdigkeiten*, II, 214–215.
[60]Werdermann, *Heeresreform*, pp. 22, 33, 47.

ranged for a joint audience with the Kaiser on the 29th. In preparation for this event Caprivi, on the 27th, sent the Kaiser a memorandum entitled, "Concerning the Further Development of the German Army." "The decisive question," wrote Caprivi, "is: can one at present in the German Reich risk a conflict with the legislative over three-year service? I believe that I can answer this question decidedly in the negative." If two-year service were to be conceded in advance, a conflict would be avoided and large concessions by the Reichstag made possible in return. The bill was to be ready for the winter of 1892–1893.[61]

As a result of this memorandum and the conference with Caprivi and Kaltenborn on the 29th, the Kaiser backed down again and agreed both that the experiment with two-year service was to be carried out as planned (the order rescinding it had meanwhile been delayed in the ministry) and that the reorganization bill was to wait until the winter of 1892–1893. But the Kaiser had, nevertheless, not really made up his mind as yet. He was uncertain as to whether the necessity of retaining Caprivi was great enough to warrant giving in to him on this issue. As late as November 1891, the Kaiser was still considering possible new candidates for the chancellorship.[62]

In December 1891 Caprivi reëstablished himself firmly with the successful passage of the first trade treaties,[63] only to have everything come crashing down in the School Bill crisis in the spring of 1892. That crisis opened on March 17 and was not settled until the 24th. On the 19th, Caprivi met with von Kaltenborn and von Schlieffen at the Chancellery and discussed the prospects of the Army Bill. After the blow which the crown had just dealt the Center and Conservative coalition in the Landtag, the Conservatives, said Caprivi, were very reluctant to envisage the introduction of the big Army Bill in the fall. The domestic situation seemed to indicate that a postponement of the measure was advisable; the Kaiser, too, was now inclined toward postponing the question. In spite of these considerations, however, all three generals were unanimous in agreeing that the introduction of the army reorganization must not be postponed but must occur the following fall as planned. All three now agreed on the necessity of coupling the reform with the reduction in the period of service to two years.[64]

But now the Kaiser was the one who held back and stressed

[61]Werdermann, *Heeresreform*, pp. 23, 25.
[62]Werdermann, *Heeresreform*, p. 25, note; Kardorff, *Kardorff*, p. 247; Waldersee, *Denkwürdigkeiten*, II, 223.
[63]See above, pp. 152–153.
[64]Werdermann, *Heeresreform*, pp. 27, 34, 49.

domestic difficulties. Supported by Minister of Finance Miquel, who was about to introduce the second part of his tax reform in Prussia and did not want it threatened by a political crisis in the Reich, the Kaiser suggested that the Army Bill be put off until the spring of 1893. He still balked, however, at giving up the three-year service. On April 6 Caprivi sent the Kaiser a new memorandum on the army reorganization:

If the desire of the Reichstag for introduction of two-year service *by law* is not at least partially met, a strengthening of the army cannot be achieved. Also, only upon this basis would a dissolution and a new election have any prospect of success . . . The question is not: is two-year service in itself preferable to three-year service, but shall we give up three-year service for the infantry in order thereby to raise the peace strength by 77,500 men.[65]

In June, just before the Kaiser's departure on his Norwegian cruise, Caprivi thought he detected a certain weakening in the imperial attitude and tried to get the Prussian State Ministry formally to request a decision from the Kaiser that the Army Bill should be introduced the following winter. But the Prussian ministry, now under the chairmanship of Botho Eulenburg and the ever increasing influence of Miquel, refused to do this, and the Kaiser put off any decision on the matter until fall.[66]

In late July and early August 1892, the Kaiser took part in the English yacht races at Cowes. On August 18, back in Berlin, he reviewed a parade of the Guards, then afterwards addressed a speech to the generals and staff officers on the army reorganization bill. He was astounded, he said, at the discussion of such technical matters in the press, especially the demands for a system of two-year service. If any such changes were to be made, he would order them himself; public discussion of the matter was quite useless. He intended, however, to retain the three-year service of his grandfather. If the Reichstag were unpatriotic enough to refuse an increase in the army on this basis, then he would get along with a small, well-disciplined army rather than make any concessions. The reverberations of this speech were many and profound. "Now that the Kaiser has publicly and decidedly repudiated the two-year system," wrote the *Vossische Zeitung*, "we are justified in asking whether Reich Chancellor Count Caprivi will remain in office." *The Times* of London remarked that apparently the Army Bill was not to be in-

[65]Keim, *Erlebtes*, p. 53; Werdermann, *Heeresreform*, pp. 34 and note, 35, 28–29.
[66]Werdermann, *Heeresreform*, p. 35.

troduced next session and the Kaiser wanted to stop discussion of it.[67]

Meanwhile Caprivi and the War Ministry had worked out a formula to save the Kaiser's face. There was to be no repeal of the constitutional provision for three-year service, but *in practice* only two years of training for the infantry were to be planned and provided for in the bill. A memorandum from the War Ministry which was sent to the Kaiser on August 27 declared under Point 14:

The existing statutory obligation of three years of service will be unconditionally retained. His Majesty's right under special circumstances to retain the third year of military service may not be encroached upon.

But once the two-year system was actually introduced, as planned, throughout the army, it would in fact be impossible to revert here and there to the old system, no matter what the "special circumstances." This was mere incense-burning.[68]

Even on this basis the Kaiser was not as yet willing to authorize introduction of the bill in the fall. But Bismarck's Vienna attack in the summer made it even more necessary to retain Caprivi. During the annual hunting holiday at Rominten in September, Phili Eulenburg submerged his own predilection for three-year service and presented the Kaiser with a memorandum urging coöperation with Caprivi. The School Bill, wrote Eulenburg, had already weakened the prestige of the monarchy. The Army Bill was of almost greater general concern.

Therefore it must be able to count on success in the Reichstag — alternatively, it *must be carried out* even in spite of the Reichstag; or else it *must not be brought in at all.*

Once introduced, the bill could not then be withdrawn, as in the case of the School Bill.

An administration of Your Majesty's which was not in a position to carry an increase of the forces regarded by it as essential would to foreign countries appear so feeble, and to the nation (which has lost the sense of its national duties) so divided, that the moment for attack might be thought to have come . . . The measure, as it now stands, represents a compromise between Your Majesty and the Reich Chancellor. That compromise will be the subject of discussion, directly any difficulties

[67]Wedel, *Zwischen Kaiser und Kanzler*, p. 198; *Schulthess* (1892), pp. 131–132; Wippermann, 8(II):2, 12; *The Times*, wkly. ed., August 26, 1892, p. 4. The version in *Schulthess* gives the wrong impression.
[68]Werdermann, *Heeresreform*, pp. 26, 29–30.

arise about the voting on the bill. The Chancellor will then revert to the two years' service, or will make concessions to the Center. Your Majesty has declared *against both* . . . On the one hand the parties are aware of the Chancellor's general tendency to yield to pressure, and especially of his liking for the two years' compulsory service; on the other the reported conclusion — to which no *démenti* has been given — of Your Majesty's speech after the Berlin review of the Forces, when Your Majesty said you preferred a small but well-trained army with three years' service to a huge force with two, has given the impression that Your Majesty sets no value on the reinforcement . . . If Your Majesty authorized the Reich Chancellor . . . to say that . . . the new measure represents what *alone* Your Majesty values, it would put an end to the dangerous myth which keeps the right-thinking elements inactive. There should not be left *the slightest room for doubt* that Your Majesty is decidedly in favor of the bill, otherwise there will be a full-dress debate, and the conflict with the Reich Chancellor will be inevitable . . . Thus alone is defeat with its incalculable consequences to be avoided.[69]

Such a defeat, warned Eulenburg, would present Bismarck with an opportunity to force reconciliation upon the Kaiser as the "saviour of the Fatherland," and would completely destroy the Kaiser's authority. In mid-September the Kaiser agreed that the bill might be introduced sometime during the coming winter. On October 15 he finally signed the bill, and the same day Caprivi submitted it to the Bundesrat.[70]

Parties and Public Opinion

The Army Bill, as introduced personally by General von Caprivi to the Reichstag on November 23, 1892, called for the effective utilization of all available manpower through an increase in the over-all peace strength of the army by some 90,000 men in all categories, or from an approximate total of 512,000 to 603,000. The term of service was also, in effect, to be reduced to two years. This reduction in itself increased the number of recruits yearly by one-third; it was considerably less, however, than one might expect because of the system currently in use of indefinite furlough after 28 months.[71] Thus this bill proposed to raise the size of the army at one stroke by more than all the increases since 1871 put together. The military budget would be raised correspondingly by some

---

[69]Werdermann, *Heeresreform*, p. 35; Haller, *Eulenburg*, I, 149–152.

[70]Werdermann, *Heeresreform*, pp. 35–36; Eulenburg to Holstein, September 30, 1892, *Holstein Papers, Correspondence;* especially the section of Eulenburg's memorandum not in Haller, reproduced in note 4.

[71]Cf. Caprivi's letter to Bennigsen, Oncken, *Bennigsen*, II, 577–579.

60,000,000 M. On the other hand Caprivi gave the liberals their long-sought-after two-year service, which also meant that the increase in cost, and ultimately in taxes, would be only half as much as the Verdy plan would have required.[72] Also Caprivi reduced the former Bismarckian *septennat* to a five-year *quinquennat,* which would correspond to the present life of the Reichstag. He introduced the measure to the new Reichstag in a speech, delivered before the formal opening of debate, two hours in length and in its careful construction, solid reasoning, and dignified, earnest delivery, one of his most notable performances. Yet, in spite of the importance of the bill and of Caprivi's careful attempts to meet the Reichstag halfway, this introductory speech was coldly received by a house which was little more than half full.[73]

There was no doubt about it, public opinion was cold and hostile to the idea of new sacrifices for the army. The business depression which had started in 1890 had continued in a downward trend throughout 1891, aggravated by unusually high food prices.[74] The winter of 1891–92 had been especially hard, with great unemployment and frequent riots in the cities. In late February mobs of unemployed workers had rioted for three days in Berlin, smashing and looting shop windows and clashing with police. Over a hundred persons had been arrested, twelve policemen had been injured, and twenty-five persons had been hospitalized with serious cuts from police sabers. In August an epidemic of cholera struck the port of Hamburg and threatened to spread to other parts of Germany. In September, the Kaiser canceled the army maneuvers to avoid the danger of further spreading the disease.[75]

The public was, therefore, in no mood to squeeze out 60,000,-000 M more for a larger army, particularly when there seemed to be no immediate danger of war. Thus Theodor Barth's Radical *Die Nation* had written on October 8:

How can a nation remain militarily effective when it is economically exhausted? . . . This process of constantly increasing military burdens must at last be brought to a halt. Whether the point where it is halted

---

[72]For a detailed outline of the Verdy plan and the changes made in 1892, see Werdermann, *Heeresreform,* pp. 55–89; for the reductions made in the cost, pp. 116–118; also *Statistisches Handbuch für das Deutsche Reich* (Berlin, 1907), pp. 532–533; Wippermann, 9(I):115.

[73]*The Times,* November 24, 1892, p. 5; *Sten. Ber.* (1892–1893), I, 7–21; Gothein, *Caprivi,* p. 63. See below, Chapter VII, section I.

[74]See above, pp. 140ff.

[75]*The Times,* wkly. ed., February 26, 1892, p. 6, March 4, 1892, p. 4; *Schulthess* (1892), pp. 72, 132, 134.

be a little further forwards or backwards is not nearly so important as the establishment, above all, of the idea that a further requisitioning of national strength for military purposes cannot be accomplished without the most severe damage to the over-all development of the German nation.

The unfavorable public opinion, wrote Barth, must necessarily be heeded by every party. Two-year service was a strong card, but it would not take every trick. "Precisely the most convinced supporters of two-year service will vote against the bill." [76]

Besides the question of cost there was the general resentment, particularly among the voters of the left, of the strong and arrogant spirit of Prussian militarism which had more and more pervaded the Reich since 1871, with its independence of the Reichstag, its domineering caste spirit, its student military "Korps," and its duels. During the past year there had been more than one instance of sentries firing on civilians who were annoying them, and, after one such incident in the spring when a sentry had killed one man and wounded another, the Kaiser had seen fit to send him his photograph, publicly commend him for his conduct, and promote him to corporal. Again, recently, in October, a sentry had fired at a fleeing drunkard in Strassburg, thus at this critical juncture for the Army Bill increasing the agitation against "militarism." [77]

Whereas the Radicals in 1890, under Eugen Richter's uncompromising leadership, had indeed not voted for the "little army bill," the clever old Windthorst had managed to use his Center votes to support the government and to attack militarism at the same time. Windthorst, however, was now dead, and the Center party had not found another single, clever hand to control it. It had been Windthorst's great achievement to steer a careful, flexible middle course, both between the parties in the Reichstag and also between the two extremes within the Center party — aristocrats on the one hand and democrats on the other. Since his death these two extremes within the Catholic fold had been left free to vie for the party leadership. At first the Silesian aristocrats, Count Ballestrem, Baron von Huene, and Dr. Porsch, maintained the upper hand. Count Ballestrem was already chairman of the party fraction and first vice president in the Reichstag; he now also took over Windthorst's vacant seat in the Prussian Landtag.[78]

[76] *Die Nation*, 10:20, 67, 84 (1892–1893). Cf. Wippermann, 7(II):59–62.
[77] Cf. Werner F. Bruck, *Social and Economic History of Germany* (London, 1938), *passim; Schulthess* (1892), p. 94; Wippermann, 8(I):272–273; *The Times*, November 25, 1892, p. 5.
[78] Bachem, *Zentrumspartei*, V, 239–242.

The aristocratic Center leaders were, from the first, more inclined to support the government in some compromise, but the opinion of the rank and file of the party, especially in South Germany, was strongly opposed. The Bavarian peasants, as agricultural prices dropped, were against Caprivi because of the trade treaties and regarded any increase in the strength of the army as an increase in the hated Prussian influence. Dr. Ernst Lieber, leader of the democratic wing of the party in the Reichstag, who had his ear to the ground, therefore opposed the Army Bill from the start.[79] The position of the Center at the beginning, then, was as usual extremely uncertain, to say the least.

One might not have expected the opposition parties to be enthusiastic; what, on the other hand, was most extraordinary was the opposition among the "state-supporting" parties, especially the Conservatives. In the first place these gentlemen took the position of many of the generals, the General Staff, and the Kaiser, that the reduction of the period of compulsory active military service to two years would ruin the army, by lessening its efficiency, by reducing its effect on "national discipline," by "betraying" the precedent of 1862, and, inferentially, by yielding the independence and dignity of the military to popular demand, thereby weakening the prestige of the crown. But however much the agrarian Conservatives might shake their heads over two-year service, the basic cause of their negative attitude lay elsewhere.

The grain harvest in 1892 yielded a much better crop than in the preceding year, and, with increased importation from new sources abroad, rapidly sinking grain prices indicated that the high prices of 1890–1891 in agricultural products had been only an exceptional, local phenomenon, not a permanent trend.[80] Farmers bringing their ample grain harvest to market found the price for a double Zentner (about 220 pounds) reduced by not only the 1½ M of the Caprivi tariff reduction but by a full 10 M. To make the situation worse, the incidence of hoof-and-mouth disease, which had been slowly advancing in recent years, rose in one jump from 394,640 cattle affected in 1891 to 1,504,308 in 1892. Chancellor von Caprivi's trade treaties, naturally, were not responsible either for the cholera, the hoof-and-mouth disease, the good harvest, or the over-all drop in prices, but, in the face of agricultural conditions which began to

[79]Bachem, *Zentrumspartei*, V, 272–273, 280; Kardorff, *Kardorff*, pp. 272–273; *Die Nation*, 10:36.
[80]Cf. Caprivi's statement in the Landtag on June 1, 1891, *Landtag* (1890–1891), V, 2448.

resemble those of the seventies, it was perhaps natural for the
Junker estate owners to seize upon the trade treaties as something
tangible that was not in their own special interest and to load them
down with the sum total of all their economic grievances, real and
imagined. Then too, by waving the flag of protection and bimetallism one could more easily attract discontented peasants to the
Conservative Junker standard and distract their attention from their
more local grievances against the landlords.[81]

The School Bill crisis had, in fact, impressed the Conservatives
with the power of mass agitation at the same time that it had delivered the party over into the hands of the Christian Socialist right
wing — that is, the Stöcker-Hammerstein-*Kreuzzeitung* group to
whom "Christian" meant anti-Semitic and "Socialist" anticapitalist.
The Conservatives had tried to revise their party program in an anti-
Semitic sense in April and May but had failed to come to an agreement on specific terms. Then in the spring and summer had come
a great wave of anti-Semitism among the German populace. In April
Rector Ahlwardt, who had been dismissed from a Berlin parish
school for dereliction of duty and had already served one prison
term for libeling the Berlin City Council, published a pamphlet,
Jewish Rifles, which accused the munitions firm of Ludwig Loewe
of deliberately supplying the army with defective rifles as an act
of sabotage. The charges raised a tremendous outcry, necessitating
official denials in the *Reichsanzeiger* of May 9 and 30. In spite of all
the denials and the denunciations in the liberal press, however,
Ahlwardt immediately became something of a national hero.[82] Then
in the summer a child had been found murdered in the little town
of Xanten on the lower Rhine, and immediately a very respectable
Jewish butcher had been accused of a "ritual murder." Although his
subsequent long-drawn-out trial firmly established his complete
innocence, a mob had meanwhile burned down his home, and public
excitement had made it necessary for him to leave the place.[83]

The waves of anti-Semitic and agrarian agitation were rising;
the Conservatives were determined to ride the waves and to sub-
merge the Caprivi tariff policy in the process. They were all the
more ready to blame everything on the government while demanding
special assistance from it, since Caprivi's New Course regime had
seemed all along to be inclining too far toward the left and toward

[81]Lotz, "Handelspolitik," pp. 103–104. See below, pp. 246ff., 289ff.
[82]*Schulthess* (1892), pp. 92, 94, 99, 100; Wippermann, 8(I):273–274, 8(II):76–
79, 87–90; *Pr. Jbb.*, 69:841ff. (1892); Eyck, *Wilhelm II*, pp. 69–70.
[83]*Schulthess* (1892), pp. 119, 342; *The Times*, wkly. ed., July 22, 1892, p. 4.

what they considered to be a dangerously soft and weak policy, rather than to be strongly upholding the truly conservative and monarchical interests in the state — namely, the Junkers. The agrarian Conservatives, therefore, were inclined to regard the Army Bill as a good opportunity to get rid of Caprivi and the New Course too.[84]

As the force of the agrarian agitation began to gather, it brought about a sharp cleavage within the small Free Conservative party, a split which was embodied in the persons of Wilhelm von Kardorff and of Baron Carl von Stumm-Halberg. Kardorff was a Junker landlord, Stumm a Saar iron and steel industrialist; Kardorff opposed the trade treaties and despised Caprivi, Stumm supported the trade treaties and admired Caprivi; Kardorff was the leader of the agitation for a double monetary standard, Stumm firmly supported the gold standard; Kardorff actively participated in the Bismarck Fronde, Stumm since July 1892 had definitely turned from Bismarck to Caprivi. Now in the Reichstag Kardorff attacked the Army Bill, while Stumm vigorously defended it.[85]

As for the National Liberals, they were for the bill in principle, but not in its particulars, and many of them felt righteously supported in their generally oppositional mood by the attitude of their old leader, Bismarck. Social Democrats were automatically against all military bills.[86]

These, briefly, were the reasons behind the cool reaction of the Reichstag to Caprivi's masterly address on November 23. A nation, suffering from the economic doldrums, having already lost its early enthusiasm for the New Course, and seemingly at peace with its neighbors, did not want to be exhorted to new and unheard of military sacrifices. From Conservatives to Social Democrats every major party was against the bill. For the Radicals it did not concede enough and went too far, for the Conservatives it conceded too much and did not go far enough. "The problem," *Die Nation* had written during the previous summer, "which Herr von Caprivi once posed for himself he has probably succeeded in solving; he has a government which stands above the parties, but also one which, for that reason, lacks the support of the parties."[87]

[84]Cf. Kardorff, *Kardorff*, pp. 272–273.

[85]Kardorff, *Kardorff*, pp. 273–275; Hellwig, *Stumm*, pp. 450–451, 459–464. On the gold standard and bimetallism, see below, pp. 289ff.

[86]Cf. Oncken, *Bennigsen*, II, 579–583.

[87]*Die Nation*, 9:669 (1891–1892). For an analysis of party opinion, see H. Goebel, *Die Militärvorlage 1892/93* (Leipzig, 1935).

Miquel and the Prussian Ministry

A further weakness in the position of the Army Bill lay in the contradictions within the government itself. In the preparation of the bill Caprivi had succeeded in winning the support of the minister of war but had quite failed to win the coöperation of the Prussian State Ministry as a whole, which was coming more and more under the influence of the finance minister, Miquel. It is doubtless significant for understanding Miquel's personal motivation to note that in November 1890, after he had been in office a few months, he remarked to the chief of the Civil Cabinet, von Lucanus, that he had discovered how things really were only since he had become a minister. Even more revealing was his complaint once to a small group of intimates, "If I only had dictatorial power I could accomplish more." [88] Miquel, it will be remembered, had started out on the left of the political spectrum but, with his party, had followed Bismarck's "realistic" policy ever further to the right. Unlike Bismarck, however, in 1890 he had believed — perhaps naïvely — that the Reich, the monarchy, and the present social order could best be defended by a policy of reform, not by extreme and violent measures. These reforms would bring together all the parties of "order" in opposition to the threat of Social Democracy. Here Miquel and Caprivi were in agreement. But soon a difference in tactics and emphasis began to make itself apparent, breaking violently into the open in the School Bill crisis.[89] Miquel, as the most important figure in the Prussian Ministry, thought in terms of Prussian policy and adapted his tactics to the climate of the Landtag, dominated by the Conservative party. Caprivi, as Reich chancellor, thought in terms of Reich policy and adapted his tactics to the climate of the Reichstag, where the Center party threw the decisive weight. Also Miquel, as a National Liberal, could not see his own party completely relegated to the sidelines. In addition, there was in his make-up the powerful factor of personal ambition, expressed through his willingness to intrigue against the chancellor by cleverly influencing the Kaiser. Real reformers — persons who want to change the world to suit themselves — frequently move from a youthful extreme of ineffective, other-worldly idealism, through a middle position of various compromises with the worldly use of power as a convenient means, to the final extreme of fascination with power itself. The

[88]See above, Chapter III, section 2, Wedel, *Zwischen Kaiser und Kanzler*, p. 131; Herzfeld, *Miquel*, II, 431.
[89]See above, Chapter V.

complexities and contradictions contained within the German governmental process during the Caprivi Era presented the dynamic and seasoned personality of the ambitious Miquel with a favorable opportunity for personal accomplishment and personal aggrandizement.[90]

For the fall session of the 1892 Landtag Miquel had planned the completion of his tax reform, that is, the transfer of the land and building taxes from state to local jurisdiction.[91] To complete the rational, over-all structure of his new tax system for Prussia was his chief and, it seemed, his only concern.[92] To put any measure through the Prussian Landtag one had to please the Conservatives; in the fall of 1892 the Conservatives were becoming more and more taken up by the agrarian movement. Therefore Miquel promised no higher taxes to meet the current and expected Prussian deficit and handed over the land, building, and business taxes to the communes, the villages, and — the "independent estates" of the Junkers. In 1861 Prussia had indemnified the Junkers for imposing the land tax on their estates; now — without calling for repayment of the indemnity — the land tax, for the Junkers, was, in effect, to be repealed.

This sugar-plum tactic was well suited to the political make-up of the Landtag, but it ran into serious trouble within the ministry. Minister of the Interior Herrfurth attacked Miquel's plan unmercifully and relentlessly. It was, he declared, "an irresponsible gift to the landlords." And in this he was strongly backed by Caprivi. In contradiction to the social reforms in the Reich and the ameliorative tendency of the previous rural-government and income-tax reforms in Prussia, the renunciation of the land and building tax would operate, not for the benefit of the poorer classes, but for the wealthy. It would create a bad impression. Herrfurth, however, to whom Miquel referred as "that little bureaucrat," by now had little influence, having suffered defeat and humiliation at the hands of the Conservatives over his Rural Government Bill. The Kaiser had already requested his removal. Nor, since the School Bill crisis in March, was Caprivi any longer in a commanding position in strictly Prussian affairs. Count Botho zu Eulenburg was now minister-president and — a Conservative — supported the position of Miquel. Other ministers — likewise Conservative — followed suit, and Miquel triumphed.[93] Also, against the ministry, his critics in the Landtag,

[90]See below, Chapter VII, section 4, Chapter VIII, section 2, Chapter IX, *passim*.
[91]See above, pp. 93–94.
[92]Oncken, *Bennigsen*, II, 574; *Die Nation*, 10:5 (1892–1893).
[93]Herzfeld, *Miquel*, II, 264–271; Oncken, *Bennigsen*, II, 564–568; Goldschmidt, *Reich u. Preussen*, p. 99, note.

public opinion, and, which was important, the Kaiser, Miquel could and did flourish the over-all logic of his reform as a whole. In the spring he had written to his eldest son: "If the thing succeeds completely then we shall have the best state and local tax system in the whole world and will lead the procession in a great social and financial reform . . . Fortunately I have the Kaiser completely on my side." [94] In August Minister Herrfurth resigned from the Prussian Ministry, and Count Botho zu Eulenburg, who had been so far without portfolio, took over his old post of the interior. The swing to the right in Prussia was further indicated by the appointment of the notorious, reactionary former minister, von Puttkamer, as governor of Pomerania.[95] Herrfurth, contrary to custom, did not keep silent after his resignation, but carried his opposition into the Landtag, where he easily obtained a seat and where, to the visible dismay of Miquel and the other ministers present and to the delight of the Radicals, he denounced the tax bill from the floor as "plutocratic" and "agrarian." [96]

It may be that, when in the midst of the School Bill uproar Caprivi had selected Botho Eulenburg to succeed him, he had thought to check the liberal — as in that particular crisis — influence of Miquel with a dependable Conservative career man. Eulenburg had been minister of the interior under Bismarck, having introduced the anti-Socialist bill in 1878, until he had been summarily dismissed by the Iron Chancellor. Perhaps this clash with Bismarck had recommended him to Caprivi. At any rate, Count Eulenburg was a smoothly diplomatic and able official, but not with the strength of character to oppose Miquel. The division created in March 1892 between the governments of Prussia and the Reich had not relieved Caprivi of Miquel; on the contrary, it had given an opportunity for a further assault upon the position of Caprivi. Caprivi, as chancellor, had retained the post of Prussian foreign minister and the right to instruct the Prussian representatives in the Bundesrat. But could he, in a serious matter, instruct them in a sense contrary to the decision of the collective Prussian State Ministry? This was a question not envisaged in Bismarck's constitution. The arena for the battle over this issue of Prussia and the Reich was, of course, the Bundesrat. There the Reich (and the president of the Reich, the German Kaiser

[94]Herzfeld, *Miquel*, II, 266. On the Miquel tax reform see above, pp. 90–91.
[95]*Schulthess* (1892), p. 130; Eyck, *Wilhelm II*, p. 52; Ponsonby, *Letters of Empress Frederick*, pp. 436–437.
[96]Cf. *Die Nation*, 9:699, 10:131; Herzfeld, *Miquel*, II, 271; *Landtag* (1892–1893), I, 94–101. On Herrfurth, cf. Bismarck, *Kaiser vs. Bismarck*, ch. IV; Eyck, *Wilhelm II*, p. 50.

and king of Prussia) was represented by the president of the Bundesrat, the Reich chancellor. But actually the Bundesrat was dominated by Prussia, a state six times larger than Bavaria, the next in size. Hence a clash in the Bundesrat between Reich and Prussia was really a clash between Prussia and Prussia. The separation of offices in March 1892, then, had not resolved the difference between Miquel and Caprivi, but had only given it constitutional recognition and additional importance.[97]

Under Bismarck much of the business of the Reich had been prepared in the separate Prussian ministries, and Prussian ministers still presided over the permanent Bundesrat committees — except the Committee for Foreign Affairs, which was specifically placed under the leadership of Bavaria. The state secretaries of the Reich were not considered to have any political importance and took a subordinate place, as technical experts, both in the Bundesrat and on special occasions, when called, in the Prussian State Ministry. The new freedom of the ministers under the regime of the New Course expressed itself as early as April 1891, when Herr von Meinecke, representing Miquel in the chair of the Finance Committee of the Bundesrat, attacked certain provisions in the Reich budget that were defended by Herr Aschenborn, representing the secretary of the Reich Treasury, von Maltzahn, and thereby provided a rather awkward display of Prussian disunity before the non-Prussian members of the committee. Chancellor Caprivi thereupon sent a directive to all Prussian Bundesrat representatives, admonishing them, if serious differences arose with the representatives of the Reich administration, first to ask the Prussian State Ministry or the minister-president (Caprivi) for instructions before expressing these views in the Bundesrat committee sessions. A special note to Miquel called attention to the specific incident and asked him politely to restrain Herr von Meinecke in the future. This directive, however, by no means settled the matter. Reich Secretary von Maltzahn tried subsequently to take over the chairmanship of the Finance Committee in the Bundesrat from Miquel, but without success.[98]

During the crisis in March 1892, Miquel told the Saxon ambassador, Count Hohenthal, that fundamentally he approved of the projected separation of the offices of Reich chancellor and Prussian minister-president, since, in his opinion, special Prussian interests often suffered from the frequently politically motivated bills of the chancellor. If the separation were carried out, however, it might

[97]Cf. Lerchenfeld, *Denkwürdigkeiten*, p. 192.
[98]Goldschmidt, *Reich u. Preussen*, pp. 96–98, 319–320.

eventually be possible, on occasion, to cast the Prussian votes in the Bundesrat against the chancellor.[99] To forestall just such pressure moves from the Prussian Ministry, Caprivi tried as much as possible to ignore Prussia in the carrying on of Reich affairs. In early April he obtained the Kaiser's permission to absent himself at his own discretion from routine meetings of the Prussian State Ministry, attending only when it seemed to him expedient in connection with Reich affairs. And on March 28, immediately after the separation, he requested an opinion on the introduction into the Bundesrat of presidential bills — that is, bills introduced by the chancellor instead of by Prussia. The opinion of the Reich Department of Justice was that bills might be introduced by the chancellor independently of the Prussian government.

The Kaiser and the Reich chancellor now hold a separate governing and executive authority in the Reich, theoretically different and separate from the authority of the Prussian state, and they represent a separate Reich policy which does not need everywhere to coincide with the policy of Prussia. It therefore follows as a matter of course that they must possess an influence on the Reich legislative processes which is independent of the Prussian state government, at least to the extent of introducing separate motions and bills.

This position, it was pointed out, had, on the whole, formerly been maintained by Prince Bismarck.[100]

The course of the 1892 Reich Army Bill illustrates the peculiarities of this situation. The bill, which was based fundamentally on Caprivi's own concepts, both military and political, was worked out in the Prussian State Ministry of War by a subordinate official, General von Gossler, working in close collaboration with the chancellor and rather over the head of the minister of war. After the approval of the minister of war, the chief of staff, and the Kaiser had at length been gained, the bill was then communicated to the ministers of war of Bavaria, Saxony, and Württemberg. It was then introduced to the Bundesrat as a presidential bill. Only at the last minute and by special request of Prussian Minister-President Eulenburg was the bill, on September 27, sent to the Prussian State Ministry "for their information." On October 3 Minister Miquel demanded that the State Ministry vote on the position which Prussia should take towards the Army Bill. A discussion of the matter followed in a meeting of the State Ministry on October 8. Miquel — who was planning

[99]Goldschmidt, *Reich u. Preussen*, p. 322.
[100]Goldschmidt, *Reich u. Preussen*, pp. 102, note, 322–324.

to repeal the land tax in Prussia — protested against any Reich measure which would bring a financial burden on the individual states. Now, strategically, Caprivi had not wanted to take up the question of how the necessary funds were to be raised until the Army Bill was accepted by the Reichstag. Reich finances were a sore point, Reich taxes being exclusively indirect and weighing chiefly, therefore, on the poorer classes, and it would be foolhardy to encumber his large-scale military proposals with the bitter complication of new taxes. But if no special taxes were provided for the 60,000,000 M, it would have to come from "matricular" payments by the member states — most of it from Prussia. This would play hob with the Prussian budget, would create obstacles to the repeal of the land and building taxes and would be generally difficult for the Prussian finance minister. Therefore the intervention of the Prussian State Ministry; therefore Miquel's strong attack on the bill. Caprivi, however, could not, after all that had gone before, allow his Army Bill to be held up now. Consequently, he was forced to set the secretary of the Reich treasury to work to discover new sources of income in the Reich to cover the cost of the bill. In the meeting of the Prussian State Ministry on the 8th von Kaltenborn was able to announce in answer to the protests of Miquel that, according to information received from the chancellor, the costs entailed in the Army Bill would be met exclusively from Reich income. The minister of finance expressed his satisfaction at this news and the State Ministry, on this condition, voted that the Prussian Bundesrat votes should be cast in favor of the bill.[101]

Opposition in the Army

In addition to the hostility to his Army Bill, implicit or explicit, from Kaiser, Prussian State Ministry, political parties, and public opinion, Caprivi also had to contend with the opposition of some of the army generals. The army, as a matter of tradition, was committed to three-year service. This weight of sentiment in the army goes far to explain the Kaiser's own fondness for and insistence on the longer term. The Kaiser's extreme statements in favor of three years, however, in turn strengthened the army opinion and, in particular, gave certain ambitious generals, such as the ousted Count von Waldersee, the notion that by bringing the weight of their opposition to bear upon the impressionable mind of the Kaiser they might get rid of Caprivi. This hostility in the army was, however,

[101]Werdermann, *Heeresreform*, pp. 78–79, 118ff. This ministerial battle was carried into the press; cf. Wippermann, 8(II):122–125.

more than a matter of mere intrigue; since it was known to the members of the various parties that the army itself was not behind the bill, this situation in turn further dampened any possible enthusiasm in the Reichstag.[102]

To give time for general debate on Miquel's tax reform, the Landtag was called into session on November 9, the Reichstag not until two weeks later, on the 22nd. Meanwhile, in October, Caprivi entered into full and frank private negotiations over the Army Bill with the leaders of the major parties. The course of these negotiations, however, was overtaken prematurely by public opinion when, in late October, the bill "leaked" out of the secret Bundesrat sessions and appeared verbatim in the *Kölnische Zeitung*. There had been some speculation and discussion on the matter since summer, but now here was something tangible, and all the party papers immediately took it up, attacking it severely from every side.[103]

Bismarck Adds His Voice

To the clamor of the various party mouthpieces was added the familiar rumble of thunder from Friedrichsruh. Prince Bismarck, who had tried to force Verdy's huge plan on the Kaiser in the spring of 1890, now scathingly attacked Caprivi's bill. In an interview with Dr. Hans Blum, leader of the National Liberal Party in Saxony, which was published in full in the *Leipziger Neueste Nachrichten,* Bismarck announced, "Precisely the first requisite for the unconditional acceptance of the military bill is lacking: necessity." Why prepare for a war on two fronts, why not three? Russia would never attack Germany, nor would France without Russia. The battles of the future would not involve millions of men but two to three hundred thousand at the most. The present size of the army was ample for a two-front war. All the anti-German feeling in the Russian press was due to the influence of Poles and Jews. On the other hand two-year service was "extremely risky." Old Kaiser William I, Moltke, and Roon were not tilting at windmills when they had fought two-year service. Bismarck then digressed to relate how at every turn in 1862 it had been he himself who had kept the king from weakening. No, he did not intend to appear in the Reichstag against the bill unless "extremely necessary." He then went on to

[102]Keim, *Erlebtes,* pp. 53–54, 75; Stein, *Es war alles ganz anders,* pp. 203–204; Schneidewin, "Briefe," p. 145; Hohenlohe, *Memoirs,* II, 452; Hellwig, *Stumm,* p. 466. On Waldersee see below, pp. 317ff.
[103]Oncken, *Bennigsen,* II, 577–579; Wippermann, 8(II):125ff.; *Die Nation,* 10:67; Keim, *Erlebtes,* p. 54; *The Times,* October 25, 1892, p. 5, October 26, p. 5, October 27, p. 5, October 28, p. 3.

describe how King William I had wanted to annex part of Saxony, Hanover, and Hesse in 1866. In a later issue of the same paper, he blamed the war scare of 1875 on General von Moltke and his own subordinates at the Foreign Office. In an interview with the professional critic of the government, Maximilian Harden, published in Harden's *Die Zukunft* at the end of October, Bismarck also, after denying it for twenty years, admitted that he had brought about the Franco-Prussian War in 1870 "for the sake of national unity" by editing the Ems dispatch. These statements were later enlarged upon in articles in the *Hamburger Nachrichten*.[104] Especially, the collective Bismarck press, with false rumors and innuendos, kept up a running fire upon the position of Caprivi.

One day it is whispered that the King of Saxony and other German Princes are at issue with the Emperor, and the story travels so widely and so quickly that the official organ of the Saxon Government is compelled to honour it with a formal contradiction. The next time it is a disparaging remark of the Emperor's which some one claims to have overheard, and the eavesdropper hastens to assure the world that the Emperor has only given a reluctant assent to the Army Bill and has merely told his Chancellor to see how far he can manage to get along with it. The idle tale falls upon such ready ears that the *Reichsanzeiger* has to be set in motion, and its *démenti* reinforced by the assurance of the *North German Gazette* that his Majesty has, on the contrary, repeatedly declared himself convinced of the necessity for the reforms . . . The air is full of such rumors, and though they may not be dangerous in themselves, like the buzzing of mosquitoes, they create and maintain a nervous irritation and apprehension which react injuriously upon the public mind.[105]

The whole atmosphere was one of confusion and dissatisfaction. Caprivi, complained *Die Nation*, had not succeeded in establishing "unified principles of government." Especially since the School Bill crisis

it has remained hidden from the public who really is man and who is master. One tinkers with this part of the state machinery, the other with that part. While an alleged deficit of 85 million Marks is envisaged in Prussia, a reform of the army is prepared in the Reich which will increase the tax burden of the nation by 65 million marks yearly. While the Prussian finance minister endeavors to release the landlords from their taxes, the secretary of the Reich treasury travels about the country to

[104]*Schulthess* (1892), pp. 140–149; Wippermann, 8(II):63–74; *The Times,* November 4, 1892, p. 5; Hofmann, *Bismarck,* II, 162ff. For a contrary opinion of Bismarck's in May 1892 see Hellwig, *Stumm,* p. 432.

[105]*The Times,* November 21, 1892, p. 5.

procure the consent of the governments of the southern states to an increase in consumption taxes on tobacco and beer.[106]

It was hardly a favorable time for the introduction of such a controversial measure. "Both Diet and nation," observed *The Times* of London, "seem for the time thoroughly out of hand." The Kaiser himself had been willing to postpone the army increases. In the midst of such a welter of oppositional forces why did Caprivi insist upon his army reform now? One may best discover the answer from his speech of November 23.[107]

[106]*Die Nation,* 10:19.
[107]*The Times,* November 24, 1892, p. 9.

Chapter VII

THE FIGHT FOR THE ARMY BILL

> One person sees the evil here, another sees it there: this one in
> the Jews, that one in the priests, this one in capital, that one in
> labor, this one in the lack of authority, that one in the lack of
> freedom — only one thing is certain: things are in a bad way. No
> one has the slightest word of praise left over for our era. It is bad,
> thoroughly bad, and is getting constantly worse. We live in an evil
> time.
>
> *Preussische Jahrbücher,* January 1893

1

CAPRIVI'S SPEECH TO THE REICHSTAG

THE Federated Governments, General von Caprivi declared
to the Reichstag on November 23, were fully aware of the gravity
of the responsibility which they had taken upon themselves in presenting this army bill. These were serious and difficult times, but the
matter simply could not be further postponed.[1]

Every year that we lose is irretrievably lost; every year in which we
hesitate to increase the number of recruits in order to spare the older
age groups cannot be made good. The Federated Governments are,
therefore, of the opinion that even if it is difficult for them to introduce
this bill it would be irresponsible now *not* to introduce it.

This was not a matter of minor details to be put over at some strategically favorable moment, but a proposal of the necessity for which
the nation could become convinced only through a full compre-
hension of the true situation.

I cannot come forward with the slogan of "War in Sight" — there is
no question of that; I shall not rattle the saber ("Bravo!"), nor indulge in

---

[1]For the following speech see *Sten. Ber.* (1892–1893), I, 7–21; Arndt, *Reden,* pp.
246–270. For press comment see Wippermann, 8(II):131–133.

pessimistic language, but as far as lies within my knowledge and conscience I shall lay before you the simple truth ("Bravo!").

The German government maintains normal and friendly relations with all other governments . . . As was declared to you once before from this same place, Germany is a satiated nation. . . . Nothing could have been more appropriate than the words of His Majesty the Kaiser in taking possession of Heligoland, that this was the last piece of German soil which we desired . . . We have no further desires, no further demands.

There had been much talk of avoiding all this increasing burden of armament by waging a preventive war which would ensure peace for twenty or thirty years. The German people would never accept such a plan. For what end?

We have no desire to annex a single square kilometer of French territory; we would be making trouble for ourselves by incorporating non-Germans into the German Reich. And even in the acquisition of French milliards we have in many respects found certain flaws (laughter). And, finally, if someone tells me to take French colonies I should answer that we have quite enough of our own (laughter) . . .

France was much better prepared and armed than in 1870. In detail the general described the new French defenses and the difficulties in breaching them. Such a war would be very costly, and it would certainly not produce peace. Its conclusion would be followed merely by a new arms race. In a weakened condition, Germany might then be in danger of attack from other quarters. They would never wage such a preventive war.

To further establish the peaceful intentions of the Reich government, past and present, Caprivi then devoted some minutes to contradicting the press reports that Bismarck had provoked the war in 1870 by falsifying the Ems dispatch.

I shall be able to prove to you on documentary evidence, first, that it was not Germany which gave the provocation; secondly, that Prince Bismarck did not falsify any dispatch; and thirdly, that it is not true, as some newspapers maintain, because they cannot make head nor tail of the affair, that old Kaiser William was too weak or that in his dealings with the French representatives he failed to take the tone consonant with the righteousness of the German cause.

Caprivi then read William I's original dispatch, Bismarck's version, the report of the ambassador in London quoting Gladstone in Germany's favor and a similar report from the Russian foreign minister, Prince Gorchakov. It was clear, declared the chancellor, that there had been no provocation, no falsification, on the part of Germany or of Bismarck. With enthusiastic applause and bravos the deputies agreed. This, as far as the Reichstag was concerned, was the most interesting and successful part of the speech. The rest was already an old story.[2]

The true story of the Ems dispatch, the general went on, showed not only that Germany's purposes, as with this bill, were purely defensive in character, but also the real danger of provocation on the part of France. "What happened once can happen again." The spirit of revenge developed in France since 1870 had been associated particularly with the "lost provinces" of Alsace-Lorraine, but would exist if these provinces had not been lost. With increasing armaments and self-confidence France had cast about for alliances.

That the predominant motivation, when France at the present day contracts an alliance, can only be to undertake a revision of the map of Europe there can be no doubt. That such an alliance concluded by France, therefore, would not have the defensive character of the alliances we have concluded there can also be no doubt.

The situation on the eastern frontier was different. Prussia and Russia had been friendly from time immemorial. Neither desired anything of the other.

The present emperor of Russia is, owing to his magnanimous character and peaceful disposition, one of the strongest bulwarks for the maintenance of peace in Europe ("Bravo!"). I am happy to be able to state on high authority that the emperor of Russia knows how to appreciate the loyal and peace-loving policy which I am pursuing at the command of His Majesty the Kaiser ("Bravo!").

It must be recognized, however, that there was also among the Russian people an anti-German feeling, the origins of which were difficult to discover, a hatred dating from the Crimean War and increased by Germany's subsequent military and diplomatic successes. There was no sign of any diminution of this feeling.

Russian policy is accustomed to deal in terms of great spans of time. The Russian military administration also looks farther ahead than others, and they are periodically but surely and purposefully proceeding in their preparations. They are not yet perfectly organized, not practically ready, . . . but what has been done suffices to arouse our serious attention. It would not be correct to conclude from this that war is looming in the

[2]Cf. *The Times*, November 24, 1892, p. 5; Thimme, "Bismarck und Kardorff," pt. II, p. 30. On Bismarck and the 1870 crisis see A. J. P. Taylor, *The Struggle for Mastery in Europe, 1848–1918* (Oxford, 1954), pp. 202–206.

near future, but it proves clearly enough that Russia believes that the next war will be waged, not on her southern but on her western frontier.

War with Russia was not imminent but must be reckoned with. The tsar could find himself in a situation which would force him into it.

The accusation has been brought against the present government that we have cut the wire connecting us with Russia.[3] This I quite emphatically deny ("Hear! hear!"). We have tried very hard to maintain this wire; only we do not want it to short-circuit the line connecting us with Austria-Hungary and Italy ("Very good!").

A French paper published an article some time ago entitled "Flirt ou Alliance," "Flirtation or Matrimony?"[4] This paper did not know, itself, in what light France should consider her relationship with Russia. If the French themselves do not know, then we may believe that the tie is not yet very strong . . . But in any case, two lovers are playing with fire; from time to time they light bonfires; the sparks fly over our house, and we have every reason to keep our fire-fighting apparatus in good condition, and, if it does not appear adequate, to supplement it . . . We do not wish to attack either France or Russia; we do want, however, in case these two nations should become more closely allied, to make use of every means at our disposal to be able to repel a possible attack. We are faced with the necessity of regarding a future war as a war on two fronts, not, indeed, as an exception, but as a probability.

To shrink before the idea of fighting such a two-front war, however, the general declared, would be sheer defeatism and unworthy of the Germany of 1813. Germany's whole position as a Power depended upon her military strength. She could thus best maintain her alliances if she herself remained strong. She, among the Powers of the Triple Alliance, would have to bear the brunt of the next conflict.

As the loser of the contest in 1871, France had made the maximum effort to rearm herself, while to maintain her military position the victor, Germany, had been satisfied with the minimum effort. She had maintained her armament, but in a halting, hesitant, piecemeal way. The resulting system was uncoördinated and full of inconsistencies, conflicts, and injustices. Older age groups had been drawn upon while younger ones were spared. On a comparatively small yearly basis the pyramid had been built increasingly higher.

[3]See above, pp. 199–200.
[4]*Le Figaro*, July 14, 1892: "We have been courting for the last year; let us raise the question of a marriage contract resolutely, as befits families who respect each other." Langer, *Franco-Russian Alliance*, pp. 255–256.

It was necessary to broaden the base of the pyramid, to reduce its height. What was envisaged was not a mere addition to the numbers of the army but a complete reorganization, which must be carried out now while there was yet time. In personnel, generals, officers, and men, the German army was still the best in the world.

But where we are lacking is in strength and organization. We are too weak, too old, and too slack in our organization for war, and we want to strengthen, rejuvenate, and improve.

The previous year he had scoffed at the rage for mass armies, but he had not meant to imply that numbers were of no importance, particularly for Germany with her troops divided between two fronts. And if they had too many troops for mobilization then they could leave the older classes at home, not call them all up together, as at present. He had nothing against the Landwehr. There was, however, no doubt that men over 30 were more encumbered with physical and moral responsibilities. Figures for the year 1885 showed that only 7.4 per cent of the 20–25 age group were married, while in the 25–30 group it was 47.8 per cent, and of the 30–35 age group, 70 per cent. This last was the age group of the reserve troops. He recalled that in the last war the first regiment of Landwehr Guards had 4,000 children for its 3,000 men. The purpose of this bill was to make possible a lessening of the military burden on the older group and to put a greater burden on the younger men.

Since a wartime force of some 4,400,000 men was envisaged, resting upon a peacetime force of 500,000, seven eighths of the total would be mobilized only in wartime. This huge swelling of the ranks could lead to severe disorganization unless some special cadres were planned which could be expanded upon mobilization. This the bill proposed to do by adding a special fourth reserve training batallion to each infantry regiment.

The general then went on to defend the introduction of two-year service, quoting General von Roon in its favor, provided, however, that sufficient "concessions" — in added numbers of troops — were granted in return. The *quinquennat,* he said, would give an adequate period for the working out of the reform plan. All these proposals came as close as possible to Windthorst's 1890 resolutions.[5] The cost had been reduced to the bare minimum, from Verdy's 117 million to 57 million.

The bill naturally is unwelcome. Nor have we been happy in introducing it. But, gentlemen, war is even more unwelcome, and a defeat

[5]See above, pp. 81–82.

would be the most unwelcome . . . The time is past when German scholars and writers could sit at home and quietly continue their work as if nothing were happening while the cannons thundered at Jena and Auerstädt. If we went through that experience now it would break our spirit, and I maintain that German science and German art would go into decline with our defeat . . . We must recognize clearly that it is a fight for existence that we must engage in — a fight for existence, politically, materially, culturally . . .

Our first duty is to God. Each nation has a place to take in world civilization. The loss of Germany could not be made up by any other nation. Unlike individuals, states are not required to sacrifice themselves for others; their first duty is to maintain themselves ("Bravo!" on the right).

Only if a state maintains itself can it remain God's instrument ("Bravo!" on the right).

We have the further duty to maintain Germany for the sake of those generations of men who have created Germany ("Bravo!" on the right), not least for those many thousands who shed their blood for the creation of Germany ("Bravo!" on the right)!

Shall it one day be said that those shed their blood for Germany and these will not give their money ("Very good!" on the right, protests on the left)? . . .

I beseech you, gentlemen, to join together with the Federated Governments to examine this bill without prejudice, to provide the nation with what it requires so that, if called once again to arms, it may go forward with the same quiet confidence displayed by the people in 1870 — with the confidence that, whatever difficult struggles might be necessary, nevertheless an ultimate victory was assured, a confidence that at home and in the field echoed itself in the words: "Dear Fatherland, no fear be thine" ("Bravo!" on the right)![6]

[6]The quotation is a line from the chorus of "Die Wacht am Rhein" (Max Schneckenburger [1840] and Carl Wilhelm [1854]). The first verse is given as follows in Max Spicker, *Songs of Germany* (New York, 1904), pp. 38–39:

> Es braust ein Ruf wie Donnerhall,
> Wie Schwertgeklirr und Wogenprall,
> Zum Rhein, zum Rhein, zum deutschen Rhein!
> Wer will des Stromes Hüter sein!

> //:Lieb Vaterland, magst ruhig sein,://
> //:Fest steht und treu die Wacht am Rhein!://

> Now thunders forth the call once more,
> Like clash of arms and waters' roar,
> The Rhine! The Rhine! The German Rhine!
> Ho! who will help to guard that line?

> //:Dear land of ours, no fear be thine!://
> //:Staunch stands and true the watch on the Rhine!://

The key sentences of this speech seem to be those referring to Germany's changed position in Europe, the danger of the Franco-Russian *rapprochement,* and the inevitability of the two-front war. Caprivi's purpose, like Bismarck's, was to maintain peace, the *status quo.* With the Franco-Russian *rapprochement* Germany's weakened diplomatic preponderance must be buttressed by a more effective effort to maintain a relative military preponderance. In 1890 the eventual reform could be postponed; by 1892 — after Cronstadt — it was dangerous to postpone it further. It would take 20 years — until 1913 — for the reform to have its full effect on the total reserve strength. "He would indeed be a bold prophet," commented *The Times,* "who should pretend to guarantee peace for a third of the intervening time." [7] This was undoubtedly the reasoning that motivated the chancellor to defy all the opposition of Kaiser, court, army, parties, public opinion, and Bismarck in bringing in his bill at such an inopportune time. As a general he could be expected to put full weight upon military necessities. And, although this new enlargement of German military power would merely further accelerate the European armaments race, the general, in this period of intense nationalistic competition, was not alone in seeking peace and security in armaments. At the end of October he had written his friend and admirer, Professor Schneidewin:

I enter upon the new and difficult struggle lying before me with the conviction that the demand is justified and necessary. I fully realize the greatness and heaviness of the sacrifice required of my fellow citizens, but I am just as convinced that we must bear the consequences of our history, and that it is our duty to fulfill our God-given tasks as long as we are able. In my opinion it is not only a question of our political and military power; but everything of value to us that is contained in the word "German" is at stake if we have become too satisfied or too feeble to make further sacrifices. In the fate of this bill may lie the decision over the future of Germany.[8]

2

COMPROMISE OR DISSOLUTION?

The Reichstag debate on the budget which began on November 30 brought out the first speeches on the Army Bill, which were con-

---

[7]*The Times,* November 24, 1892, p. 9.

[8]Schneidewin, "Briefe," p. 137. Cf. the statement of the *Norddeutsche Allgemeine Zeitung,* January 28, 1893, Wippermann, 9(I):113.

tinued with the first reading, from December 10 to 14. Eugen Richter led the opposition with a speech on November 30, brilliant, witty, sarcastic, in which he effectively compared Caprivi's speech in November 1891 [9] with that of November 1892. It was difficult to believe that this was the same chancellor who had then made light of large masses of troops, of Russian troop movements, and had spoken of the "uneasiness bacillus." Caprivi II was now unsaying everything that Caprivi I had so solemnly preached only twelve months before. But meanwhile nothing striking had occurred. The chancellor spoke at length of the strength of French armaments but said nothing of those of Germany. If his statements concerning Germany's weakness were true, then they were an open invitation for France and Russia to attack while Germany was "still the weak, defenseless country Count von Caprivi makes her out to be." But France and Russia would do no such thing; they knew only too well "with what sauce military bills are served up, to build upon the chancellor's lamentations." Germany, said Richter, was quite strong enough to take care of herself. As for her lost military supremacy on the continent, "I protest that we never claimed such a supremacy. It is foreign to the ideas of the German people." Under Richter's attack Caprivi, controlling his temper with difficulty, answered that his remarks had been distorted and quoted out of context. The Radical party, he pointed out, had a long record of voting against military defense measures.[10]

Two days later the growing split within the Radicals was clearly evidenced when Deputy Rickert protested that when Caprivi spoke of a negative record he should not include those Radicals who were former National Liberals, but only the old Progressives. For his part he was sure Caprivi would never treat the Reichstag as Bismarck had in 1887. Chancellor Caprivi thanked Rickert for his dispassionate approach and expressed the hope that he might be convinced of the validity of the government's arguments in the committee sessions. At this point Richter shouted, "Other people have a say in that too!" [11]

In general, both Center and Radicals were willing to grant enough funds to provide for the introduction of two-year service, but none for any increase in numerical strength. On November 30, Richter declared, "In recent years the huge demands for military purposes have already considerably threatened Germany's taxable

[9] See above, pp. 135–138.

[10] Cf. *The Times,* December 1, 1892, p. 5; *Sten. Ber.* (1892–1893), I, 49–63; *Schulthess* (1892), pp. 187–190.

[11] *Sten. Ber.* (1892–1893), I, 109; *Schulthess* (1892), p. 191.

capital wealth. If this continues, the defensive strength of the country, in spite of a greater number of soldiers, will ultimately not be strengthened but weakened because of the sapping of its economic strength. To hinder this process I consider an imperative and a patriotic duty." The Centrist Dr. Lieber was even more explicit. "The question," he declared on December 14, "is simply can we, ought we, may we ruin ourselves now in peacetime in order to prepare for a possible war? We can put the question in no other way! And if the question is put in this manner, we can make no other answer: we may not ruin ourselves now in peacetime; that would not help us in time of war." The Conservatives were noncommittal, while von Kardorff intimated that the agrarians would not vote for the Army Bill unless the government made special concessions to agriculture.[12] On the other hand, the Social Democratic leader, Liebknecht, in a speech on December 1, attacked in succession the selfishness of the agrarian Conservatives, the greed of the industrial National Liberals and Radicals, the immorality of Bismarck, who not only provoked the war in 1870 but had admitted as much, and the militarism of the new regime, different only in name from that of the old. "It is the spirit of militarism which has divided us into two peoples — one with arms and one without arms." The Social Democrats would not vote a penny to support the present capitalistic, militaristic system. Germany, maintained the Social Democrats, could best be defended by a popular, democratic militia. If Germany took the initiative in appealing for an end to standing armies and to the armaments race, other nations would surely pay her heed.[13]

The prospects for a majority for the bill seemed extremely dim. More and more it appeared that a dissolution of the Reichstag would be necessary; while the stronger the parliamentary opposition appeared, the more impatient the Kaiser, in the midst of his military entourage, became. Had not Bismarck himself warned him that a conflict with the Reichstag was inevitable and that the sooner it came the less bloodshed there would be? He had, he told Phili Eulenburg in January, met all parties in a friendly spirit and by the extension of social legislation shown his sincere desire to help things on, and all the thanks he got was curt rejection, enmity, and intentional misunderstanding. Phili managed to calm him down, but wrote to Caprivi, "How can I be certain that the idea of a conflict will not again be put into his head by someone or other? The Kaiser

[12]Cf. Huene and Richter, *Sten. Ber.* (1892–1893), I, 228–233; also *ibid.* (1892–1893), I, 60, 330, 67–78; *Die Nation*, X, 176; Kardorff, *Kardorff*, p. 272.

[13]*Sten. Ber.* (1892–1893), I, 75–84; *The Times,* December 2, 1892, p. 5.

is so extremely impulsive! The aides-de-camp who are now in
H. M.'s suite will not be on *our* side . . . I confess I don't know
what can be done about that. . . ." As early as November 24 Kardorff had written gleefully to his wife, "If Caprivi decides to make a
deal then the Kaiser will let him go, and if he doesn't do it he can't
possibly get a majority." Kardorff's own solution, expressed in a
letter to Stumm on December 17, was to make Botho Eulenburg
chancellor and reduce the Army Bill to 35 or 40 million Marks.
Meanwhile, he wrote gloomily, France was growing so strong that
she might attack any day, "and perhaps that would be the final
means of putting an end to our political fragmentation." [14]

Meanwhile, in a by-election in the rural Brandenburg district of
Arnswalde-Friedeberg, the anti-Semitic Rector Ahlwardt, on December 5, was elected overwhelmingly to the Reichstag, having
secured the support of most of the Conservatives of the district, including the government officials. On December 9 Ahlwardt was sen-
tenced for libel to five months in prison for his pamphlet, *Jewish
Rifles.* After much protest in the liberal press, Count Eulenburg sent
the Arnswalde district president a stiff reprimand for his active support of Ahlwardt in the election.[15]

On December 8 the German Conservative party met at the Tivoli
Hall in Berlin to consider a new program. There, amid cheers and
applause for Ahlwardt, an uncompromisingly anti-Semitic plank
was adopted into the platform. A contrary resolution in favor of
the previous program, signed and sent in by the former moderate
leader, von Helldorff, and twenty others, was received with groans
and hisses. On December 12 the most interesting session of the Army
Bill debate was provided, not by any development directly connected with the bill itself, but by two interpellations on seemingly
extraneous matters — one on the rifles sold to the army by Loewe
and Co. and one on the line being pursued by the German representatives at the Brussels monetary conference. In replying to the
second of these interpellations Chancellor von Caprivi explained
that he was giving the matter this attention because

I see clearly how throughout the country efforts are being made to
harness bimetallism and anti-Semitism to the same wagon ("Oho!" great
disturbance on the right. "Hear! hear!") and to drive it on by cracking

---

[14]Cf. *Die Nation,* X, 97–98; Haller, *Eulenburg,* I, 153, 155–156; Kardorff,
Kardorff, pp. 273–274; Thimme, "Bismarck und Kardorff," pt. II, p. 30; Hellwig,
Stumm, pp. 461–462.

[15]*Schulthess* (1892), pp. 191, 194; *The Times,* December 6, 1892, p. 5, December
8, p. 5. On anti-Semitism, see also above, p. 218, and below, pp. 250–251.

the whip of popular agitation . . . Events in recent weeks which have been among the most depressing that I, as a patriot, have ever experienced ("Very true!" on the left), seem to me to make it necessary for the Reich government, not to conceal its opinion, but to state its position on these things ("Bravo!").

I can perhaps comprehend that a person may be anti-Semitic; I can perhaps understand that a person may be bimetallist; I can also comprehend that a person may be both together. But when anti-Semitism or bimetallism is directed and manipulated in a demagogical way, then it is impossible for the Reich government not to set itself against it, and I cannot understand how patriotic men can go along with it ("Hear! hear! Very good!").

This exchange, which enraged the Conservatives, especially endeared Caprivi to the Radicals. His remarks, said *Die Nation*, had hit the bull's-eye.

The way in which he expressed himself had a dramatic interest. . . . The disinclination to go into the details of the incidents intensified into an impossibility. He could not utter a certain name; he could not describe fully the events which he had in mind and which were known to everyone. In all this there was nothing artificial; it was the instinctive recoil which an honorable man feels when he unexpectedly comes up against something evil.[16]

All these developments did not seem to discourage Caprivi. This Army Bill was largely his, and he defended it energetically and with determined optimism. "An absolute confidence in the justice of his cause was necessary to take on such a tremendous task in the midst of such a confusion of adverse circumstances, and only a real man of extraordinary will power and with the courage of his convictions could carry it through. That was Caprivi." [17] It was Caprivi who, to the complete exclusion of War Minister von Kaltenborn, defended the bill in the debates in the Reichstag; it was Caprivi who appeared before the committee; it was Caprivi who, throughout the winter, carried on endless negotiations with party leaders to try to find some way out of the impasse.

To one who was in a position to observe him closely during those ten months it was wonderful with what tirelessness he tried to get a hearing for his practical arguments. If he did not lose courage, then he was called an optimist, if he tried to win over the liberal opposition . . . then he appeared to many as too conciliatory; if he could not agree to a com-

[16]*Sten. Ber.* (1892–1893), I, 258, 273; Arndt, *Reden*, pp. 287–293; *Die Nation*, X, 175; Wippermann, 8(II):79–87. On bimetallism and the agrarians, see below, pp. 289–290.

[17]Hammann, *Der Neue Kurs*, pp. 44–45.

promise proposal, his attitude was called "obstinate and unyielding." Nothing discouraged him, each disappointment made him more tenacious in his persistence.[18]

The committee for the Army Bill held its first session on January 12, 1893. In this session, General von Caprivi explained the political and military situation of Germany with the utmost frankness. France, following the Panama scandals, was in a dangerous state of ferment. Russia was a growing power and soon to become the most powerful military state on the continent. Chiefly for military reasons Russia had historically pushed toward the Dardanelles. The German alliance with Austria, therefore, had produced the conviction in certain Russian circles that the road to Constantinople no longer lay through Vienna but through the Brandenburg Gate. The guiding principle of Germany's foreign policy was and must remain the preservation of Austria-Hungary as a great European power. They could not sacrifice Austria to gain temporary concessions from Russia. Caprivi did not know what engagements existed between France and Russia but declared that it was highly probable that military agreements for operations by land and water had been made. Germany must, therefore, count on a two-front war. Since she was the strongest of the Triple Alliance powers she also would bear the brunt of the main enemy attack. For political reasons the war must be short and the victory quick and lasting. The long eastern frontier could not easily be defended. For these reasons Germany must prepare an offensive strategy which, to be successful, demanded a numerical preponderance. In actual fact, France and Russia together had more trained soldiers than the three Triple Alliance powers, and their reserves were younger and better trained. Although the general requested that his remarks be kept confidential, a fairly complete report of his words immediately appeared in the *National Zeitung* and created a tremendous sensation throughout the foreign press. They had very little effect, however, on the position of the parties in the military committee.[19]

[18]Hammann, *Der Neue Kurs*, p. 54; cf. Keim, *Erlebtes*, pp. 53–54; Lerchenfeld, *Denkwürdigkeiten*, p. 373.

[19]*Schulthess* (1893), pp. 2–3; *The Times*, January 20, 1893, wkly. ed., pp. 1, 41; Thimme, "Bismarck und Kardorff," pt. II, p. 32; *Die Nation*, X, 251; *DDF*, 1 ser., X, 167. In 1892 the German army had an over-all peace strength of 511,600 men, the French army 570,600 men, and the Russian army 843,000 men. The French chief of staff, the same year, estimated that in wartime the Triple Alliance could muster a total of 2,810,000 men, France and Russia 3,150,000. The Military Convention agreed upon by the French and Russian General Staffs in August 1892 provided that France would mobilize a total of 1,300,000 men on Germany's western front and Russia 700,000 to 800,000 men on Germany's eastern front. *Statesman's Yearbook* for 1892; Langer, *Franco-Russian Alliance*, pp. 237, 260.

The military committee dragged out its examination of the bill from January into March, through some twenty-eight sessions of futile debate. As the lines became more clearly drawn, the deadlock appeared the more unbreakable and the more disastrous. The opposition of the Conservatives, to be sure, was soon overcome. A letter to the Kaiser from Phili Eulenburg in late December suggested that he make it absolutely clear in his New Year's speech to the commanding generals that he stood behind Caprivi's bill. "The bill may be *defeated* if these gentlemen cherish the slightest doubt of Your Majesty's complete identification with the Reich Chancellor's declared standpoint." The result was that in his speech the Kaiser not only identified himself with the bill and instructed the generals not to oppose it, but declared that he would "send the half-crazy Reichstag to the devil" if it did not pass the bill. This declaration, although so exaggerated as to embarrass Caprivi, nevertheless showed the Conservatives how the land lay and gave them an opportunity to rally gracefully to the side of the monarchy. On the Kaiser's birthday, the 27th, four generals, including Waldersee, spoke in favor of the Army Bill in their toasts to the Kaiser.[20]

Caprivi's own efforts had also begun gradually to take effect; his arguments, his facts and figures in his Reichstag speech and in the many committee sessions were hard to refute. He had also begun at last, reluctantly, to try to reach the public through the press. Very soon after Bismarck's departure the *Norddeutsche Allgemeine Zeitung*, in whose offices the court *Reichsanzeiger* was also published, left his support and took up its old semiofficial position with the new government. For a long time Caprivi limited relations with the press to the *Norddeutsche* and the *Reichsanzeiger*. At the very beginning he had stopped the payment of subsidies from the notorious Guelf fund, and, after long and delicate negotiations, had finally, in March 1892, gotten rid of this fund entirely by restoring it to the Duke of Cumberland.[21] It was all the easier, therefore, for Bismarck,

[20] For the committee sessions see Wippermann, 9(I):45–61. *DDF*, 1 ser., X, 265; Haller, *Eulenburg*, I, 154–155; *Schulthess* (1892), p. 1; Waldersee, *Denkwürdigkeiten*, II, 274; *Die Nation*, X, 219–220, 283. The Kaiser at this time also told the Austrian ambassador that the new Reichstag building would make a good embassy for him; he was going to get rid of the Reichstag. Langer, *Franco-Russian Alliance*, p. 300, note.

[21] Cf. Wedel, *Zwischen Kaiser und Kanzler*, pp. 78, 79, 124; *DDF*, 1 ser., VIII, 25; Keim, *Erlebtes*, p. 50; *Schulthess* (1892), pp. 73–75, 83; Hale, *Publicity and Diplomacy*, p. 66. Reich Chancellor Prince Chlodwig zu Hohenlohe-Schillingsfürst wrote to his son Alexander in 1896, in connection with Baron Marschall and the Lützow case, "That Caprivi gave up the Guelf Fund is in itself sufficient proof of the political ineptitude of my worthy predecessor." *Denkwürdigkeiten des Reichskanzlerzeit*, p. 269.

in retirement, to construct a powerful press network to support his campaign against the Kaiser and the New Course. In no time the Foreign Office had collected twenty-five volumes of newspaper clippings charting the success of the old master's efforts. This press campaign of Bismarck's forced the general to reconsider the relation of government and press. At the height of the reconciliation campaign in the spring of 1892 he called young Julius von Eckardt from the Marseilles consulate and gave him the run of the Foreign Office files to prepare a defense, but then the campaign died down and Caprivi called it off. In addition, through Holstein's friendship with Dr. Fischer, the *Kölnische Zeitung* had been used occasionally to plant government-inspired articles.[22]

The questionable fate of the Army Bill obviously demanded further efforts. In the fall of 1892 articles were placed in the military journals; these, however, had a rather negative effect, due to the fact that in explaining the reform they attacked the popular Landwehr. Then Caprivi summoned to the Chancellery a Major August Keim, who had done some previous military writing, and put him in charge of publicity and information for the bill. It was also at this time that he engaged the services of the journalist Otto Hammann, who assisted Keim on the Army Bill, and who in 1894 became head of a unified press bureau for both foreign and domestic affairs. Major Keim was installed in a room in the upper story of the right wing of the Chancellery, and all journalists and deputies seeking information were sent to him. He also published a series of pamphlets supporting and explaining the army reform. His efforts were especially effective during the subsequent election. In discharging him from his special duty in July 1893, Caprivi recommended him for the Order of the Crown, third class, and declared in his memorandum to the chief of the Military Cabinet, "I do not hesitate to say that *the adoption of the Army Bill would have been put in question without his assistance.*" In addition to the labors of Keim and Hammann a whole series of authorities were lined up to write articles in the bill's defense, Baron von der Goltz-Pasha, General von Boguslawski, General von Leszcynski, General von Kameke, and others.[23]

There were thus many patriotic deputies among the Center and the Radicals who wanted very much to find some way of supporting

[22]Hale, *Publicity and Diplomacy*, pp. 66–67; Eckardt, *Aus den Tagen*, pp. 44–66; Keim, *Erlebtes*, p. 50; Hammann, *Der Neue Kurs*, pp. 61, 73–77; Haller, *Eulenburg*, I, 154–155.
[23]Werdermann, *Heeresreform*, pp. 90–93; Keim, *Erlebtes*, pp. 41–42, 46–47, 49–54, 59, 73; Hale, *Publicity and Diplomacy*, p. 67; Hammann, *Der Neue Kurs*, p. 48; Wippermann, 8(II):129–131, 9(I):56, 107ff.

Music of the Future (Leitmotif from "Das Rheingold").
Kladderadatsch, September 28, 1890

A Mole at Work. *Kladderadatsch*, February 22, 1891

The Trojan Horse. *Kladderadatsch*, July 16, 1893

Laßt euch nicht vexiren!

Don't Be Vexed! *Kladderadatsch*, March 18, 1894

The End of the Struggle, or The Victor. *Kladderadatsch*, November 4, 1894

the government, particularly since it became abundantly clear that if the bill were defeated and the Reichstag dissolved, such a dissolution and new election — fought on an issue of patriotism and at the height of the agrarian reaction — could only weaken their own parties and strengthen the Conservatives. This almost certain prospect of rejection and dissolution had made it that much easier for the Conservatives to swing over to support of the bill. They confidently expected to make the most of agrarianism, bimetallism, and anti-Semitism in the resulting election and hoped that, one way or another, they would in the process get rid of Caprivi, the man of the trade treaties. It was clear enough that, if his bill were finally defeated, Caprivi would not accept a weak substitute, but would resign. With Caprivi out of the way the Conservatives were looking forward to a complete victory over the Reichstag, including an agrarian chancellor and the abolition of universal suffrage.[24]

The situation was very difficult for the Radicals. On the one hand, Caprivi certainly was no liberal; this stiff, elderly Prussian general could never lead the movement to transform the aristocratic, paternalistic Bismarckian Reich into the Radicals' ideal of a liberal, parliamentary democracy. His support of the Prussian School Bill in the spring and his introduction of this huge military measure now certainly could not be taken to indicate a liberal attitude. Was not the fight against militarism also a fight against government by paternalism, by the dictation of an aristocratic, military clique? Was it not a fight for authority and dignity for the Reichstag, a fight for a government responsible to the people, for democracy? Certainly this was the time when the government was weak and on the defensive and when a fight could best be made.[25] On the other hand, might not the general's departure be an opening for something worse? After all, against the rising flood of the reaction, with its special agrarian demands for tariffs and subsidies and bimetallism, its anti-Semitism, and its contempt for liberal principles, who was there to stem the tide but the Radicals and — Caprivi? National Liberals had long since come under Conservative domination and were still held enthralled by the spell-binding voice from Friedrichsruh. They might rise up in liberal wrath in the School Bill fight, but that was partly because they were afraid of being displaced in their favored position of handmaiden to the ruling class; and, besides, the important realities were economic. The Center had its own

[24]Cf. General von Loë to Stumm, Hellwig, *Stumm*, p. 468, Kardorff to Stumm, *ibid.*, p. 461; *Die Nation*, X, 98.
[25]Cf. the report on sentiment in South Germany in *Die Nation*, X, 133.

special interests and could best satisfy these through an alliance, not with the liberals, but with the more clerical Conservatives, as in the School Bill fight and even now in the pending tax reform. And the Social Democrats insisted on talking in terms, not of liberal reform, but of revolution.

In the December 10 issue of *Die Nation*, Theodor Barth published an article entitled "Political Dry Rot." This condition, he wrote, was brought about by "dampness, lack of light, and a certain warmth." It thrived in Germany in the "foul atmosphere of special interest politics, Stöckerism, and phrase-making nationalism" resulting from the Bismarck regime.

Moral and political diseases usually develop slowly and often break out violently just when the first timid attempts are being made to cure them. The administration of Count Caprivi made a start towards such a cure, but the good intentions did not develop into energetic acts. Then came a period of vacillation, of indecision, of misunderstandings, of intrigues, and today we stand in the middle of — a political bog. That Count Caprivi can lead us out of it appears every day less likely. He had a chance, such as few statesmen have had, if he had declared immediate war with liberal measures upon the whole Bismarckian domestic policy. To do this, however, he would first have had to free himself from the prejudice that today's Conservatives belong to the "state-supporting" parties . . . And from the point of view of tactics alone these elements were not necessary to him. The campaign of the new trade treaties showed the complete powerlessness of this party as soon as the government opposed it energetically. And this powerlessness would have regularly repeated itself as often as the Reich chancellor introduced a liberal measure . . . For Count Caprivi can never make enough concessions to enable him to win the confidence of the agrarians. In the eyes of these special-interest politicians he remains always the man of the trade treaties, who is suspected, furthermore, of placing the general welfare above the special interests of a class or a clique . . . In reality, from the beginning Count Caprivi has had real friends only in the liberal camp. Here one knew well enough how to value the difference between the corruption of the Bismarckian regime and the political integrity of the present chancellor; and here one hoped for a gradual development, through a natural opposition to the Bismarck intrigues, of Count Caprivi as the leader of a resolute anti-Bismarckian policy.

This hope, wrote Barth, had largely disappeared. The dry rot, apparently, would continue to grow.[26] On February 4, however, *Die Nation* wrote:

[26]*Die Nation*, X, 158–159; cf. Count Hatzfeldt's letter to Holstein, July 10, 1892, *Holstein Papers, Correspondence*.

[Count Caprivi] is, indeed, conservative, but he is a political gentleman, as his predecessor was not, and as his successor also is not likely to be. Further, the present Reich chancellor is no passionate advocate of special agrarian interests, no colonial visionary, no promoter of anti-Semitism; he is, on the other hand, the representative of a commercial policy which is, at least to a certain degree, in line with moderate liberal opinion. If Count Caprivi resigns things will get worse.[27]

In the face of the growing threat from the right, would it not be catastrophic to force a dissolution and a new election? The reaction was too strong; the forces of liberalism were too weak; the compulsion of patriotism was too great; and the military arguments were too impressive. Should one commit political and national suicide for an ideal? Eugen Richter was ready with an unqualified "yes," but many of the right-wing Radicals were very tired of Richter's dogmatic leadership. Would it not be more practical, more responsible, and more truly progressive to support this honest, enlightened conservative chancellor now in his Army Bill, thus avoiding a dissolution and thereby strengthening his hand against the reaction? Barth and his friends tended basically to agree with Caprivi's own point of view, as expressed to Hammann in February:

The Radicals could now show that they are capable of governing. They probably won't do it. This semiparliamentary system of government has the disadvantage that leaders like Richter can continue always to say no without running the danger of having to take over the government and discrediting themselves in short order.[28]

Government, Radicals, and Center party all wanted desperately to avoid a dissolution, but prolongation of the crisis did not bring them any closer together. In the last sessions of the committee, on March 16 and 17, the National Liberal leader von Bennigsen introduced what he hoped would be a successful compromise, an amendment which cut the government demands approximately in half and gave the change to two-year service a formal constitutional sanction. The Bennigsen amendment, however, was too much for Richter, not enough for Caprivi — it would spoil the reorganization plan — and the Conservatives, who wanted a dissolution, would not agree to a formal sanctioning of two-year service. On March 17 the government bill and the amendments were all voted down by the committee in its final session. Back in the Chancellery Hammann found

[27]*Die Nation*, X, 286.
[28]*Die Nation*, X, 482; Hammann, *Der Neue Kurs*, p. 50.

General von Caprivi pacing up and down the room. "We have bad days ahead of us! — I must save Germany!" [29]

Meanwhile, the agrarian movement had shifted into high gear with the publication in mid-January 1893 of an appeal by a Silesian tenant farmer named Ruprecht:

> We must shout so that the whole nation hears it, we must shout so that it echoes in the parliaments and the ministries — we must shout so that it is heard even at the steps to the throne! But at the same time, so that our shouting is not once more ignored, we must bargain. We must bargain by ceasing, as we have heretofore done unquestioningly, to campaign for the government in our electoral districts; we must refuse all posts of honor, etc., which we are not legally compelled to accept; . . . I am suggesting nothing more nor less than that we join the Social Democrats in a solid front against the government, to show them that we do not wish to be handled so badly in the future and to let them feel our power.[30]

In December and January several thousand miners had struck in the Saar and in the Ruhr. On January 12, 1893, an interpellation of the Social Democrats came up for discussion which demanded, "What measures have been, or are going to be taken by the Federated Governments to counteract the distress which is widely spread throughout the land in consequence of the continued lack of labor, the frequent reduction of wages, and the general depression of trade?" On January 18 four large mass meetings were organized by the Social Democrats in Berlin to demand relief measures. On January 18 and 20 the Saar and Ruhr strikes were successfully broken without government interference. But the Social Democratic interpellation was the spark which set off a large-scale debate on the effects of the depression, involving both Reichstag and Landtag and lasting past the middle of February. Each party defended its own special interests and ideology and called for government assistance in its favor. The Social Democrats spoke for labor: the government had recognized its obligation to care for the working classes in the decrees of February 1890; let it keep its promises! All the other parties, led by Stumm and Eugen Richter, joined solidly together in heaping scorn on the Socialist "New Order," but among themselves they were just as divided. The agrarians demanded high tariffs, bimetallism, and laws tying the agricultural population to

[29]*Die Nation*, X, 483; *Schulthess* (1893), pp. 26–30; Oncken, *Bennigsen*, II, 584–586; Hammann, *Der Neue Kurs*, p. 49.
[30]*Schulthess* (1893), pp. 5–6; Wippermann, 9(I):138ff.

the soil. The Catholic clericals called for a revitalization of handi-
crafts and guilds. The industrialists of the National Liberals and
Free Conservatives, led by Stumm, called for government interference to discipline the strikers and break up the unions. And the
Radicals insisted on no government interference whatever, whether
by control or subsidy, but on the old-fashioned political and economic freedom of the individual.[31]

The later weeks of the debate were dominated by what
amounted to a great agrarian demonstration against the government,
Caprivi personally, and the trade treaty with Russia, then in negotiation. While, at the end of February, Conservative deputies attacked
the trade treaties in Reichstag and Landtag, in one week five different agrarian organizations held meetings in Berlin: the Farmers'
League, the German Peasants' League, the Union of Tax and Economic Reform, the Farmers' Congress, and the Association for International Bimetallism. At all these different meetings the same group
of Conservative agrarians appeared, remarked *Die Nation* tartly,
"and all these leagues, unions, congresses raise only one demand:
it is the duty of the government to pump money out of the pockets
of the rank and file and into the pockets of the big Conservative
landlords." On February 22 a deputation from the East Elbian
Central Agricultural Society presented a long memorandum on the
plight of agriculture to the Kaiser. The height of the demonstration
came with a big parade of "suffering farmers" and, on February 18,
a meeting attended by 4,000 persons, at which was organized the
new and inclusive Farmers' League.[32]

The program of the Farmers' League called, among other things,
for no trade treaty with Russia and for the introduction of a bimetallic monetary standard. One of its first acts was to send a telegram of
allegiance and greeting to the Kaiser. At Chancellor Caprivi's request, however, this telegram remained unanswered. To the chancellor, bred in the loyal conservative tradition of the Prussian office-
holding nobility, this gross agrarian agitation was dangerous and

---

[31]Hellwig, *Stumm*, pp. 494–495; Thimme, "Bismarck und Kardorff," pt. II, pp.
33–34; *The Times*, wkly. ed., January 6, 1893, p. 2, January 20, 1893, p. 45;
Schulthess (1893), pp. 6, 8–9; *Die Nation*, X, 254–255, 271–272, 300–301, 303;
Sten. Ber. (1892–1893), I, 429ff., 706ff., II, 755ff., 808–901, *Anlageband* I, 417;
Landtag (1892–1893), I, 384ff., 457ff., II, 662ff.

[32]*Schulthess* (1893), pp. 9, 10–17; Wippermann, 9(I):141–151; *Sten. Ber.* (1892–
1893), II, 1017–1123; *Landtag* (1892–1893), I, 468, II, 662ff., 765ff., 853ff.; *Die
Nation*, X, 319, 330–331; *The Times*, wkly. ed., February 17, 1893, p. 123, February
24, p. 146. See below, p. 289. On the Farmers' League see Tirrell, *German Agrarian
Politics*, pp. 158ff.

anything but conservative. On February 17 he declared in the Reichstag:

> The Reich government has had to withstand the sharpest attacks, on individual officials as well as upon the Reich chancellor, and it is necessary to inquire where these originate and what their purpose may be . . . For months past such strong indications of mistrust have been expressed and these last few days so collected together and condensed, that I cannot avoid concluding that, perhaps not with all, but certainly with part of the gentlemen who have attacked the government the intent has been to mount a general attack against the government, perhaps to overthrow it (disturbance).

He would prefer that, instead of continual complaints against the government, they would advance some positive and practical proposals for settling the agricultural problem. He could not, declared Count von Caprivi, abolish the world market, which was the cause of the depression of German agriculture.

> Can I compel our working class to work where they do not want to work and not to work where the work appears more pleasant and more profitable? The government has no such right.

The count then delivered a sermon on conservatism.

> I believe that I am a conservative man through and through. One asks what is meant by "conservative" . . . In my opinion conservatism is the manifestation of an over-all philosophy of life. If one proceeds on the assumption that the world is guided according to a definite plan, that what has developed historically possesses by reason of its existence a certain justification which ought to be denied it only if there exist compelling reasons for change, if one believes that for us Germans a Christian-monarchical state is the state which the Conservative party and conservative men have an interest in supporting, then I am a conservative through and through (lively applause on the right).
> I must admit that I am no agrarian — I own no plot of ground, no blade of straw [*kein Ar und keinen Strohalm*], and have no idea how I could possibly become an agrarian. I am well aware that in the conservative movement and with conservative people support of the different lines of business enterprise . . . must occupy a principal place. But it seems to me that it should not occupy a position of such importance that precisely that element in conservatism which is concerned with the preservation of the state is thereby submerged.

Von Kardorff had said that all office holders should be landholders, but he disagreed. It would be better for the chancellor not to be agrarian.

The more our political parties are governed by economic interests so much more must the government try to maintain a clear and unhampered view over a wide field, over the state and the Reich, in order to procure for them their rights . . . Economic interests are always more or less based on self-interest — one says usually enlightened self-interest — while the state demands sacrifices and idealism from its citizens. The more the parties become involved in economic affairs and interests, that much more must it be the duty of the state government to represent the more idealistic interests. We shall protect all property — that is the duty of the government — the agrarian as well as the industrialist and capitalist; we shall do it justice and shall try in every way to see that it continues to be protected. But we are also obligated to take care of the propertyless . . . The agitation which has been provoked in Germany and which is inspired by many forces has, it seems to me, gone far beyond the limits of what is reconcilable with the good of the state ("Hear! hear!" on the left) . . . Spirits have been conjured up which one will perhaps not be able to control . . . [It is not] because I am being attacked that I wish to put a stop to this agitation. There is, gentlemen, no question of that! If I were persuaded that in giving up my office the slightest profit would accrue to Germany, internally and externally, I should not wait an hour before sending His Majesty my resignation.

The weight of the burden which I bear is so heavy that I shall bless the day when I am relieved of it. But I shall not take such a step, I shall remain at the helm, I shall carry out my bounden duty, adhering to the ancient Prussian traditions in which I have been trained. Not for myself, to be sure, but for Kaiser and Reich! . . . Therefore I shall remain. But I most earnestly desire that the representatives of the agrarian interests take counsel with themselves and reflect deeply upon whether the course they are pursuing is compatible with the interests of the state.

It is not a question here of a man — what is one man overboard? — but only of whether the ship can go on its way; it is a question of this Ship of State which flies the German flag (enthusiastic "Bravo!" on the left).[33]

During January and February there were rumors that a new party was to be founded, combining agrarianism, anti-Semitism, and an active colonialism with allegiance to Bismarck. Nothing tangible, however, resulted. It was, indeed, wrote *Die Nation*, a very confused situation:

The bitterest opponents of the Reich chancellor support his military bill and — hope that it will not pass; for therein lies the prospect of the fall of Count Caprivi. On the other side the chancellor's most disinter-

---

[33]*Schulthess* (1893), p. 9; Hellwig, *Stumm*, p. 469; *DDF*, 1 ser., X, 243–244. For the Farmers' League cf. E. v. Oldenburg-Januschau, *Erinnerungen* (Leipzig, 1936), pp. 36–40, 58. *Sten. Ber.* (1892–1893), II, 1114–1116; Arndt, *Reden*, pp. 303–309.

ested friends do not find themselves in a position to go beyond a definite limit in the military question, although they know that this reserve may under the circumstances result in a dissolution of the Reichstag followed by the resignation of the chancellor.[34]

Hard upon the agrarian outburst came a new anti-Semitic demonstration, when, on March 20–21, Rector Ahlwardt entered the Reichstag for the first time and denounced the "Jewish conspiracy" from the tribune. All kinds of corruption had occurred in the setting up of the Reich invalidity insurance fund:

I have documents signed by gentlemen now sitting here and by one gentleman who still holds a high position in the government which prove that among other things the worst kind of deals have actually been perpetrated (great disturbance on all sides of the house; shout: "Name names!"). It is impossible to start a long debate now so close to adjournment. But the name of the present Prussian finance minister is among them (great disturbance) . . . You will see that the German people have been cheated out of hundreds of millions! Here on all sides of this house friends of Judaism are sitting who are betraying their own people (laughter and great commotion; shout: "Shut up! Down from the tribune!")!

To its credit the Reichstag, in 1893, did not cringe or remain fearfully silent before the crudity of these accusations. All sides of the house, including even the Conservatives, agreed with Eugen Richter's declaration that if they did not compel Ahlwardt at once to substantiate these charges, the financial administration would be placed in the same jeopardy before the public as had already been the case with the army and its rifles. On the following day Ahlwardt appeared in the Reichstag with a bundle of documents which were only part, he said, of a collection in his possession weighing over 200 pounds. On the motion of Count Ballestrem the session was forthwith adjourned one hour while the Senioren-Konvent examined the documents on the spot. At the end of the hour Count Ballestrem reported to the Reichstag that not the slightest evidence of irregularities had been found. During the debate even the Conservatives had not cared to defend their protégé. Rather, by carefully differen-

[34]*The Times*, wkly. ed., December 30, 1892, p. 3, February 24, 1893, pp. 146, 155; *Die Nation*, X, 236–237, 331; L. Maenner, *Prinz H. zu Schoenaich-Carolath* (Stuttgart, 1931), p. 63; Waldersee, *Denkwürdigkeiten*, II, 265, 285. The January *Preussische Jahrbücher* made an interesting attempt to postulate possible cabinet combinations and coalitions for the Reichstag as it would be under a parliamentary system and arrived at the conclusion that a stable majority was impossible (71:190–191). The situation, it declared in February, would have been much more favorable if Caprivi had not been defeated in the School Bill affair the previous year (71:378ff).

tiating between anti-Semitism as a movement and Ahlwardt as a person, Deputy Stöcker sought to salvage as much as possible from the proceedings. When, on April 25, Ahlwardt repeated his accusations against a long list of personages, including Miquel, Bennigsen, and Rickert, the Reichstag appointed a special committee to investigate the charges, which reported back the following week that they were absolutely without foundation. This report was accepted by a unanimous vote. Ahlwardt, by this time, had become somewhat of an embarrassment to the anti-Semites.[35]

The rejection of the Army Bill by the committee on March 17 was followed by further delay. The report of the committee did not appear until April 24. During the ensuing time, although he did not believe a dissolution could be avoided, Caprivi made extreme final efforts to reach a compromise, especially with the Center. Both the Kaiser and Caprivi had expected with some confidence that the aristocratic element would, in the nature of things, carry the day in the Center party. Baron von Huene was also a personal friend of Caprivi's, having served with the general on the staff of the Tenth Army Corps in 1870. The Silesian aristocrats, indeed, did all that they could to influence the party in favor of the bill, including Cardinal Kopp of Breslau, who was hoping for a repeal of the anti-Jesuit law. Dr. Lieber, however, refused to be persuaded and supported himself, ironically enough, on a rigid interpretation of the resolutions by which the aged Windthorst had rescued the "little army bill" in 1890.[36] At the end of April the Kaiser and the Kaiserin attended the celebration in Rome of the silver wedding anniversary of the king and queen of Italy. During his stay there the Kaiser paid a courtesy call on Pope Leo XIII. He also found occasion to request Cardinal Ledochowski, who had suffered in the Kulturkampf, "to forget the past." Subsequently, mild pressure was exerted from Rome for some compromise between the Catholic party and the government. But German Catholics were none too pleased over the recent pro-French attitude of the Vatican, and the pressure from the agrarian movement among the Bavarian peasants on the one side and the challenge of the Social Democratic campaign against "militarism" in the cities on the other was too strong; Lieber would not be moved. In a speech in Bavaria he declared: "Even if all the

[35]*Sten. Ber.* (1892–1893), III, 1796ff., 1990ff., 2131, *Anlageband* II, 1147; *Die Nation*, X, 392–393, 467, 471; *Schulthess* (1893), pp. 30–31, 32–33; Wippermann, 9(I):132ff. The *Schulthess* account of the scene in the Reichstag on March 21, which has been followed in this instance, is somewhat more detailed in its description than the official transcript.

[36]See above, pp. 81–82.

demands of the Federated Governments in this military bill were completely justified politically and militarily, the continuation of a party such as the Center, as it now is, would still be more important for the Reich than the authorization of the military bill." [37]

In late March Caprivi requested Kaltenborn to see whether the bill could be reduced in terms of men and money. Then new negotiations were undertaken with Huene. With the help of the War Ministry Huene prepared a compromise bill which called for a reduction of about 14,000 men in the total peacetime strength envisaged in the original bill, or a new total of 589,000 men, an increase of about six sevenths of that provided for in the Caprivi bill.[38]

Meanwhile everyone was speculating on the outcome in the Reichstag, and all sorts of opinions and rumors flourished. Everyone except the Conservatives was afraid of dissolution. There was some sentiment in the Prussian Ministry for postponement of the whole affair until fall. The South German representatives in the Bundesrat were not enthusiastic about the idea of dissolution. The French ambassador reported that the Kaiser himself, under the influence of the grand duke of Baden, was said now to favor Bennigsen's compromise rather than risk a dissolution and that there was a chance Caprivi would resign and be replaced by Bennigsen or by Miquel.[39] Actually, the Kaiser at first refused to approve support of the reduced Huene bill. But Caprivi enlisted the aid of Cardinal Kopp, who in a three-hour talk persuaded the Kaiser to give his assent.[40]

3

DISSOLUTION AND ELECTION

On May 3 the second reading of the Army Bill opened in the Reichstag, Huene introduced his amended version, and Chancellor von Caprivi announced that the government would support it. Debate continued for four days. It was obvious that the bill would not be passed. On May 6 the chancellor came into the session with the

[37]Werdermann, *Heeresreform*, pp. 96–97; Keim, *Erlebtes*, pp. 54–55, 59–60; Bachem, *Zentrumspartei*, V, 275–286; *Schulthess* (1893), pp. 32, 43–44, 50–51; Wippermann, 9(I):123.

[38]Werdermann, *Heeresreform*, pp. 98–100; *DDF*, 1 ser., X, 417; Ziekursch, *Geschichte*, III, 68; *Statistisches Handbuch*, pp. 532–533.

[39]*Die Nation*, X, 403; Werdermann, *Heeresreform*, p. 99, note; *DDF*, 1 ser., X, 272; Keim, *Erlebtes*, pp. 64–65. Cf. *The Times*, wkly. ed., March 17, 1893, p. 206; Oncken, *Bennigsen*, II, 583, note, 584.

[40]Bachem, *Zentrumspartei*, V, 280–281. Cf. Wippermann, 9(I):111, 238–239.

familiar red dispatch case containing the signed decree of dissolution. The vote was taken: 210 to 162 against the Huene bill. Against it had voted all the Social Democrats and most of the Center and the Radicals; for it all the Conservatives, Free Conservatives, National Liberals, and Poles, and, in addition, twelve members of the Center, including Huene, Ballestrem, and Porsch, and seven Radicals. A last-minute attempt to attract a large bloc of Radical votes through a new compromise, granting the government its essential demands as embodied in the Huene bill but conceding statutory two-year service, was frustrated by the defeat of a motion for adjournment by the votes of the Center and the Conservatives. Caprivi then arose and read the decree dissolving the Reichstag. Three days later at Tempelhof field the Kaiser declared to the generals, after a review, that he hoped the new Reichstag would pass the bill but, if not, "I am determined to use every means in My power to achieve My purpose." [41]

In the evening of the same day the German Radical party (*Deutschfreisinnige*) deputies held a crucial party caucus. Seven members had broken party discipline and voted for the Huene bill. Eugen Richter demanded that these renegades be expelled from the party. The accumulated resentment of Richter's dogmatic policies and dictatorial methods, however, now brought an irrevocable breach. Richter threatened to resign if his expulsion motion were not accepted. The opposition threatened to walk out of the party en bloc if it were. The seventy-year-old Ludwig Bamberger, who was presiding, declared that if the party split he would not run again for the Reichstag. Both groups refused to yield, Richter's motion passed by a 27 to 22 vote, and the minority — including mostly former National Liberal "Secessionists," Rickert, Barth, Bamberger, Schrader — withdrew from the party. For the election campaign Richter's majority group took the name of Radical People's party (*Freisinnige Volkspartei*), Barth's group that of Radical Union (*Freisinnige Vereinigung*). The split, said Richter, had endangered the prospects of the party in the election and demonstrated that the party no longer possessed the requisite ideological unanimity. It was a question, said Barth, not of purposes but of methods; a truly liberal party must preserve freedom of action and of opinion for its own members:

[41]*Sten. Ber.* (1892–1893), III, 2214–2217; *Die Nation*, X, 495, 540; Maenner, *Carolath*, p. 62; *Schulthess* (1893), pp. 51–52, 54; Langer, *Franco-Russian Alliance*, p. 310, note; *DDF*, 1 ser., X, 346–347. Cf. the version of the Kaiser's speech published in the *Norddeutsche*, Wippermann, 9(I):242.

"Only a liberalism free from all narrow-mindedness can protect the German Reich from a disastrous future." [42]

Given the undoubted eagerness among Center and Radicals, in much larger numbers than became apparent, to find some way to support the government, and the fact that Conservatives, Free Conservatives, and National Liberals all finally voted for the bill, one wonders why in all these weeks of negotiation some practical compromise was not found. The answer seems to lie in the key point of statutory two-year service. A large part of the opposition might have voted the government demands in men and money if all uncertainty had been removed by a definite legal stipulation of a reduction to two years. But precisely this empty shell of three-year service in principle had been the price by which, the preceding fall, Caprivi had finally won the reluctant support of the Kaiser. Now, with sufficient parliamentary backing, the general could doubtless have made the Kaiser yield the appearance after having already yielded the substance, but this support the Conservatives would not give. They were the one party which expected to profit by a dissolution, and therefore it may be fairly stated that the dissolution would probably not have been necessary if the Conservatives had not forced it. The unbridgeable gulf thus existing between left and right was well illustrated by the miserable failure of the National Liberal attempt at compromise. After strongly attacking the government measure and introducing a drastic reduction as a compromise, the National Liberals meekly voted for the Huene bill. As a moderate liberal party they had long since lost any position of leadership.[43]

The subsequent election campaign differed markedly from that of 1887. Then, under Bismarck's spell, the whole country was aroused by the fervor of patriotism and the fear of war; there were only two parties, the "patriots" and the "enemies of the Reich." This time there was no attempt to play upon an immediate danger of war. Caprivi had declared in the Reichstag that he recognized the patriotism of all the parties. The election fight, therefore, was something of a free-for-all, with each party fighting mostly for itself, and the government fighting only for its bill, regardless of who its

---

[42]"Die Auflösung des Reichstages und die Spaltung der freisinnigen Partei" (Barth), *Die Nation*, X, 494–496; *Wahlaufruf* of Radical Union, *ibid.*, X, 496; *Wahlaufruf* of Radical People's party with open letter of Richter on the party crisis, *ibid.*, X, 497; also *ibid.*, X, 582; Ullstein, *Richter*, pp. 151–163; *Schulthess* (1893), p. 52; Wippermann, 9(I):173–177. The seven voting for the bill were Brömel, Hinze, Birkenfeld, Maager, Meyer, Schröder, Siemens. Stillich, *Politischen Parteien*, II, 313.

[43]Cf. *Pr. Jbb.*, 72:565–571; Leuss, *Hammerstein*, p. 106; *Schulthess* (1893), p. 344.

prospective supporters were. Everywhere the agrarians were especially active, campaigning against Caprivi's trade treaties but for his Army Bill. The picture was very confused. Never had there been so many candidates in so many districts representing so many parties.[44]

Within the limits set, the government did its utmost to carry its cause to the public. Major Keim threw his propaganda machine into high gear, making more use of government organs in the districts than could be officially approved by the more scrupulous Caprivi. The government was also considerably assisted in its propaganda efforts by the excesses of the French press, which, having carefully guarded itself all during the winter and spring, now, after the bill's defeat, freely expressed its great relief and somewhat over-confident exultation. French papers hailed the defeat of the bill as a victory for France and praised the "loyalty" of the Alsace-Lorraine deputies who voted against it. *La Patrie* raved:

In an hour, which is perhaps not distant, this apparent façade of power and despotic tyranny will with one blow unexpectedly collapse under the impulsion of events whose development no one may halt or retard. Then we shall see the victory of Right over Might, then we shall see Prussian domination reduced to more modest circumstances and the map of Europe reorganized according to the precepts of justice, of reason, and of truth.[45]

The election of 1893 took place on June 15. That night Major Keim was up all night tabulating the returns as they came in and trying to figure out possible majorities. The results were extremely difficult to interpret. Obvious enough was the catastrophic defeat of the Radicals. Torn between the anti-Semitic agrarian agitation on the right and the antimilitarist socialist agitation on the left, they had lost seats both to National Liberal and Anti-Semitic supporters of the Army Bill and to its Social Democratic opponents. On the initial ballot the Radical Union had won only 3 seats, and the Radical People's party none at all, not even Richter. These were increased in the run-off balloting to 13 and 24, respectively, or a total of 37, as opposed to 66 in 1890. The weakening of the liberals meant a strengthening of the extremes. On the extreme right the Anti-Semites increased their seats from 5 in 1890 to 16 in 1893, and their popular vote from 50,000 to 260,000. On the extreme left the Social Democrats, again polling the largest vote of any party, increased

[44] *Pr. Jbb.*, 72:564–565; *Die Nation*, X, 551; *Schulthess* (1893), pp. 55ff.; Wippermann, 9(I):169–173, 177–220.

[45] Keim, *Erlebtes*, pp. 66–67; Hammann, *Der Neue Kurs*, pp. 52–53.

their seats from 35 to 44, their popular vote from 1,400,000 to 1,700,000.[46]

But here the returns took leave of the obvious. The National Liberals lost 180,000 votes, but increased their number of seats from 42 to 53. The Conservatives, on the other hand, gained 140,000 votes, but, in spite of all their agitation, had their representation reduced by 1, from 73 to 72. Their espousal of anti-Semitism, ironically, had helped the Anti-Semites but not themselves. Stöcker lost his seat, while Ahlwardt was elected in two districts. The Free Conservatives lost 40,000 votes, as against 1890, but raised their number of seats from 20 to 28. The Center gained 125,000 votes but lost 10 seats, from 106 to 96 in 1893. Huene and his Silesian friends were not elected.[47]

It was plain, however, that the forces of the right — those supporting the Army Bill — had gained slightly in strength. The agrarian campaign also had been much more successful than the figures showed. Many new Conservative and Center agrarians entered the Reichstag, including Count Herbert Bismarck. Thus, the prospects for the Army Bill were better but still dubious, and the strengthening of the right meant a strengthening of the forces opposing Caprivi. What, moaned Ludwig Bamberger in *Die Nation*, had influenced the minds of the electorate? Certainly not the debates in the Reichstag.

How utterly defeated Ahlwardt seemed! . . . Now he laughs over that unanimous vote of the Reichstag . . . And that great day of Eugen Richter's when, to the thundering applause of right and center he reduced Bebel and his socialist New Order to dust and ashes. On the minds of the wisest and the most foolish the question must force itself, what, then, actually sways the opinion of the masses? In any case anything but logic! . . . The conflict of interests that is entering more and more into parliamentary life the world over finds a particularly fertile ground on German soil, provided by the inner tendencies of the national character . . . The German character is the least political in Europe . . .

The Radicals, wrote the aged Bamberger sadly, had failed because they were the only "purely political" party left in Germany.[48]

The new Reichstag was opened with a speech from the throne on July 4. The speech briefly rehearsed the situation and the reasons

---

[46]Keim, *Erlebtes,* p. 69. *Statistisches Handbuch,* pp. 530–531; Specht, *Reichstagswahlen,* p. 104. Figures for popular votes are approximate, that is, in round numbers.

[47]Cf. Ziekursch, *Geschichte,* III, 67–68.

[48]Cf. Eyck, *Wilhelm II,* pp. 72–74; *Die Nation,* X, 585.

for dissolution, stated calmly that the international situation was still good, there was no danger of war, but that because of her geographical position and the preparations of her neighbors Germany's armaments must be increased to keep her strong and to maintain peace. There was no excitement in the speech, there were no threats. It was received with great applause. After the applause had died the Kaiser added extemporaneously:

Now gentlemen, go forth; the Good Lord [*unser alter Gott*] looks down upon you, he grants you His blessing so that a worthy deed may be accomplished for the welfare of our Fatherland. Amen.[49]

Since everything had been said many times over in the previous session, the debates on the bill were brief. As promised, the government adhered to the Huene bill. To the last the outcome was most uncertain, and the line-up close enough so that the few votes of any one splinter party — Radical Union with 13, Anti-Semites with 16, or Poles with 19 — could decide the issue one way or another. The Poles took advantage of this situation to approach Caprivi and to try to get a pledge of special concessions before the vote, but were met with a stiff and dignified refusal. The Radical Union group were still intent on getting a more definite pledge on two-year service as long as the envisaged peace strength and reorganization were in effect. This amendment, however, was voted down with the help of the Center and Richter's Radicals who, apparently, were afraid that if it were accepted the Conservatives would vote against the whole bill and precipitate a new crisis. In general, the opposition did little to delay or to impede passage of the bill out of fear of another dissolution. And the Bismarck Fronde seemed, in Count Herbert's short maiden speech — which was loudly cheered by the agrarians and interrupted by cat-calls on the left — to be finally yielding, if ungraciously, to the call of patriotism. To satisfy the Radical Unionists, Caprivi gave a declaration that there was no intention and small likelihood of reintroduction of the three-year term. He also dropped the tax proposals of the last session and assured the Reichstag that the new taxes to be proposed would fall only on the strongest shoulders of the population. The third reading of the bill came on July 15. It passed by the slim margin of 201 to 185 — that is, 16 — votes. The Poles had voted for the bill. The Reichstag was forthwith adjourned. To Chancellor von Caprivi the Kaiser issued a congratulatory cabinet order.

[49]*Sten. Ber.* (1893), pp. 1–2; cf. *Schulthess* (1893), pp. 79–80; Wippermann, 9(II):1–2; *Die Nation*, X, 611.

The accomplishment of this great work is due, above all, to you . . . It is my pleasant duty to express to you my full appreciation and my lasting gratitude with the wish that your inestimable services may be long preserved to Me and to the Fatherland.

Yours affectionately,
WILLIAM I. R.

The Kaiser, who, in spite of an admonishing letter from Phili Eulenburg, had not stayed for the vote but had already started off on his Norwegian cruise, telegraphed decorations to Baron von Stumm and to "Admiralski" Koscielski — in both cases a rather fatal gift politically.[50]

4

VICTORY OR DEFEAT?

Considering the unfavorable circumstances, the extreme political confusion of the period, the passage of the bill after such a long battle was a personal victory for Chancellor Count von Caprivi. But it was a Pyrrhic one. His over-all political position was worse, not better. In the Reichstag and in the Reich the whole affair had served to strengthen the hand of his worst enemies, the Conservative agrarians. Capitalizing upon the general dissatisfaction throughout the country and joining forces with the Bismarck Fronde, this movement had begun to develop rapidly into an all-out frontal attack, not only upon the trade treaties, but upon the New Course as a whole and upon Caprivi in particular. During the January debate the Conservatives in the Prussian Landtag had attacked Minister von Berlepsch and the whole idea of social reform, which Baron von Minnigerode had denounced as "fanatical humanitarianism" (*Humanitätsfanatismus*). They had voted against the provisions for industrial arbitration courts in the budget. But their most important and most characteristic coup at this time — and one which passed almost unnoticed in the midst of the clamor over the Army Bill — was the law to reform the Prussian electoral system.[51]

From the very beginning of the New Course reform in 1890–1891, with the passage of Miquel's income tax, it was obvious that something would have to be done about the Prussian three-class

[50] *Sten. Ber.* (1893), pp. 11–14, 97–101, 139–140, 143; Hellwig, *Stumm*, pp. 475–477; Kardorff, *Kardorff*, p. 282; Thimme, "Bismarck und Kardorff," pt. II, pp. 28, 43; Keim, *Erlebtes*, p. 70; *Die Nation*, X, 628–629, 633; *Schulthess* (1893), pp. 83–84, 92–94; Haller, *Eulenburg*, I, 211–212.

[51] *Die Nation*, X, 359, 364. *Landtag* (1892–1893), I, 338, III, 1346; *Schulthess* (1893), p. 18.

voting system. When the system of dividing the electorate politically in thirds according to the amount of taxes paid was put through in 1849, it resulted in the upper third of the tax list representing 5 per cent of the electorate, the second 15 per cent, and the third 80 per cent. With the growth of great industrial wealth, however, by 1888 the first property class contained only 3.5 per cent of the electorate, the second 11 per cent, and the third 86 per cent. There were, by now, more districts than ever in which the electors for the first class were chosen by one wealthy man, who could thus practically dictate the choice of candidate. Thus, although in theory the suffrage was universal, in practice the votes of the lower classes, the vast majority of the population, did not count. There was, therefore, an increasing lack of interest in elections for the Landtag. In 1874 25 per cent of the qualified voters voted under the three-class system while 21 per cent voted under universal and equal suffrage in the Reich. In 1893 participation had dropped to 14.5 per cent in Prussia and increased to 72.1 per cent in the Reich. A franchise which gave the appearance of political representation to the poorer classes but not the reality was more frustrating and dangerous than none at all. "This Prussian suffrage," wrote the *Preussische Jahrbücher* in September 1892, "is a continual provocation and insult to all of the less well-to-do." Miquel's graduated income tax naturally had aggravated the existing irregularities of the three-class system. In 1892 in one Berlin district, of the qualified voters there were 1 in the first class, 22 in the second class, and 1,400 in the third class. Twenty-three people thus controlled a district of 1,400 voters.[52]

The central theme of the original New Course program had been to reconcile the diverse groups in the Reich, to rally all classes to the support of the nation. This meant, practically, an attempt to satisfy the lower classes, not only through the labor-protection bills, but also through the trade treaties, and Herrfurth's rural-government reform. But if the lower classes were to be wooed away from the Social Democrats and in any real way attracted to the support of the government, a reform in the franchise that would give them more of a real voice in the political life of the state was obviously in order. Herrfurth realized this and, with Caprivi's backing, wanted to introduce — not universal and equal suffrage, to be sure! — but a change in the law, fixing the size of the three classes at the original

[52]On the three-class system see Lowell, *Governments and Parties*, I, 303–308; Ziekursch, *Geschichte*, III, 49–50; L. Herrfurth, "Die Wahlreform in Preussen," *Deutsche Revue*, 18(II):230–250 (1893); *Die Nation*, X, 86–88, 252–254, 537; *The Times*, wkly. ed., January 20, 1893, p. 45. See above, pp. 36, 93.

ratio of 5 per cent, 15 per cent, and 80 per cent of the population.
This would mean a departure from the property basis of the suffrage
and would tend to diminish the plutocratic tendencies of the system.
It was not a radical proposal, but would have been an honest attempt to carry over into political realities the progressive conservative pretensions of the New Course. Herrfurth, however, already in
his rural-government bill had come up against the unyielding opposition of the Junker Conservatives. And already in 1891 the one
avowed liberal in the ministry, Miquel, had deserted Herrfurth and,
for the sake of his own tax reform, had rallied strongly to the Junker
point of view and the *status quo*. Electoral reform was a hot issue;
Miquel was able to persuade the conservative members of the
ministry not to endanger the tax reform by introducing it now but to
postpone it for a while. Miquel was afraid, and rightly so, that Herrfurth's mild bill would alienate the Conservatives without winning
over the Center and Radicals, who were pledged to universal suffrage. In the winter of 1891–1892 everything had to yield to Zedlitz's
School Bill, which necessitated the coöperation of the Conservatives
with the Center. After the School Bill debacle, the beginning of the
agrarian and anti-Semitic agitation, Herrfurth's resignation from the
ministry, and Caprivi's handing over of the minister-presidency to
Botho Eulenburg, the Prussian Ministry came more and more under
the influence of Miquel and of the Conservatives, with whom he was
now working hand in glove. First, he had to finish his tax reform;
secondly, there was the chance of successfully riding the agrarian
wave to overwhelm the Reich and eventually to replace Caprivi.[53]

Since the land tax was now being dropped for state purposes,
however, some "adjustments" would be unavoidable in the election
law. The Conservatives wanted to retain the *status quo;* Center and
Radicals wanted universal suffrage, although the Center, under the
leadership of the aristocratic von Huene, was not too serious about
it. Also, by hastening to coöperate with the Conservatives, the
Center could jockey the National Liberals out of position in the
Landtag. The result was an unedifying comedy in which a compromise bill was worked out by Conservatives and Center, fixing the
ratio of the three classes on the property basis as before, but in a
ratio of 5/12–4/12–3/12 rather than in thirds. This was a feeble
gesture indeed, albeit in the right direction, but much to the chagrin
of the Center these changes were wiped out of the bill in the Conservative House of Lords, and the bill was then calmly passed by

[53]Herzfeld, *Miquel*, II, 292–293, 309–310; *Landtag* (1892–1893), I, 347–350; L.
Herrfurth, "Wahlreform," pp. 230–250.

Conservatives and National Liberals in the House. Everything was thereby returned to the *status quo ante* with the apportionment still by thirds. The old system, after all, had so far kept Social Democrats out of the Landtag. Under the rising Socialist threat National Liberals, too, were ready to support the *status quo.* Junker interests, however, were carefully preserved by including county, commune, and district taxes for electoral purposes in addition to state taxes. Owners of "independent" estates, who now paid no actual communal tax, were allowed to figure in a fictitious tax, so that the Junker landlords continued to dominate their districts and, through them, Prussia, on the basis of a tax which they did not pay. While the Reichstag was battling with the questions of the day, the Landtag — now rid of both Caprivi and Herrfurth — had become an agrarian backwater. It was like another world, wrote *Die Nation* in January, and quoted Storm's lines:

> Kein Hauch der aufgeregten Zeit
> Drang noch in diese Einsamkeit.

"In the House the *Bourgraves* debate, who barely comprehend that the political world has changed in the last five hundred years, and who, in any case, would very much like to see to it that it does not change in the next five hundred." [54]

This ignominious end to the fond hopes of a progressive electoral reform was accepted by Botho Eulenburg and Miquel without a murmur. In fact, to lead the attack upon Caprivi, the Conservatives, in the summer of 1893, were looking confidently to Miquel. He was the Moses who had obtained for them the sustaining manna of the land-tax repeal, and he would lead them out of their agrarian woes and into greener pastures. It was the hour of Miquel's triumph. His tax reform was finished. The Kaiser presented him in August with the Grand Cross of the Order of the Red Eagle and compared him to Stein and Hardenberg. Behind him was all the force and confidence of the Conservative agrarian movement. Could he not now carry his success over into the Reich and, by forcing out Caprivi, unite the two governments once more under one person — himself?[55]

The previous March, under the stress of the agrarian agitation, a wide crack had appeared in the Reich façade when the prime minister of the little state of Anhalt had opened his Landtag with

[54]Herzfeld, *Miquel,* II, 310–313; Bachem, *Zentrumspartei,* V, 271; *Die Nation,* X, 255.

[55]*Die Nation,* X, 331, 376; Herzfeld, *Miquel,* II, 277, 287–290, 324; Wehrmuth, *Beamtenleben,* p. 198.

an attack on the trade treaties and on the Army Bill. To be sure, Caprivi had sent an official off posthaste from Berlin to demand an explanation, the erring minister had quickly recanted, and the *Reichsanzeiger* had publicly announced that in the Bundesrat Anhalt had not voted against the trade treaties. But for a moment it seemed as if Prussia were successfully organizing the smaller states against the Reich government. Now, in the new Reichstag, Conservative agrarians and the Bismarck Fronde united against Caprivi and behind Miquel. The extreme agrarian Wilhelm von Kardorff was elected chairman of the budget committee. On July 14 an "Economic Union," with Bismarckian overtones, was formed among the Reichstag members. Kardorff managed to get Stumm to join this union so as to soften its strictly agrarian character. The Reich tax bill which von Maltzahn had quickly scraped together the year before, after Miquel's protest in the Prussian Ministry, had died in committee in the previous Reichstag. Originally von Maltzahn had tried to meet a large part of the cost of the Army Bill through a 50 per cent reduction in the notorious government subsidy — "Liebesgabe" — to the distillers. This proposal, however, had been resisted in the Bundesrat by Bavaria, under the influence of the agrarian agitation, and had been dropped. The left, which would have been pleased by this sort of thing, was thus strengthened in its opposition to the bill as a whole. Now von Maltzahn's failure was Miquel's opportunity. Pressing the interests of Prussia in the matter, he compelled Caprivi to allow him practically to take over the question of the new taxes for the Army Bill plus a general reform of the Reich finances. These new taxes, declared Caprivi in the Reichstag on July 7, to the cheers of the agrarians, were being worked out "hand in hand" with the Prussian Finance Ministry. The way into Reich politics seemed wide open. On August 12 von Maltzahn resigned from his post as secretary of the Reich treasury and was succeeded by Count von Posadowsky-Wehner. As a new man, Posadowsky, at least for a while, would have to follow Miquel's lead. On July 19 von Kardorff wrote to Bismarck:

In my opinion, after he was compelled to declare that Miquel would prepare the tax bill, Caprivi has already abdicated, and I regard the ascendancy of the former, because of the furious hatred existing between him and Caprivi, as the best result attainable at present.[56]

[56]Hohenlohe, *Memoirs*, II, 457; *Die Nation*, X, 159, 255–256, 633; Kardorff, *Kardorff*, pp. 282, 284–285; Thimme, "Bismarck und Kardorff," pt. II, pp. 42–44; *Sten. Ber.* (1893), p. 13.

On July 21, in a speech to a deputation of Brunswickians at Friedrichsruh, Bismarck declared that the Reichstag had abdicated its "authority" by accepting the trade treaties in so hasty a manner at the command of the government. The vote of the Poles for the Army Bill he regarded with suspicion as a Greek gift. The power vacuum left by the "abdication" of the Reichstag would not be filled by the monarchy, but by the bureaucracy. Here Bismarck was repeating a theme already elaborated in a masterly speech on July 8 to a delegation from the principality of Lippe-Detmold. Their ancient hero, Hermann, he had said then, had delivered the first blow for German nationalism by resisting the Roman bureaucracy in the Teutoburger Wald.[57] The seventeen small German states which possessed only one vote in the Bundesrat must not be underestimated. They were the mortar between the stones. By adding their seventeen votes to the seventeen votes of Prussia they could always control the Bundesrat!

What power, therefore, lies in the small states! I marvel that in none of them has there been a politician who has put it to use.

He had intended the Bundesrat to take a prominent part in national life, and he was disappointed that it had not done so. Bundesrat members always had the right to speak in the Reichstag. He would like to see the representatives of the smaller states speaking out for their point of view in the Reichstag, when they had found no consideration for their grievances in the Bundesrat. The "blood of national feeling," however, was too concentrated in the head and heart. The Landtags of the separate states should also concern themselves more with Reich affairs, and should call their Bundesrat representatives to account.

At present the danger exists that [the bureaucracy] will again win domination over us, not by bloodshed but by suffocation, and that the achievements of the sword will perish, I will not say through the pen of the diplomats, but nevertheless through the operation of the bureaus, the rule of officials, and the lazy expectation that some one else will do what is necessary. "The government will take care of it!" But who is the government? Yes, if the princes could manage it themselves, they are all well-meaning gentlemen, but they must necessarily depend on their officials, their ministers, their first and second counsellors.

My fear and concern for the future is that the national consciousness will be choked to death in the coils of the bureaucratic boa constrictor, which has grown hugely in recent years.

[57] A famous battle near Paderborn where the legions of Augustus were defeated in A.D. 9.

On August 20 to a deputation at Kissingen Bismarck declared:

I regret very much the separation of the office of Reich Chancellor from the presidency of the Prussian Ministry . . . The Kaiser has no vote in the Bundesrat, only the king of Prussia. And, therefore, it is necessary that nothing should be introduced in the Bundesrat which has not previously been approved by the Prussian State Ministry . . . It was quite incidental that I usually carried the title of Reich Chancellor, my authority lay in my capacity as leading minister in Prussia, whose instrument I was as Reich Chancellor.

And on August 27 in a speech to a delegation from Frankfurt he added:

I hold it to be urgently necessary that the Reich Chancellor, as official head of the government, should not emancipate himself from the control of the Prussian State Ministry, which is a collegiate group of ten expert ministers who are usually better acquainted with affairs. I am alarmed by a chancellor, who asks no one's opinion but his own and his adjutant's (laughter).

If, when he gave up his office as Prussian minister-president while consenting to remain in the Reich, Caprivi, as appears likely, had hoped to straighten things out later, take back the minister-presidency again, as well as bring an end to the opposition between Kaiser and Bismarck: to do this after some victory in the Reichstag — say, after the successful passage of the army reform — if this had been his intention, it was now further from realization than ever. Now it was Prussia which was threatening to take over the Reich. His hard-won victory in the Army Bill had left the general even more on the defensive.[58]

[58]*Schulthess* (1893), pp. 83–84, 86–89, 95–99, 108–113, 114–117; Wippermann, 9(II):42ff.; Eyck, *Wilhelm II*, p. 74; Jagemann, *75 Jahren*, p. 112; Hutten-Czapski, *Sechzig Jahre*, I, 159.

PART THREE
THE FINAL BATTLE

Chapter VIII

ENGLAND, RUSSIA, AND THE PRICE OF WHEAT

> The Prussian Kraut-Junker, on the other hand, who possesses hardly any of the merits of the English or French nobility, whose manners are unpleasant, whose intellectual cultivation is slight, whose means, in part, are scanty, has . . . not only maintained his position, but — thanks to the powerful assistance of the greatest Junker of them all, Otto von Bismarck-Schönhausen — has, indeed, entrenched himself in it. This historical success has tremendously increased the Junker's self-confidence, which was never small, . . . Coldbloodedly like a Cooperian Indian on the warpath, he will lie in wait for the opportunity when he can get rid of the hated Reich chancellor who will not allow himself to be reduced to a tool of Junker politics.
>
> *Die Nation,* May 1893

I T HAD been largely an impersonal economic development — the world-wide depression, the deflation of money at this time, and the consequent fall in agricultural prices — that had deprived Caprivi of the fruits of his Army Bill victory. Politics is thus a seamless web; there is no single issue that does not have its general orientation and its several impacts. In addition to the general interrelation of issues, however, the life of the state is further complicated by the fact that it follows simultaneously two separate careers in two different but allied realms: it has a domestic life and also an external life among the nations. For General Count von Caprivi this conduct of affairs both at home and abroad was another "two-front" contest that was not to be avoided.

With the agrarian movement now at full force, the most elementary prudence would dictate that in domestic affairs the government should proceed very cautiously, endeavoring to placate the agrarians, at least to some degree, and certainly doing nothing to excite them further. It was thus of the utmost fatefulness for the

Caprivi regime that the logic of its foreign policies should develop in 1893–1894 in such a way as to exasperate and stimulate the agrarians to further heights of passionate opposition. Perhaps, logically, this foreign policy, in its inherent principles and tendencies, should not have excited their opposition. The fact is that it did. Thus, trying to hold to a reasonable, moderate course, dedicated to national security, Caprivi found himself once more swept onward by forces that he could not control.

1

ENGLAND OR RUSSIA?

While, from School Bill to Army Bill, the crisis had been gathering in internal German affairs, conditions outside in the world of European power politics had not stood still. The display of Franco-Russian enthusiasm at Cronstadt in July 1891 had not led to a binding diplomatic alliance between the two states. Part of the credit for this failure was due to the clever diplomacy of Lord Salisbury, who, correctly gauging the reluctance of the French to join Russia irrevocably against England, arranged that the fleet of Admiral Gervais on its return from Cronstadt should stop off at the British port of Portsmouth to be cordially received by Queen Victoria. Simultaneously the British prime minister delivered a speech at the Mansion House in which he declared he had no knowledge of the terms of the Triple Alliance and had not asked to know them. The association of England with the Triple Alliance powers, which so alarmed the Russians, had apparently been grossly exaggerated. The accord reached in August 1891 by the governments of France and Russia was merely a general agreement to concert views and measures in case of a serious threat to the peace. Russia had no intention of fighting Germany to regain Alsace-Lorraine for France, and France, as yet, was unwilling to join with Russia in an anti-English policy.[1]

Throughout the summer of 1891, however, Europe tensely awaited a Russian move against Constantinople and the Straits. This move did not materialize, and in the fall and winter Russia was seriously weakened by the development of a very severe famine, accompanied by an epidemic of cholera.[2] But the Russian famine

[1]Langer, *Franco-Russian Alliance,* pp. 185–194; cf. Reuss to Caprivi, *G.P.,* VIII, 69–71; Dugdale, *German Diplomatic Documents,* II, 138.

[2]Langer, *Franco-Russian Alliance,* pp. 201–207; Köhler, *Revanche-idee,* pp. 342–345; S. I. Witte, *Memoirs of Count Witte* (London, 1921), pp. 35, 48; *The Times, passim.*

did not lead to a relaxation of the international tension; on the contrary, it increased it. In Russia the court, government, and people were convinced that the Kaiser would now take his revenge for Cronstadt by making war on Russia when she was weak and helpless. In Berlin, on the other hand, there was a widespread conviction that the famine would provoke Russia to declare war on Germany to avoid internal revolution. The press of both countries, therefore, was extraordinarily touchy and ready to scent treachery and masked plotting in the other side's uneasiness. In November 1891 an appeal published by prominent Germans for help for the starving Russians was attacked in such insulting terms by the Russian press that the attempt was given up.[3]

In the German Foreign Office two views were in conflict. The most extreme group, led by Holstein, hoped for a Russian economic and political collapse and feared a Russian attack. Caprivi, on the other hand, held out against Holstein, the Kaiser, and the more excitable generals the milder and more sane opinion that Russia was so incapacitated by the famine that there was nothing to fear from her in the way of foreign adventures. At the time, however, Caprivi was engrossed in the preparation of the first trade treaties and their debate in the Reichstag and, later, with the School Bill affair.[4]

The Kaiser was especially excited over the fact that twice, in September and October, the tsar had passed through Germany on his way to and from Denmark and had made no move to pay his respects to the Berlin court. Actually, the rather rude and simple Alexander III did not want to have to discuss Cronstadt. The Kaiser, who was persuaded with great difficulty through the special efforts of Phili Eulenburg not to force himself on the tsar when he went through Danzig, was convinced that the tsar's impoliteness was a deliberate insult. Also, Berlin was uneasy over the visits, during the fall, of Russian Foreign Minister Nicholas de Giers to Paris and to Rome.[5]

In actual fact, Giers had made his trip to the western capitals with the idea of holding back any threat to peace in the Mediterranean while Russia was in such a weakened condition. In October

[3]Cf. particularly Schweinitz's report of his conversation with the influential Pobyedonostsyev, G.P., VII, 367; also G.P., VII, 368, 372, 374–382, note; P. Bigelow, *Prussian Memories* (New York, 1915), pp. 104–106; Langer, *Franco-Russian Alliance*, p. 225; *The Times*, wkly. ed., November 13, 1892, p. 8.

[4]See above, Chapter IV, section 3, Chapter V; Langer, *Franco-Russian Alliance*, p. 226 and note.

[5]Langer, *Franco-Russian Alliance*, pp. 223, note, 213–220; Haller, *Eulenburg*, I, 130–133; L. Raschdau, *Bismarck u. Caprivi*, p. 242; G.P., VII, 306, 309, 169.

a Russian loan was floated in Paris but so unsuccessfully that a large amount of it had to be bought back by the Russian Finance Ministry. When Giers stopped off in Berlin on his return trip to Russia, he tried to interest the Germans in a tariff agreement and a loan. Here, apparently, was an opportunity to reverse the trend begun in 1887, when Russian securities had been attacked by Bismarck, and to weaken the economic ties uniting Russia and France. Both Caprivi and Marschall, however, took a very reserved attitude. The loan, Marschall explained, would be welcome to the German bankers, but was rendered impossible because of the state of public opinion. In March Shuvalov received instructions to begin negotiations for a trade treaty but did not meet with much enthusiasm in the German Foreign Office. Caprivi, it was reported, was willing to give Russia most-favored-nation status on grain in return for reductions in her rates on iron and textiles, but Holstein, at this time, balked at any concession to Russia. On March 25, 1892, Holstein wrote:

After the German government prevented an Anglo-Russian war for the first time in 1878 and for the second time in 1885 [the Afghan question] and in addition put a stop to the Franco-Chinese war through its mediation also in 1885, now for the fourth time Providence comes to our aid in the shape of the Russian famine. Let us hope that we do not frustrate this benevolent Providence for the fourth time by in any way helping the Russians financially and economically.[6]

The Caprivi trade treaties with Italy and Austria had placed Russia in an unfavorable position economically. It was, therefore, natural that the Russians, in their weakened and touchy condition, should regard Germany's negative attitude in the matter of a trade agreement and a loan in a hostile light. In addition, there was Caprivi's new policy towards the Poles, who were obviously hoping for the reconstitution of their kingdom with the help of a German war against Russia. These suspicions were only confirmed by Bismarck's loud denunciations of Caprivi's Polish policy as being anti-Russian. Then, in February 1892, came the Kaiser's "days of glory" speech to the Brandenburg Diet which, again, the Russians took as directed against them, although it was aimed at the School Bill. And with the resignation of Caprivi in the School Bill crisis in March, it seemed that the Kaiser was trying to get rid of the one person in the

[6]Langer, *Franco-Russian Alliance*, pp. 210, 221–222, 228 and note; *G.P.*, VII, 227–230, 402; cf. Köhler, *Revanche-idee*, p. 359; Rogge, *Holstein*, p. 164; also cf. Rogge, pp. xxxvii, 150; Bülow, *Memoirs*, IV, 607.

German government in whose peaceful intentions the Russians had complete confidence.[7]

With this tension in existence between Berlin and St. Petersburg, the French attempted to make capital out of it to turn their loose entente with Russia into a military alliance. But the Russians were so weak and so afraid of a German attack that a military alliance with France — which might leak out and become known — was the last thing they wanted. In spite of the efforts of the pope to encourage the union, nothing definite resulted. A French draft of a military convention was presented to the tsar in 1892, but nothing was done. Currently involved on their eastern frontier with the English, against whom the French showed no willingness to assist them, the Russians had no interest in provoking the Germans on their western frontier by a military agreement with the French.[8]

Under the circumstances the tsar preferred to try to improve relations with Germany. At his request a meeting between himself and the Kaiser was arranged at Kiel for June 7, 1892. In spite of the skepticism of the Germans, this Kiel interview went much better than expected. The emperors carefully refrained from political discussions and got on quite well together. The reëstablishment of the personal connection between the two royal personages could easily become the groundwork for a general improvement in relations.[9]

In late June 1892 came the Bismarck trip to Vienna and his blast in the Vienna press featuring the broken "wire to St. Petersburg." It was quite obvious to the tsar that the Kaiser's reconciliation with Bismarck was now impossible, and the Russian press unanimously condemned Bismarck while praising Caprivi. Russo-German relations continued friendly. Under the circumstances the French were worried, and it was in this atmosphere that the *Figaro* article of July 14, 1892, "Flirt ou Alliance?," was published. The tsar was not pleased by the French insistence, but the French, nevertheless, could not be completely repulsed. Thus, during the summer of 1892, General Boisdeffre entered into negotiations in St. Petersburg with the Russian generals, and a compromise military agreement provid-

[7]See above, Chapter IV, section 2, Chapter V, sections 6 and 7. *G.P.*, VII, 382–386; Langer, *Franco-Russian Alliance*, pp. 228, 232–233 and note; Schweinitz, *Denkwürdigkeiten*, II, 433–441. On the margin of a report of Shuvalov's in February the tsar wrote, "One must always believe Caprivi." *G.P.*, IX, 87.

[8]Langer, *Franco-Russian Alliance*, pp. 235–241.

[9]For the interview at Kiel see *G.P.*, VII, 407–409; Waldersee, *Denkwürdigkeiten*, II, 241–242; Raschdau, *Bismarck u. Caprivi*, pp. 262–263; Langer, *Franco-Russian Alliance*, pp. 243–245.

ing for simultaneous mobilization was eventually drawn up. This draft was agreed to by the tsar "in principle" on August 17. It was then, however, handed over to Giers, who was ill in Finland, and a further period of inaction resulted.[10]

The exact developments in the relations between France and Russia were, of course, not known to the German government. To them, as to the other European governments, the most important international event of the summer of 1892 was the British general election in mid-July, which returned the eighty-three-year-old Liberal idol, Gladstone, to power. Gladstone, unlike Salisbury, was known to be generally uninterested in overseas empire, anti-Turkish, unenthusiastic about holding Egypt, and generally pro-French. To be sure, he was forced to entrust the position of foreign secretary to Lord Rosebery, an admirer of the policy of Lord Salisbury, but it was very doubtful if, in a pinch, Gladstone and the cabinet as a whole could be counted on to back Rosebery in continuing a policy favorable to the Triple Alliance. The New Course, since 1890, had conducted its foreign policy with a western orientation, implying a certain amount of British support. The anti-German inclinations of the Liberal cabinet, however, now threatened these assumptions. On July 18, 1892, Ambassador Count Hatzfeldt was instructed from Berlin to draw up a report on "how far the now evident result of the British election will probably affect England's continental policy. The above with special reference to her attitude towards Italy and Turkey." A calm and carefully reasoned memorandum by Raschdau of July 20 on "The Influence of the English General Election on the Foreign Policy of the Country," based on Hatzfeldt's report, declared that, even if there were no real change in policy, a change in method would tend to amount to the same thing:

Under Gladstone's leadership the desire for action will be much less to the fore than under Salisbury's . . . other Powers, France and Russia in fact, will henceforward be guided in their actions by the diminished fear of England's interference . . . To sum up — if, as I wrote above, there is no real alteration in the theoretic basis of British foreign policy, the executive will not improbably exhibit a kind of hypocritical tendency, which will encourage the bold ones amongst England's rivals. Hence we may look on it as fortunate that the new ministry comes at a time when Russia is least capable of taking action.[11]

[10]Langer, *Franco-Russian Alliance*, pp. 253–265; see above, Chapter VII, section 1.

[11]Langer, *Franco-Russian Alliance*, pp. 252–253, 286–287; Taylor, *Struggle for Mastery*, pp. 341–342; *G.P.*, VIII, 75–80; Dugdale, *German Diplomatic Documents*, II, 163–167.

Just as in 1890 the change of government in Germany had resulted in a shift of diplomatic preponderance from Germany to England, so now the change in government in England destroyed the strong position held for two years by Lord Salisbury and restored Germany to the position of European arbiter and balancer. This was all the more true since the great Panama scandals had already begun in France, and, in short order, revealed to the tsar not only the weakness and corruption of the French Republic, but also the peculiar susceptibility of his own Russian officials to French francs. On the other hand, with Germany and Russia becoming more friendly, England was in grave danger of complete isolation at a time when she was coming more and more into conflict with Russia and France overseas. Caught as he was between the skeptical coolness of the conservative Triple Alliance Powers on the one hand and the cautious and suspicious attitude of his own Liberal cabinet colleagues on the other, Lord Rosebery's position was not an enviable one. As for the Caprivi government in Berlin, it was now in the very strong position of being able to balance off both England and Russia. If Gladstone's majority in Parliament seemed likely to hold together for a while, Count Hatzfeldt wrote to Caprivi on November 24, 1892:

[then], if Your Excellency will permit me to express an opinion, I should think the time come to leave Mr. Gladstone in no doubt that we and our allies cannot hold ourselves bound to act in the interests of England and expose ourselves to dangerous European complications, so long as we are not quite certain, in what way, if at all, England means to do her part.

The negotiations for a trade treaty with Russia, which had become bogged down in the spring were taken up again in August. In October Baron von Marschall told General von Schweinitz, "I realize now that the one reasonable policy for us is that which tries for good relations with Russia." In November 1892 the pro-Russian General von Werder was appointed to succeed General von Schweinitz at St. Petersburg as a personal favor to the tsar.[12]

The effect of the new German attitude upon relations with England was quickly and bluntly documented in January 1893 by the Baghdad Railway incident. In 1888 Sultan Abdul Hamid, distrustful of the English and French, had given the Deutsche Bank the concession for a railroad line from Ismid to Angora. By 1890 the first section of this line had been completed, and the Sultan, who

---

[12]Langer, *Franco-Russian Alliance*, pp. 288–290, 286, 296–297; *G.P.*, VII, 242, VIII, 96; Dugdale, *German Diplomatic Documents*, II, 205; Schweinitz, *Denkwürdigkeiten*, II, 443–445; *G.P.*, VII, 412–414.

wanted to extend the line eventually to Baghdad and the Persian
Gulf, tried to interest the German bankers in a further concession.
Through his ambassador in Berlin, he even directly solicited the
personal interest and support of the Kaiser for the project. The
Deutsche Bank was not very enthusiastic, but with some encouragement from the Wilhelmstrasse, finally agreed to extend their Anatolian Railway line from Eskishehir to Konia.

So far, all the negotiations had been carried on between the
Germans and the sultan personally, without the knowledge of the
grand vizier. In December 1892 the news got out and immediately
caused a sensation in English and French financial circles, since the
proposed extension of the Anatolian line to Konia would cut through
the hinterland of their own lines extending inland from Smyrna
(Izmir). Under pressure from British and French interests, the
British ambassador, Sir Clare Ford, demanded that the concession
to the German company be held up and went so far as to threaten
the sultan with a fleet demonstration.

News of Ford's action reached Berlin on January 6 and produced
a small hurricane in Wilhelmstrasse 76. Baron Marschall immediately summoned the British ambassador, Sir Edward Malet, and
protested that Ford had turned a business affair into a matter of
politics. Such a protest by England against German economic
activity was not only impolite but an unfriendly act. Germany had
heretofore supported English interests in the east to maintain the
present alignment of the European powers. But if England were
now going to use this alignment against German interests, Germany
would have to reconsider her whole policy. Since the sultan had
engaged the interest of the Kaiser in the project, failure now to
award the concession would be a personal insult to His Majesty.
Marschall telegraphed substantially the same message to Count
Hatzfeldt, to be relayed to Lord Rosebery. Simultaneously, without
waiting for Rosebery's answer, he telegraphed the German consul
in Cairo to withdraw the consent recently given by Germany to an
English proposal to increase the size of the Egyptian army. Since
the French had refused their permission for this increase, the
English in Egypt were quite dependent upon the friendly support
of Germany, and Lord Cromer immediately wired Lord Rosebery
urging the importance of Anglo-German coöperation.

This Egyptian threat was very effective. Lord Rosebery wired
on the 9th that he had no intention of opposing German interests in
Turkey, and the Turkish railroad concession was granted in due
course. But Marschall's action was significant. He had thrown his

cards on the table face up, so that the English could see just how strong a hand Germany possessed. By driving home the lesson, however, in so crude, so brutal a fashion, by not even waiting for a reply to his protest before he ordered his counterthrust in Egypt, he did more than merely call the attention of the Liberal cabinet to the value of German friendship; he alienated their feelings. Rosebery himself was piqued, and other members of the cabinet and of the Foreign Office staff felt insulted and hurt in their national pride by the German crudeness. Here was Bismarckian ruthlessness, but with a bludgeon, not a rapier. One feels safe in ascribing this quick, nervous, suspicious, extreme, and even vindictive action to Baron von Holstein. It is doubtful that Caprivi was exactly aware of what was going on. It was during these days that he was busily engaged in defending his Army Bill in the Reichstag committee. Marschall's action was significant also in another respect. It was the first time that the German government had allowed purely economic interests to impel it to positive political action at Con- stantinople — a place where heretofore it had tried to maintain a neutral, disinterested policy. The forces of German economic na- tionalism were moving out beyond the boundaries of the old Bis- marckian political concepts. Nationalism was the one sentiment over which there was no dispute in Germany, not even in the Wilhelmstrasse. It lay at the very basis of the New Course and of the Caprivi regime.[13]

The shift of the Berlin government away from England was evidenced in their attitude toward Austria's Balkan interests and, particularly, Bulgaria. Whereas in 1890 Berlin had supported Austria and Ferdinand, now, in January 1893, the Kaiser personally

[13]*G.P.*, XIV, 441–464, VIII, 184–187, 191; Dugdale, *German Diplomatic Docu- ments,* II, 180–183, 279–280; J. B. Wolf, "The Diplomatic History of the Bagdad Railroad," *University of Missouri Studies,* XI (1936), 12–18; K. Helfferich, *Georg v. Siemens* (Berlin, 1923), III, 58–69; Langer, *Franco-Russian Alliance,* pp. 291–294; cf. Sir Eyre Crowe's well-known memorandum of 1907, G. Gooch and H. Temperly, *British Documents on the Origin of the War* (London, 1926–1938), III, 416; Raschdau, *Bismarck u. Caprivi,* pp. 257, 297–298; Sir E. Grey, *Twenty-five Years* (New York, 1925), I, 7–10; Wippermann, 9(I):238. Wolf's study has in some respects superseded E. M. Earle's *Turkey, the Great Powers, and the Bagdad Railway* (New York, 1923). On March 22, 1893, Count Hatzfeldt warned Holstein against a policy of "threats" in dealing with the Gladstone government. "Rosebery," wrote Hatzfeldt, "*who is personally extraordinarily sensitive and resentful,* might be driven by *repeated* threats of this sort onto undesirable paths." Germany should expect favors from the English in exchange for those granted, but should proceed on the basis of frankness and politeness, not "general and vague threats" in the Bismarck manner. This criticism of Hatzfeldt's evidently put Holstein in a temporary huff, against which his old friend felt it necessary to defend himself vigorously. Hatzfeldt to Holstein, March 22, September 17, 1893, *Holstein Papers, Correspondence.*

prevented Ferdinand's marriage to a Bavarian princess, and, in April, Caprivi absolutely refused to receive Stambulov in Berlin. In January Holstein succinctly expressed the new Foreign Office attitude in a letter to Phili Eulenburg.

We desire good relations with Russia, *but without committing political adultery.* The existing treaties must be observed, as long as they last and as far as they go. But to go beyond that, there is no call. If Russia attacks Rumania, Austria would *certainly* be on the defensive if she advanced against Russia. If Russia attacks Bulgaria, Austria would *perhaps* be on the defensive. But Austria would *not* be on the defensive if Russia delivers a direct attack by sea against Turkey proper. In that case let those fight who wish; *we* are under no obligation to fight. No *casus foederis.*

The Germans, in fact, were hoping with some confidence that, with the aid of the Panama scandals, they could put an end to the Franco-Russian rapprochement. The Russian ambassador in Paris, Baron Mohrenheim, was currently being accused in the French press of having received Panama funds.

On January 24, 1893, Tsarevich Nicholas arrived in Berlin for the wedding of Prince Frederick Charles of Hesse to the Kaiser's youngest sister, Margaret.[14] On the evening of the 24th the Kaiser had a long intimate talk with Nicholas about the European situation. His father, said the tsarevich, had made a "terrible scene" over the report of Mohrenheim's implication in the Panama scandals. What, asked the Kaiser, did they think in St. Petersburg the result of the affair would be in France? A military dictatorship, replied the tsarevich, leading to war. And what would Russia do in such a war? Why, then, the tsarevich said, there would have to be another coalition of all the powers against France, as in 1813–1815. That was exactly the basis, responded the Kaiser, of the Triple Alliance — a mutual guaranty of the territorial *status quo,* protection of monarchical principles against radicalism, socialism, nihilism, and so on, and creation of mutual material benefits through trade agreements to combat the threatening Pan-American imperialism of the United States. There was always room in this alliance for other like-minded states. The tsarevich, impressed, replied that he had not thought of the Triple Alliance in exactly this way before; was His Majesty sure it had no anti-Russian tendencies? Absolutely not! said the Kaiser.

[14]Langer, *Franco-Russian Alliance,* pp. 295–301; *G.P.,* VII, 425–426, IX, 97–98; Haller, *Eulenburg,* I, 139–141. Cf. the German text of Haller, *Aus dem Leben des Fürsten P. zu Eulenburg-Hertefeld* (Berlin, 1926), pp. 83–84.

Germany had nothing to gain from war with Russia. Their interests were both conservative. The revolutionary danger emanated from France. The Kaiser then obtained the tsarevich's promise to talk the matter over with the tsar and presented him with a written memorandum, which had been worked out in the Foreign Office, to base his arguments on. Five days later Holstein wrote to Phili Eulenburg:

You want to know what I think of it all? Well, I believe that the Russian tempest raised by Bismarckian influences had reached its climax at Kronstadt. Kiel was the turn of the tide. I question if today the tsar would stand during the playing of the Marsellaise.

The renewal of the Triple Alliance was essential, because thereby we gained time to wait quietly for the turn of the tide. Whether a second renewal would be useful, I — poor blind mole! — am in no longer a position to judge; but *you* are.

Either the new treaty can be limited to the territorial *possessions* of the contracting parties (therefore excluding Bulgaria and Rumania), or it can be arranged with Russia *before* the treaty expires to sign an agreement *after* its expiration. If Austria submits to the above limitations, one can perhaps negotiate with Austria *and* Russia, otherwise, if one is sure of the tsar *and* the tsarevich, only with Russia. But in any case the existing treaties must be maintained *as long as they last,* just as the old landsknechts used to do. No Haugwitz policy as in 1890.

We must keep Austria on its feet as long as we can, with or without a treaty. That it was not yesterday that I began to uphold this program, you can see from the fact that I was for Kiel and — the first to be so — for Werder.

There seemed every reason to believe that a reconstitution of the Three Emperors' League — to the exclusion of France — was imminently possible.[15]

The days and weeks went by, however, and no word came from St. Petersburg. The tsar never mentioned the matter. When pointedly asked about his Berlin trip, the tsarevich replied only that he had enjoyed it very much. The Kaiser and the Foreign Office had obviously overplayed their hand. Germany, at this time, was in the throes of the Army Bill crisis. Only two weeks before the tsarevich's arrival in Berlin, on January 11, Caprivi had made his frank and open statement to the Reichstag committee about the necessity of preserving Austria as a great power, of the probability of a two-front

---

[15]*G.P.,* VII, 243–244; Haller, *Aus dem Leben,* pp. 83–84; *Eulenburg,* I, 141. Cf. *Schulthess* (1893), pp. 7–8; Waldersee, *Denkwürdigkeiten,* II, 277, 284; Langer, *Franco-Russian Alliance,* pp. 301–303. Count Christian von Haugwitz was Prussian foreign minister, 1792–1804, 1805–1806.

war, and of the necessity of preparing an offensive strategy.[16] Just before the tsarevich's arrival, on January 22, the Kaiser had toasted the visiting duke of Edinburgh with the statement that, if some day it should be necessary for the English and German fleets to fight shoulder to shoulder together against a common enemy, "then will the famous watchword given out by England's greatest naval hero before the battle of Trafalgar, 'England expects every man to do his duty,' find an echo in the patriotic heart of the German fleet." And, on the Kaiser's birthday, the 27th, while the tsarevich was still in Berlin, fiery speeches in support of the Army Bill had been made by various generals, including General von Schkopp, governor of Cologne, who said, in part, "War is coming! May God grant that it finds the German nation rallied around its princes. If not, . . . then adieu, fair land!" The right hand of the Berlin government did not seem to know what its left hand was doing. And, in any case, who could tell what the result of the Army Bill deadlock would be? Dissolution of the Reichstag appeared inevitable. The tsar had every reason to wait quietly and observe.[17]

On March 30, 1893, the Ribot government fell in France and was succeeded by a combination of Dupuy as premier and Dévelle as foreign minister. Special attempts had already been made to regain the confidence of the Russians, including a direct apology from President Carnot to the tsar for the recent Panama excesses. The press was also held back during the spring from making any provocative comment on the German Army Bill. On the other hand, the French did all they could diplomatically to impress the Russians with the threat of the German army reorganization and of the need for precautionary measures. Also Caprivi, under pressure from the Conservatives, whose votes he needed for the Army Bill, and from the friends of the Conservatives within the Prussian Ministry, had not been able to offer sufficient tariff concessions in the spring of 1893 to bring the new, strong-minded Russian finance minister, Count Witte, to a trade agreement. In June, after the election had shown the strength of the agrarian movement, and with the Army Bill still hanging in the balance, Caprivi defied a Russian threat to raise their tariff rates, and an all-out tariff war resulted. On June 25

---

[16]See above, p. 240. Cf. Waldersee, *Denkwürdigkeiten*, II, 276; Thimme, "Bismarck und Kardorff," pt. II, pp. 27, 33. Ambassador Shuvalov was especially distressed by Caprivi's statement.

[17]Langer, *Franco-Russian Alliance*, pp. 304–310; Wippermann, 9(I):112, 230; *Die Nation*, X, 283; *G.P.*, VII, 418–428 and notes; Taylor, *Struggle for Mastery*, pp. 340–341. General von Werder, too, was much distressed by the occurrences enumerated.

the Russians announced a new differential tariff with a maximum some 30 per cent higher than their already very high rates. On July 25 the maximum rate was applied to Germany. On July 28 Germany retaliated by raising her tariffs on Russian exports 50 per cent. To this Russia replied on August 1 with a further special boost of her maximum tariff of 50 per cent against German exports. By way of contrast, the French concluded a tariff treaty with Russia in June. Of little economic importance, it was part of the French diplomatic campaign.[18]

In early July 1893 extensive rioting in Paris was suppressed rigorously by the government, a fact that impressed the tsar. On July 15 the German Army Bill was finally passed by the votes of the Poles, a fact that, along with the decoration of Koscielski, could not fail to impress the Russian court. Of primary importance, however, for the more favorable attitude of the Russians toward the French was the much stiffer attitude of the new French ministry toward England. Since the beginning of the construction of the Trans-Siberian Railway in 1892, Russia had turned her attention more and more to the east. The European press was full of articles, not on Bulgaria, but on new Russian expeditions in the Pamirs. Now in July 1893, the French suddenly began pressing west from Indochina into Siam, which the British preferred to preserve as a buffer state. As border clashes began to multiply, Lord Rosebery, nervous and uncertain, began to make confidential overtures to the Italian and German ambassadors. The British press mentioned the possibility of a quadruple alliance if the French went too far.[19]

These advances, however, were greeted in Berlin with coolness and suspicion. In a typical memorandum of July 27 Holstein questioned whether Rosebery's "somewhat dramatic confidences" to the German and Italian ambassadors were really, as Count Hatzfeldt reported, to bring pressure on his colleagues or were aimed rather

at covering and, in fact, making possible England's retreat by the introduction of a third party.

It is a matter of life and death for Italy not to leave England unsupported in a war against France. For this, however, one of two conditions must exist:

Either hostilities have already begun, in which case England can no

---

[18]Langer, *Franco-Russian Alliance*, 311–313, 305–306; Witte, *Memoirs*, pp. 63–69; *Schulthess* (1893), pp. 99, 287. For a résumé of the German-Russian tariff negotiations see *Schulthess* (1893), pp. 99–103; *G.P.*, VII, 443, note.

[19]Langer, *Franco-Russian Alliance*, pp. 313–324; *G.P.*, VII, 103–105, 203, note, 204; Dugdale, *German Diplomatic Documents*, II, 191–192, 236–237.

longer withdraw; or England has made a firm treaty with Italy, which must bear *Gladstone's* signature.

If Italy joins diplomatically in the Anglo-French quarrel before one of these suppositions is fulfilled, it will serve as a lightning rod for England, that is, England will probably slip out of the affair scot free, while France will suffer a diplomatic check, but in the process will have made up its mind to settle with Italy at the first opportunity. Recent experiences make it less likely than ever that a Gladstone ministry would then come to the aid of Italy *of its own free will* . . .

It is, therefore, directly to our interests that Italy does not worsen her relations with France without being certain of England's support *in fact or by treaty.*[20]

Meanwhile two French gunboats had advanced up the river to Bangkok, delivered an ultimatum to the Siamese, and, having received an unsatisfactory reply, had declared a blockade of the city. Such a blockade could only hurt the English, who carried on about 90 per cent of the trade there. On July 30, a Sunday, Lord Rosebery, alone in London, received a telegram from the captain of the British gunboat off Bangkok reporting that the French commander had asked him to withdraw his ship outside the blockaded area. All of Rosebery's cabinet colleagues were in the country for the weekend. In the Foreign Office there was only an old scrubwoman. On his own responsibility Rosebery sent off a telegram ordering the British commander to reject the French demand. Then he tried to contact Gladstone. For all he knew, his action might mean war. He sent off a telegram to Queen Victoria:

French Government demands we withdraw gunboats from before Bangkok. I have refused this. Desire to see Count Hatzfeldt in London immediately.[21]

The evening of July 30 His Majesty, the German Kaiser, who had come to Cowes for the yacht-racing, was dining there at a late hour with the prince of Wales and their suites. Suddenly the queen's private secretary, Sir Arthur Ponsonby, entered, obviously distraught, and handed Lord Rosebery's telegram to the Kaiser. The news fell like a bombshell among the company. The Kaiser retired to the *Hohenzollern,* called Phili Eulenburg into his cabin, and completely broke down.

[20]*G.P.,* VIII, 105, notes, 106; Dugdale, *German Diplomatic Documents,* II, 237–238.

[21]*G.P.,* VIII, 111–112, note, 107–108; Dugdale, *German Diplomatic Documents,* II, 239–240. For a full résumé of the Siam incident see Langer, *Franco-Russian Alliance,* pp. 324–330, especially 328, note.

I really have never seen him so overcome . . . The Kaiser exclaimed that England's fleet was weaker than the Russian and French fleets in combination. Even with the aid of our little fleet England would still be the weaker. The French (he said) wanted to drive Russia to some action — which, considering the tsar's hostile attitude toward us, they might succeed in doing. Our army was not strong enough to fight simultaneously against France and Russia. It was impossible to sit still and let the tempest break on our heads. All Germany's prestige was gone if we could not take a prominent part; and not to be a world power was to cut a deplorable figure. What were we to do?

With the help of Kiderlen, Eulenburg finally succeeded somewhat in calming the Kaiser down.

But he looked very wretched — pale, and biting his lips nervously. I felt dreadfully sorry for him. He, coming here with his big talk about our ships, felt driven into a corner as it were, and politically put in his place. And to be put in one's place is always a bitter pill for one's poor dear vanity.[22]

In Berlin they took the matter seriously but more calmly. On a well-reasoned dispatch of Count Hatzfeldt's, warning that the incident might develop into a general war and inquiring whether such a war would suit Germany politically and militarily at present, Caprivi commented that at present, as far as domestic affairs were concerned, a war would be "not undesirable," as far as military preparation was concerned, "as good now as later." In general, Berlin took the cautious attitude that England must be irrevocably engaged one way or another before Italy or the Triple Alliance could be allowed actively to enter the fray. Caprivi wrote:

For us the best beginning for the next great war would be for the first shot to be fired from an English ship. Then we are sure of being able to convert the Triple Alliance into a Quadruple one. We must avoid sending Italy forward alone. The blows would fall on her, and it would be all the worse for us later. Thus, first let England be engaged irrevocably, then, however — whether Russia comes in later or not — let all the Triple Alliance Powers or Italy + Germany go into action. That is the correct military sequence, and diplomacy must act in accordance with it.[23]

Before the crisis really got under way, however, suddenly it was over. Reports from Bangkok, Rosebery explained to the somewhat incredulous Germans, had been much exaggerated. All talk of a

[22]Haller, *Eulenburg*, I, 142–144.
[23]*G.P.*, VIII, 108–110, notes; Dugdale, *German Diplomatic Documents*, II, 241–242.

quadruple alliance quickly ceased. No matter what Rosebery said, it looked to many outsiders as if England had backed down before the French. The Germans, who had significantly enough naturally accepted the idea that they would ultimately go to the aid of England, but whose suspicion of the motives of the Gladstone government in the affair seemed almost pathological, found these suspicions all confirmed in the event. With the Kaiser, especially, the vivid memory of the fatal hour at Cowes and of his own ignominious panic rankled painfully. When Rosebery explained that, because of the Kaiser's presence in England, he had thought it only proper that his own telegram to the queen should be communicated to him, the Kaiser scribbled on Hatzfeldt's report:

What a yarn! That doesn't have to be done through a deathly pale private secretary at 12 o'clock at night.[24]

The Russians were, of course, greatly pleased by these new developments. Within a week of the Siam incident they promised the French to send a naval squadron to Toulon in October. During September the whole European press busied itself excitedly over this Russian visit and especially over the announced intention of the Russians subsequently to establish a squadron, with the help of French bases, permanently in the Mediterranean. If this actually came about, Caprivi told the Austrian ambassador, it would be a more serious threat to the general peace of Europe than any event in the last twenty years. French-Russian naval coöperation would outbalance the English in the Mediterranean, as elsewhere in the world, and might lead to a fundamental readjustment of the balance of power. Caprivi, resting at Carlsbad in September 1893, sent a note to Marschall expressing deep concern over the potentialities of the coming Toulon visit as a provocation to the Triple Alliance.[25]

On October 13, 1893, the Russian Admiral Avellan arrived at Toulon with five warships, and the festivities began. The admiral and his men were feted in Toulon, Marseilles, Lyon, and Paris. Russian and French flags blossomed everywhere, banquets and demonstrations abounded. The spectacle was unprecedented and

[24]*G.P.*, VIII, 107–116; Dugdale, *German Diplomatic Documents*, II, 239–245; Eyck, *Wilhelm II*, pp. 111–112; *G.P.*, VIII, 107, note. On the Siam crisis see also Hatzfeldt to Holstein, August 2, 7, September 17, October 19, November 8, 18, 1890, *Holstein Papers, Correspondence*.

[25]Langer, *Franco-Russian Alliance*, pp. 332–347; *G.P.*, VII, 247, VIII, 119–122; Dugdale, *German Diplomatic Documents*, II, 247. For Queen Victoria's reaction, see Hatzfeldt to Holstein, August 7, 1893, *Holstein Papers, Correspondence*.

made a great impression on the whole continent. The point of it all was further driven home by a personal visit of the tsar to a French ship at Copenhagen on the same day the Russian ships arrived at Toulon. There was, however, no anti-German flavor throughout the affair. The French had, in fact, been making friendly gestures towards Germany, and the final telegram of the tsar to President Carnot at the end of the celebration could be variously interpreted.

The evidences of sincere sympathy, which have once again been manifested so eloquently, will add one more link to the chain which unites our two countries and will, I hope, help to strengthen the general peace, the object of our constant efforts and prayers.[26]

The Toulon demonstration, with its direct bearing on the naval situation in the Mediterranean, was, in fact, clearly directed against England. There it was so recognized, and a tremendous agitation arose in press, Parliament, and naval circles for increases in the navy, which, at length, forced the resignation of the elderly Gladstone in March 1894. In Germany this development, after Siam, was taken rather coolly. The chief tie to England was through the Mediterranean interests of Italy. Any attack on Italy by France would automatically bring in Austria and Germany. Berlin realized that during the Toulon days the tsar had held back the French from any anti-German or anti-Italian expressions. A Russian-inspired article in *Figaro* on October 13 had declared pointedly that the tsar wanted Europe to know that Russia would support France if attacked but would not support her in any aggressive action. Whereas in early September, before Toulon, the Kaiser, in connection with the German army maneuvers, had made characteristically bellicose speeches in Lorraine with the crown prince of Italy by his side, later during the height of the Toulon festivities he had sent a telegram of condolence on the death of Marshal MacMahon. This telegram was very favorably received by the French press. The Toulon affair, Secretary Marschall said to the Belgian ambassador on October 25, was a greater threat to England than to the Triple Alliance. France and Russia did not have any interests in common on the European continent, but did have common interests in the Mediterranean and the Far East. England, on the other hand, did not want to or could not tie herself closely to the Central Powers, although she would

[26]Langer, *Franco-Russian Alliance*, pp. 348–349; *G.P.*, VII, 247–253; *Schulthess* (1893), pp. 239–242; Dugdale, *German Diplomatic Documents*, II, 246–247.

like to depend on them in a crisis, and the Central Powers had no interest in defending England's interests overseas.[27]

During the fall and winter, in fact, the European diplomatic picture began to take on more the aspect of a five-power continental association against England. Forewarned by the Siam episode, Germany was not going to allow England to use her as a cat's-paw or as a "buffer" against the French or the Russians. They must be wary, Marschall wrote to Hatzfeldt, of a country which was not looking for allies but for lightning rods. The Gladstone ministry would always be inclined to a do-nothing policy, and Lord Rosebery had demonstrated in the Siam affair neither the power nor the will to go his own way. Under the circumstances Berlin preferred to cultivate the friendship of the French and Russians, to try energetically to negate the Franco-Russian rapprochement or at least to render it harmless to themselves. In November 1893 Germany and England signed an agreement delimiting the western boundary of the German African colony of Cameroons but leaving the eastern boundary open, thus cutting off France from expanding eastward into the Sudan and to the upper Nile. But in March 1894 Germany came to an agreement with France limiting the eastern Cameroons boundary and opening the way once more for French expansion into the Sudan.[28]

The fate of the English in the Mediterranean might leave the Germans unmoved; it could not be regarded with equanimity, however, by Austria. An English abdication in the Mediterranean in favor of France and Russia would on the one hand undermine Italy's position in the Triple Alliance, making an agreement with France imperative for her, and on the other hand would leave Austria to face alone the intermittent pressure of Russia at the Straits and in the neighboring Balkans. During the winter of 1893–1894, therefore, Count Kálnoky did his utmost to extract a pledge from Lord Rosebery that England would follow her own interests in supporting Italy against France in the Mediterranean and Austria against Russia and France at the Straits. In response to these efforts, Rosebery merely pointed out that the English were determined, as before, to oppose a Russian advance on the Straits, but that they could

[27]Langer, *Franco-Russian Alliance*, pp. 355–365, 350–353; *The Times, passim; Schulthess* (1893), pp. 121ff., 240; *G.P.*, VII, 337–338; Köhler, *Revanche-idee*, pp. 382–396, quote from Marschall, p. 388. It is interesting that at this time the Germans were encouraging the English to build up their navy: see Hatzfeldt to Holstein, December 13, 1893, *Holstein Papers, Correspondence.*

[28]*G.P.*, VIII, 124–127, 413–423, VII, 335–336 and note; Langer, *Franco-Russian Alliance*, p. 353.

not hold the Straits against the fleets of both Russia and France. Consequently, they would need the assistance of the Triple Alliance to hold back France in a position of neutrality.[29]

The problem thus inevitably boiled down to a question of the attitude of Germany. But when, in February 1894, the Austrians approached Berlin on the question, they found very little to encourage them. The previous September at the Austro-Hungarian army maneuvers at Güns the Kaiser had told Emperor Francis Joseph that Germany had no direct interest in the Straits question and could not support Austria there. In December Holstein had written to Hatzfeldt, "In no case, however, do *we* put ourselves forward in Balkan or Mediterranean affairs. If we see that the interested parties are doing nothing, then we turn aside, i.e., let the Russian stream flow calmly into the Mediterranean and await the results." Now, in February, in reply to Rosebery's suggestion, Caprivi said flatly that there could be no question of risking war with France over a Russian threat to the Straits. He did not believe that the Russians intended a move there soon, anyway, and if Russia did raise the Straits question, it would be better to settle the problem peacefully by reciprocal compensation. If England would formally join the Triple Alliance, all well and good, but otherwise Germany would only be placing her own fate and that of her allies in English hands. It was quite obvious that Caprivi, at this point, had little faith in England, but, more important, he and the other Berlin officials were completely absorbed in trying to weaken the Franco-Russian relationship by promoting a close rapprochement with Russia. In a memorandum summing up the decisive conversation with the Austrian ambassador in April 1894, the chancellor wrote:

> Having given our reasons for avoiding any engagement with England, I added that we were trying to turn Russia away from France and that we might succeed in this in the course of the year. But we should risk failure, if we made it possible for England to denounce to Russia any words of ours unfavorable to her on the Dardanelles question.[30]

Since the early days of 1890 and the decision not to renew the Reinsurance Treaty, the foreign policy of the New Course had swung halfway around the circle — now everything appeared up-

[29]Langer, *Franco-Russian Alliance*, pp. 367–381; *G.P.*, IX, 123–129; Dugdale, *German Diplomatic Documents*, II, 259–261.

[30]Langer, *Franco-Russian Alliance*, pp. 381–389; *G.P.*, IX, 101–102, 105–109, 134–146; Caprivi quote, p. 144; Holstein to Hatzfeldt, December 9, Holstein memorandum, December 8, 1893, Hatzfeldt to Holstein, February 15, 28, 1894, *Holstein Papers, Correspondence*.

side down. Whereas then it was a secret agreement with Russia which might shatter the Triple Alliance and alienate England through some indiscretion, now it was a secret agreement with England which — through an "indiscretion" — might alienate Russia. Whereas then the new policy tended to support Austria at the Straits without injuring Russia, now it had swung back remarkably close to the old Bismarck policy of supporting Russia without injuring Austria. To no one was this shift so clear as to Count Hatzfeldt, whose sympathies tended to adhere to the land to which he was accredited. He complained in a private letter to Holstein in December that Sir Philip Currie, the new English ambassador to the Porte, would not be encouraged to oppose Russia energetically there when he discovered

[that] Radolin alone offers him neither advice nor the slightest political help, that is to say, *very much less* than we offered to Salisbury's representative, White. I refer to the Bulgarian Bishops and similar matters.[31] It is known that at that time I had to represent the view *here* that we could not stand in the *foreground* but eventually would stand behind our friends. I do not pretend to judge whether it is correct for us to cling to our present reserve in Constantinople, because I have not the necessary means for seeing the whole situation . . . I regret to see in the final sentence of one of Reuss's latest reports, that he is faithful to the old Bismarckian policy of a separate understanding of Austria with Russia and considers it *especially desirable*. He probably says so to Kálnoky — I am all the more determined to keep silence, for words would fail me, if my opinion were asked for.

If Italy falls away and England throws up her part, we naturally shall be quite right, as I often said to Salisbury, *de retirer notre épingle du jeu* [to extricate ourselves]. But I cannot describe the political situation, which would then follow in Europe, as a *desirable* one. In my opinion — and the Emperor Francis Joseph appears to agree with me — Austria would merely be buying a reprieve for her existence as a Great Power, and this latter factor, apart from all others, seems to me an essential condition for the greatness and welfare of the German Empire.

Hatzfeldt's question was indeed a fundamental one. Could the sprawling empire of the Habsburgs, now in a state of progressive decay, survive intact the attainment of hegemony over the Straits — and, therefore, the Balkans — by Russia? And had not Caprivi himself declared the year before that it was in Germany's fundamental interest to maintain Austria-Hungary in her status as a Great Power? Temporarily, of course, Caprivi was right in regarding the question

[31]See above, p. 114.

as secondary and academic; Russia had definitely, for the time being, shifted her interest from the Near to the Far East. But the fundamental conflict inherent in the Balkan question was a permanent factor which would come up again. Meanwhile, however, Count Hatzfeldt found no sympathy for his fears. The Berlin government was earnestly intent on winning back the friendship of Russia. The most obvious and effective way of winning Russian friendship, of course, was to put an end to the tariff war which had broken out in the summer of 1893 and to conclude the long-pending trade treaty.[32]

2

TRADE TREATIES (II)

On November 16, 1893, the Reichstag was opened with the usual ceremony. The main business for the new session consisted of a second string of trade treaties, the so-called "little trade treaties" with Spain, Serbia, and Rumania, and Miquel's new Reich tax measures. Here, at once, the growing but heretofore hidden conflict in the government, the struggle between Reich and Prussia, between Caprivi and Miquel, came openly to the fore. For the approval of his trade treaties, Caprivi must withstand the passionate opposition of the right and look for his support on the left, whereas Miquel could hope to find support for his new taxes only on the right. Before the Reichstag, in the initial debate, Caprivi defended his tariff policy with the very able assistance of Baron Marschall, whose interest in things economic and whose experience as a state's attorney here stood him in good stead. The tax program was defended energetically by Count Posadowsky, whose position before the house and whose responsibility for the tax legislation, however, were obviously subordinate to that of Prussian Finance Minister Miquel.[33]

With the passage of the Army Bill in the summer, the Reichstag had been promised that the necessary new taxes would fall only on the "strongest shoulders" of the population. To the parties on the left this principle, if it were to be fully carried out, meant the introduction of direct taxes into Reich financing, a Reich income tax

[32]Langer, *Franco-Russian Alliance*, pp. 391–392; *G.P.*, IX, 117–122; Dugdale, *German Diplomatic Documents*, II, 254–259; Hatzfeldt to Holstein, December 13, 1893, *Holstein Papers, Correspondence*.

[33]*Schulthess* (1893), pp. 151f., 153–156, (1894), pp. 4–14, 17–23; *Sten. Ber.* (1893–1894), I, II, III; *DDF*, 1 ser., X, 552; Raschdau, *Bismarck u. Caprivi*, pp. 227, 231; Hammann, *Der Neue Kurs*, p. 91; *Die Nation*, XI (1893–1894), 96–97, 129–131.

or, at least, a Reich inheritance tax. The new tax proposals, as prepared by Miquel, did not, however, interpret the statement in such an extreme fashion. Bismarck had originally intended Reich finances to be supported by "matricular" cash payments by the federal states. Then, however, to create a more independent financial position for the Reich, he had developed a system of indirect Reich taxes. His protectionist high-tariff policy, inaugurated in 1879, had fitted nicely into this search for independent revenue. At the same time, to mollify the states, the "Franckenstein clause" was passed (1879), which provided that any surplus amount of Reich income over 130 million Marks would be given over to the states. Thus, balancing "matricular contributions" from the states to the Reich over against the "Franckenstein" payments from the Reich to the states, in any one year — depending on how both the Reich and the member states' budgets happened to balance, the extent of Reich income, and the size of the matricular payments — the Reich might contribute a net payment to the states' finances or the states make a net payment to the Reich. For example, in 1890–1891 Prussia had benefited by a net receipt of 46 million M *from* the Reich, whereas in 1893–1894 Prussia made a net payment of 20 million M *to* the Reich. This arrangement did not make sound financial practices in the states particularly easy, and it was from the point of view of the states that Prussian Finance Minister Miquel now approached the Reich finances. Prussian revenue was derived from direct taxes on income and property, affecting mostly the upper classes. In insisting that the Reich live off its own revenue — derived from indirect taxes, falling most heavily upon the lower classes — Miquel was protecting both Prussia from paying large matricular contributions and the propertied classes from paying higher taxes. Miquel's tax scheme proposed to raise 100 million M additional revenue from new taxes, 60 million to be applied to the Reich budget and the remaining 40 million to be given as a fixed yearly payment to the states, thus replacing the Franckenstein clause provision. This prospect of an assured and fixed income for the states from the Reich Treasury gave the bill a marked particularist character. It was well received by the Bundesrat, and Miquel was given a free hand by Caprivi to take the bill through the Reichstag. The new taxes, as before, were to be indirect. Instead of von Maltzahn's beer and brandy taxes Miquel proposed taxes on tobacco and wine, as well as assorted stamp duties. The taxation of the "stronger shoulders" was supposedly indicated by the shift from beer to wine! But a tax on consumption was not to be reckoned — at least by the parties of the left — as a tax affecting the higher income levels. Nor could the slogan, let the Reich pay its own way, hide the fact that Reich and Prussian taxpayers were largely identical. The heightening of Reich taxes, including the assured payments to the states, with the practical elimination of matricular payments, thus meant in over-all effect that the smaller, comparatively stable state budgets for schools and police would be met by direct taxation on property and income, while the huge, rapidly swelling national budget for the army and navy would be met by indirect taxes on articles of mass consumption. It was clear that Miquel's scheme very skillfully combined a particularist (Prussian) outlook with a policy favorable to the propertied classes. It was Miquel's attempt to carry over into the Reich the conservative property-conscious policy which had made him so popular in Prussia.[34]

There was no doubt about it, however much it might be overlooked by the liberal press — a severe crisis actually existed in agriculture. Whether it was the result of overvaluation and overindebtedness of the big estates, competition from the virgin soil of the United States and Argentina, a general sinking of prices due to the limited world supply of gold, no matter what the cause of the crisis, the average price of a metric ton of rye, which over the decade of 1880–1889 had held an average level of 154 M — and in 1891 had reached the extraordinary height of 208 M — had by 1894 fallen to 118 M. Wheat, quoted for 1880–1889 at 185 M — 222 M in 1891 — had dropped in 1894 to 135 M. Under normal harvest conditions it was in many cases impossible, with such prices, for proprietors to cover their costs of production.[35]

Under the pressure of declining prices and mounting debts the landed proprietors became more and more enthusiastic in the cause of a bimetallic monetary standard. The old "normal" relation of gold to silver of 1:15 had fallen by 1893 almost to 1:30. Silver, in other words, was worth only half of what it had been twenty years before; or, conversely, gold was twice as dear. All over the world expanded economic activity seemed to have outrun the gold supply, causing a gradual rise in the value of gold-backed currency and an accompanying general decline in prices. This deflationary trend hit the heavily indebted farmer especially hard. Interest rates on his mort-

[34]*Die Nation*, XI (1893–1894), 130–131; Geiger, *Miquel*, p. 69; *Schulthess* (1893), pp. 154–156, (1894), pp. 34–42; Herzfeld, *Miquel*, II, 350–360; *Pr. Jbb.*, 74:585–586.

[35]Von der Goltz, *Geschichte der dtn. Landwirtschaft*, II, 390ff.; Bachem, *Zentrumspartei*, V, 252; Lotz, "Handelspolitik," pp. 103–104, 112–113; *Pr. Jbb.*, 74:583–585. Kardorff in the Reichstag, *Sten. Ber.* (1892–1893), I, 67.

gages and loans remained high, whereas, especially in good years, his crops brought less and less cash on the world market. Consequently farmers everywhere, whether in Germany, France, or the United States, whether conservative Junker aristocrats or radical, independent "dirt farmers," turned for economic salvation to the sponsoring of a government policy of "cheap money," that is, to a currency based on silver — cheaper and more plentiful — or on both silver and gold — a bimetallic monetary standard.[36]

Whereas in 1891 Caprivi had been able to shrug off Kardorff and his bimetallist friends with the statement that they represented only a "small isolated group," in 1893 he felt it necessary to insist that in the monetary question he was "not at all unyielding" and was at all times willing to be persuaded, and in February 1894 he appointed a commission to investigate and to discuss measures for relieving the silver crisis. More and more the agrarians — now in their new "economic association" including some 150 members of the Reichstag, from the Conservatives and Free Conservatives to the National Liberals and Center — were inclined to set up bimetallism as the price for their support of the government's trade treaties. Since, however, as Caprivi repeatedly emphasized, very little could be done towards adopting a bimetallic standard without some similar action abroad and particularly in England, and since this was extremely unlikely with a Gladstone government in England, the all-or-nothing attack of the agrarians on the trade treaties took on the character of a general and relentless campaign not for any practical advantage but merely to oust Caprivi. The system of reciprocal trade treaties had been endorsed by the Reichstag in 1891 by an overwhelming majority, including a sizable number of Conservative votes. Once such a system had been adopted it would be economically and, in the end, politically unwise and futile to refuse to extend it to include this nation or that. The attack on the Caprivi treaties served very well, however, as a rallying cry for the agitation of the Farmers' League among the peasantry and as a means of bringing political pressure to bear upon the Caprivi regime.[37]

[36]Cf. A. Wagner's article, "Die neueste Silberkrisis u. unsere Münzwesen," *Pr. Jbb.*, 74:138–166, 242–284. American agrarians founded the new Populist party in 1892, and in 1896 the agrarian populists captured the Democratic party, nominating their man, Bryan, for the presidency after his famous "Cross of Gold" speech. Cf. J. D. Hicks, *The Populist Revolt* (Minneapolis, 1931).

[37]*Sten. Ber.* (1890–1892), V, 3336, (1893–1894), I, 454; *Schulthess* (1893), pp. 166–167, (1894), pp. 69–70; Wippermann, 10(I):44–51, 290–291. Cf. Thimme, "Bismarck und Kardorff," pt. II, pp. 154–155.

The Rumanian Treaty

It was the Rumanian treaty which, in the fall of 1893, provoked the full fury of the agrarians. Rightly, they claimed that a treaty with Rumania was only the first step towards a treaty with Russia. If the conventional tariff were granted to Rumanian grain, it would be impossible to maintain a high rate against Russia. Also, since the beginning of the tariff war with Russia the previous summer, Rumania had become an important exporter of grain to Germany. Whereas in 1889 Russia had supplied 58 per cent of German wheat imports and Rumania only 5 per cent, in 1893 Russia was supplying only 3 per cent and Rumania 20 per cent. The United States and Argentina, however, which, in 1893, were contributing respectively 45 per cent and 22 per cent of the wheat imported, already enjoyed the conventional rate through most-favored-nation agreements.[38]

Since the Reichstag itself had previously granted most-favored-nation status provisionally also to Rumania during negotiation of the treaty, the bitter debates during November and December 1893 must be regarded not so much as an attack on the Rumanian treaty itself as a general test of agrarian strength. The agrarians accused Caprivi of telling Baron von Manteuffel in a private conversation that agrarian distress was due to overvaluation of their estates and that, although this was regrettable, there was nothing the government could do about it; the Junkers must either live less expensively or liquidate some of their holdings.[39] The *Kreuzzeitung* wrote articles attacking the dangerous liberalism of the "bureaucracy," which had ignored the plight of agriculture. The simple peasant, it wrote, could not understand why the Kaiser should permit such an economic policy.

He figures that not only must he buy the friendship of the Austrians and Italians with his hard-earned money but that now we must pay this tribute to make the Russians peaceful. These people are not so far wrong, but what would Frederick the Great, what would the Great Elector say if he heard his men of the Mark talk this way, the Brandenburg peasants with whom he mastered the whole world. Buying peace! Pfui, shocking words for every Prussian! — But are we so far removed from this? . . .

We must rip up the trade treaties with Austria and Italy, if necessary with sword in hand! Better an honorable battle for life and death than this living starvation![40]

[38]*Sten. Ber.* (1893–1894), *Anlageband* I, 81ff., II, 1210ff.; Lotz, "Handelspolitik," pp. 110–111.

[39]*Schulthess* (1893), pp. 152–153; *Pr. Jbb.*, 74:583–584.

[40]*Schulthess* (1893), pp. 146–147, 154.

In the Reichstag von Manteuffel declared that in voting for the trade treaties in 1891 he had made a political mistake. There had been talk then of the new trade treaties strengthening the Triple Alliance; this could hardly apply to the extension of the system to include every power in Europe. The government was merely continuing to make blunders which were the necessary results of such a mistaken policy. "From this moment," he declared, "I separate myself from the Federated Governments." The Conservatives, warned von Plötz and von Hammerstein, had made possible the passage of the Army Bill; the government could not continue to rule without the Conservatives. The Farmers' League, declared Deputy von Plötz, had 160,000 members, two newspapers, over 1,000 district leaders, and over 10,000 workers.[41]

The Farmers' League might go as far in its agitation and its statements as it pleased. There was no way in this semiparliamentary state of calling it to account. No matter what happened, it was the government, the bureaucratic officials of the crown who would bear the responsibility. Hammerstein or Kardorff had as little prospect of having to head a ministry and defend their agrarian policies from the government table as did Eugen Richter or the Social Democrats their negative attitude towards military defense. With no final responsibility attached to its decisions the Reichtag was fast becoming a mere arena for the conflict of special interests, intent on forcing the government to their point of view. As long as there was no connection between the governing bureaucracy and the parties the sky was the limit for pressure politics. Let the government decide on actual policy.[42]

Caprivi did not take the agrarian attack lying down, but opposed it as vigorously as he could.

I have directed myself, and do so again today, against these agitational methods which have been adopted. Again today I repeat: it is not conservative to battle with majorities against authority ("Very true!"). It is not right to battle with the masses against the authority of the government. The government must support itself upon a large segment of the population. In our existing party situation it is impossible for a government, whether in the Reich or in an individual state, to support itself upon a single party. Upon which one, then, gentlemen? Are you able to give the government a majority it can govern with? No! Therefore, since I have had the honor to hold this office there has been no alternative but

---

[41]*Sten. Ber.* (1893–1894), I, 450, 46, 66, 45; Lotz, "Handelspolitik," pp. 113–114; *Schulthess* (1893), pp. 162–165.

[42]Cf. Lotz, "Handelspolitik," pp. 114–115.

to attempt to achieve what the Federated Governments believe to be right with whatever support is available to us at the time.

The Farmers' League in the recent election had thrown its votes only to those candidates who would pledge themselves to vote against the Rumanian and the Russian trade treaties. This limitation on the freedom of the deputy, said Caprivi, was contrary to the spirit of the constitution, where it was stated specifically that the members of the Reichstag represented the whole nation. The Reichstag should represent the best and wisest of the nation; its members should be free to make their own decisions. Members should not become completely dependent on their constituencies. They must consult the voters' interests, yes, but they must also teach and instruct them on the basis of their own greater knowledge of affairs. It was, therefore, the duty of the deputies to keep the agrarian movement within bounds.

But what I gather from the cat-calls and your laughter here shows me that you do not share this opinion, and from this I conclude correctly that what you do is dangerous and that you have no will to resist it ("Very true!" on the left), you want to be led by the masses, you see in the masses a power which drives you on! [43]

This sharp language of a conservative Prussian nobleman, official, and army general could not be expected to please the Conservative agrarian nobles against whom it was directed. On December 20 the *Kreuzzeitung* delivered a formal declaration of war.

The action of Reich Chancellor Count Caprivi against the Conservatives has created an unbridgeable gulf between him and the Conservatives. The origin of this breach goes further back; the statements with which the Herr Reich Chancellor greeted the Tivoli Program of the Conservatives gave rise in Conservative circles to the idea that the party unfortunately would not be able further to carry on a fruitful policy with the head of the government. How justified this interpretation was recent occurrences have clearly shown. The tie between the Reich chancellor and the Conservatives has been severed by the former. There can be no doubt on this score.

It follows necessarily from this that the Conservatives no longer possess any confidence in the head of the government.

Conservative interests coincide with the vital interests of the state; for this reason no party interests as such exist for us, and the accusation of demagoguery is, therefore, meaningless.[44]

[43]*Sten. Ber.* (1893–1894), I, 452–454; *Schulthess* (1893), pp. 165–166.
[44]*Schulthess* (1893), p. 168; Wippermann, 9(II):97–98.

With the parties of the right irreconcilably opposed to the trade treaties and to Caprivi personally, with the parties of the left generally disposed in favor of the treaties, everything depended, in the Reichstag, upon how the members of the middle parties cast their votes. The majority of the Free Conservatives, under the leadership of von Kardorff, lined up solidly with the Conservatives and the Farmers' League. A handful of industrialists followed the lead of Baron Carl von Stumm-Halberg, who strongly supported the treaties. The clash between agriculture and industry waxed hotter within the Free Conservative party as Stumm got control of the party organ, the *Post*, and began to use it to advance his own special philosophy of severe but benevolent industrial paternalism.[45] The National Liberal leadership supported the treaties, but many of its deputies had made campaign pledges against the treaties to the Farmers' League. The same situation existed within the Center. During the Army Bill debate in July Caprivi had accused the Center of going democratic under Lieber's leadership. This accusation had been stoutly denied at the time, although it was a fact that the pro-Army Bill aristocrats had lost their seats in the election. Since then, with his rivals gone from the Reichstag, Dr. Lieber had become convinced that a policy of fruitless opposition would be fatal to the party in the long run and that a return to the traditional Windthorst policy of gaining important concessions by supporting the government was in order. Also, there was the ominous probability that if he were defeated on the Rumanian treaty Caprivi would not risk another dissolution at the height of the agrarian agitation but would resign. Another chancellor would hardly be as well disposed towards the Center party. But even Lieber could not completely offset the effects of the agrarian movement, especially among the Bavarian deputies. The outcome of the struggle was, therefore, in considerable doubt up to the last minute.[46]

The decisive vote came at the end of the second reading of the Rumanian treaty on December 13, when it was approved by the Reichstag by a vote of 189 to 165. Against the bill had voted practically all the Conservatives (64), the Anti-Semites (13), the majority of the Free Conservatives (18), a minority of the National Liberals (13), and slightly more than half (49) of the Center, plus some

---

[45]Thimme, "Bismarck und Kardorff," pt. II, pp. 154–155; Kardorff, *Kardorff*, p. 286; Hellwig, *Stumm*, pp. 479–482.

[46]*Sten. Ber.* (1893), p. 44; cf. Schneidewin, "Briefe," p. 139; Bachem, *Zentrumspartei*, V, 306, 314–316, 318–319, 328–335; Wippermann, 9(II):100; *Pr. Jbb.*, 74:586; *Die Nation*, XI, 164–165. For a more detailed report of the Reichstag debates see Tirrell, *German Agrarian Politics*, pp. 207ff.

scattered splinter party votes. For the bill had voted all of the Social Democrats (38), both groups of Radicals (37), the Poles (15), the South German People's party (8), the majority of the National Liberals (34), the minority of the Center (45), 6 Free Conservatives, and 2 "wild" Conservatives.[47]

Most noteworthy was the solid support of the government by the Social Democrats. In 1891 their support could easily have been dispensed with. This time their vote could easily have defeated the government. For a truly revolutionary party there could be few more favorable opportunities. A dissolution and new election on the trade-treaty issue could only further strengthen the left; the acceptance of defeat by the Caprivi government on the issue without a dissolution could only produce even worse confusion and, most probably, a new government, which would be a clear victory for the Reichstag. These waters were certainly troubled enough, but the Social Democrats resolutely refused to fish in them. They would be faithful to their allegiance to the free-trade principle. Also, there were other considerations. Freed from the repression of Bismarck's anti-Socialist law, the Social Democrats in 1891 had united triumphantly at Erfurt behind a bold new program of theoretical Marxism, combined with concrete demands for responsible, democratic government. But already their new freedom and their growing strength in the Reichstag were producing within their ranks severe divergencies over tactics. Between the demand for direct action of the Berlin "Jungen," who busied themselves organizing demonstrations of the unemployed and holding mass meetings, and the conservative demands of Georg von Vollmar, who was concerned with the plight of the peasant and with practical agrarian reform, the old leadership of Liebknecht and Bebel had difficulty steering a middle course. There was always the possibility that extremism might provoke a new reaction and new repressive measures. The way of parliamentary action seemed safer and surer. "Their own following demands from them practical achievements that benefit the present generation and not some distant and uncertain future . . . They are afraid of the anger of the industrial workers in the districts where the rejection of the treaties would bring about lay-offs and don't dare to calm the comrades with the orthodox teaching that the sooner they become a ragged proletariat the sooner the all-saving revolution will come." [48]

The victory in the Rumanian trade treaty could hardly be regarded as comforting to the government. The outlook for the more

[47]*Schulthess* (1893), pp. 161–162; Bachem, *Zentrumspartei,* V, 335.
[48]*Pr. Jbb.,* 75:203–204. See above, p. 129, and below, p. 334.

crucial Russian treaty looked extremely dubious. Many of those voting for the Rumanian treaty had specifically reserved for themselves a free hand on the Russian treaty.[49] Both sides now redoubled their efforts. Local government officials in Prussia were openly following the line of the Farmers' League and agitating against the government. On December 22 Caprivi succeeded in extracting an executive order from Count Botho Eulenburg calling attention to Bismarck's order of 1882, commanding full support of government policy by all officials. To this the *Kreuzzeitung* replied with a rather involved constitutional argument, invoking the current dichotomy between Reich and Prussia, that stated, in brief, that the decree of 1882 applied only to Prussia and could not possibly have a bearing on the trade-treaty policy, which was a Reich affair.[50]

In early January Caprivi took the initiative by publishing in the *Reichsanzeiger* an exchange of letters between himself and the East Prussian Conservative Association, which, a moderate group, had not coöperated with the extreme program of the Farmers' League. In his letter Caprivi announced that the government was considering repeal of the identity declaration for exported grain and investigation of the bimetallism question by a special commission. Through discussion of bimetallism in a commission he obviously hoped to illumine its essential impracticality and thus render it useless as a propaganda slogan. The repeal of the identity declaration, on the other hand, would be of considerable practical value to eastern grain growers.

Heretofore the government had lifted the import duty on grain which was reëxported if the exporter could show that it was the same grain. Now this proof of identity requirement was to be repealed, which meant, in effect, that the East Elbian proprietors could ship their grain overseas to Scandinavia and England immediately after the harvest for ready cash at a cheap transportation cost and then replace it later with foreign grain imported in the west *duty free,* and sold there at the higher, protected German market price. The saving in internal transportation costs thus realized by this double transaction meant that the Junker could make more money from the 3½ M Caprivi tariff than he had from the previous tariff of 5 M. The Junker class had, in the past, been given all sorts of privileges. Even now, with the remaining tariff on grain, the liquor subsidy, the general emphasis on indirect taxation in the Reich, unequal election districts in the Reich, and the old three-class voting system still in

---

[49]*Die Nation*, XI, 160.
[50]*Schulthess* (1893), pp. 168–169; Hohenlohe, *Memoirs,* II, 463.

operation in Prussia, the Junkers, as a class, occupied a very special economic and political position. Inasmuch as these gentlemen were the proprietors of large agricultural estates and could claim to speak for agriculture, the nation as a whole might possibly be convinced that the necessity of maintaining German agriculture, of assuring an adequate food supply in time of war, was sufficient reason to give them special favors. With the repeal of the identity requirement, however, the resulting quick export of grain after the harvest would actually, in the future, leave Germany every year in a most precarious and vulnerable position.[51]

The proposed repeal of the identity declaration was, thus, an important concession to agrarian interests, which might break the opposition to the Russian treaty, or at least take some of the sting out of the movement. The Conservatives, however, had no intention of weakening in their campaign. On January 10 they were instrumental in cutting down the budget of the Reich Office of the Interior in the Reichstag Budget Committee — now chaired by von Kardorff. For this action the *Konservativer Korrespondenz* gave the following explanation:

He who has eyes to see cannot close them to the fact that only Jews and middle-class and socialist democrats are "satisfied" with the present situation. If to disturb this satisfaction is demagoguery, then indeed — but only then — is the Conservative as a Christian and a monarchist by the purest standard a nasty demagogue. Is this, perhaps, the only way in which government and liberal circles now also look at the situation? If so, then many things will have to be explained.[52]

Difficulties now began to multiply within the federal machinery; namely, in Bavaria and Prussia. The Bavarian Landtag passed a resolution sponsored by representatives of the Center party demanding that the grain tariff should be maintained at a high level in the treaty with Russia and opposing the repeal of the identity declaration. To satisfy Bavaria and maintain peace within the Bundesrat and also to gain needed Center votes in the Reichstag, Caprivi now proposed to repeal the special graduated freight rate introduced on the Prussian railroads in 1891 to ease the grain shortage by encouraging long distance shipments from the east. Here, however, the Prussian State Ministry objected that Prussia needed this revenue and that the chancellor in tampering with the Prussian railroads was exceeding his proper jurisdiction and invading Prussian domes-

---

[51]*Schulthess* (1894), pp. 2–3; Wippermann, 10(I):37–40; *Die Nation*, XI, 217–220; Lotz, "Handelspolitik," pp. 129–131; Ziekursch, *Geschichte*, III, 60–62.
[52]*Schulthess* (1894), p. 4.

tic affairs. Since failure to conciliate the Center might lead to the fall of the Crailsheim government in Bavaria, the loss of Center votes in the Reichstag, and defeat for the Russian trade treaty, Caprivi countered this Miquel-Eulenburg obstruction in the ministry with the threat of his own resignation. With the aid of Phili Eulenburg the Kaiser was persuaded to back Caprivi, and the Prussian railroad freight rate was sacrificed. Eastern grain growers were thus to be conciliated through the repeal of the identity declaration, western grain growers through the repeal of the Prussian graduated freight rate.[53]

Reconciliation with Bismarck

At this juncture the tenseness of the political atmosphere in Berlin was brought to explosive proportions as the Kaiser suddenly reconciled himself — at least outwardly — with Bismarck. In the late summer of 1893 the seventy-eight-year-old Bismarck had fallen critically ill with inflammation of the lungs and shingles. His illness, however, had been kept a close secret by his family, and reports of it had not reached the government until mid-September, when the medical crisis was long since past. Lacking exact information, however, Berlin circles had immediately become anxiously concerned over the effects on public opinion if the old man should die while in official disfavor. Caprivi had promptly called a council of select advisers, with the result that on September 19 the Kaiser, at the Austrian maneuvers in Hungary, had sent a telegram of congratulation to Bismarck on his recovery, offering him the use of one of his castles for the winter. Bismarck had replied courteously, declining the offer, and for a while the papers had been full of new reconciliation rumors. Shortly, however, with increasing health, the old man had renewed his vitriolic attacks, and reconciliation had receded into the background.[54]

Various pressures on the Kaiser for a reconciliation with the prince, however, had not ceased. And with the growing strength of the opposition to Caprivi, with which Bismarck was associated, the

---

[53]*Schulthess* (1894), pp. 29, 68, 95; Wippermann, 10(I):41–43; Bachem, *Zentrumspartei*, V, 346; Thimme, "Bismarck und Kardorff," pt. II, p. 160; Kardorff, *Kardorff*, p. 290; Haller, *Eulenburg*, I, 119; Tirrell, *German Agrarian Politics*, pp. 272–273.

[54]*Schulthess* (1893), pp. 118, 128–129; Wippermann, 9(II):37, 58–61; *DDF*, 1 ser., X, 549–550; Hammann, *Der Neue Kurs*, p. 27; Haller, *Eulenburg*, I, 176–177; Raschdau, *Bismarck u. Caprivi*, pp. 300–302; Wedel, *Zwischen Kaiser und Kanzler*, p. 206. Raschdau claims that Holstein and Marschall were on leave at this point and were furious at the action taken, but cf. Jagemann, *75 Jahre des Erlebens u. Erfahrens* (Heidelberg, 1925), p. 118, quoting Marschall as in favor of such action.

Kaiser was more and more anxious to achieve some resolution of a situation which was seriously infringing upon his own personal popularity. The difficulty was to avoid playing into Bismarck's hands by making the reconciliation seem like capitulation to both the old man personally and to the anti-Caprivi opposition. Thus leading agrarians were ready in the winter of 1893–1894 to vote for the Russian treaty if Bismarck made a declaration in favor of it, and Bismarck suggested through private channels that he would give such a declaration — if the Kaiser requested it. So much had passed between Bismarck and the New Course government in the way of attacks and counterattacks that a reconciliation now without political consequences was almost impossible. For this reason the Kardorff agrarians, aided by the influence of Miquel and Botho Eulenburg, were most anxious to bring it about.[55]

On January 18 Herbert Bismarck, formally invited apparently by mistake, suddenly appeared at an official court function, where his friends quickly tried to maneuver him into the presence of the Kaiser. The Kaiser, taken unawares, deliberately ignored these advances and avoided speaking to Herbert. Then, on January 22, while this incident was still reverberating, the Kaiser suddenly sent his wing-adjutant, Count Kuno Moltke, who was an old and intimate friend of Phili Eulenburg, to Friedrichsruh with a bottle of "Steinberger Kabinett" wine for the prince, a most solicitous inquiry as to his health, and an invitation to attend the celebration in Berlin on the 27th of the Kaiser's twenty-fifth "military anniversary."[56] To this Bismarck replied that in view of his ill health he could not attend a formal function, but would like to express his thanks to the Kaiser personally in Berlin. The Kaiser then telegraphed a favorable reply.[57]

Under the circumstances the news of this action hit the Wilhelmstrasse like a bombshell. The Kaiser had informed no one of his intention. Immediately the Foreign Office prepared a statement for the *Kölnische Zeitung* to the effect that the Kaiser's action was officially sanctioned. But the Kaiser would not allow such a cover-up. In spite of some harsh words from von Marschall he insisted on publishing in the official *Reichsanzeiger* a specific denial that the government had any knowledge of his invitation to Bismarck, which

[55]Cf. Lucius, *Bismarck-Erinnerungen*, pp. 587–589; *Schulthess* (1893), pp. 62–63; Thimme, "Bismarck und Kardorff," pt. II, pp. 38–39; Hutten-Czapski, *Sechzig Jahre*, I, 225, 160.

[56]Eulenburg, *Aus 50 Jahren*, pp. 265, 256ff. Hohenzollern princes traditionally were inducted into the army at the age of ten.

[57]*Schulthess* (1894), p. 30; Wippermann, 10(I):20–22.

had proceeded entirely from his own personal initiative. By all the rules of politics this public disassociation of the Kaiser from his government officials in the very act of reconciling himself with their foremost critic and political opponent should have meant a complete change of government. The Reichstag was in an uproar, Caprivi's enemies were jubilant. Bismarck, it was variously reported, would now come back to the Wilhelmstrasse; no, he would not officially return, but Caprivi, Marschall, Holstein, Bötticher, and Berlepsch would be dismissed; Bismarck would certainly move back to Berlin, but would limit himself to giving advice. Botho Eulenburg, wrote von Kardorff to his wife, would now be chancellor and Herbert Bismarck foreign secretary. In the ministries fear of Bismarck's return and of his revengeful wrath spread like a prairie fire. Each official tried to outdo the other in professing loyalty to Bismarck and in disassociating himself from the present government. Holstein, who did not know the Kaiser personally, was sure a palace conspiracy was afoot against Caprivi and expected that Bismarck would bring to Berlin a complete list of names for a new ministry. It would be *"Finis Caprivii et Germaniae!"* In the four days from January 22 to 25, six letters and five telegrams went out from Holstein, Kiderlen, and Marschall to Phili Eulenburg, imploring him to do something. Caprivi was more calm but was nevertheless quietly worried.[58]

Phili Eulenburg took it all very calmly. He knew William II's unpolitical mind. And he himself had long been in favor of an unpolitical reconciliation. As far as the Kaiser was concerned, that was exactly what it was to be. He had merely extended his benevolent favor once more to his "subject," Bismarck. Also, by reconciling himself with the old man he might remove the weight of his influence from the opposition to the Russian treaty. For this stupendous act of magnanimity, however, there was to be no sharing of applause with the government; he was determined to take all the bows alone. On the morning of Bismarck's entry Phili Eulenburg appeared at the Foreign Office with assurances that the visit of the prince had no political significance.[59]

[58]Alexander v. Hohenlohe-Schillingsfürst, *Aus meinem Leben* (Frankfurt a. M., 1925), pp. 259–261; Raschdau, *Bismarck u. Caprivi*, p. 330; Bülow, *Memoirs*, IV, 656; Hohenlohe, *Memoirs*, II, 465, *Denkwürdigkeiten des Reichskanzlerzeit*, p. 40; Jagemann, *75 Jahre*, pp. 117–118; Eulenburg, *Aus 50 Jahren*, pp. 256ff.; Eyck, *Wilhelm II*, pp. 81–82; cf. Hutten-Czapski, *Sechzig Jahre*, I, 224–225; Wippermann, 10(I):22–24.

[59]Eulenburg, *Aus 50 Jahren*, p. 267; Zechlin, *Staatsstreichpläne*, p. 100; Eyck, *Wilhelm II*, 82–83; Raschdau, *Bismarck u. Caprivi*, p. 331.

Shortly after noon on January 26, 1894, Bismarck made his triumphant entry into Berlin, where he was met with a royal welcome — so royal that the king of Saxony protested to Prince Hatzfeldt-Trachenberg that "such honors belong by rights only to one of us." Met at the Lehrter Bahnhof by Prince Henry of Prussia, Bismarck was accompanied to the Schloss by a military escort, while Berlin officialdom vied for prominent places on strategic balconies, and the less favored crowded the streets. At the Schloss, while the crowds outside cheered and sang endless renditions of "Die Wacht am Rhein" and "Deutschland, Deutschland, über alles," Bismarck and sons were graciously received by the Kaiser and family. Nothing was said of politics. During the afternoon select persons called on Bismarck to pay their respects, including Botho Eulenburg. Caprivi and Marschall sent their cards. Late in the afternoon, while Bismarck was still in the palace, the Kaiser emerged with his suite for his afternoon ride. The crowd cheered excitedly; one thin man in a black frock coat and top hat ran up and shouted, his face tense with emotion, "We thank you, Kaiser!" The following day the *Kölnische Zeitung* rhapsodized:

If today the heartstrings of the nation resound once more with a full, clear note reminiscent of Germany's most stirring and glorious days, we have our Kaiser to thank for it. *The Kaiser has fulfilled the desires of the nation. . . . And so today the most powerful feelings affecting the German Nation in its innermost depths,* loyalty to Kaiser and Reich and gratitude to Prince Bismarck, mingle harmoniously together to the sound of the festive bells with which today Germany celebrates its Kaiser's birthday.

On February 19 the Kaiser returned Bismarck's visit at Friedrichsruh. Here also there was no question of politics. The reconciliation, it was clear, was only an outward one. "Now they can erect triumphal arches for him in Vienna and Munich," said the Kaiser shortly thereafter to Prince zu Hohenlohe, "I am always a horse's length ahead of him." Bismarck, however, possessing a very keen political mind, was quite pleased with the whole affair. The public gesture was, indeed, symbolic. The Kaiser had begun, psychologically, to yield to the opposition.[60]

For the present the political effect of the visit was to encourage

[60]For Bismarck's Berlin visit see especially Alexander Hohenlohe, *Aus meinem Leben*, pp. 259–264; Kardorff, *Kardorff*, pp. 288–289; Thimme, "Bismarck und Kardorff," pt. II, pp. 156–158, 163, 167; Ebmeyer, "Caprivis Entlassung," p. 209; Zechlin, *Staatsstreichpläne*, p. 100; *Die Nation*, XI, 249–250; Hohenlohe, *Memoirs*, II, 466; Wippermann, 10(I):2–6, 8, 24–29.

the opposition in the belief that Caprivi's fall was imminent. The break of the Conservatives with Caprivi, as announced in the *Kreuzzeitung*, indeed went deeper than the Russian treaty or the depressed state of German agriculture. Upon the fate of agriculture, particularly the grain market, rested the fate of the whole structure of social and political privilege enjoyed by the landowning Prussian aristocracy. Over against the rising power of German industry they felt their own position gradually weakening. Caprivi, in attempting to carry out his trade-treaty program against the opposition of the agrarian Conservatives was, in effect, trying to rule Germany against the interests of the Junker class — or at least what they believed to be their interests. And this defiance of Junker interests, which could have been taken easily from a liberal or a radical, was insufferable and infuriating from a man who was himself a conservative, an aristocrat, a Prussian, and an army general! Being all these things, in his denunciation of the irresponsibility of the agrarian agitation, in his emphasis on his own personal disinterest, he only emphasized the self-interested egoism of the agrarians and enraged them the more. Their opposition to Caprivi was more than merely political, it was deep and personal; he had betrayed his class. Against him, after the *Kreuzzeitung* article, they imposed a social boycott — very effective, since they were "society." They attended no Chancellery functions, they refused to deal with the chancellor, or even to speak to him. On February 19 Kardorff wrote to his wife, with sadistic satisfaction:

At a dinner at Stephan's [state secretary of the Reich Postal Department] all the Conservatives again treated Caprivi as if he were air, and Mirbach told very comically how, when they were standing around before and after dinner, there was nowhere he could turn without half of the group turning their backs to him. The minister of war [General Walter Bronsart von Schellendorf], who sat across from him at table, spoke very loudly across the table that he had "Halm und Ar" and knew quite well how miserable the state of agriculture was.[61]

The more bitter the Conservatives became toward Caprivi the more hopeful and enthusiastic the parties of the left became in his support. In December 1893 *Die Nation* wrote:

The Prussian Junkers, who with their widely ramifying connections in the army and the bureaucracy provide the real support for the agrarian movement, realize full well that their whole political position is en-

[61]*Die Nation*, XI, 279; Barth, *Politische Porträts*, pp. 35–37; Wahl, *Geschichte*, III, 560; Thimme, "Bismarck und Kardorff," pt. II, pp. 159, 162; Kardorff, *Kardorff*, pp. 289–291. See above, p. 248.

dangered if the present Reich chancellor remains at the helm after the difference between the Junkers and the first agent of the throne has come so clearly into the open.

Yet this line-up of Caprivi with the left against the right could not be very comfortable for the count personally. The left complained that he was too soft towards the right opposition, and Richter remarked in the Reichstag that there was more joy in the Chancellery over one repentant Conservative than over one hundred faithful Radical and National Liberal supporters. In fact, during February Caprivi went to heroic lengths, considering his pride, to try to persuade von Kardorff to negotiate with him, but von Kardorff held himself firmly aloof.[62]

The Russian Treaty

The Conservatives had, indeed, placed themselves in what was, for the moment, a very peculiar position. As the government pointed out again and again, the essential "sacrifice" of agricultural interests, the reduction in the grain tariff from 5 to 3.5 M, had been made in the Austrian trade treaty in 1891. Since then this rate had been spread far and wide through the most-favored-nation proviso, and, most recently, through the Rumanian treaty. There was no additional sacrifice in including Russia in this system; the concessions made to German industry in the proposed Russian agreement actually were sheer gain. During the tariff war between the two countries, in spite of a tariff of 7.5 M on Russian grain, the difference in price between the internal German and world grain market had not risen even to the treaty rate of 3.5 M. Even Conservatives recognized that if the German tariff wall already had twelve holes in it, it would not make much difference to add a thirteenth. Also, an outright refusal to include Russia in the treaty system would amount, at this stage, to a political snub. Such a repudiation of the friendship of Europe's most conservative Power could, in the long run, not be in truly conservative Prussian Junker interests.[63]

Here, as Caprivi guardedly indicated, entered important considerations of foreign policy. The treaty, he declared on February 27, was intended to constitute "a bridge for the friendly intercourse of two great nations. It is in this connection a project of unusual im-

[62]*Die Nation,* XI, 191, 299; *Sten. Ber.* (1893–1894), I, 172, II, 1481; Thimme, "Bismarck und Kardorff," pt. II, pp. 161–162; Kardorff, *Kardorff,* p. 291. See also Hatzfeldt's interesting letter to Holstein on Bismarck, Caprivi, and the Conservatives, July 10, 1892, *Holstein Papers, Correspondence.*

[63]Lotz, "Handelspolitik," pp. 120, 129; Hammann, *Der Neue Kurs,* p. 93; *Pr. Jbb.,* 75:579.

portance." Without paying any price for it they were extending the chain of trade treaties by one more and final link. There was no conflict between the political aim of strengthening the Triple Alliance, given for the treaties of 1891, and the present treaty with Russia. The general purpose of German foreign policy was peace, and all the trade treaties, including this one, were aids toward this end.

For what is it that we desire? We do not strive for military glory. We desire the glory of cultural achievement, of furthering the civilization of Europe, of making more easy the peaceful coexistence of nations, of welding together the strength of Europe for a later time, when it may be necessary in the interest of European economic policy to unite together in establishing a larger complex of states ("Very good!" on the left).

Failure to ratify the treaty would play into the hands of the Moscow industrialists and encourage isolationism and Pan-Slavism in Russia.

If the hand which Russia is stretching out toward the West is refused then it is left to its own resources, then it will become Pan-Slavistic, and then will enter all the dangers which in our minds are connected with that word, with that phenomenon.

The New Course had been accused of breaking the wire to St. Petersburg.

If you reject this treaty, gentlemen, which I believe to be a strong, powerful new wire, then not only will the new wire not be strung, but you then also cut the old wires — and you, not the government, will bear the responsibility.[64]

At a dinner of the diplomatic corps, celebrating the Kaiser's birthday, the very next day after Bismarck's Berlin triumph, Count Shuvalov, apparently upon direct orders from St. Petersburg, had pointedly made a toast to the health of Chancellor von Caprivi. Even Bismarck, always inclined toward Russia, did not come out strongly against the treaty, but suggested that it might be accepted with special compensations for agriculture. In particular, it was this foreign-policy aspect which held the Kaiser in Caprivi's support in spite of the Bismarck triumph. By bringing Russia and Germany closer together perhaps it would be possible to alienate Russia from France. In characteristic fashion the Kaiser devoted himself to winning over the Conservatives, declaring to their representatives

[64]*Sten. Ber.* (1893–1894), II, 1449–1451; cf. R. Ibbeken, *Das Aussenpolitische Problem Staat u. Wirtschaft in der deutschen Reichspolitik, 1880–1914* (Schleswig, 1928), pp. 180–183.

at a dinner at the Chancellery on February 5 that "he had no desire to go to war with Russia because of a hundred stupid Junkers." If the treaty failed to pass, there would be war in three months, and the eastern provinces would probably be the first to be sacrificed! He also threatened Count Kanitz with the loss of his court position as Vice Grand Master of Ceremonies if he voted against the treaty. With the Kaiser's backing, opposition within the government was kept to a minimum, and Caprivi could announce in the Reichstag to the cheers of the left that the Prussian State Ministry and the Bundesrat had both voted *unanimously* for the treaty.[65]

In addition to these forces working in the treaty's favor, industrial and commercial circles, suffering as they were from the tariff war, began for the first time to become actively vocal in the government's support. Baron von Stumm was especially active in and out of the Reichstag. On February 21 the Central Association of German Manufacturers came out strongly for the treaty. Petitions and resolutions poured in from other industrial and commercial organizations. As the new Russian finance minister, Count Witte, had foreseen, the damage done to Russian agriculture in the tariff war had been overshadowed by the damage to German industry. The Russian market for German industrial products was already in danger of being captured by French and English competition.[66] Also, Caprivi's concession to agriculture in lifting the identity declaration on grain export was admitted even by Kardorff to far outweigh the possible disadvantages of the treaty for agriculture. He could easily vote for the treaty, he wrote, except for his "protectionist principles."[67]

Of more practical importance than the rather secondary economic considerations was the effect of a possible defeat for the treaty on the general party situation. If the treaty were defeated as a result of Conservative and agrarian opposition, then, as the seventy-year-old von Bennigsen warned the Conservatives on February 27, with a dissolution of the Reichstag the new election would be fought with a solid liberal bloc, from National Liberals to Social Democrats, against the Conservatives. The Conservatives could not desire such a campaign. Secretly, they would be grateful

[65]Wippermann, 10(I):4–5, 6–7, 10–11, 51–52; Thimme, "Bismarck und Kardorff," pt. II, pp. 159–160; Kardorff, *Kardorff*, pp. 289–290; Hofmann, *Bismarck*, II, 241–245; *G.P.*, VII, 451–452; Szögyény to Kálnoky, Langer, *Franco-Russian Alliance*, p. 383; Waldersee, *Denkwürdigkeiten*, II, 306; Hohenlohe, *Memoirs*, II, 467; *Sten. Ber.* (1893–1894), 1449.

[66]*Schulthess* (1894), pp. 54, 68–69; Wippermann, 10(I):55–77; *Die Nation*, XI, 295; Witte, *Memoirs*, pp. 67–68; Lotz, "Handelspolitik," p. 121 and note.

[67]Thimme, "Bismarck und Kardorff," pt. II, pp. 160, 163–164; Kardorff, *Kardorff*, pp. 290, 292.

and relieved if the left were able to muster a majority and avoid a dissolution by passing the treaty. If, on the other hand, a dissolution and new election brought a victory and a majority for the left, it would be fine for the trade treaty, but for other measures like taxes and the military budget extremely dubious. "What," demanded Bennigsen, "could one do with such a Reichstag (much laughter)?" [68]

Whereas many members of the Conservative party may have felt as Bennigsen surmised, the extreme agrarian leadership, encouraged by the Bismarck reconciliation, were obviously expecting the result of their rejection of the treaty to be, not the dissolution of the Reichstag, but the dismissal of Caprivi. On February 12, however, the Kaiser finally had personally intervened to bring the Prussian Ministry unitedly behind the trade treaties and had sent the following note to Miquel:

Dear Miquel!

Great things are at stake. You have always appeared to me as a shining example of the broad point of view; will the greatest finance minister of the century endanger his Kaiser's very own undertaking over a little question of the tariff? When, with all my regiments in close ranks, I begin the attack will the "golden" Miquel regiment refuse to heed the signal "gallop"?

The result was that on March 1 Miquel spoke on the Russian treaty in the Reichstag, where, to sympathetic applause from the Conservatives, he devoted most of his speech to the necessity for assistance to agriculture, only at the end recommending the passage of the Russian treaty. Thus he publicly supported the treaty and at the same time once more clearly disassociated himself from Caprivi. Privately he passed the word around that the Conservatives would be fools to vote for it.[69]

The final debate on the treaty in early March was more heated, more extreme than ever. The agrarian leaders all extolled Bismarck while damning Caprivi. Although Bismarck, declared Count von Mirbach sarcastically, had been hampered in his judgment by the possession of thousands of acres of land (*Aren*), nevertheless he had received a certain recognition from the German people. As for the trade treaty, Germany needed nothing from Russia but caviar. Whereas Secretary Marschall had declared that the treaty would

[68]*Sten. Ber.* (1893–1894), II, 1466; cf. *Die Nation*, XI, 299.

[69]Thimme, "Bismarck und Kardorff," *passim;* Herzfeld, *Miquel*, II, 329ff.; *Sten. Ber.* (1893–1894), II, 1516–1518; cf. *Sten. Ber.* (1893–1894), II, 1760; *Die Nation*, XI, 328; Hammann, *Der Neue Kurs*, p. 96.

be a milestone, it would rather, said von Hammerstein, be a tomb-stone,

upon which on one side may be set the inscription: here German agricul-ture was brought to its grave ("Bravo!" on the right). The other side will remain bare for a while — then will be written on it: and German in-dustry followed it (much laughter on the left).

Count von Arnim complained that the Reich was forcing Prussia to repeal the railroad freight rate, and Count von Kanitz explained that the Conservatives had voted against an insignificant item in the army budget for the first time because the extreme poverty of agri-culture caused by the trade treaties necessitated economy. On the other side, Dr. Lieber, in his enthusiasm, went to the extreme of declaring the conclusion of the Russian treaty a greater victory for Germany than that of 1871. In spite of — or because of — the Con-servative barrage, in the decisive vote on Article I in the second reading on March 10 the Reichstag approved the treaty with the comfortable majority of 200 to 146. For Caprivi it was another hard-won victory.[70] The new pro-Russian policy was successfully launched and, for the next few years, relations between the two countries would be considerably improved. Yet, ironically, the German step came just a little too late to achieve any lasting result. The military convention sealing the alliance between France and Russia had finally been signed by the tsar in December.[71]

[70]Thimme, "Bismarck und Kardorff," pt. II, p. 164; Kardorff, *Kardorff*, p. 292; Wahl, *Geschichte*, III, 561; *Sten. Ber.* (1893–1894), II, 1417, 1423, III, 1904, 1745, 1924, 1750–1752; *Die Nation*, XI, 557–558. For the practical arguments pro and con, cf. the summary in Lotz, "Handelspolitik," pp. 122ff., also Tirrell, *German Agrarian Politics*, pp. 248ff.

[71]Langer, *Franco-Russian Alliance*, pp. 354–355; Ibbeken, *Staat u. Wirtschaft*, p. 184.

Chapter IX

THE CONSERVATIVE TRIUMPH

The German Kaiser may not fight with the king of Prussia.

Preussische Jahrbücher, 1892

1

COURT, CABINETS, AND CLIQUES

CHANCELLOR Caprivi's personal position seemed stronger than ever. He had completed perhaps his greatest accomplishment in rounding out his system of trade treaties, and these treaties had begun to bring him a certain popularity, especially among the coastal trading towns. In the Reichstag he had withstood the fire of the strongest attack which the powerful Junker agrarians could muster and had come out victorious, supported both by the sheer logic and reasonableness of his program and by the personal respect he had acquired among the parties of the left. Within the government he had managed to maintain a certain semblance of unity, his own position, and the support of the Kaiser in spite of all the intrigues of the agrarian and Bismarck forces in and around the court.[1]

Also, Caprivi's chief political opponent, Miquel, had not succeeded in his bid for recognition in the Reich. The Reichstag, Miquel had discovered, could not be managed as easily as the Prussian Landtag. His tobacco and wine taxes found almost no support, and his over-all reform scheme was defeated resolutely by the Center. Miquel's political successes in Prussia, by their very nature, could not, in fact, increase his following in the Reich. In Prussia he had consistently followed what may be regarded as a Kartell policy, based essentially on coöperation with the Conservatives. For this policy, even after the election of 1893 — as the

[1] Cf. *Die Nation,* XI, 327, 389; Wippermann, 10(I):76–77.

majority for Caprivi's Army Bill, a very special and unusual one, clearly showed — there still was not a majority available in the Reichstag. Also, Miquel's action in the School Bill affair, combined with the Conservative treachery in the suffrage reform, had deeply embittered the Center. Miquel, characteristically, had carefully cultivated Dr. Lieber and managed to secure his backing for his Reich finance bills, but the Center party would have none of it. They threatened Lieber with the loss of his seat, and in the future the good doctor learned to be more careful in his relations with the wily Prussian minister of finance. Even the National Liberals had begun to be uncomfortable over Miquel's Conservative leanings. The Radicals had no faith in him whatever. The left was able with very good effect to quote in the Reichstag tax debates the position formerly taken by Miquel, the National Liberal party leader, as against the present conservative program of Miquel, the minister. To embarrass Miquel further, not only with his Conservative friends but also with the Kaiser, in October 1893, at a meeting of the Social Democrats, August Bebel had read one of Miquel's letters to Karl Marx. Written in 1850, it testified to young Miquel's communistic sympathies and activities. To this challenge the minister of finance replied with a statement of defense in the Reichstag on November 27, repudiating his youthful frivolities, and, most important, with a letter of explanation to the Kaiser. The latter elicited a comforting reply by imperial telegram:

> From the mountain to the sea, from youthful
> dreams to manhood's sober acts, that is the
> answer of your Hohenzollern king.
>   William I. R.

The incident, nevertheless, was most unpleasant for the darling of the Conservatives. In the end, the hostility of the Reichstag left Miquel's tax legislation in ruins. His attempt to bring Reich and Prussia together once more by means of the dynamic agrarian movement and under his own leadership had miserably failed. It was the first great defeat of his official career. For the Reich, in 1894, Caprivi's compromising, shifting, paradoxical policy was more realistic.[2]

Defeat on the Russian trade treaty did not dampen the ardor of the agrarian attack, however, but rather heightened it. Caprivi had

[2]Bachem, *Zentrumspartei*, V, 336–337; *Die Nation*, X, 376; *Sten. Ber.* (1893–1894), I, 118–119, 170; Herzfeld, *Miquel*, II, 363–367. Cf. Miquel's letter of explanation to Hammerstein, Leuss, *Hammerstein*, pp. 110–111.

repeatedly accused the agrarians of offering no positive program; now, in April, Count von Kanitz introduced a motion, immediately brought to debate by action of the Radicals, calling for a government monopoly of all grain imports, the grain to be resold at a fixed minimum price, some 60 per cent higher than current prices and 10 M above the 1880–1890 average. The motion was immediately denounced by Caprivi on the grounds that such a step, by circumventing the tariff reduction, would make foreign nations lose faith in German sincerity in concluding the trade treaties, that it would be a great burden on the lower classes by raising the price of bread, that, since 69 per cent of the persons living off the land were small holders (*Parzellenbesitzer*) who had no grain to sell, the measure would benefit only the large estates and not agriculture as a whole. It would, on the other hand, awaken resentment against agriculture and, therefore, actually benefit the Social Democrats. The other parties reacted to the Kanitz motion with shocked disapproval, regarding it as a kind of agrarian socialism, while the Social Democrats opposed it because it would raise the price of bread. Logically, commented the astute *Preussische Jahrbücher,* such a measure must lead to a system which would also arbitrarily fix commodity prices and guarantee a minimum wage for labor. Meritorious, perhaps, in themselves, such measures, it explained, were quite impractical. It was fairly plain that the Conservatives themselves did not take the Kanitz motion too seriously. Its overwhelming defeat by a vote of 156 to 46 was not unexpected. But the motion was a call for positive action and, now that the trade treaties were for a while a dead issue, a further claim on the government. It made an excellent political rallying point, and the Conservatives were determined to make the most of it. "To us," orated Count von Kanitz in the Reichstag, "belongs the confidence of the public, to us belongs the future (enthusiastic 'Bravo!' on the right)!" [3]

While offering the Kanitz motion as their positive program, negatively the agrarians continued to snipe at the government by voting down items in the budget, including some pet projects of the Kaiser's, and by helping defeat the Dortmund-Ems ship-canal bill in the Landtag. Meanwhile Miquel and Botho Eulenburg secured the Kaiser's backing for a general Prussian state program of agrarian reform. To impress public opinion, in the Miquel fashion, an agricultural conference was called to meet in late May in Berlin, under the sponsorship of Prussian Minister of Agriculture von

[3] *Sten. Ber.* (1893–1894), III, 2096–2101, 2133–2134; *Schulthess* (1894), pp. 104–109; Eyck, *Wilhelm II,* 80–81; *Pr. Jbb.,* 76:370–379.

Heyden, to discuss the proposed government measures. The decision to call this conference was taken and the invitations sent out without the knowledge of the Reich chancellor, and, since the list of those invited included some of his most violent agrarian opponents, Count von Kanitz, Baron von Gamp, and Adolf Wagner, Caprivi was furious and immediately lodged a vigorous protest with the State Ministry. In the ministry Reich and Prussian officials lined up against each other in bitter opposition. While Count Botho zu Eulenburg apologized politely for the slight to the chancellor's dignity, he smoothly suggested that it was too late now to countermand the action taken. The majority of the ministers agreed that, after the bitterness of the Russian treaty fight, something ought to be done to soothe the agrarians.[4]

On April 20 Bismarck spoke at Friedrichsruh to a delegation of twenty-eight National Liberal Reichstag deputies. His speech laid the basis for a four-pronged attack on the Caprivi government. First, the fate of 20,000,000 farmers could not be ignored; something must be done for agriculture. Second, the Social Democratic threat could not in the long run simply be hushed up, "but sooner or later it must be actively confronted." Third, the "weak" Polish policy had not worked and must be revised. Fourth, the existing separation between the offices of Reich chancellor and Prussian minister-president could not continue without falsifying the constitution and weakening the "authority of the Reich." After the reconciliation with the Kaiser in January, Bismarck, speaking with even more authority in his rôle of revered elder statesman, declared, "A Reich chancellor who is not supported by the authority of the Prussian State Ministry is poised precariously in the air as on a tight-rope [*schwebt mit der seinigen in der Luft wie ein Seiltänzer*]." It was clear, he went on, that a chancellor enjoying the support of the collective Prussian administration would carry more weight than one "who is thrown upon only the resources of his own personal department and of the personal experience accumulated during his military career." The first and foremost political aim should be to end the separation of these offices.[5]

The ever sharpening conflict between the governments of the Reich and of Prussia had, in fact, inevitably created a strange state of confusion within the Bundesrat. In rather interesting conformity with Bismarck's suggestions the previous summer, von Mittnacht,

---

[4]Thimme, "Bismarck und Kardorff," pt. II, p. 167; *Schulthess* (1894), pp. 121, 123; Herzfeld, *Miquel*, II, 325–327, 332–333.

[5]*Schulthess* (1894), pp. 113–115; Wippermann, 10(I):32–34; cf. 293–294.

the chief minister of Württemberg, had in January carried his opposition to the wine tax to the unprecedented extreme of speaking against it in the Reichstag. And in the Reichstag von Kardorff had taken this golden opportunity to deplore the lack of solidarity within the Bundesrat.[6]

When, in the meeting of the State Ministry on May 26, Chancellor von Caprivi protested against the action of the ministers of agriculture and finance in calling the conference on agriculture without his knowledge, Minister-President Eulenburg retorted that a Bundesrat ordinance recently had been passed and published before it had been discussed by the Prussian Ministry. To this Caprivi replied that it was obviously impossible for the State Ministry to decide on how the Prussian delegates should vote before every decision of the Bundesrat. As Prussian foreign minister, he himself must take the responsibility for how the Prussian votes were cast. On June 14 Eulenburg replied in a memorandum that the Prussian foreign minister must decide whether or not his instruction of the Prussian vote required a decision of the State Ministry. He (Caprivi) could be all the more certain of making a correct decision by calling upon the advice of the Reich secretaries, who as Prussian Bundesrat representatives, wrote Eulenburg smoothly, were obliged to represent the interests of Prussia. Also, the Prussian ministers might report on whether the business of their separate ministries in the Bundesrat might require a Prussian ministerial decision. At this point Caprivi called a conference with Reich Secretaries Bötticher, Marschall, and Nieberding and sent an answering memorandum to Eulenburg on June 23. In case of doubt, wrote the chancellor, the Reich secretaries would try to make sure of the attitude of the State Ministry and, if necessary, to obtain a discussion of the matter. "In other respects, however, I recognize with Prince Bismarck that it is the minister of foreign affairs who, as the voting representative of Prussia, instructs the Prussian vote in the Bundesrat." He put special importance on this responsibility, wrote Caprivi. It might, for instance, require that the foreign minister contest the decision of the State Ministry in a matter of Reich or international importance, and thus require another consideration of the matter by the State Ministry or a decision by the king. It was the duty of the Prussian ministers who chaired the Bundesrat committees to vote in ac-

[6]See above, p. 263. For this very interesting incident see *Sten. Ber.* (1893–1894), I, 763–771, and cf. 387; *Schulthess* (1894), pp. 26–29; *Die Nation*, XI, 255–256. Kardorff demanded immediate adjournment but was met by the solid opposition of Reich officials, Radicals, Center, and Social Democrats. Singer's answer to Kardorff is especially notable. Cf. below, pp. 321, 354.

cordance with the attitude of the State Ministry and, if in doubt, to request clarification. A further exchange with Eulenburg, in which the minister-president tried to pin the responsibility for the decision on whether a Bundesrat vote should be brought before the State Ministry entirely on the foreign minister, resulted in Caprivi's issuing, on July 5, two decrees to Reich officials, copies of which were sent to Eulenburg. The first repealed Bismarck's order of May 25, 1885, prohibiting direct intercourse between Reich and Prussian officials. The second directed the Reich officials who were also members of the Bundesrat for Prussia to make certain of the attitude of the Prussian State Ministry, or, if in doubt, to bring about a decision of the matter by the State Ministry. In an accompanying note to Eulenburg Caprivi declared that he retained the right to collaborate as Prussian foreign minister and, where the interests of the Reich were involved, as Reich chancellor.[7]

In this whole veiled struggle with Botho Eulenburg one can see the Reich chancellor trying energetically to preserve the interests and independence of the Reich free from Prussian interference, and in this attempt becoming badly entangled in the meshes of the web of the Bismarckian constitution. If, as he at first attempted, he placed all his authority as Reich chancellor entirely upon his position as Prussian foreign minister then, as a member of the Prussian State Ministry, he would place Reich decisions in the hostile hands of that collegiate body. So in the end he tried to dodge the difficulty, to belittle it, to throw it back at the ministry, to let it be fought out at a lower level by subordinate officials. But by thus repealing Bismarck's order requiring all transactions between Reich and Prussia to pass through the hands of the Prussian foreign minister, Caprivi made it all the easier for Prussian ministers to circumvent and to oppose Reich policies in the Bundesrat. In this battle of the administrations, "Reich authority," as Bismarck had so cleverly and astutely observed, was, indeed, being threatened. But the threat existed in the deliberate campaign being waged against the Reich government by the agrarian-Junker forces in Prussia, led by Botho Eulenburg, Miquel, von Kardorff, and by Bismarck himself.[8]

In his memorandum of June 23 Caprivi had mentioned, as a last resort in case of disagreement between the Prussian foreign minister and the State Ministry, the possibility of a decision by the crown.

[7]For this exchange see the documents reproduced in Goldschmidt, *Reich u. Preussen,* pp. 324–327, notes. Cf. Thimme, "Bismarck und Kardorff," pt. II, p. 167; Kardorff, *Kardorff,* pp. 295, 298.
[8]Cf. Goldschmidt, *Reich u. Preussen,* p. 103.

This, indeed, was the obvious key to the problem. How could there be a conflict between the administrations of the Reich and Prussia when both answered to a single emperor-king? The Kaiser could not remain long in conflict with the king of Prussia. Yet, in the spring and summer of 1894 he was, indeed, in just such a conflict with himself. As Kaiser he gave his full approval and energetic backing to a Reich administration which was fighting with all its strength against the Conservative agrarian agitation, while simultaneously as king of Prussia he eagerly sanctioned a program of appeasement of these same agrarians. No doubt the personality of William II made such inconsistency easier; within himself he reflected and expressed the contradictions existing within the state. But even William II surely could not pursue diametrically opposed policies indefinitely. It seemed certain that one or the other of them must finally gain the upper hand. The conflict between Prussia and the Reich, between agriculture and industry, between reactionaries and liberals, between the camps of Eulenburg, Miquel, Bismarck and of Caprivi, thus resolved itself finally into a struggle for the person of the Kaiser and king. The chief battleground was, thus, not the Landtag nor the Reichstag, but the Berlin court. It was an atmosphere especially favorable to intrigue.

When he first entered office, Caprivi had declared that the hardest part of his new position would be his relations with the Kaiser. He had tried especially hard to meet this problem, first, through building a spirit of independence and solidarity among the ministers. But the ministers he had inherited from Bismarck had no real spirit of independence; those who did take independent positions, such as Herrfurth and Zedlitz, came into conflict with the parliament, and in the School Bill crisis the ministry cracked wide open and had since been a breeding ground of conflict with the Kaiser rather than a support against him. Personally, Caprivi, as was necessary and natural for his soldierly instincts, had tried to hold himself aloof, to maintain his dignity — a difficult thing in Berlin — by seeing the Kaiser as little as possible. This attempt was rendered easier by the Kaiser's frequent absences from Berlin, for hunting or traveling, and his general lack of sustained interest in the business of government. Caprivi had early discovered that he could not read through or discuss long documents fully without boring His Majesty, and so he had adopted the practice of presenting a report in summary which the Kaiser, as was his wont, could quickly grasp and approve with a few trenchant comments. Caprivi's policy of reserve, however, entailed the grave dangers of being negative and remote. By approaching the Kaiser only occasionally and for important reasons he could more easily influence and control him at those times. But meanwhile, in between, during the incessant hunts, parties, voyages, maneuvers, and train trips, the Kaiser was being exposed to and influenced by all manner of people, many of whom were not averse to using their influence for a purpose. Caprivi could always, of course, when confronted with a contrary policy — as in the long-drawn battle over two-year service — bring the Kaiser back to his point of view by threatening resignation. But this was a last resort, a serious step, and must be kept for serious occasions. There were many lesser crises over which it would be petty and irresponsible to threaten to resign. This was especially true of appointments to government or court posts.[9]

One day, for example, in January 1893, a certain infantry Captain von Natzmer appeared at the Chancellery and announced to the astonished Caprivi that he had just been appointed governor of the colony of Cameroons. The chancellor at first thought he was insane and tried to humor and to soothe him in a friendly way. But, as the captain related, most rationally, the details of the occasion at a party in the New Palace the night before, when the Kaiser had appointed him to the then vacant post, it became painfully apparent that he was quite sane indeed. Caprivi summoned Marschall, together they drove over to Potsdam, and that was the last that was heard of Captain von Natzmer. On this occasion, Caprivi had raised the question of confidence in himself as responsible head of the government and, as usual, had won. But this could not always be done. In the summer of 1891 when the Kaiser, just before his state visit to England, announced to a group of friends at a reception in the Chancellery garden that he intended to participate in the yacht-racing at Cowes, Caprivi voiced strong objections. English public opinion was not particularly friendly, and, one way or another, the outcome of the races might have political effects damaging to Hohenzollern popularity in England. Obviously vexed, the Kaiser retorted, "The Hohenzollerns have never been popular in England, I am going to Cowes for the races, and that's all there is to it." Coldly Caprivi replied, "Then, Your Majesty, I have done my duty and must decline further responsibility." Short of actual resignation, the responsibility of the chancellor was not so easily renounced. One could not very well resign, however, over a yacht race.[10]

[9]Cf. Waldersee, *Denkwürdigkeiten*, II, 6–7; Wertheimer, "Ein k. u. k. Militärat-taché," *Pr. Jbb.*, 201:282.

[10]Stein, *Es war alles ganz anders*, p. 190; Thimme, "Bismarck und Kardorff," pt. II, p. 32; Kardorff, *Kardorff*, p. 277; Ebmeyer, "Caprivis Entlassung," p. 208.

It was all the more difficult to influence the Kaiser personally because of the ceremonial formality and institutional apparatus surrounding his person as supreme head of the Prussian state and Reich. There were, first, his own Military and Civil Cabinets, each with its own chief. Since the introduction of constitutional government in 1848 these cabinets had gradually revived and increased in importance, but under Bismarck, as with everything else, they had been kept in the shadow. Bismarck himself, however, had encouraged every tendency of William II to heighten the appearance of his own monarchical authority, and since 1888 the cabinets had come again very much to the fore. Being closest to the Kaiser, they were a good deal more than a mere secretariat. The two chiefs, General Wilhelm von Hahnke for military and Hermann von Lucanus for civil affairs, had the right to attend every audience of any official with the Kaiser which affected their separate spheres. Only the Reich chancellor could report to the Kaiser alone. Normally all written reports of the ministers were presented to or summarized for the Kaiser by the two cabinet chiefs. Conversely, all imperial decisions were transmitted to the ministers through the same cabinet channels. Hahnke and Lucanus were thus the official liaison between Kaiser and government, and many were their opportunities for influencing the course of business. The cabinet chiefs also constituted a separate channel of approach to the Kaiser for extraneous influences, including subordinate officials, who could thus appeal a policy over the heads of their superiors to the Kaiser personally. This great possibility for influence was considerably limited in practice, however, by the fact that the Kaiser did not care for criticism or for independent opinions in his entourage. Cabinet influence remained, therefore, largely negative. Lucanus could, and did on occasion, fail to inform the chancellor of the contents of an approaching imperial speech, and he had added his voice to the attack on the Zedlitz School Bill. General von Hahnke had strongly upheld the more conservative anti-Caprivi position in the matter of two-year service for the army. Both were sympathetic with the Conservative Junker cause and worked for reconciliation with Bismarck.[11]

More important than the influence of the cabinets was the whole

[11]Cf. especially F. Hartung, "Verantwortliche Regierung, Kabinette u. Nebenregierungen in konstitutionellen Preussen 1848–1918," *Forschungen zur Brandenburg-Preussischen Geschichte*, 44:2–28, 318; R. Schmidt-Bückeburg, *Das Militärkabinett der preussischen Könige und deutschen Kaiser* (Berlin, 1933), pp. 96ff.; Craig, *Politics of the Prussian Army*, pp. 237–242; see above, pp. 000, 000–000; Raschdau, *Bismarck u. Caprivi*, pp. 198–200; Haller, *Eulenburg*, I, 210; Wedel, *Zwischen Kaiser und Kanzler*, pp. 197–198, 206; Eulenburg, *Aus 50 Jahren*, p. 255.

complex of military influence resulting from the Kaiser's independent position as commander-in-chief of the army and navy. Military affairs were somewhat vaguely divided between the minister of war, the chief of the General Staff, and the chief of the Military Cabinet. The Military Cabinet controlled the important area of army personnel, the General Staff that of organization and strategy, while the minister of war, as a member of the "responsible" Prussian State Ministry, was supposed to handle the political aspect. Obviously, these three areas seriously overlapped. Before and during Bismarck's rule the minister of war, as was logical, maintained the dominant position. But already in 1889 Chief of the General Staff General von Waldersee, as part of his intrigue against Bismarck, managed to gain the upper hand over the minister of war, including the right to report directly to the Kaiser. This led to the resignation of the war minister (the elder Bronsart) and the succession of General von Verdy du Vernois, who was definitely a creature of Waldersee's, all this done more or less over Bismarck's head.[12]

Waldersee also further buttressed his own influence at court by means of the military attachés stationed at the most important embassies. He tried very hard to have their reports sent through the General Staff or to the Kaiser directly, rather than through the regular diplomatic channels to the Foreign Office, where they came under the scrutiny and control of the chancellor. Such a state of affairs, under the ambitious, warmongering Waldersee, would amount to the setting up of an independent military foreign policy. Bismarck fought an energetic rear-guard action against Waldersee on this score, but some reports nevertheless managed to get through to the Kaiser without going through the Foreign Office.[13]

After Bismarck's dismissal, with a general in the Chancellery, the road seemed open for the expansion of army influence. But Waldersee soon discovered that Caprivi, backed by Holstein, had no intention of allowing any sort of dual regime. Already, in August 1890, Caprivi ordered the military attachés to refrain from political reports where their opinion differed from that of the ambassador. Since Waldersee was determined to fight back, the clash between

<hr/>

[12]Hartung, "Verantwortliche Regierung," pp. 306–307; Waldersee, *Denkwürdigkeiten*, II, 14, 18–22, 24–27, 43, 48; Schmidt-Bückeburg, *Das Militärkabinett*, pp. 96–185; Craig, *Prussian Army*, pp. 227–232.

[13]On the problem of the military attachés see especially Waldersee, *Briefwechsel*, I, *passim*, *Denkwürdigkeiten*, II, 30–31, 83–84; G. Craig, "Military Diplomats in the Prussian and German Service: the Attachés, 1816–1914," *Political Science Quarterly*, 64:65–94 (1949), also *Prussian Army*, pp. 266–272; Hartung, "Verantwortliche Regierung," p. 307; Hutten-Czapski, *Sechzig Jahre*, I, 176–177.

him and Caprivi grew, in spite of an attempt to patch up their relationship at Kiel in August 1890. In December 1890 Caprivi prepared an order formally subordinating the activity of the military attachés to the Foreign Office and obtained the Kaiser's approval. This success was really the climax of the affair and spelled defeat for Waldersee, who lost his head and bitterly accused Caprivi to the Kaiser of intriguing against him. Since Caprivi, on the contrary, had said nothing to the Kaiser, but had operated, as usual, in a restrained and formal way, this outburst could only damage Waldersee himself in the Kaiser's estimation. Waldersee's restless ambition had, in fact, accumulated a large body of opposition. In October 1890 von Holstein wrote to Phili Eulenburg: "Waldersee must go . . . In general, take a stand against the idea that military men are more reliable than civilians." Von Hahnke also worked against him. Also, by forming close connections with the Stöcker-Hammerstein right wing of the Conservatives, Waldersee drew upon himself the active enmity of the moderate leader, von Helldorff, who in 1890–1891 was still a political power and whose advice was valued by both Caprivi and the Kaiser. Court circles were tired of the general's intrigues and were convinced that there would be no clarity, no stability in the political situation until he was removed. In early 1891 the New Course was still young, the reform program was in full swing, the Bismarck Fronde was not yet strong, and the Kaiser was still relatively popular; the general had no real backing for his intrigues, not even in the army. In addition, he had inevitably come into personal conflict with the Kaiser, with whose personality he had become, in course of time, profoundly disillusioned and disgusted. In September 1890, during the army maneuvers in Silesia,[14] it had fallen to Waldersee, as chief of staff, to criticize the day's exercises, which he had done tactfully but truthfully, so that the Kaiser's insufficiencies as a military leader were nevertheless glaringly exposed. The Kaiser immediately suggested to Caprivi that Waldersee be placed in command of the vacant army corps in Stuttgart. Caprivi, however, thought that this should be a free choice on Waldersee's part, although he went so far as to urge him to take it. But Waldersee, although he himself clearly saw the handwriting on the wall, would not give in gracefully and refused. The result was that in January 1891 he was finally dismissed, in spite of angry protests on his part and much agitation on the Kaiser's, and given command of the army corps at Altona. Here he immediately made a rapprochement with his old enemy, Bismarck,

[14]See above, p. 114.

in nearby Friedrichsruh, and became a bitter enemy of the Caprivi regime.[15]

With Waldersee's departure the military attachés lost their main support. Nevertheless, the difficulties in controlling their influence on the Kaiser by no means ceased. Certain of them, such as von Huene and later von Funcke in Paris, or von Engelbrecht in Rome, were also wing-adjutants at court and could thus manage to report directly to the Kaiser in defiance of Foreign Office and chancellor. Their reports, often deliberately sensational, were likely especially to please the Kaiser, and it was thus difficult to remove them. The Kaiser's military suite of adjutants and aides-de-camp, generally young men chosen for their congeniality, constituted, in fact, a sort of permanent camarilla. Their influence was mostly negative, but very difficult to combat. By making jokes about the more elderly and less dashing ministers and civilian officials they entertained the Kaiser but also tended to undermine his confidence in and respect for the responsible officers of his government. How much trouble an aide-de-camp could cause the Foreign Office and Chancellery by personally influencing the Kaiser has already been described in the von Huene incident of 1891, which was all the more noteworthy since von Huene at that time was no longer in office.[16]

Even if his frank, open nature had not precluded any such attempt, the demands on his time and energy caused by his position as chancellor, combined with the public, formal nature of the office, rendered impossible any attempt by Caprivi closely to influence the Kaiser. At various times he was aided by royal personages, such as the Kaiser's wife, Kaiserin Auguste Victoria, and the king of Saxony, but such royal figures could not always be depended upon. A person was needed who was personally close to the Kaiser and whose official duties would afford frequent contact with him. For this delicate task Caprivi was forced early, as has been seen, to use the natural talents of the professional amateur, Count Philipp zu Eulenburg-Hertefeld. In the following years Eulenburg worked closely with the Foreign Office. He, Kiderlen, and Holstein formed a sort of team, a shock troop, to protect and advance the chancellor's

[15]See above, pp. 133, 194–195, 210; see below, pp. 328, 348–349. Waldersee, *Denkwürdigkeiten*, II, 135–137, 139–141, 144–148, 154–155, 165, 173, 175–183; Haller, *Eulenburg*, I, 282; Kiderlen to Holstein, July 19, 1890, Eulenburg to Holstein, August 1, 1890, Holstein to Maximilian von Brandt, December 26, 1890, *Holstein Papers, Correspondence*; Schweinitz, *Briefwechsel*, p. 276; Wedel, *Zwischen Kaiser und Kanzler*, pp. 123–124, 126–127, 133, 138, 140–148, 150–151; Wippermann, 7(I):136–139.

[16]Hutten-Czapski, *Sechzig Jahre*, I, 177, 179; Hartung, "Verantwortliche Regierung," pp. 307, 318, 320; Eulenburg, *Aus 50 Jahren*, p. 255. See above, pp. 118–119,

policies and interests. Eulenburg and Kiderlen provided the contact with the Kaiser; Holstein was the political brain and the hidden director of operations. By and large their efforts were successful, enough so as to make their services almost indispensable to the smooth running of the government.[17]

Less than three weeks after Caprivi's appointment as chancellor, Eulenburg wrote to Holstein:[18]

Tomorrow you will receive a survey of opinion prepared for the Kaiser. It is better for me to write you and for H.M. to receive this letter through *Caprivi*. We must see that H.M. becomes as friendly as possible [*möglichst warm*] with Caprivi — and it will strengthen H.M.'s trust in C. not a little if he sees that my letters follow this route.

Is this not your view?
Cordially yours,
P E.

Here was a camarilla in a very special sense — semiofficial, as it were. It faced fundamentally three dangers: one, that it might lose the confidence of either Kaiser or chancellor; two, that its operations might become known to the public; three, that the three collaborators might become too ambitious and fall out among themselves. By the summer of 1894 the system was threatened by all three.

As has been noted, it was particularly difficult for Caprivi to control the Kaiser's appointments. A policy left traces, and responsibility for it might be tracked down, but just for what exact reason, from which of a number of sources the Kaiser derived his confidence in this person or his distrust of that one, was impossible to tell. For this game of personality politics the soldierly Caprivi was particularly unskilled. Thus the Holstein-Eulenburg team had a golden opportunity to further their own private ends without the chancellor's noticing it. As early as 1892 Phili Eulenburg sent the following delicately modulated warning to Holstein:

Because of the great increase of appreciation which I perceive in the Kaiser with regard to you I want to beg you more than ever to take care that we do not go against Caprivi and Marschall, or give any color to the suspicion of a dual régime. That there is such a suspicion I can scarcely doubt . . .

[17]See above, pp. 64–65, 49–51, 60–61. Letters of Kaiserin Auguste Victoria and the king of Saxony in Caprivi Papers, Hauptarchiv, Berlin. For the king of Saxony see also below, pp. 339, 341.
[18]*Holstein Papers, Correspondence,* April 8, 1890.

And, when in December 1893, Eulenburg finally succeeded in preventing the promotion of the military attaché, von Engelbrecht, to succeed Count Solms zu Sonnenfelde as ambassador in Rome, Holstein wrote:

Again you have been foremost in this business. The chancellor guesses it too. When he told me yesterday of the course of events he said, "Eulenburg will have a hand in this!" I said nothing . . . We must not deprive him of the little self-confidence he has. Marschall knows nothing either.[19]

In spite of these attempts at self-restraint, the temptation to further private ends was not altogether resisted. In 1892 Holstein was able, with Eulenburg's help, to reshuffle the ambassadors, getting rid of the more loyal Bismarckians who also happened to be his own personal enemies. Thus Ferdinand Stumm was removed from Madrid, Kurt von Schlözer from the Vatican (to make room for Eulenburg's friend Bernhard Bülow), and Radowitz demoted from Constantinople to Madrid. In 1894 Prince Reuss was finally replaced in Vienna by Phili Eulenburg himself.[20] Again, in the summer of 1893, another opportunity arose through a severe crisis in the relationship of the chancellor to the Kaiser. Instigated apparently by the military, a misunderstanding had arisen over the army maneuvers to be held in Württemberg. Caprivi, in good faith, opposed them for that year in the belief that he was following the wishes of the Württemberg government only to be deserted by the Württembergers at the decisive stage. Eulenburg was able to calm the Kaiser's wrath but in the process persuaded Caprivi that his "honor" demanded the removal of the Württemberg ambassador to Berlin, von Moser. Into the vacancy thus artificially created Eulenburg was then able to push his old and intimate friend, Baron von Varnbüler.[21]

Yet the triumvirate of the Foreign Office often sacrificed their

[19]Hutten-Czapski, *Sechzig Jahre,* I, 185; Haller, *Eulenburg,* I, 196, 142.

[20]Cf. Hammann, *Der Neue Kurs,* pp. 59–60; Hutten-Czapski, *Sechzig Jahre,* I, 221–223; Wedel, *Zwischen Kaiser und Kanzler,* pp. 205, 207–208, 210–214; Raschdau, *Bismarck u. Caprivi,* pp. 195, 207, 308–309; Holstein to Hatzfeldt, December 9, 1893, Holstein memorandum, December 8, 1893, Bülow to Holstein, December 10, 1893, Reuss to Holstein, January 3, 1894, Bülow to Holstein, January 14, Polsdorff letter, February 2, Reuss to Holstein, April 19, von Ratibor to Holstein, October 22, 1894, *Holstein Papers, Correspondence.*

[21]Haller, *Eulenburg,* I, 248–251; Hohenlohe, *Memoirs,* II, 459, 461–462; Raschdau, *Bismarck u. Caprivi,* pp. 304–308; Wedel, *Zwischen Kaiser und Kanzler,* pp. 203–205; Caprivi to Eulenburg, November 14, 1893; Caprivi memorandum, November 16, 1893, Polsdorff letter, February 2, 1894, *Holstein Papers, Correspondence.*

own opinions to the service of Caprivi and the Reich. Thus Eulenburg coöperated up to a point on the two-year service and Bismarck issues, and, in spite of his aristocratic sensibilities, refused to have anything to do with the Farmers' League; and Holstein, who fought for Caprivi doggedly to the end, as an old Prussian aristocrat with scant knowledge of economics, did not agree with the chancellor's Polish or trade-treaty policies. Nor did they always have things their own way. In 1896 Holstein wrote to Eulenburg, "That I feel myself to be *de facto* director of the political department is true enough. In that capacity I had frequent battles with Caprivi . . ." [22]

By 1894 the close collaboration of Holstein and Phili Eulenburg was beginning to show signs of a basic cleavage. In the pulling and hauling between court and government it was perhaps inevitable that the inherent differences in the personal motivation of these two mediators, who bore a considerable part of the strain, should be forced to the surface. Each began to be basically dissatisfied with the other's weaknesses. Holstein saw clearly that Eulenburg was letting his mystical romanticism and his feelings of personal affection influence him too much in the Kaiser's favor. Too often he was willing to defend or tolerate acts, such as the staging of the Bismarck reconciliation, that benefited the Kaiser personally but were detrimental to the government and to the long-term national welfare. Eulenburg's own essential weakness tended in the long run to accentuate the Kaiser's weaknesses. In turn, Eulenburg, who later in his memoirs referred to Holstein vindictively as a former "house dog on Bismarck's leash," began to distrust Holstein's increasing hostility towards the Kaiser, not appreciating that it may sometimes be advisable to sacrifice a king to save a monarchy. Also, Holstein, with his deep cynicism and his morbid suspicions, was extremely difficult to work with. His absolutely solitary life, his monomania for work warped his otherwise keen intelligence. Everyone with whom he came in close contact came to regard him as mentally unbalanced. He was too inclined to regard his own office in Wilhelmstrasse 76 as the center of the universe from which everything must proceed, must be controlled. Every influence which did not come under his control he suspected. He saw a conspirator behind every bush. Like his master, Bismarck, he tended too much to identify his own personality with the work he performed. He took everything personally. Thus he was likely suddenly to acquire a hate against some ambassador who had recommended a policy he disagreed with and to punish him by not sending him any important reports. He liked

[22]Haller, *Eulenburg*, I, 116, 341; Rogge, *Holstein*, pp. 199, 207.

particularly to get the ambassadors to deal with the most important matters through private correspondence with himself, these letters being filed or not as he saw fit. Hence, in September 1891, when Count Hatzfeldt had an important report to make and found that Holstein was on leave, it was possible for him to write to the under-secretary, von Rotenhan:

My inquiry yesterday about the return of Baron von Holstein was called forth by the fact that I have important communications to make, which are perhaps not yet suitable for the archives. I therefore make the urgency of the matter my excuse for begging you to inform the chancellor as follows: . . .[23]

Holstein's idiosyncrasies were not confined to his personal relations but expressed themselves also in the conduct of foreign policy: for example, the quick, indirect retaliation in Egypt against England in the Turkish railroad affair, in preference to a direct approach. In May 1894 the British government, preoccupied with blocking the French advance, leased some territory in central Africa to the Congo Free State, taking in return the lease of a corridor of land west of German East Africa, thus connecting British possessions north and south, from "Cape to Cairo." The German Foreign Office, considering this to be deliberate treachery and "encirclement" of their colony, lodged a joint protest with France, threatened action in Egypt, and thus brought about the abrogation of the treaty. On a particularly harsh note to be sent to the British Caprivi wrote: "I should like the note in a somewhat more polite form and have marked a few places to be toned down." Again, in the summer of 1891 in connection with Anglo-French rivalry in Morocco, Marschall wrote to Hatzfeldt, "Lord Salisbury would probably have been more reserved if he had realized our wish that England should set herself in acute and lasting rivalry with France by seizing Tangier and Spartel. . . . In your next conversations with Lord Salisbury I beg you . . . to continue to avoid arousing the suspicion that it is not the natural development of world events, but the policy of Germany that is forcing on Anglo-French rivalry in the Mediterranean." As against this Bismarckian idea that other nations must continually be provoked and set against each other by a policy which emanated from Berlin, thus maintaining Germany in a position of supreme arbiter, Caprivi took a more relaxed and saner view.

[23]Haller, *Eulenburg*, I, 340, 342, 303–310; Eulenburg, *Aus 50 Jahren*, p. 251; Hutten-Czapski, *Sechzig Jahre*, I, 251; Lerchenfeld, *Denkwürdigkeiten*, pp. 386–387; Hammann, *Der Neue Kurs*, pp. 58, 67–69; Eyck, *Wilhelm II*, p. 26; Dugdale, *German Diplomatic Documents*, II, 87.

In a memorandum written shortly afterwards for Rotenhan and Holstein he wrote: "Had we not better let matters proceed quietly there [in Morocco]? So long as England and France still *want* something in that part of the world, the uncertainty will keep them in rivalry. But if they *get* it they will live at peace beside one another — a condition which we ought not to hurry on." Here there is implied the whole conflict between the dynamic and provocative diplomatic manner of Holstein and the objective and restrained manner of Caprivi. It was a conflict between the traditional Bismarckian attempt to avoid a final conflict by setting the potentially aggressive forces against each other so as to create a stalemate and Caprivi's own less traditionally diplomatic attempt to avoid a conflict by calmly preparing for the worst and meanwhile trying as far as possible to restrain and deëmphasize the potentially aggressive forces. Hence Caprivi's trade-treaty policy, in its relaxing, conciliatory diplomatic tendency, was diametrically opposed to Holstein's forceful Foreign Office manipulations.[24]

Caprivi particularly disliked Holstein's meddling in matters outside of his jurisdiction and his liking for secrecy and intrigue. As early as the summer of 1890 Caprivi complained to Waldersee that Holstein was carrying on private correspondence behind his back. But when in 1892 General von Schweinitz, upon his retirement, said quite bluntly in a private conversation with Caprivi that "a personality not quite right in the head" had too much influence in the Foreign Office, Caprivi answered that he knew very well that Holstein had great faults and was affected by personal prejudices, but that it was impossible to get along without him. The chancellor had no interest or special ability in diplomacy and knew it. Phili Eulenburg later declared from the perspective of some twenty-five years that he had never tried to remove Holstein because

I had no doubt whatever that Holstein, despite his pathological and other traits, was indispensable. No chancellor would or could have done without him; it was clear to every one of them that in view of the stupendous difficulties caused by the Kaiser's meddlings and private policies, which were incessantly putting the Foreign Office into the tightest sort of holes, Holstein *alone* possessed the qualities to steer the ship of state *tant bien que mal* out of the Imperial whirlpool without veering from Scylla to Charybdis.

[24]*G.P.*, VIII, 1847ff., 2024ff.; Dugdale, *German Diplomatic Documents*, II, 314, 142–143 for quotes; Langer, *Franco-Russian Alliance*, p. 408; Holstein to Hatzfeldt, March 23, 1891, *Holstein Papers, Correspondence;* Eyck, *Wilhelm II*, p. 113. **Cf.** Wahl, *Geschichte*, III, 155.

In brief, Holstein's faults were his greatest virtues. It was the great subtlety of his highly political mind and his passion for intrigue which, after Bismarck, exactly fitted the needs of the Reich and, operating tirelessly and clandestinely, served to keep the machinery from flying apart at the center.[25]

In January 1894 the humor magazine *Kladderadatsch* began a series of attacks, which, without naming names, accused Eulenburg, Holstein, and Kiderlen of forming a secret camarilla. The attacks took the form of humorous verses, dialogues, and stories in which the principals bore various names, such as Count Troubadour (for Eulenburg, a singer-composer), Baron Austernfreund (oysters' friend — for Holstein, a gourmet), and Count Spätzle (a Swabian dumpling — for Kiderlen, a Swabian and rather stout), and were depicted sitting in a rathskeller wearing false whiskers or in search of a fourth for skat. These pieces were, of course, completely meaningless to the uninformed, but to those in the know it was obvious that the unknown author possessed a very good source of information. The motive behind the attacks was clearly indicated in a fable published in the January 21 number, entitled:

THE THREE MEN IN THE FIERY FURNACE

Once upon a time there was a king who possessed many true and honest servants. But there were three who were not very honest and deceived their master and did many evil things, for they slandered many of the truest knights so that they lost their positions and were sent away from the palace. The names of these unfaithful servants were Insinuans, Intrigans, and Calumnians. And not the most evil but probably the most dangerous of them was Insinuans, inasmuch as he saw the king more often than the others and also because he skillfully played the lute and sang to it bewitching melodies.

Then, however, a "true and simple" hero arose and by spreading humorous writings throughout the land exposed their evil deeds so that they were dismissed from office and placed in a fiery furnace, where to increase their discomfort Insinuans had to listen continuously to the lies of the others and they to his songs.[26]

As the attacks continued week after week the humor wore a bit thin. References to Eulenburg — who stood closest to the Kaiser — soon ceased completely, the pieces concentrating more and more on

[25]Hammann, *Der Neue Kurs*, p. 104; Waldersee, *Denkwürdigkeiten*, II, 140; Schweinitz, *Denkwürdigkeiten*, II, 443; Haller, *Eulenburg*, I, 308.

[26]*Kladderadatsch* (Berlin, 1848–   ), 47:10, 15; J. Hohlfeld, *Deutsche Reichsgeschichte in Dokumenten 1849–1926* (Berlin, 1927), I, 279–281; Hammann, *Der Neue Kurs*, p. 59; cf. Kardorff, *Kardorff*, p. 297.

Holstein. Kiderlen, at first, was able to take it all as a joke and would say, "So, now I put on my false whiskers and go to lunch." But Holstein was sure the attacks emanated from a high and secret source and, in his frustrated rage, went to ridiculous lengths to avenge himself. At the same time an attack had appeared in one of the Bismarck papers recalling Holstein's part in the Arnim affair, and Holstein sent his seconds to demand satisfaction from Count Herbert Bismarck, who, he was sure, was the instigator. Count Herbert, however, denied any connection with the Arnim article or with *Kladderadatsch*. Next, Holstein — who was half-blind from cataracts — challenged Count Guido Henckel von Donnersmarck, the pro-Bismarck publisher of the *Berliner Neueste Nachrichten*, to a duel on the ground that the attitude of his paper proved his complicity. But Count Henckel refused to accept the challenge. Then Holstein sent a Prussian general to threaten the publisher of *Kladderadatsch*, without result. Finally, one of the editors of the magazine was foolish enough to name names in a letter published in the *Frankfurter Zeitung*, and Kiderlen successfully challenged him to a duel. After that the matter gradually subsided. Whether or not the authors of the *Kladderadatsch* articles — apparently two subordinate Foreign Office officials — had, in reality, a formal connection with the Bismarcks is impossible to tell. But there is no doubt that the attacks came in conjunction with Bismarck's reconciliation with the Kaiser, that they represented the point of view of the Bismarck party — to which the chief officials "conspired against," such as Stumm, Rantzau, Schlözer, and Reuss, belonged — and that they were made much of by the Bismarck press. They seemed to have no effect whatsoever upon the Kaiser, who knew how valuable his advisers were.[27]

Holstein, who hated publicity, was much hurt by the whole affair. In a letter of March 5, 1894, which might very well be taken as his own "apology," he wrote:

I have never in my life been ambitious. Twice I could have become state secretary. But I have been in the way of all sorts of people and am hated for it. Also for many years, and now also for reasons of health, I

[27]See especially *Holstein Papers, Correspondence*, January-April 1894, most notably Polsdorff's accusatory letter of February 2 and Eulenburg's letter of April 5 describing the Kaiser's reaction, also further correspondence with Bissing, August-September 1898; Hammann, *Der Neue Kurs*, pp. 60–66; Haller, *Eulenburg*, I, 124; Rogge, *Holstein*, pp. 169–170; Thimme, "Bismarck und Kardorff," pt. II, p. 165; Kardorff, *Kardorff*, p. 297; Waldersee, *Denkwürdigkeiten*, II, 312; *Die Nation*, XI, 326, 342.

have led a lonely life. Out of a hundred people who hear me complained against perhaps one knows me, and he does not necessarily like me. I shall, therefore, if I ever figure in history, probably be described as an intriguer, although I have always done my duty as I understood it.

Frustrated in his attempts at revenge, he struck out blindly in all directions. "If H. M.," he wrote Eulenburg, "does nothing against Henckel, he ranges himself with my enemies." And again to Eulenburg, "As I perceive you are working for the Foreign Office and against me, I shall be obliged to show my claws in some way." In the summer of 1894 Holstein went so far as to suggest that Eulenburg submit all his important reports from Vienna to himself personally by private letter;

thus letting me in for the Reich Chancellor's displeasure! If poor Caprivi got hold of this letter, friend Holstein's days would certainly be numbered! But since we cannot — I had almost written, alas! — do without him, I shall pay no attention to this hint, nor shall I show the note to good Caprivi. My God! What a drama! [28]

The *Kladderadatsch* affair went quite against the grain with the punctiliously correct Caprivi. The time had come, he decided, for the good of the service, to let Holstein go. But Marschall interceded for the old Geheimrat, insisting that he could not continue in office without him, and Caprivi let the matter drop temporarily. In fact, during the past year, as the Miquel-Junker-Bismarck attack mounted in fury, Caprivi had been forced more and more to rely upon the Eulenburg-Holstein clique. He had, to be sure, consistently found majority support for his program in the Reichstag, but the most recent majority of the left was a patch-work affair, which, running the gamut from Social Democrats to National Liberals, possessed no unity, no strength of its own. It was, for Caprivi, no real political support, particularly since most respectable Germans must look askance at a government, which, since 1890 under an avowed program of uniting all parties against the socialist threat, was now depending for its successful continuation upon the votes of the Social Democrats. Nor, particularly since the Bismarck reconciliation in January, could Caprivi find support now in the ministry. In January Hutten-Czapski wrote to Prince zu Hohenlohe:

My impression — based upon the remarks of various ministers — is that in case Count Caprivi should lose his support with the Kaiser he would be deserted by all of his Prussian colleagues.

[28]Rogge, *Holstein*, p. 168; Haller, *Eulenburg*, I, 285–287, 283.

On March 4 von Kardorff wrote to his wife:

The split between Caprivi and the Prussian State Ministry and the disintegration of the Bundesrat (etc.) becomes more and more obvious. But whether Caprivi falls or Miquel remains doubtful.

And on April 10:

Who is man, who is master, one knows even less now than before, and if one asks three ministers about the government's future plans, one can be sure of getting three diametrically opposite answers.[29]

With uncertain support in the Reichstag and no support in the ministry, Caprivi was, indeed, almost as isolated as Bismarck had indicated sarcastically in his "tight-rope walker" speech. All the influences at court now worked against him. Unlike Holstein in the Foreign Office, he had done nothing to remove hostile elements and to create a personal following for himself at court. The army, from Chief of the Military Cabinet General von Hahnke on down, still smarted over two-year service and wanted nothing more than to get rid of this chancellor who was also a general and who supervised military affairs with too tight a rein. The Kaiser's military suite found ever increasing occasions to make jokes at Caprivi's and especially Marschall's expense. General von Waldersee had extended his own intrigues to include the federal princes. And through the whole court ran the smoldering hatred of the land-owning Junker aristocracy for the landless career man (whose ancestors were of Italian or Slavic origin and had, after all, been ennobled only in the seventeenth century) who dared to try to govern Germany against their will. This Junker opposition dominated not only the parliaments and the court, but the bureaucracy as well, which traditionally had been recruited almost entirely from this class. Caprivi's manner was incisive and direct, with no circumlocutions, no temporizing, little capacity for tactful persuasion. His habit of thinking and acting had, no doubt, been too much molded by his army training, where hesitation or vagueness of decision is always disastrous, and where a decision once made immediately becomes an order. For this reason the solitary general in the chancellor's palace could never capture the imagination or enthusiasm of his administrative subordinates. Within the bureaucracy opposition to Caprivi found its roots not only in the

[29]Polsdorff letter, February 2, 1894, *Holstein Papers, Correspondence;* F. Thimme, "Fürst Bülow u. Graf Monts," *Pr. Jbb.,* 232:22–23; Hammann, *Der Neue Kurs,* p. 64; Lerchenfeld, *Denkwürdigkeiten,* p. 384; Raschdau, *Bismarck u. Caprivi,* pp. 350–351; *Die Nation,* XI, 327; Hutten-Czapski, *Sechzig Jahre,* I, 224–225; Thimme, "Bismarck und Kardorff," pt. II, p. 164; Kardorff, *Kardorff,* pp. 293, 298.

agrarian Junker interests, but in veneration — and now fear — of Bismarck. The Foreign Office was not the only ministry where subordinate officials tried privately to sabotage policies and personalities which they believed to be "un-Bismarckian" or unagrarian. Thus subordinates in the Reich Department of the Interior obstructed trade-treaty negotiations, and the Prussian political police — under Botho Eulenburg's protection — spread rumors and slanders through their agents in the press. This clash of competing and conflicting interests had, by the spring of 1894, made any kind of orderly government almost impossible. On March 6 Phili Eulenburg wrote to his friend Varnbüler:

I have been in Berlin and had a horrible time, for the nervousness and irritability of the parties, politicians, court officials, etc., is at fever height. The Russian commercial treaty, Gladstone's retirement, Kálnoky and his huffs, *Kladderadatsch*, the [Kaiser's] trip to Abbazia, and so on and so forth — it begins to feel like a lunatic asylum; and my equilibrium was not restored until I went out to Liebenberg with Cuno [Moltke], shot some pheasants, talked, slept, and had some music.[30]

The precariousness of his position forced the chancellor more and more upon the support of the crown, and the fact of this dependence weakened his own personal standing with Phili Eulenburg and the Kaiser himself. The more Caprivi tried to please and humor the Kaiser, the less disinterested he appeared, and the less the Kaiser respected him. The Kaiser had, in fact, long since grown tired of the stiff and unyielding old general. Since he had been forced to give up three-year service for the army their relations had never been the same. It was clear that the Kaiser had been ready to change chancellors since the end of 1893. Already then he had begun to cover Caprivi's memoranda with caustic marginal comments. Early in the summer of 1894 he told a friend, "I get along with Caprivi but he is not congenial to me. The man has no imagination and does not understand me when I tell him of my wider thoughts. For his successor I shall take a younger man who will be closer to me personally and will not have any past experience to oppose to me; he shall be my man alone." This "younger man," wrote General von Stosch to Bennigsen, would very likely be Phili Eulenburg or Bernhard Bülow. Eulenburg, however, had no intention of becoming chancellor, but,

[30]Schmidt-Bückeburg, *Das Militärkabinett*, p. 195; Hohenlohe, *Memoirs*, II, 461–462; Eulenburg, *Aus 50 Jahren*, p. 255; R. Geis, "Der Sturz des Reichskanzlers Caprivi," *Historische Studien*, 192:59–61, 65 (1930); Waldersee, *Denkwürdigkeiten*, II, 209, 297, 316; Wehrmuth, *Beamtenleben*, pp. 190, 196–197; Ebmeyer, "Caprivis Entlassung," pp. 210–211; Haller, *Eulenburg*, I, 182; cf. Wippermann, 10(I):12–16.

sensing His Majesty's restlessness under Caprivi, began as early as the fall of 1893 to make soundings in favor of his cousin, Botho. At the very time when Caprivi most needed the support of his agent at court, this agent, also, had begun to desert his standard.[31]

The more dependent Caprivi became upon the Kaiser the more obsessed with his own importance, the more arrogant and overbearing the Kaiser became. In his Brandenburg speech in February 1894, as an illustration of the properly exalted place of the monarchy in the life of the Reich, the Kaiser told the story of an old Dutch woman who pointed to the bullet hole in the wall of the house where William the Silent had been murdered and exclaimed, "Dat is Wilhelm!" After that, whenever the Kaiser did something striking or appeared in public, "Dat is Wilhelm!" was the watchword.[32] The public did not quite go along with the Kaiser's mood. In May 1894 a pamphlet appeared entitled *Caligula, a Study in Roman Megalomania*, which, significantly, became widely known only after it was reviewed at length in the *Kreuzzeitung*. As the author told of Caligula's ostentation, his mania for building, his desire to control the seas, his pleasure in military maneuvers, the comparison with William II was glaringly obvious. He even quoted the words, "There is only one ruler, only one king!" In August the *Vossische Zeitung* published its own computation from official sources that the Kaiser had spent at least 199 of the past 365 days in travel. In Berlin the saying went the rounds, "I have no time to rule!" [33]

No matter how tired of Caprivi the Kaiser might be, he could not very well get rid of his chancellor as long as there was no positive political alternative, that is, no candidate available who could muster an opposition wide and determined enough to defeat Caprivi's program in the Reichstag. The Radical Unionists, with their little bloc of thirteen votes, might, as Caprivi's enemies declared sarcastically, constitute the chancellor's only dependable following, but, with the exception of the Conservatives, there were very few who really wanted him removed. The Conservatives, by concentrating so narrowly and fanatically on agrarianism, had alienated their industrial, upper-middle-class friends and had thereby ensured Caprivi's victory.

[31]Wedel, *Zwischen Kaiser und Kanzler*, pp. 200–205; Hutten-Czapski, *Sechzig Jahre*, I, 224; Raschdau, *Bismarck u. Caprivi*, pp. 337, 347–349; Oncken, *Bennigsen*, II, 591–592; Hohenlohe, *Memoirs*, II, 461.

[32]Raschdau, *Bismarck u. Caprivi*, pp. 333–334; *Schulthess* (1894), p. 74; Wippermann, 10(I):11–12. By this reference in his speech the Kaiser meant to emphasize the contribution of his grandfather, Wilhelm I, to national feeling, but the connection with himself was too obvious to be easily resisted.

[33]Kardorff, *Kardorff*, pp. 294–295; Waldersee, *Denkwürdigkeiten*, II, 313, 320; Eyck, *Wilhelm II*, p. 85; Wippermann, 10(I):273–274.

Really to defeat Caprivi they would have to win back some middle-class support. To frighten the middle class into coöperation there were in their political closet the familiar, old, rather worn and dusty, but still effective bogies of military defense of the Fatherland against the threat of foreign attack and defense of property against the internal threat of socialist revolution. These were the two issues which the master manipulator Bismarck had planned to use in 1890. Then he had been defeated by the optimism of the parties, each looking to the young Kaiser to lead them into a new era. This new era, with its confusions and startling paradoxes, had then come and had pleased nobody. Now, in 1894, it was time, once more, for pessimism. The military issue had been settled for a while the year before. The threat of socialist revolution remained. In May Bismarck had already pointed to stronger anti-Socialist measures as the chief plank in the anti-Caprivi platform. Yet the threat of revolution — without government coöperation — could not be made real enough sufficiently to frighten the middle classes without, as in 1878, some shocking incident. As luck would have it this incident was shortly provided.[34]

2

THE REVOLUTION BILL

During the past two years there had been a succession of anarchist bombings and dynamitings, especially in Italy and France, which had occupied the attention of all Europe. In November 1893 two time-bombs had been mailed to the Kaiser and Caprivi from Orléans, but had been detected before any damage was done. On June 16, 1894, there was an unsuccessful anarchist attempt on the life of the Italian premier, Francesco Crispi. Then, on June 24, President Sadi Carnot of France was fatally stabbed by an anarchist in Marseilles. All Europe was deeply shocked. The Kaiser sent a telegram of sympathy to Mme. Carnot. In France, Spain, and Switzerland laws against anarchists were quickly passed. In Germany the press, led by the *Kreuzzeitung* and the *Hamburger Nachrichten*, took up the cry and demanded that the government do something. The general demand was for a new, exceptional law, not only against anarchists, but against Social Democrats as well. A position against such a law,

[34]Cf. Hohenlohe, *Memoirs*, II, 462; Wedel, *Zwischen Kaiser und Kanzler*, pp. 201–202; Eyck, *Wilhelm II*, p. 81; Wippermann, 10(I):269–274. In 1878 Bismarck put through his anti-Socialist law after an unsuccessful attempt on the life of old Kaiser William I.

said the *Hamburger Nachbrichten*, should at least not be taken
a priori. Almost without exception the press of the "middle parties"
— the upper middle class — joined in. In fact, they were the ones
who called loudest and longest for the strongest measures. Among
them only the *Preussische Jahrbücher* advocated moderation. The
papers of all parties — except Radicals and Social Democrats —
called for "action." There was, of course, some disagreement on what
kind of action would be most appropriate. The Center, afraid of
forging weapons for a new Kulturkampf, did not go along with the
middle-party papers in advocating laws curbing the press and the
right of assembly. It put its hopes rather in a new Zedlitz school
law. The fight for religion, explained the *Germania*, could not be
fought with the irreligious liberals but must rather be fought against
them. It would be better to line up with the Conservatives, who
were a Christian party. On the other side the *Kreuzzeitung* soon declared that it could not fight for religion by the side of atheists and
Jews. It would prefer to work with the Center. As for the National
Liberal papers, they clamored most loudly for some kind of action
but did not seem to have any specific measures in mind.[35]

Within the government Miquel also seized upon the opportunity
presented. Since the Reichstag had been so unkind to his tax legislation and financial reform he had become disillusioned with universal
suffrage. At least part of the Reichstag, he believed, would have to
be chosen by the Landtags. In July he inspired articles in the *National Zeitung* and *Kölnische Zeitung* advocating, in case the Reichstag failed to pass repressive measures, dissolution and eventual
abolition of universal suffrage. To Raschdau, in July, Miquel predicted that the necessary attempt to strengthen the state against
revolutionary elements would be the occasion for a change in the
government. He agreed with Bismarck, also, he said, on the Polish
question. On his return to Berlin in August he wrote, "I want to
bring the matter to a head, as the present situation can no longer be
tolerated and has become quite untenable and, besides, is tottering
badly." Miquel, however, did not push himself forward. Rather it
was Botho Eulenburg, the author of Bismarck's anti-Socialist law of
1878, who was encouraged to champion the new repressive legislation and thus to put himself at the head of the agitation. Was not
this much more careful and discreet for Miquel? If Caprivi opposed
a program of repression and the anti-Capriviites received sufficient
backing, they might force Caprivi out on the issue. If Botho Eulen-

[35]*The Times, passim; Schulthess* (1893), p. 154, (1894), pp. 131–132, 136–137,
143–144, 163; Wippermann, 10(II):63ff.; Zechlin, *Staatsstreichpläne,* p. 102.

burg then became chancellor, Miquel's influence would rule Germany. If Caprivi, however, accepted the task of putting through the repressive legislation, he himself would be tarred with the black brush of reaction and, if the program, as was quite possible, should subsequently arouse heated liberal opposition — say, as in the School Bill affair — Miquel could then change tactics and come forward again in the role of liberal statesman. In any case, things could not go on as they were, and by keeping in the background he was saving his own neck. With the Conservatives, the agrarians, and the Bismarckites, Miquel was firmly convinced that all the misfortunes of the government since 1892, the split between Reich and Prussia, public dissatisfaction, the increasing confusion within the parties, the confusion and backbiting within the government itself, the intrigues around the court — all this was due to Caprivi's stupidity and general lack of political ability. The difficulties of Caprivi's position, Miquel told Waldersee in January at the height of the battle over the Russian trade treaty, were due entirely to his "vanity and belief in his own infallibility." The removal of Caprivi would in the eyes of his opponents take away the sole obstacle to a complete triumph of order, stability, and monarchical solidarity, a firm control over Socialists, Poles, Jews, and atheists — and victory for the interests of the agrarian Junkers.[36]

For Caprivi the situation was extremely difficult. As a conservative he did not deny that forceful measures against the threat of revolution might, one day, again become necessary. In the winter of 1892–1893, at the time of the Saar strike, Caprivi, apparently under the strong influence of von Stumm-Halberg and Krupp, had taken an extreme position in the ministry, advocating not only action against Social Democratic "agitators" in the union but action against all members to break up the union itself. With the sacrifice of the anti-Socialist law, said Caprivi, all other means of fighting the Social Democrats must be applied even more vigorously. The state mines must take a strong stand to encourage private operators. At that time, the strike having already been broken, Berlepsch's milder view found more support, and Caprivi yielded to the majority. In the summer of 1893 Stumm's influence with the Kaiser increased, and, with the anarchist excitement abroad, in November 1893 the Kaiser suggested to Caprivi that special legislation against anarchism

[36]Herzfeld, *Miquel*, II, 374–378, 309–310; Wippermann, 10(II):73–74, 76; Raschdau, *Bismarck u. Caprivi*, p. 355; Zechlin, *Staatsstreichpläne*, pp. 104, 112–113; Haller, *Eulenburg*, I, 251; Hohenlohe, *Memoirs*, II, 462; Keim, *Erlebtes*, p. 79; cf. Hutten-Czapski, *Sechzig Jahre*, I, 267.

in Germany might be in order. At this point, apparently foreseeing the general trend and effects of such a policy, Caprivi began to put on the brakes and to resist the movement. Forceful measures might sometime be necessary, but they did not, he profoundly believed, provide a solution to the problem, nor should they be used except as a last resort. He had taken up the government of the Reich in 1890 on the basis of the Kaiser's program, expressed in the February decrees, of uniting all classes behind the monarchy through a program of conciliation and reform, tying himself to the interests of no particular party, and having special consideration for the weaker elements of the population. In every important measure since then — including the big Army Bill with its reduction of service to two years — he had in some degree tried to pursue this purpose. Now to swing over completely to a policy of repressive, exceptional legislation would contradict the whole course of policy pursued by him — and by the Kaiser — during the past four years.[37]

It was in some measure a clash of basic attitudes on the proper treatment by the state of avowed revolutionary parties. The Bismarck-Junker group demanded that such parties be legally outlawed and forceably repressed. There seemed much justification for this point of view. Anarchists, said the middle-class papers, could not be kept down as long as the free activity of the Marxist Social Democrats undermined the authority of the state. Since the expiration of the anti-Socialist law in 1890 Social Democrats had been in a strong and triumphant mood. The Marxist dogma of revolution, adopted at Erfurt, had begun to take hold of the imagination of the masses. And, under the aegis of universal suffrage — and despite unequal districting — the number of Social Democrats in the Reichstag was growing larger and larger with every election. In May 1894 the Social Democrats in Berlin had replied to the joint action of the owners against the demands of brewery workers by a city-wide boycott on beer, which was still continuing. Against the revolutionary threat the right demanded a declaration of war.[38]

On the other side, Caprivi and Berlepsch believed that forceful measures — as under Bismarck — would only strengthen and solidify the revolutionary movement, that in the long run the only effective method was to combine a firm stand on the basis of the legal main-

[37]Hellwig, Stumm, pp. 494–498; Zechlin, Staatsstreichpläne, p. 93. Cf. Caprivi's statement in the State Ministry, October 12, Zechlin, op. cit., p. 193; see below, pp. 345–346.

[38]See above, Chapter IV, section 2. Cf. Hammann, Der Neue Kurs, pp. 131–139; Ziekursch, Geschichte, III, 55–56; Schulthess (1894), pp. 120–130; Wippermann, 10(I):288–290; 10(II):67.

tenance of law and order with a serious attempt to undermine the movement by removing its causes — by granting justified demands and righting social and economic wrongs. A year later Caprivi wrote to Dr. Schneidewin:

I do not believe that the "Guards" can solve the social problem. Let us hope that this problem never brings them into action, that it will be possible without bloodshed to create a place in our political life for whatever is justified in the movement and to suppress everything that is unjustified by legal means. I refuse to give up hope that this will succeed. . . . I cannot deny that it seemed undesirable to me to remove the Social Democrats from the Reichstag. Better not to plug up this safety valve.[39]

On July 4 an article appeared in the semiofficial *Norddeutsche Allgemeine Zeitung* which read in part:

There is as little possibility of providing an absolutely certain means for protecting the state and society against waves of assassinations as there is of finding radical preventives for other crimes. . . . Anarchists who have sealed their political creed with an *act* and have placed themselves in the hands of the law we already know how to deal with: we give them short shrift. *More severe treatment is impossible . . .* It could, therefore, be a matter only of persons who so far have revealed their anarchist convictions merely with *words*. Within them *may* lie concealed the germs of bloodthirsty fanatics and assassins, germs which the first favorable occasion will ripen; *but they may also all their lives remain blusterers,* inwardly trembling wretches intoxicating themselves with bloodthirsty tirades and horrifying fantasies, or after a few years they may have cleansed their minds of the wild nonsense *and transformed themselves into useful citizens.* Shall all these types, which at first glance exactly resemble each other and between which only later experience of their actions will draw sharp distinctions, shall all these be handled in the same way? It will be hard to answer this question in the affirmative; it will be considered *too severe* that a man, sometimes needlessly, should atone for the mad dreams of his youth with the annihilation and extinction of his whole social existence.

Horrified, the Conservative *Kreuzzeitung* commented on the 8th that it could not believe its eyes to see such "humanitarian phrases" in an official paper. The government, it declared, was in danger of "sinking to the level of the most wretched democratic radicalism." [40]

Out of all the clamor of conflicting opinions in the press two points of view clearly emerged. The one boiled down to taking away the right to vote from the Social Democrats and depriving them of

[39]Schneidewin, "Briefe," p. 249.
[40]Wippermann, 10(II):65–66. Italics in the original.

representation in the Reichstag. The other point of view, held almost exclusively by the official press, was most clearly elaborated in a series of articles by the former head of Reich press affairs, Dr. Konstantin Rössler. In an article in the *Wiener Politische Korrespondenz* he declared that the "social question" was actually on the point of solution, that, although the Social Democrats were still increasing in number their program and tactics were becoming less and less revolutionary, that to the present extreme demands Caprivi would oppose the "courage of deliberation." The present fright and clamor for action by all the different party factions in so many different keys, he hinted, seemed to indicate that what they really wanted was a dictatorship. As a positive program, he suggested, in brief, that universal and equal suffrage be extended to the Prussian Landtag. The *Preussische Jahrbücher,* which had been running a series of articles defending the Caprivi Polish policy, suggested, in calling attention to Rössler's argument, that the main threat to German national feeling in Posen was the Germans in Posen themselves, who had been so protected by the government as to lose all independent initiative. They had begun to wake up only when the government had begun to deal kindly with the Poles. It might, it suggested, be the same with the squabbling and divided middle-class parties and the socialist menace.[41]

Rössler's "courage of deliberation" raised a great hue and cry. Baron von Stumm-Halberg wrote to Caprivi on July 6, protesting over the article, which mentioned Caprivi's name and appeared to be officially inspired. "Nor can I to the best of my conscience make any reply to the negative criticism other than it is impossible that that article should have been inspired by Your Excellency or expressed your intentions." In a letter of July 8, Caprivi replied to Stumm that he had not, in fact, inspired the article, which had been written independently by a supporter of the government, who, however, had often been used by the government for such purposes before. As to the question at hand, wrote Caprivi, it was, for him, a matter of what could or could not be done with the Reichstag and whether a dissolution should be risked. He was not nearly as confident as Stumm that all the "state-supporting parties" would be in favor of strong measures. When the actual proposals for changes in the criminal code, for dynamite laws, assembly and press

---

[41]*Pr. Jbb.,* 78:361–367; Hammann, *Der Neue Kurs,* p. 98. For opinions on the social question and the success of the New Course policy, cf. Berlepsch, *Sozialipolitische Erfahrungen,* pp. 21–22; F. Meinecke, *Staat u. Persönlichkeit* (Berlin, 1933), p. 179; Lotz, "Handelspolitik," p. 69.

laws, were advanced, all the parties which would find themselves affected by them would protest. But there would be no use in passing an anti-Socialist law like the previous one, since that had "prevented neither the growth of the Social Democrats nor assassination attempts against the old Kaiser." If any such law were to be passed now it would have to be more severe to be effective. But National Liberals and Free Conservatives had not voted for the last one; would they vote for more severe measures now? He would not mention the obvious technical difficulties in apprehending anarchists *before* they committed crimes, but would confine himself to the Reichstag. The situation was not such that a repressive measure could be introduced and then dropped if defeated. Once the government had taken the position that more severe legislation was needed it would have to go through with it, to dissolution and even worse. The question must first be asked, then, how and whether the government would carry its program through from there.

The question cannot be evaded; if an anarchist or socialist law were rejected and the succeeding elections brought no improvement in the Reichstag, would we not merely be playing the game of the Social Democrats, increasing the dissatisfaction, egging on their followers? These are, indeed, very serious questions which one must be sure about before one takes the first step.

If the Social Democrats remained "unmolested as at present," replied Stumm, he doubted if a *coup d'état* could be avoided. There would be less chance of one if a positive step were taken now against the Socialists by the government.[42]

It was all very well for Caprivi to wish to avoid the extreme policy demanded by the reactionary elements, now making the most of the anarchist scare. But he could not expect to achieve any following of his own with merely a negative program or no program at all. By 1894 his policy of the just mean, of compromise and balance, with limited and specific aims, had been proved insufficient. His government-above-the-parties had alienated the nationalists with the colonial and Polish policies, the liberals with the School Bill, the agrarians in the right and center with the trade treaties. The policy his Junker adversaries now advocated was reactionary and extreme, and could not finally be approved by the bulk of the nation. Was not the present state of general confusion and discontent especially opportune for creating a new political line-up by launching a new,

[42]Hellwig, *Stumm*, pp. 499–503; Zechlin, *Staatsstreichpläne*, pp. 184–186; Wippermann, 10(II):64ff.

hopeful, progressive program of moderate reform? Since the fight on the Rumanian treaty, the Radical Unionists Alexander Meyer and Theodor Barth had been trying to educate Caprivi to this point of view. To carry on a constructive program, they wrote in *Die Nation*, a government must be supported by a firm majority, and if one was not available, it *must create one*. It was not yet too late to create such a following; all that was needed was a leader with a strong enough will to carry it through.

A government that wishes to capture people's minds and spirits must possess initiative. It must undertake reforms. And there is always need for great reforms. . . . A statesman who conducts a positive policy will always win a significant following, and a statesman who conducts an intelligent policy will always find this following among intelligent people. . . . It is not enough for [the government] to reveal its immediate objectives from time to time, it must also reveal the long term objectives toward which it is striving. It must not appeal solely to sober reason but must also understand how to appeal to the heart. . . . If today there still existed among us a party such as the National Liberal party was during the first half of the seventies, in such a party the Reich chancellor would find his natural support.

There is some evidence that Caprivi by the summer of 1894 had come to agree with these writers that if he were to go on governing he must create a following for himself. He was willing to try to appease the popular demand for action against revolution with a mild strengthening of existing laws. Might he not offset the weakness of this negative program by balancing it with new positive reforms, coupled with a strong propaganda attempt to create a new political grouping around a moderately progressive policy? The key reform in such a program, as Rössler had suggested, would be a new attempt at suffrage reform in Prussia. Caprivi was not averse to such a measure. To sponsor it he would have to recapture the presidency of the Prussian Ministry. But if he were to continue to head the Reich government these self-assertive steps would be almost inevitable. The Bismarck-Junker opposition would force him to it.[43]

If, in the summer of 1894, Caprivi's only chance to continue long in office was to introduce a positive program in the fall, his political opponents were determined to force him out before things got that far. They had the great initial advantage of having the Kaiser, whose concern for his personal safety played a prominent part, on their side.

[43]*Die Nation*, X, 205, 209, XI, 161, 175–176, 191; cf. Schneidewin, "Briefe," pp. 257–258; Wippermann, 10(I):276–277, 10(II):29–31, 135, 140–141; see below, p. 364; Ebmeyer, "Caprivis Entlassung," p. 196.

He quite agreed that "something should be done," and found the moderate tone of his own official press quite distressing. Fortunately, during July he was away on his Norwegian cruise, accompanied as usual by Phili Eulenburg and Kiderlen. Nevertheless, on July 16 Kiderlen telegraphed instructions to Caprivi from the Kaiser, the tenor of which coincided exactly with the arguments of Bismarck and Stumm. He was glad to see, said the Kaiser, that the middle classes were excited and demanding energetic measures. Exceptional laws must not be rejected a priori! Caprivi was to work out a bill to bring before the Bundesrat and Reichstag in the fall. Meanwhile the press must keep middle-class feelings in a state of sufficient excitement. In private telegrams to Holstein and Rotenhan Kiderlen warned that the Kaiser was greatly excited because the official press was taking a line contrary to his own attitude, which was known to the chancellor. He advised caution and that it would be wise to go along with the Kaiser's slogan of defense against anarchists and socialists and utilizing aroused middle-class opinion. The Kaiser had said nothing about the content of the bill.[44]

On July 19 Caprivi submitted a report by telegraph going along with the Kaiser's idea of the necessity for action, but recommending, since the prospects for approval of such measures in the Reichstag were slim, that — as he had suggested the previous year — the program should be put through the Prussian Landtag. Thus, with the approval of his advisers, Holstein, Marschall, and Göring, he temporarily avoided entanglement in the issue by pushing it off on the Prussian ministry.[45]

Botho Eulenburg was quite willing to accept the challenge. When, in mid-August, the Kaiser returned from Cowes, he declared to him in Berlin and later, in early September, at the army maneuvers at Königsberg that action taken by the Prussian Landtag would not suffice but would be partial and premature. The social question was essentially a Reich problem, and sooner or later a conflict with the Reichstag must be faced. Several dissolutions, perhaps a *coup d'état* and alteration of the suffrage, might be necessary. At Königsberg the Kaiser also conferred with the kings of Saxony and Württemberg, who agreed with Eulenburg's proposals. Things, said King Albert of Saxony, could not go on as they were. There would be no difficulty with Bavaria; he would see to that. "None of us," remarked

[44]Text of Kaiser's instructions, Zechlin, *Staatsstreichpläne*, "Anlage 6," pp. 186–188, also pp. 189, 101–103; Wippermann, 10(II):1.

[45]Zechlin, *Staatsstreichpläne*, pp. 188–189, 191, note; cf. *Norddeutsche* article, August 5, Wippermann, 10(II):71.

the king of Württemberg, "has taken an oath to uphold the Reich constitution, therefore it can be changed." [46]

On September 6, 1894, at a banquet in the Königsberg castle for the representatives of the province of East Prussia, the Kaiser delivered a speech, destined to produce long-lasting effects upon the internal politics of Germany. The first part of the speech he devoted to castigating his Junker audience for their opposition to his government. "For the Prussian nobility to oppose their king is an absurdity!" Then, looking around at that unbroken sea of hostile faces, he abruptly changed his tone and ended the speech with a reference to the threat of revolution and an appeal for unity. "Onward to battle for religion, for morality and order against the parties of revolution!" [47]

3

CAPRIVI'S FALL

The Crisis

On August 27, 1894, Chancellor von Caprivi, as in previous years, had gone to Carlsbad for the cure, where, accompanied only by a small suite consisting of his adjutant, Major von Ebmeyer, a code officer from the Foreign Office, and his personal valet, he had taken simple quarters in the "White Lion," an inn located on the market square and operated by an elderly lady, Frau Winter. The chancellor was in a distinctly depressed mood. Quite contrary to his usual manner, he was moody, introspective, and taciturn. His silence at length became so noticeably oppressive that he himself apologized for it to Major Ebmeyer and explained that recent developments in domestic politics were so much on his mind that he could not find room for a relaxed conversation. There was, indeed, much in the past four years to weigh him down. He had tried to conduct a policy, moderately conservative, but carefully adjusted to divergent views and open to compromise, to hew a middle line, and for this moderate policy of reasonable, careful, honest compromise he had found almost no support. Recently the Conservative party, those who were supposed to be the staunchest upholders of the state, had been his strongest and most bitter opponents. During these days he wrote to Professor Schneidewin,

[46]Zechlin, *Staatsstreichpläne*, pp. 106–107, 189–192.
[47]*Schulthess* (1894), pp. 139–141; Wippermann, 10(II):3–5, 79–91; Hammann, *Der Neue Kurs*, p. 99; Zechlin, *Staatsstreichpläne*, pp. 105–106; Ebmeyer, "Caprivis Entlassung," pp. 203–204. Cf. Waldersee, *Denkwürdigkeiten*, II, 322.

I believe that with the Army Bill and the trade treaties I have deserved credit from Germany, and that with many other things which people find fault with I knew no better solution. If I find no recognition, then I must put up with it. I did not expect it when I entered office.

But the parties were not all. His had been a war on two fronts: for every battle with the Reichstag he had had to fight a running battle in the rear against the Kaiser and the influences around the Kaiser. He was a man who loved clarity and decisiveness. With parties and issues he could deal, but in this constant guerrilla fighting of personal influences and intrigues he found no joy of battle. And recently it had been worse. Against military suite and court officials and Prussian ministers the constant and necessary defensive action had monopolized his time and worn away his energy and his will to resist. He was sixty-three years old, tired, and in ill health. Must he go on with it? [48]

It was in this mood that Caprivi learned of the Kaiser's speech at Königsberg on September 6. Two days later a coded message came in by telegraph from the Kaiser describing his interviews with Botho Eulenburg and with the kings of Saxony and Württemberg:

I was pleased to see how clear the king was on the political situation and that his opinions fully agreed with mine. . . . He declared emphatically that if the Reichstag refuses repeatedly to accept measures for the protection of society it has forfeited its right to exist. Then the moment will have come when the bomb must burst and the Bundesrat [i.e., the German princes] must introduce or, as the case may be, dictate a new suffrage law. In other words, the *ultima ratio*, a *coup d'état*. . . . He stands with his Saxons completely at my disposal and has not the slightest doubt that the Bundesrat will support it *in toto*. . . . I could only declare myself in agreement with everything. . . .[49]

Thus the Kaiser — who as early as 1892 had declared that he had had "just about enough of the liberal era" — now enthusiastically recommended to Caprivi the identical program over which he had forced Bismarck's resignation in 1890. It was one of those historical ironies, amusing but not particularly comforting. But to Caprivi it meant more than a denial of the policy which he had pursued for the last four years; in approving a policy of reaction the Kaiser had publicly identified himself with the Bismarck-Junker opposition, the chancellor's enemies. Caprivi's first reaction was immediately to write out his resignation, and, deaf to all arguments, he gave it to

[48]Ebmeyer, "Caprivis Entlassung," pp. 193–194; Schneidewin, "Briefe," p. 140; Zechlin, *Staatsstreichpläne*, pp. 108–110.
[49]Text in Zechlin, *Staatsstreichpläne*, "Anlage 9," pp. 191–192.

Major Ebmeyer to send off to Berlin. The next day he thought better of it, and, since the major had disobeyed and had not sent the letter, was able to retract it. He had resigned himself to see the fight through to the end.[50]

The Königsberg speech found a mixed reception in the press. The papers of the left welcomed the attack against the Junker opposition in the first part and overlooked the rest, while the papers of the right welcomed the call to arms against revolution and overlooked the first part. As for the middle-party press, it took its lead from the *Hamburger Nachrichten*, which declared that the inner meaning of this "significant" and "well-considered" speech was, through the call to battle against revolution, to end past disputes and to forgive past differences. The press battle had, in fact, become centered in a contest between the official press and Bismarck's *Hamburger Nachrichten*. The government was attacked for its "weakness," its "excess of silly humanitarianism [*Humanitätsduselei*]." To the reiterated argument of the *Norddeutsche Allgemeine Zeitung* that a reactionary program could not muster a majority in the Reichstag the *Hamburger Nachrichten* replied grandly that a really responsible government should never be prevented by the possibility of failure from pursuing a measure with determination if it was right and necessary. Severe laws would do no good, said the *Norddeutsche*, as long as the middle-class parties were in their present state of confusion and dissolution. The government, retorted the *Hamburger Nachrichten*, was merely concealing its own weakness and disinclination to act behind the obstreperousness of the Reichstag. The New Course was afraid to fight strongly in the defense of the nation and the crown, afraid that a crisis might endanger the perpetuation of its own career. Thus the anarchist-socialist issue was used to create a general attack on the "weakness" of the New Course as a whole.[51]

Then, to complete the picture, Bismarck, on September 16, delivered to a delegation of Germans from the province of Posen a speech attacking government policy towards the Poles. "It is lack of political skill or political ignorance to depend on the Polish nobility to secure the eastern frontier." In fact, simultaneously with the conclusion of the trade treaty with Russia, the Polish party had itself begun to shy away from the government, a development which led

[50]Waldersee, *Denkwürdigkeiten*, II, 223; Ebmeyer, "Caprivis Entlassung," pp. 194–195.

[51]*Schulthess* (1894), pp. 141–142; Wippermann, 10(II):69–71; Zechlin, *Staatsstreichpläne*, pp. 95–98, 110–111; Hofmann, *Bismarck*, II, 260. Cf. Radical and Center opinion that the whole agitation was for the purpose of embarrassing and ousting Caprivi, Wippermann, 10(II):76.

to the repudiation of the leadership of "Admiralski" Koscielski and his resignation from the Reichstag in March. In September, at a meeting in Lwów, in Austrian Poland, Koscielski had declared that in spite of the map there was one Polish nation, "one blood and one heart," which everywhere beat as one. On September 22 the Kaiser, speaking at Thorn, reprimanded the Poles sharply for not acting "like full Prussian citizens . . . What I have said today should be heeded. I can also be very disagreeable." This outburst was warmly commented on the next day in another speech by Bismarck to a delegation of West Prussians. The Polish nobility, he said, was also a "revolutionary party . . . May God give the Kaiser advisers and servants who are ready, and show this readiness, to act in accordance with this imperial program." He ended the speech with a "Hoch!" for the Kaiser.[52]

On September 24 Caprivi left Carlsbad for Berlin, cutting short his leave by a week, and on October 5 he went out to see the Kaiser, then hunting at Hubertusstock. A tired, stubborn old man, not easily given to flattery, cajolery, or bootlicking tactics, Caprivi now was in no mood to mince words. It was time to clarify things. Stiffly he adhered to his former position. He would be willing to introduce a bill mildly strengthening the criminal code, but no more. He would not go along with Botho Eulenburg's severer measures. He complained of the Kaiser's Königsberg speech. The Kaiser replied that, on the contrary, he had done Caprivi a service there, that his speech had been very well received by the Conservative and the Bismarck press. With this speech, he said, he had "won over" these people to support of the government, which Caprivi himself had not been able to do. Unfortunately, it was clear enough who had been "won over" — the reverse was the case. At Hubertusstock Caprivi again offered his resignation, and again it was declined. The Kaiser hoped that Botho Eulenberg and Caprivi might work out some sort of compromise. He was furious with Caprivi's stiffness of manner at this meeting. "The Chancellor apparently intended to *browbeat* me!" he said later to Phili Eulenberg. "Do tell your cousin that he must hold himself in readiness." As for Caprivi, he returned rather downcast and discouraged to Berlin, yet clinging to the hope that the Kaiser would, upon reflection, be convinced by the facts of the case and would at length listen to reason, as he had so many times in the past. Here the general underestimated two factors: the extent to which

[52]*Schulthess* (1894), pp. 149, 152, 153–157; Wippermann, 10(I):284–285, 10(II):7, 14–24, 45ff., 91ff.; Tims, *Germanizing Prussian Poland*, pp. 21–30; Ebmeyer, "Caprivis Entlassung," p. 206; cf. *Pr. Jbb.*, 76:173ff.

the Kaiser had become alienated from him personally, and the influence of the "permanent camarilla" of the Kaiser's entourage.[53]

Now Holstein entered the fray. He and Marschall, Chief of the Chancellery Göring, and the *Kölnische Zeitung* correspondent, Fischer, were convinced that a strong stand by Caprivi could only win in the end, since the Kaiser could not afford to let him go in a manner which would label the Kaiser as the sponsor of a reactionary policy. A victory of Caprivi over Botho Eulenburg would mean the retirement of the latter and the reuniting of the Prussian and Reich governments under Caprivi. They hoped that the opposition, by overplaying its hand, would lose the game. Holstein thus began a battle against Miquel and Botho Eulenburg in the press. In particular, he worked on Phili Eulenburg, even traveling out to his estate at Liebenberg to talk to him, to try to convince him that a conflict with the Reichstag not only would endanger the Reich but would threaten the position of the monarchy and of the Kaiser personally. On October 3 Holstein wrote to Bernhard Bülow — urging him to write to Eulenburg — that he was firmly convinced that

the Dissolution Regime, whether Botho or whoever, will last only three months at the most. Then, when particularism begins to show itself, the clamor of those loyal to the Reich for Bismarck will become *so* great that H. M. will have no choice but to shoot, to abdicate, or to yield. In the latter case I envisage, for example, Schweinitz as chancellor and Herbert as foreign secretary. After 4½ years of independent rule, H. M. would thereby declare his political bankruptcy. The effect this would have abroad is not difficult to imagine.

Holstein also tried at this time to get Marschall a seat in the Prussian State Ministry, to counteract the influence of Miquel.

Holstein did not, however, wholly succeed in his efforts with Phili Eulenburg, who found himself in a difficult position. He was aware of the danger of an extreme policy, but he did not want to go against his cousin Botho, and he suspected Holstein's determination — unexpressed — to bring the latter down. He knew, as no one else, how tired the Kaiser was of Caprivi; he hoped that his cousin might succeed as chancellor, but he did not dare approve the reactionary policy which his cousin advocated. And so he encouraged the Kaiser in the impossible attempt to reconcile the two irreconcilable parties,

[53]Zechlin, *Staatsstreichpläne*, pp. 110, 115–116; Hammann, *Der Neue Kurs*, p. 100; Haller, *Eulenburg*, I, 255–256; Holstein to Bülow, October 6, 1894, *Holstein Papers, Correspondence*.

to bring cousin Botho and Caprivi to compromise and coöperation.[54]

On October 12, 1894, the Prussian State Ministry met to discuss the proposed "revolution bill." It was a decisive occasion for all concerned. The collegiate ministry had to act unanimously on important questions. Usually, as now, some sort of compromise was sought to produce the desired unanimity. If compromise was impossible it then became a question of resignation for the individual minister. Since 1892 Caprivi had held only a subordinate position in the ministry, which was headed by his opponent, Botho Eulenburg. According to Caprivi's own order of April 1890, reaffirming the order of 1852, he was morally responsible to Eulenburg for his opinions as over against the Kaiser.[55] His real authority came, however, from his position in the Reich, and it was a Reich affair which was under discussion.

General von Caprivi opened the discussion with a massive frontal assault. He wished to ascertain, he said, to what degree the State Ministry supported the continuation of the policy which he had so far conducted with the approval of His Majesty. This policy was a moderately conservative one, depending upon no one party, and favoring the weaker elements of the population. An extreme program, however, such as called for in the Kaiser's Königsberg speech, could not yield before a rejection by the Reichstag, but must go on to dissolution and a change in the suffrage. He believed that forceful measures should be avoided as long as possible. Prince Bismarck, at the end of his career, had maintained that the Reich constitution, which had been agreed to by the princes, could be altered by them at any time. He believed this view to be "legally untenable and politically dangerous" and had said so to the Kaiser in writing in June 1891, and in 1892. The possible advantages of a *coup d'état* were, in the present instance, so outweighed by the dangers that he must urgently advise against taking even the first step which could lead to such a result. Even for such a first step he would have to refuse to take the responsibility. The German Reich was a loose association which would be easy to dissolve but very difficult to put together again. In such a case he feared that the individual state parliaments would take the lead in a democratic movement which would deprive the imperial crown of many of its prerogatives. The

---

[54]Zechlin, *Staatsstreichpläne*, pp. 115, 117; Haller, *Eulenburg*, I, 254, 256–257, 266; Hutten-Czapski, *Sechzig Jahre*, I, 225; Eulenburg to Holstein, September 26, Holstein to Bülow, October 3, 1894, *Holstein Papers, Correspondence*.

[55]See above, pp. 42–43.

Reich had its origin less in the initiative of the federal princes than in the will of the nation and the Hohenzollerns. If it was to remain strong, then in the future also it must be backed by the national will. A *coup d'état* would endanger Germany's position abroad, but particularly the position of the Kaiser. He could not take the responsibility for these dangers.

As far as the Reichstag was concerned it was doubtful if even the entire Conservative party would vote for an antirevolution bill, particularly since they had themselves recently gone in for popular agitation. They would make agrarian demands which he doubted could be satisfied. The Anti-Semites would vote against it. The Free Conservatives would vote for it, but would demand a halt in social legislation, "which would not correspond to the Kaiser's program." The National Liberals had recently spoken for measures against revolutionary tendencies, but had always insisted that these must not be reactionary. With the exception of the Social Democrats, all of the parties at the moment were in a state of disintegration, and it should be considered whether such a moment was appropriate for large-scale legislative reform. The Conservatives, Free Conservatives, and National Liberals had not possessed a majority in the Reichstag for some time. One could not count on the Poles, Guelfs, and Alsatians. He had been assured privately that the Center would not approve extreme measures. Such measures would also alienate the Radicals, who in many places outside of the Reichstag were energetically opposing the Social Democrats. Extreme measures would weld the Social Democrats together, whereas recently large elements of the party (for instance, von Vollmar's following) had become more moderate. He would not deny that present legislation, which in some cases was too elastic, might be improved, but he could not go along with any return to the policies of the "old course." He would not support a dissolution of the Reichstag on the issue, since he believed that a new election would not alter it appreciably, would at most strengthen the Social Democrats and Radicals. He was having a bill of his own prepared in the Reich Department of Justice which was not yet ready, but he would like to know the opinion of the ministers so he would know where he stood.[56]

In the subsequent discussion, Botho Eulenburg stood by his bill but denied that it would necessarily lead to a *coup d'état.* "The dangers accompanying the previous policy of *laisser-aller* were not less than the dangers of a *coup d'état.*" Germany was at present "in

[56]Protocol of the ministerial session of October 12, 1894, Zechlin, *Staatsstreich-pläne,* pp. 193–198.

a state of latent anarchy." Backing Caprivi, von Berlepsch made a strong plea for the continuation of the program of social legislation. The parties supporting repressive measures were opponents of social reform. Forceful measures had not kept down the Social Democrats in the past. The present excitement was the result of anarchist crimes which had not occurred in Germany. Von Bötticher and von Bosse also indicated support for Caprivi. The greatest surprise was the position taken by Miquel. On September 30, at their meeting at Frankfurt, he had managed to get the National Liberal party to vote for strong antirevolutionary measures, but only by a small majority, and since then a split had threatened in the party over the issue. It was very doubtful, for instance, whether the aged Bennigsen would support such a program. Consequently, Miquel left Eulenburg high and dry, beating a graceful retreat. The possibility of rejection of the bill, dissolution, and a *coup d'état,* he said, must be carefully examined. Perhaps it would be safer to be satisfied with a milder measure. Public opinion among the classes upon which the government must lean was not yet sufficiently united to support a *coup d'état.* Miquel had taken the matter more lightly in the beginning and had believed it would be possible to put through extensive measures, but the more he had noted the comment in the press the more doubtful of success he had become. He hoped — in words that would look good in the record — that under the leadership of the socially minded monarchy (*des sozialen Königthums*) the present great crisis would pass without revolutionary outbreaks. With this general discussion the matter rested. It was agreed to go into a detailed discussion in the next session on the 19th.[57]

Caprivi went away from the session dissatisfied; the crisis had been only postponed, not resolved. But during the following week his position gradually strengthened. The former Conservative leader, von Helldorff-Bedra, sharply warned the Kaiser about the results of an extreme policy. Botho Eulenburg now made soundings among the Conservatives as Miquel had done with the National Liberals. At a secret meeting of Conservative leaders it was announced that Eulenburg was ready to take over the chancellorship from Caprivi upon the condition that the Bundesrat immediately suspend universal suffrage. The Kaiser had agreed to this, but Eulenburg would go ahead only if he had the united backing of the whole Conservative party. Most of those present, including Stöcker himself, were willing to support this program. But two of the younger leaders of the

[57]Zechlin, *Staatsstreichpläne,* pp. 199–204, 112, 121–123, 125 and note; Wahl, *Geschichte,* III, 573; Oncken, *Bennigsen,* II, 593; Eyck, *Wilhelm II,* p. 91.

Stöcker Christian Socialist group, which sought its following among the masses, Helmuth von Gerlach and Oberwinder, editors of *Das Volk*, violently opposed the plan. They threatened to carry their opposition to the city party organizations, and they would not compromise. Hammerstein then arose, white with anger, and declared, "The plan is done for. If we are not absolutely united it won't work. For me the matter is settled. I am going at once to Eulenburg to tell him so." On October 18 the Conservative organization of the Hallescher Tor passed a resolution warning against middle-class attempts at a *coup d'état,* and on the 19th *Das Volk* editorialized in the same sense.[58]

At the meeting of the Prussian ministry on October 19 Botho Eulenburg withdrew his bill, and the ministry agreed to accept the milder Caprivi-Nieberding bill as a basis for discussion. Since Eulenburg still insisted, however, that preventive and repressive laws governing association and assembly should be passed, even at the cost of a conflict, Caprivi suggested that the chief ministers of the Federated Governments be invited to Berlin to a special conference on the issue, which was approved. Thus against Prussia Caprivi called up his Reich reserves.[59]

The whole development was a clear and decisive victory for the chancellor. The grandiose Bismarck–Junker–Eulenburg–Miquel barrage, with its journalistic flares and rockets, had amounted in the end to a mere puff of smoke, which, being blown away by the prevailing winds, had revealed the old general-chancellor still occupying the position he had taken up at the beginning. The Foreign Office strategy was working brilliantly. Caprivi had won the battle.[60] But the essential hostility, the underlying political divergence, remained. The government, divided thus into two hostile camps, could not continue to conduct affairs for long. One must finally yield the field completely to the other. To strike once more before it was too late, to draw the general from his impregnable position to a spot where he was more vulnerable, the reactionary party now resorted to diversionary and provocative flank attacks.

On October 18 the army leaders, in combination with General von Waldersee, arranged for the Kaiser to present new flags to the new battalions created by the Caprivi Army Bill of 1893. These new

[58]Zechlin, *Staatsstreichpläne,* pp. 127–128; Haller, *Eulenburg,* I, 257; H. v. Gerlach, *Erinnerungen eines Junkers* (n.d.), pp. 86–87; Leuss, *Hammerstein,* pp. 116–117; Wippermann, 10(II):135–136.

[59]Zechlin, *Staatsstreichpläne,* p. 129.

[60]Cf. Wippermann, 10(II):139.

battalions had been created for the special purpose of providing cadres for use in general mobilization and were organized for that purpose only in two companies, at half strength. The Kaiser's military entourage now suggested to him that it was a shame that these battalions had been left at half strength, that they really should be made complete. And, indeed, as they paraded past the Kaiser at the monument to Frederick the Great, their two little companies tacked on to the end of each regiment did not look very impressive. As a result, the Kaiser in his speech said that he hoped they would soon be brought up to full strength, a statement which, to the public, made the Caprivi reorganization look like a mere trick to prepare the way for further army increases. It was thought that the Kaiser was announcing a new army bill for the coming session of the Reichstag. At the reviewing stand the Kaiser so openly snubbed Caprivi that the chancellor — who had fought and won the military battle for him in 1892–1893 — soon absented himself from the Kaiser's entourage and did not hear the speech. At the subsequent dinner at the New Palace in Potsdam, however, the Kaiser pointedly toasted Caprivi last and then with the insolent words, "I shall thank you only when the half-battalions have become complete." [61]

Two days later, on October 20, the day following the second and decisive meeting of the ministry, while Reich Chancellor von Caprivi was receiving at the Chancellery honorary citizenship at the hands of a delegation from the politically Radical city of Danzig in recognition of his achievement for German commerce in concluding the trade treaty with Russia, over at Potsdam the Kaiser, attended by Prussian Minister-President zu Eulenburg, Prussian Minister of Agriculture von Heyden, and Chief of the Civil Cabinet von Lucanus, was receiving a delegation of the Farmers' League. This reception of the chancellor's bitterest political enemies, apparently arranged with the help of Court Marshal August Eulenburg, brother of Botho, was obviously intended as a provocation to Caprivi.[62]

The combination of the two incidents was too much. Caprivi had had enough. Early in the morning of October 23, 1894, he wrote out a letter of resignation and sent it to the Kaiser at Potsdam. Briefly he surveyed, in his letter, the results of the last meeting of the ministry, which had decided to accept his bill, and continued:

[61]Wippermann, 10(II):8–9; Haller, *Eulenburg*, I, 257–258; Ebmeyer, p. 203; Waldersee, *Denkwürdigkeiten*, II, 327; Keim, *Erlebtes*, p. 82; Zechlin, *Staatsstreichpläne*, pp. 129–131.

[62]Ebmeyer, "Caprivis Entlassung," p. 205; Zechlin, *Staatsstreichpläne*, pp. 131–133; Wippermann, 10(II):136–138.

Although in the bill which I presented I had gone to what I believe to be the farthest possible extreme in conciliation, and the majority of the ministers were led by similar motives, yet from these discussions I was unable to avoid the conclusion that between my own views and those of part of the ministry, in particular those of Minister-President Count zu Eulenburg, an unbridgeable gulf exists. . . . These fundamental differences remain directly opposed to each other in spite of the formal agreement.

My long-standing conviction has thus been strengthened that the opinions of the minister-president and myself are too divergent to be reconciled upon the basis of the Reich policy heretofore approved by Your Majesty. That is a situation which is not to the long-run advantage of Your Majesty's service. The times are too difficult for it not to be necessary to avoid with determination all friction within the government. Already today, following from the open divergence in the opinions of the highest officials, a confusion of minds has resulted which threatens to cripple and to defeat every productive activity. Above all, the coming parliamentary program demands the united coöperation of all the government's forces; it demands, on the other hand, also men who thoroughly believe in the cause. The possibility of compromise among statesmen finds its limits in the necessity not to sacrifice one's own character. I could not deny my convictions on fundamental questions without losing all value for the office and the tasks in which Your Majesty has placed me. But not only that: I should only be a hindrance to Your Majesty if Your Majesty were inclined to a change in the direction and methods of Reich policy. To shift now over to another course, to accommodate myself to the tendencies of the minister-president, is impossible for me. . . . The basis for any further fruitful coöperation is, therefore, lacking. . . .

Furthermore, I am in doubt as to whether I still possess the confidence of Your Majesty, which from the beginning has been for me the indispensable supposition for every productive activity, in sufficient measure to be able to continue my work with any success. Your Majesty has recently made basic decisions in matters of far-reaching consequence without previously hearing my respectful opinion. The basis of my position as the first, responsible official of the Reich is thereby severely shaken. As difficult as it is for me to leave Your Majesty's service, after mature consideration I can only make the most respectful request that Your Majesty may be graciously pleased to retire me from service with Your Majesty's favor and with the prescribed pension according to paragraph thirty-five of the Reich Civil Service Law.[63]

[63]Copy of letter in Caprivi Papers, Hauptarchiv, Berlin; reproduced in Zechlin, *Staatsstreichpläne,* "Anlage 11," pp. 204–207; the final paragraph printed in facsimile in Goldschmidt, Kaiser, and Thimme, *Ein Jahrhundert deutscher Geschichte . . . 1815–1919* (Berlin, 1928).

The Kaiser, who had not believed Phili Eulenburg's grave warnings of a new crisis, but had told him gaily two nights before at the theater that "everything was all right" and that he was altogether "too gloomy," was, of course, completely unprepared for Caprivi's step, which, he later declared, had "burst on him like a bomb." Shortly after noon Chancellor von Caprivi received a telegram from Potsdam: "Message received. Refuse approval. Rest orally." Almost immediately thereafter the Kaiser drove up in front of the Chancellery in his carriage with the white horses, greeted Caprivi heartily in the vestibule, and accompanied him into his office — Bismarck's old work-room — on the ground floor. Cigarettes and port wine were called for. For an hour, while subordinate officials strained their ears in the adjoining rooms, the Kaiser talked with the chancellor, using all his very considerable charm and persuasiveness to try to make him alter his decision. To Caprivi's repeated assertions that he did not possess the Kaiser's confidence in the necessary degree, the Kaiser insisted emphatically that he had full confidence in Caprivi, as much as ever. His reconciliation with Bismarck had nothing to do with Caprivi's position, and Caprivi had even approved of it. As for his reception of the members of the Farmers' League, this was the beneficial result of his Königsberg speech, and Caprivi should be glad that these people were now willing to coöperate. The Kaiser's ear was always open to the pleas of all his subjects, and Caprivi should be glad to have him create better feeling among the Conservatives. As proof of his confidence he would grant Caprivi any wish or guaranty that he should desire. Caprivi, he declared, must send a copy of his resignation to Botho Eulenburg with an accompanying note that it had not been accepted because he, the Kaiser, agreed with it. "Send the letter off today, so that Eulenburg will know where he stands." [64]

Under these circumstances Caprivi felt compelled, once more, to yield. He decided, however, to send the letter to Eulenburg. His adjutant, Ebmeyer, warned him that he would thus bring about a breach with Eulenburg, but Caprivi was determined to go ahead. The situation must be clarified. Holstein, on the other hand, was convinced that Caprivi should have asked the Kaiser directly for Eulenburg's resignation during their interview. That would have

[64] For Caprivi's version of this interview see Ebmeyer, "Caprivis Entlassung," pp. 196–197; Haller, *Eulenburg*, I, 260. For the Kaiser's version cf. reports of Counts Lerchenfeld and Hohenthal, Zechlin, *Staatsstreichpläne*, pp. 209–211, 217–218. Cf. Eyck, *Wilhelm II*, pp. 93–94; Haller, *Eulenburg*, I, 258–259.

clearly established and consolidated his victory. But Caprivi, whose
attitude towards Eulenburg had been stated clearly enough in his
resignation, had modestly refrained from making any such harsh
demand. Eulenburg, therefore, might still slide out of the crisis.
Holstein would have preferred some sort of insurance. On October
25 an article appeared in Fischer's *Kölnische Zeitung* giving a
résumé of the crisis, including an account of the Kaiser's talk with
Caprivi:

The renewed assurance of the imperial confidence and agreement
which has been imparted to Reich Chancellor Count Caprivi in connection with his proposals for further combating the revolutionary parties
will contribute very happily [*in sehr erfreulicher Weise*] towards clarify-
ing the situation. It is known that the Reich chancellor is a decided opponent of exceptional laws and that his experience of the last four years
has also not been able to alter his conviction. . . . In so far as it appears
necessary to stop up loopholes in existing Reich legislation, the Reich
chancellor has always maintained as the decisive point of view that it is
urgently desirable to bring all middle-class parties to a common agreement in the fight against the parties of revolution, not, however, to provoke them by exaggerated measures into a battle among themselves.
Count Caprivi has repeatedly asserted in this connection that it is better
and more effective to achieve something positive with the greatest possible united agreement of all the parties of law and order than to make
far-reaching proposals which give the appearance, but only the appearance, of great determination and power, but which actually merely break
up the middle class parties and in this way only further the ends of the
revolutionary parties themselves. . . . An uncompromising position
against this point of view was taken by Prussian Minister-President Count
Botho Eulenburg. He had made proposals which, it must have been clear
to him beforehand, could not be passed by the present nor by a newly
elected Reichstag. . . . The Reich chancellor held fast to the position
that no kind of measures might be proposed which in their practical
application by courts and officials might tend to be applied, in time of
tense political conflict, also against the middle-class parties. In the hour-
long conference which he had yesterday with the Kaiser, we are informed
confidentially, all these opinions received complete acceptance. The
Kaiser thoroughly approved them and assured the chancellor of his full
support. Since, according to our information, a large majority of the
ministers of the Federated Governments will speak in this morning's
Bundesrat session for a restriction of the program to what may be
achieved in the present Reichstag, we may hope that thereby the desired
unity will be achieved and ensured in the first half of the legislative body
of the German Reich.

After the publication of this article, bearing so clearly all the marks of official inspiration, it would be next to impossible for Botho Eulenburg to continue in the government. This, apparently, was Holstein's insurance.[65]

On the evening of the 23rd the Kaiser, going out to Liebenberg for a hunting party, greeted Phili Eulenburg at the railroad station with the words, "I bring you the joyous news of the end of our ninth crisis." [66] When, therefore, Botho Eulenburg arrived in the middle of the shooting party the following day with his resignation in hand, the Kaiser was most painfully surprised. "The Kaiser came up to me," wrote Phili, savoring the situation with sympathetically mournful relish, "with that pale, pinched look so familiar to me from all the innumerable bad hours we have been through together." Cousin Botho had pointed out to the Kaiser Caprivi's mention of an unbridgeable gulf and the impossibility of their further working together, points which the Kaiser had apparently overlooked. As the Kaiser and Phili stood alone together in the butts, the Kaiser asked Phili dejectedly what was to be done. "Whom can you suggest? I have no idea whom I could call upon. Don't you know anyone?" Phili had his answer ready. "A man who is neither conservative nor liberal, neither ultramontane nor progressive, neither ritualist nor atheist, is hard to find." Then he suggested the stadtholder of Alsace-Lorraine, Prince Chlodwig zu Hohenlohe-Schillingsfürst. Hohenlohe was a Bavarian who had, however, served Bismarck and the Reich for years in the diplomatic service, a Catholic, but more liberal than conservative, a blooded aristocrat who was still on good terms with Friedrichsruh. He would serve as a stopgap until a younger man (Bülow) was ready. Not once did Phili try to back up Caprivi — and not only because he knew that the Kaiser really did not want to keep Caprivi. The development of the political crisis had resulted in a clear opposition of the interests of the Reichstag as represented by Caprivi to the interests of Prussia and of the Junker ruling class as represented by Botho Eulenburg. To dismiss Caprivi alone would have meant, not only a victory for Eulenburg and his reactionary crisis program, but a direct challenge to the existing parliamentary

---

[65]Hammann, *Der Neue Kurs*, pp. 103–104; Ebmeyer, "Caprivis Entlassung," pp. 199–200; Hutten-Czapski, *Sechzig Jahre*, I, 226, 238. Text of the *Kölnische Zeitung* article in *Schulthess* (1894), pp. 168–169; Wippermann, 10(II):139–140; Hohlfeld, *Geschichte*, I, 292–293; Ebmeyer, *op. cit.*, pp. 200–201. Discussion of Holstein's authorship of the article in Zechlin, *Staatsstreichpläne*, pp. 147–149.

[66]According to Marschall, via Raschdau, Caprivi handed in his resignation ten times in four and a half years. Raschdau, *Bismarck u. Caprivi*, p. 357.

and democratic forces in the Reich by the interests of the Junker aristocracy of Prussia. This dangerous way out — approved by Bismarck — had been finally defeated by Caprivi, discredited and officially disapproved. To dismiss Eulenburg alone, however, would be a victory for the Reich over Prussia, of the left over the right, of the parliament over the court (and the Kaiser), of democracy over aristocracy and monarchy. In Bismarck's Reich such a victory would amount in its implications to a constitutional change. Phili Eulenburg, as a Prussian Junker and a personal friend of the Kaiser, could not join in what would have been inevitably a parliamentary victory. He would not "sing to Holstein's tune," he said. Neither he nor the Kaiser had any thought of a liberal change in the constitution. The German Kaiser could not, in the end, go against the interests of the Prussian ruling class. Both parties, Prussian Junkers and Caprivi bureaucrats, had gravitated into upholding extreme, diametrically opposed positions, each demanding a crystallization of the conflict, a victory for one side or the other, a constitutional decision. The Kaiser's eager acceptance of Hohenlohe's candidacy for the chancellorship meant that there was to be no such crystallization, no victory, no decision. Somewhat haughtily Phili Eulenburg wrote later to Bernhard Bülow, "To no one had the most obvious of solutions occurred — namely, that if the Kaiser was driven into a corner, the only thing he could do was to part with both statesmen." [67]

On October 25 the Kaiser returned to Berlin, still cherishing the hope that a compromise nevertheless might be reached between Botho Eulenburg and Caprivi. Count Botho had agreed at Liebenberg that he would consent to remain in office if Caprivi would expressly request it. This was the least, said the Kaiser, that Caprivi could do as a gentleman. Before the Kaiser reached Berlin someone handed him a copy of the *Kölnische Zeitung*. As he read he exclaimed, "My private conversation with Caprivi is in the paper!" There was no question of keeping Eulenburg now. [68]

On the morning of October 26, 1894, the chief ministers of the federal states called at the Chancellery in the Wilhelmstrasse to take official leave of the chancellor. The previous day they had met and, with the exception of Württemberg's von Mittnacht, had supported Caprivi's viewpoint, that no bill concerning laws governing associ-

[67]Haller, *Eulenburg*, I, 260–270; Zechlin, *Staatsstreichpläne*, pp. 138–140. Cf. Kardorff's reaction to the appointment of Hohenlohe, Thimme, "Bismarck und Kardorff," p. 168.
[68]Haller, *Eulenburg*, I, 269–270.

ation and assembly should be introduced to the Reichstag, that the proposed changes in the criminal code should not go beyond the bounds of the attainable. Whereas the federal princes at Königsberg had been all for a *coup d'état*, their governments, especially the Bavarian, would have none of it. The whole session had been a strong vote of confidence in Caprivi. As they took their leave on the morning of the 26th rumors of Botho Eulenburg's resignation were already in circulation. The Bavarian minister, Count Crailsheim, told Caprivi that he hoped that he would now again take over the minister-presidency of Prussia.[69]

Later in the morning Chief of the Civil Cabinet von Lucanus appeared at the Chancellery and inquired whether Caprivi had written or inspired the article of the day before in the *Kölnische Zeitung*. No, said Caprivi, he had not. Would he in any case, said Lucanus, returning a second time, issue a denial or a correction, particularly of the references to Count Eulenburg. No, said Caprivi, he had nothing to deny or to correct; everything the article had said was true. As for Eulenburg, it was impossible to work with him further, and the same went also for Miquel. If the Kaiser had had no other way out, Caprivi's strong stand might even yet have prevailed. But now he had his way out. The answer had been given the day before at Liebenberg. The crisis now proceeded with typical Wilhelminian dispatch. At 1 o'clock in the afternoon Caprivi and Ebmeyer attended a special prayer service at the Russian Embassy for the dying Tsar Alexander III. During the service Caprivi received a summons to appear at the Schloss. At 2 o'clock Chancellor von Caprivi was received by the Kaiser and his resignation accepted. At 2:15 Minister-President zu Eulenburg was received and his resignation accepted. At 2:30 the ambassadors of Bavaria, Saxony, Württemberg, and Baden were received and given a résumé and an explanation of the change in government.[70]

Now that everything at last was settled, the Kaiser was in a good humor and ready to show himself quite the master of the situation. Standing with a cigar in his hand, he acknowledged good-naturedly to the federal ambassadors that Caprivi was completely honest and loyal, but declared that he had suffered terribly from his

[69]Jagemann, *75 Jahre*, pp. 121, 123–125; Zechlin, *Staatsstreichpläne*, p. 143; Ebmeyer, "Caprivis Entlassung," p. 199.

[70]Ebmeyer, "Caprivis Entlassung," p. 202; Jagemann, *75 Jahre*, p. 125; Zechlin, *Staatsstreichpläne*, pp. 140, 143–145. For a condensed but interesting version of the crisis, see the Kaiser's telegram to the grand duke of Baden, Zechlin, "Anlage 12 C," p. 221; also Phili Eulenburg's revealing summary in a letter to Bülow, Haller, *Eulenburg*, I, 263–270.

obstinacy. With every little difference in opinion Caprivi had tendered his resignation. That had happened at least five times.[71] He had become quite weary of these everlasting battles, and he hoped he would finally get a chancellor who would make his life a little easier. Caprivi's lonely life as a bachelor and his ill health had no doubt had a bad effect upon his character. Also he had not understood how to listen to the soul of the nation. And so he himself, the Kaiser, had had to intervene, as at Königsberg. "One can't get anywhere with these virtuous, hypercritical bachelors," he said laughing. "I won't take any more of them." Caprivi had suggested Botho Eulenburg as his successor, but he had at once replied, "If you go, then Eulenburg must go too; otherwise the public will say, Eulenburg is staying on to make a *coup d'état* with the wild young Kaiser." He had, on the contrary, no thought of a *coup d'état*, but put his trust in the German people, who in time of danger would rally around their princes, which, of course, was not to say that it might not sometime be necessary to resort to arms. If the revolution came it must not come from below as in 1789 but from above. He had no idea of dissolving the Reichstag and was in full agreement with Caprivi's program. A century which was coming to its end brought all sorts of unrest and strange ideas to the surface. Prince Chlodwig zu Hohenlohe-Schillingsfürst had been asked to take over both offices of chancellor of the Reich and minister-president of Prussia.[72]

Later, Caprivi gave his own version to the federal ambassadors. Since the reconciliation with Bismarck, he said, his life had been a succession of surprises, and he had felt that he no longer possessed the full confidence of the Kaiser. In the first two years of his career he had thought that the Kaiser would gradually get used to the idea of consulting him first on important decisions. But His Majesty wanted to take all the responsibility on himself. This did not conform to his interpretation of the Reich constitution, nor to his own feeling of responsibility. Consequently, there had been constant differences of opinion between them. He could not smooth over things with words and phrases like Eulenburg and Miquel. If Prince Hohenlohe did not take care, Miquel would soon be the most powerful man in Prussia. Lacking the Miquel smoothness, he had often had to offer his resignation (*die Cabinets-frage zu stellen*), and the Kaiser had

[71]See above, p. 353 and note.
[72]Reports of this interview by Counts Lerchenfeld and Hohenthal, Zechlin, *Staatsstreichpläne,* "Anlage 12 A, B," pp. 207–221, also pp. 146–147. Cf. Jagemann, *75 Jahre,* pp. 124–125.

said repeatedly, "Caprivi, you get terribly on my nerves," whereupon he had always answered, "Your Majesty, I have always been a very uncomfortable subordinate." His dismissal had been caused primarily by the Kaiser's wish to reconcile himself with the Conservatives. He had approved of this wish in principle, but not of the Kaiser's timing. The differences between the Reich and Prussian officials over the "revolution bill" could easily have been resolved with a little good will, but this good will was lacking. During this interview, Count Hohenthal wrote in his report to the Saxon government, he had been forcefully reminded of his last interview with Bismarck.

Then, as now, the movers were already in all the rooms, the writing desk, at other times so laden with documents, completely empty; then, as now, we sat in the same remote corner of the reception room on the same chairs. The great difference, aside from the political aspects of the situation, consisted only in that Prince Bismarck was extremely excited and heaped bitter complaints upon the Kaiser, while Count Caprivi in more cheerful calm was happily looking forward to Lake Geneva.[73]

To the sudden ending of his public career General von Caprivi's first reaction, at least outwardly, was one of intense relief. "You won't believe," he wrote in a note to Major Ebmeyer during the afternoon of the fateful day, "how good I feel." This sense of sudden release attested eloquently to the heavy weight of the burden he had carried for four years. He had decided to go immediately to Montreux in Switzerland, where, after the 1870–1871 war, he had stayed with a convalescent comrade-in-arms. He seemed eager to shake the dust of Berlin from his feet and with it all thoughts and memories of the last four years. "You will never hear from me again," he told Count Lerchenfeld. "My administration and I personally have suffered too much under the attacks of Prince Bismarck for me to want to follow his example." When Major Keim, summoned by telegraph, arrived at the Chancellery at midnight of the 26th, he found that the general had been burning his private papers; the ashes were still smoking in the fireplace. Caprivi said to him, "I have often quarreled with you over questions of personalities, but you have, nevertheless, usually seen more clearly than I. When you took your leave of me in the summer of 1893 . . . you said then, 'If Your Excellency doesn't wring the necks of the Eulenburgs as soon as possible, these gentlemen sooner or later will manage to do it to you.' That is the 'process' I have been put through to-day."

[73]Reports of Counts Lerchenfeld and Hohenthal, Zechlin, *Staatsstreichpläne,* "Anlage 13, A, B," pp. 222–225.

On October 30 General von Caprivi took his formal leave of the Kaiser and, on October 31, quietly and unannounced, left Berlin for Montreux, accompanied to the station only by Göring and Ebmeyer. His last official act had been to instruct his press officer, Otto Hammann, to see to it that the papers friendly to the government did not blame the Kaiser for the crisis but treated it simply as a matter of dispute between himself and Botho Eulenburg. The Kaiser's bestowal upon him of the diamond insignia of the Black Eagle with a handwritten note of appreciation for his services was left unpublicized.[74]

The press reaction to Caprivi's dismissal was generally in agreement as to his integrity of character and his energetic initiative, but revealed a wide divergence as to his policies.

> Count Caprivi [wrote *Die Nation*] has for four and a half years protected Germany from convulsions and adventures both at home and abroad. That, in spite of extraordinary difficulties, this man, hated by the influential Prussian Junkers, bitterly attacked by the agrarians and anti-Semites, constantly harried by the criticism of Bismarck, attacked from the rear by false middle-party worthies [*Biedermännern*], supported only half-heartedly by the German middle class out of a lack of appreciation of its most fundamental political interests, that he was able for more than four years to keep the helm in his hands: that is an achievement the greatness of which can be evaluated completely only when it becomes apparent what his successor will — and will not — be able to accomplish.

Wrote the *Kölnische Zeitung:*

> Count Caprivi was a real man and a real minister. . . . He defended his independence towards those above him as towards those below him, as a genuine statesman should and must, and when he believed he was in the right he went ahead with determination and self-confidence.

Richter's *Freisinnige Zeitung* wrote:

> Even Count Caprivi's political opponents cannot upon his retirement refuse to testify that he has shown himself an honorable and loyal statesman and has demonstrated his independence also of the highest circles. Every successor will find the comparison to him very difficult.

The Catholic *Germania* declared that they would never grant to a successor the antirevolutionary measures asked by Caprivi, since they had been confident that Caprivi would never have misused such authority. The *Kreuzzeitung*, however, declared:

[74]Ebmeyer, "Caprivis Entlassung," p. 203; Lerchenfeld, *Denkwürdigkeiten*, p. 369; v. Schulte, "Erinnerungen an Graf Caprivi," *Deutsche Revue*, 24(II):229 (1899); Keim, *Erlebtes*, p. 81; Raschdau, *Bismarck u. Caprivi*, p. 364; Hammann, *Der Neue Kurs*, pp. 104–105.

We are convinced that the result of his policy has been that the dissatisfaction in Germany has grown to alarming proportions and to the same degree public confidence has sunk, and that this has occurred precisely among those elements of the Nation upon which the monarchy and the Fatherland must look above all for support.

Wrote Stöcker's *Das Volk:*

Only the Jews and part of the liberals among us will be sorry to see Count Caprivi go.[75]

Among less partisan observers, Empress Frederick wrote to Queen Victoria:

Caprivi was looked upon by most sensible and reasonable people as a drag on the wheel of the Government and a guaranty that no very sudden adventure would be plunged into. The very quick, easy and unceremonious way in which he was removed (at least to all appearances) made many sections of the public apprehensive as to what might follow. . . . Poor Prince Hohenlohe has no easy task.

The general satisfaction over the reuniting under Hohenlohe of the administrations of Prussia and the Reich was without any basis, declared the *Preussische Jahrbücher.* Prince zu Hohenlohe, at seventy-five, was older than Bismarck in 1890 and could not possess Caprivi's forcefulness and initiative. This weakness of Hohenlohe's, combined with the fact that Miquel was to continue in office in Prussia and Marschall and Holstein in the Reich, meant that the split between Reich and Prussia, patched over only superficially, would, in fact, continue to gape and even to widen. Caprivi, wrote the *Preussische Jahrbücher,* because of his succession to Bismarck and because of the economic depression, had inevitably been unpopular. He had, in the end, found only hatred among his natural supporters and sympathy only among the opposition.

He must bear the unpopularity; only the retrospect of history, which no longer has to reckon with feelings, will do him complete justice.

The foreign press, astonished and uneasy at Caprivi's unceremoniously precipitate dismissal at the moment of his apparent triumph, universally deprecated his departure and praised his administration. "The general," wrote *The Times* on October 29, "quits the political field . . . with all the honours of war."

For four-and-a-half years he has maintained the prestige of the Empire at home and abroad with a dignity and skill which history will

[75]*Die Nation,* XII, 57–61; *Schulthess* (1894), p. 170.

probably recognize more fully than his countrymen appear inclined to do at the present moment. In the domain of foreign politics he has won the confidence of rulers and nations as a man of peace. . . . At home the conciliatory methods which he adopted with so much success abroad have not proved so effectual. Probably his greatest mistake has been to under-rate the potency of the nefarious influences which have been brought to bear against him, even in the highest quarters. Having lived the greater part of his life as a soldier and a student, entirely outside the atmosphere of politics, he took up his new duties with the serene optimism of a philosopher into whose calculations the passions and weaknesses of human nature are scarcely allowed to enter, or perhaps it would be more correct to say with the generosity of a singularly noble character, which naturally, and as a matter of course, credits others with the possession of its own virtues. Those of Count von Caprivi are, above all, transparent singlemindedness, intense honesty of purpose, and the love of truth for its own sake, and he seems to have been blissfully unconscious of how rare they are, especially in the world of politics. . . . That he should have had to take up an inheritance wrested from Prince Bismarck's living hands, and that he should have borne such a burden without ever faltering under its weight, alone sufficiently entitles him to a high place in the annals of his country.

In a leading article in the same issue *The Times* editorially summed up Caprivi's political career in words such as might be prized by any statesman:

He has served his country wisely and well, and he has made for him-self the reputation not only of a prudent, far-seeing statesman, but also of a singularly noble, upright, honest man, true to his Sovereign and at the same time true to himself.[76]

"The Rest is Silence"

Caprivi remained at the Pension Lorius in Montreux until the spring of 1895. Major Ebmeyer came and visited him for two weeks, but the general consistently refused all invitations to Berlin and gradually severed all connections with the official world. His reso-lution to forget the past, taken with such a sense of spontaneous relief at the time of his departure from Berlin, he found difficult to keep. Every day he read the *Frankfurter* and the *Kölnische Zeitung,* as well as the *Deutsche Revue.* And there were the constant curious inquiries of the other guests, which it was difficult always to avoid. In the spring of 1895 [77] he wrote to Major Keim:

[76]*Die Nation,* XII, 57–61; *Schulthess* (1894), p. 170; Ponsonby, *Letters of Empress. Frederick,* p. 449; *Pr. Jbb.,* 78:541–549; *The Times,* October 29, 1894, pp. 5, 9.
[77]Keim erroneously dates the letter 1896.

Many thanks, my dear Keim, for your friendly remembrance on my birthday. It is natural that my thoughts should go back often to the past and should also linger with gratitude upon you. For I still continue to take pleasure, in spite of the complaints, in the Army Bill and the trade treaties, and to continue to believe that it would have been difficult to put through the former without your help. I am only sorry that I was unable to put through that position of department head for you, for which Count Schlieffen gave me some expectation. . . . *I thank God that I am now out of the impossible situation in which I finally found myself!* I have only one wish, never again to have to come before the public in any way. Here I carefully avoid speaking of politics. Unfortunately I cannot avoid thinking about it *and having gloomy thoughts over the future of the Reich.* I am helped finally by my belief in the providential rôle of Prussia and of Germany. I don't take it hard that agrarians and Bismarckians complain about me wherever they can. Perhaps a later time will be more just to me. The "Revolution Bill" affair reminds me of old General v. Schachtmeyer, who said quite loudly in the marketplace in Nordenheim, "I don't believe in God — two years in prison." [78]

At the end of 1894 he wrote to Professor Schneidewin thanking him for his latest pamphlet on Caprivi as a speaker. ("If I have accomplished anything in this direction it must come under the heading of the 'unconscious.'") He was grateful for Dr. Schneidewin's support of his political efforts. If in the present, "so dominated by partisan viewpoints," there was little hope of an objective judgment, "to a future historian you demonstrate that a more favorable attitude towards my accomplishments is also possible. Your writings will make it necessary for him to examine things, will prevent an adverse judgment a priori." It could not be good for the German nation to believe that its second chancellor was "such a miserable official."

It was the National Liberals who contributed the most to this sorry picture of the chancellor, whereas their national standpoint should have made them either support this weak chancellor or overthrow him. That they successfully attempted the latter only after 4⅘ years, at a time when they could no longer be in doubt that I was pursuing a course which according to their principles they could and must support, is still for me an unsolved riddle.

He would like to enlighten his friend somewhat on his political difficulties and motives but had decided not to,

because I believe that it would cause more harm than good. I could not speak of myself without also speaking of others, and, in addition, I would run the danger that the devil of self-conceit would lead my pen astray

---

[78] Von Schulte, "Erinnerungen," pp. 229–235; Keim, *Erlebtes*, pp. 81–83.

[*führte und verführte*]. I must at length put up with what is dealt out to me and be content that men whose judgment I value greatly, as I do yours, concede me the *laudanda voluntas* and the *integer vitae*.

He had decided to settle down at Skyren, near Frankfurt an der Oder, "in the midst of nieces and nephews, grandnieces and grand-nephews." The place had recently come into the hands of his nephew, and was said to be very attractive, affording many pleasant walks. He was hoping, he told Schneidewin, that his love of good literature and of nature would be a help to him now. By February 1895 he had begun to tire of the Swiss winter and wrote, "I do not look cheerfully at the future and have to gather together all the optimism, all the belief in Germany I can muster up." He regretted that he had never met Schneidewin face to face and asked him for a photograph.[79]

In March he wrote that he had not been able to accept the request of the *Berliner Morgenzeitung* for an article,

because I cannot speak out loud about Prince Bismarck and the shady side of his politics. Nor would it do any good at present, rather harm. And above all, I cannot describe the motives of my actions without explaining my relationship to H. Majesty. Precisely in this relationship, which amounted often to the most difficult part of my task and which caused me the most troubled times, lay often the deciding motives. But that can be published neither now nor later. If unfavorable opinions of me grow out of it, I must bear it.[80]

At Skyren, hidden deep in a pine forest, the old general's life became more and more isolated. Even in 1896, when Bismarck revealed the terms of the secret Reinsurance Treaty and its non-renewal, and the Hohenlohe government met the interpellation in the Reichstag largely by putting the responsibility on Caprivi, even then curious journalists were unable to seek him out. To a man, however, who had led an active life the satisfactions of retirement were insufficient. While he was still in the Chancellery he had written to Schneidewin that the prospect of being a burden on some-one, "whether through physical disability, or through the inability to earn one's daily bread, . . . does not make me want to become very old." In February 1897 he wrote, "Now and then I feel old age to be very tedious. I had thought it would be better. Nevertheless I am thankful for what God has given me; it is, in any case, much more than I deserve." In July he wrote, "It is rather monotonous living

[79]Schneidewin, "Briefe," pp. 141–144.
[80]Schneidewin, "Briefe," p. 146.

here, but what I see and hear of public life is no more pleasant." More and more, as time went by, the past which he had wanted to forget filled and dominated his thoughts. In January 1898 he wrote:

If you have derived from my previous letter the feeling of a certain depression you will scarcely have been mistaken. I can hardly find pleasure in my own existence now; I also have many worries in my family, and I can hardly work myself up now to any great enthusiasm [erwärmenden Freude] over politics.

It was, he admitted, refreshing when a man like Bennigsen could begin the study of Kant in his old age — "but can he have any consciousness of thereby being of use to the community? Hardly." His self-imposed silence he found hard to bear. The ignorance, the maliciousness, the misrepresentations in the press were a strong temptation, a goad to self-defense. He finally found himself wanting to answer back, wanting to write his memoirs. He would like, he wrote Schneidewin, to defend again before the public the principles he had defended as chancellor, for the sake of future generations. But it was too late, he was too old and feeble. And he no longer had the basic materials. When he resigned he had not kept even the Kaiser's letters. "I have literally no notes at all." Nor did he now have access to the archives or a staff of assistants to hunt up documents for him. There was much in the idea of writing his memoirs that was attractive. They would not have to be boring. He could write, not only of his years in the Chancellery, but of those in the Admiralty, of his experiences in the three wars and in the War Ministry. But here too he would have to name names. "By my nature I have found myself often in a position of opposition to authority." In writing of his entrance into and departure from the Chancellery he would have to mention the Kaiser,

which, however, according to my own view of the duty of an officer or an official I find quite impossible. I must, therefore, deny myself any excursion into literature, and if it rains on me in the press, why I shall get wet. . . . Now as before, I believe that the single service I can still do my Fatherland is to carry through to the end my thankless rôle as an honorable man, selflessly placing the state above the individual. If I lose thereby the freshness of intellect which I might still have been able to retain, the loss is, indeed, a relatively minor one. . . . There is, therefore, now as before, no doubt that nothing remains for me to do but to be silent, and to be silent precisely where silence works to my disadvantage. . . . In short, the gods are against me, and I must bear my fate with as much resignation as possible.[81]

[81]Schneidewin, "Briefe," pp. 255–257 (January 15 and March 5, 1898).

In March 1898 he wrote that on his birthday four of the children had been ill nearby. For some time one nephew had been slowly wasting away with tuberculosis. "I myself am gradually falling more and more a prey to the weaknesses and infirmities of old age." He was oppressed increasingly with a sense of personal failure. Had not his political career ended precisely as it had started in 1890, with the "social question" and the threat of a *coup d'état?* Had he accomplished anything at all towards his goal of general reconciliation and increasing the self-confidence, health, and vigor of German political life? It would not appear so. Characteristically he blamed himself. It would have gone better if he had been more skillful, if he had not made mistakes. In November 1898 he wrote:

My life with a little more skill could easily have turned out differently and more fortunately. I did not know how to go about it. . . . At the beginning of my career I did not have the indispensable know-how and was too unfamiliar with the practical techniques. . . . If I had been more familiar with things nothing would have been easier for me. I belonged to none of the existing parties; I could have formed one of my own. But then the possibility of the formation of a strong [*lebensfähigen*] party coincided with the collapse of my political career, and it was too late.[82]

On February 6, 1899, Count Georg Leo von Caprivi, General of Infantry, Knight of the Order of the Black Eagle, former Chief of the Admiralty, and former Chancellor of the German Reich, died of a stroke at Skyren, thus surviving by only six months Prince Otto von Bismarck, his great predecessor.

[82]Schneidewin, "Briefe," pp. 256, 258.

EPILOGUE

Chapter X

AN APPRAISAL

THE Caprivi Era abounded in contradictions, perplexities, and paradoxes, not all strictly of German origin. The staggering growth of industrialization and the relative decline of agriculture, the opposition of the power of capital to the rights of labor, the defense of the tenet of private property against the claims of socialism, the losing struggle of humanitarianism with the forces of imperialism and racism, the rear-guard battle of religion against materialistic rationalism — all these conflicts and cross-currents were common to the culture of the West and to the *fin de siècle*. Intertwined inextricably with these were problems with a peculiar German slant, such as the conflict between monarchy, aristocracy, and democracy, between Prussia and Germany, and the question of what sort of political system would succeed to Bismarck. In the face of all the issues and currents of the day, the primary problem of the Caprivi Era was how to handle a complex political creation which had finally escaped from the control of its creator. It was an open question in 1890 how much of the dissatisfaction and frustration under the Bismarck regime would naturally disappear with the removal of his personality and how much would be found to be inherent in the Reich structure itself. The post-Bismarck period started with high hopes which, for one reason or another, were soon blighted. The history of the era is largely one of the slow and often painful awakening of the German Nation to the real nature of the constitution of its Reich.

General von Caprivi's disavowal of any intention of "inaugurating a new era" was honestly meant. The conservative general had, at the beginning, not the slightest idea of basically altering the structure of Bismarck's Reich. It was strong enough, he said, to "withstand the wind and the weather." [1] Not intending to change the system, he was, however, determined to alter the method. To soften the animosities, to reconcile the deep divergencies which had resulted

[1] See above, p. 43.

from the Bismarck era, he had appealed to a spirit of patriotism, of nationalism, which could unite the warring factions in loyal service to the Nation. He had tried to conduct a national policy. With his army increases he had sought to strengthen the nation's military might, with his trade treaties its economic power, and in the latter case to help the lower classes by providing jobs and decreasing the cost of bread. To turn labor away from the socialists and reconcile it to the state he had sponsored paternalistic labor laws and tax and administrative reforms. Even his foreign policy had served national sentiment, had departed from the Bismarckian cabinet diplomacy by dropping the secret treaty with the hated eastern enemy. In 1893, unlike Bismarck in 1887, the general had defended his Army Bill by open reference to Russia as well as to France. This attempt to rally the nation behind the government in a new spirit of coöperation and confidence worked rather well for two years. By then it came up against the underlying limitations existing in the Bismarckian constitutional structure, as well as those existing in the multiplicity of conflicting party policies, themselves shaped and accentuated by that constitutional structure. In the resulting stress of the School Bill crisis, caused in large measure by the divergence in composition and interests between Prussian Landtag and German Reichstag, the government collapsed and flew apart. With the School Bill crisis the New Course proper really came to an end; that anything at all was accomplished after that was a miracle.

Caprivi's national policy was necessary in dealing with a Reichstag where the oppositional parties possessed a majority. Thus in his introductory speech he had promised equality of treatment — he would take the "good," he said, from whatever source it might come. But as Caprivi in the course of his administration found it necessary to work with ever changing majorities — with the Kartell for the Miquel tax reform, the Center and the Radicals for the Herrfurth Rural Government Bill, the Center and Conservatives for the Zedlitz School Bill, and, finally, Center, National Liberals, Radicals, and Social Democrats for the later trade treaties — it became obvious that the definition of the "good" for his government-above-the-parties was in the end a matter of his personal decision alone. Thus Caprivi treated the parties almost as cavalierly as Bismarck had done. For Bismarck's dictatorship of ruthless, unscrupulous opportunism Caprivi merely substituted his own unique dictatorship of strict honesty and essential good will. If it had worked it might in the end have been more detrimental, more demoralizing to the parties than the former, since it attempted to be rational, just, and dispassionate.

Yet, it is obvious that for the Caprivi Administration dictatorship is too strong a word. It was the difference in method which in the end turned out to be its most important aspect, a case wherein the means did, indeed, determine the end.[2]

Bismarck, in domestic as in foreign policy, had followed the principle of divide and rule. He had encouraged alien forces and pitted them against each other in a precarious balance well suited to the maintenance of his own position of supreme arbiter and balancer. To maintain the tension and thus the hegemony of Germany in Europe and of Prussia and Bismarck in Germany no attempt at a resolution of opposing forces was envisaged. But international peace is more than a diplomatic checkmate, and the greatest brilliancy of maneuver in maintaining the domestic political *status quo* cannot substitute indefinitely for a progressive, productive policy. A healthy government must be more than a rigid power mechanism for holding hostile forces in check. It must provide means for the resolution of such forces and opportunity for free, organic development. It is no doubt unfortunate that Bismarck could not have continued his leadership in foreign affairs until the essential sterility and failure of his policy had become more evident. In domestic affairs the twenty-eight years of his rule in Prussia and the Reich were marked by the continual weakening and fragmentation of the parties which were loyal to his government, so that in the end it was only the "enemies of the Reich," the Center and Social Democrats, which remained unweakened and strong. In 1890, when he finally fell, his opportunism was in such ill repute that even the parties of his own Kartell remained passive or assisted actively in his overthrow.[3]

It was, on the contrary, not Caprivi's method to intensify existing conflicts, to attempt by force to overwhelm or trick the opposition. In foreign as in domestic policy it was his tendency rather to accept existing conflicts, and then to try to reconcile, to compromise, to conciliate. This virtue of Caprivi's may, indeed, have been his greatest weakness. He was, perhaps, too much the fatalistic soldier who, knowing war to be an ugly business, nevertheless wages it brilliantly "for the greater glory of his general." [4] He possessed, perhaps, to too great a degree the sharpness of intellect and clarity of perspective which sees all sides of a problem and renders any great willful, imaginative action impossible. Thus in 1890 he had taken on his

[2]Cf. *Die Nation*, X, 98, XI, 327.
[3]Cf. Hartung, "Verantwortliche Regierung," p. 310; Taylor, *Bismarck*, pp. 150–151. See above, pp. 15–26.
[4]Schneidewin, "Briefe," p. 247.

office clearly foreseeing that he would "fall ingloriously" and in the event had proved himself to be a good prophet. That sentence written near the end of his life, "The gods are against me, and I must bear my fate with as much resignation as possible," although obviously tinged with the bitterness of ill health and old age, may have been indicative of his general fatalism. Certainly it expresses most aptly the brief course of his political career. He was too honest, too reasonable to be a good politician.[5] This reasonableness did convince him, however, that the government must always be in line with the national will, that he must try to get along with the Reichstag, which was the expression of that will.[6] All political manifestations which he believed to be wrong, whether socialism, anti-Semitism, or agrarianism, he opposed with reasonable, energetic argument, clearly, openly. And in his attempt to rule with the Reichstag he succeeded remarkably well. For every important piece of legislation he was able, without resorting to threats or deliberately arousing passions, to find the necessary majority, some of them surprisingly large. But the attempt to work with the parties, not against them, necessarily led to a situation which tended toward parliamentary government. The constitution of the Reich, however, was meant to be only superficially parliamentary, and it was here that Caprivi's national program came up against the Bismarckian constitution itself when, heeding the call of the necessary majority in the Reichstag, his Reich tactics ran up against the special interests of Prussia. This conflict of interests between Reich and Prussia, which was only implicit in the School Bill affair, came fully into the open with the Rumanian and Russian trade treaties.[7]

According to Bismarck's constitution the Reich chancellor was responsible to the Kaiser, who was president of the Federation, and in legislative matters to the Bundesrat. The Bundesrat, however, in actual fact had no life of its own. None of the smaller members would dare to go against the wishes of Prussia. If some of them actually disapproved of a measure, they would prefer to hope that it could be stopped in the Reichstag. Since the Bundesrat sessions were secret, no one ever knew who had voted for or against a measure. This fact made control of the Bundesrat difficult also for the Landtags of the member states, which could not, in any case, meddle effectively or with justification in Reich affairs. The Bundesrat, then, in effect, was a very clever institution for sup-

[5] Cf. Hammann, *Der Neue Kurs*, pp. 106–107; Herzfeld, *Miquel*, II, 339–340.
[6] Cf. Bachem, *Zentrumspartei*, V, 121.
[7] Cf. "The Ruler in Berlin," *The Times Literary Supplement*, December 11, 1948.

porting and concealing the political predominance of Prussia. In
Prussia, however, the popularly elected Landtag was limited by the
three-class system of voting to representatives of the upper classes.
Nor was Prussia ruled finally by the Landtag. The final authority in
Prussia was the crown, and the crown ruled traditionally in the
interests of the Junker aristocracy which dominated the bureaucracy
and the army, both of which, in turn, were independent of parliamentary control. In effect, then, the Reich government had been
shaped to represent Prussian interests, and when Chancellor von
Caprivi led Reich policy in Bundesrat and Reichstag against Prussian
interests, as vehemently proclaimed by the Junker leadership, he
may have been in line with the national will, but he was going
against the political substance of the constitution. In his final battle
for the interests of the Reich as over against the special interests of
Prussia he found insufficient practical support in the Reichstag, since
the Reich government was not responsible to the Reichstag, but to
the crown, and as a minister of the crown he could not really be
parliamentary.

There were, as Caprivi had himself declared in 1892,[8] really only
three possible solutions to the German political conundrum: to try to
continue to rule paternalistically with majorities formed of changing
coalitions, which satisfied nobody and alienated everybody; to let
the parties capture the government through a parliamentary regime;
or to have the government itself sponsor and control a party or
parties. Bismarck had attempted the latter with his Kartell, but had
failed to inspire continuing faith in his program or his leadership.
In 1894 Caprivi — egged on, interestingly enough, by Barth's
Radicals — had himself finally arrived at the conclusion that he
must form a party of his own to back his government in the parliaments, but did not have time enough left to attempt it. The ideal
solution in Caprivi's mind (and in the mind of the Radicals?) thus
would appear to have been an independent, bureaucratic government attracting popular support and enthusiasm by conducting a
nationalistic, middle-of-the-road policy and organizing parliamentary
support for this policy through a "government party" of the "King's
Friends." When one remembers the enthusiasm for the leadership
of the new Kaiser in 1890 and the continuing notions of "democratic
monarchy" and the "people's Kaiser" endemic in Germany before
1914, it seems entirely possible that some such single-party system
of frock-coated totalitarianism might have succeeded in establishing
itself. As it was, however, Caprivi did not have sufficient knowledge

[8]See above, p. 157.

or experience to take advantage of the situation, Bismarck's attacks threw the parties into confusion, and the underlying divergencies of interest and outlook were too deep to be easily resolved. Only a large-scale catastrophe could have produced the necessary unity of feeling. There is small likelihood that Caprivi, with a few more months of government in 1894–1895, could really have organized a new government party of sufficient strength adequately to support his regime.

As Bismarck himself so keenly pointed out in 1893, Caprivi's government was really a government of the bureaucracy. The corps of ministers and secretaries which Bismarck had used as a passive instrument for his personal rule Caprivi, to fill the vacuum in the state, had tried to raise to the level of an independent power. But in 1892 he had lost the ministry to Miquel, and at the end only the staffs of the Chancellery and Foreign Office — this was Holstein's rôle — supported him in his battle for the national interest. The bureaucracy in itself did not represent effective political power, except as its individual members represented the dominance of the Junker class — and in a fight *against* Junker interests this latter factor was a liability, not an asset. The only possible support for a bureaucratic government was the crown. But the crown, being at once the center and pinnacle of power, was in a very vulnerable position and — even with some other monarch than William II — was extremely susceptible to all the shifting winds of public sentiment. In such a system it was the government officials themselves, caught between crown and Reichstag, who became expendable. Thus Herrfurth was sacrificed to the Conservatives and Zedlitz to the liberals. In 1894, to preserve the system and to appease both left and right, Botho Eulenburg and Caprivi himself became finally expendable. Such sacrifices became inevitable for a government that had to straddle two houses of different political composition and base its support on shifting party coalitions. This exposed position of the ministers, however, did not encourage individual initiative in the bureaucracy, nor the general stability of the government. Yet the bureaucracy was the only body of men sufficiently conversant with affairs to be able to preserve an over-all view and thus to try to steer in some fashion between the special interests in order to keep the Reich ship afloat. It was not merely coincidence that, after Caprivi, subsequent chancellors were drawn exclusively from the bureaucracy, and the chancellorship itself became merely the highest rung on the bureaucratic ladder.

The basic evil of the system was the complete lack of any clear line of responsibility. In the careful balance between monarchic, aristocratic, democratic, state, and national interests each element could shift the blame upon the other while itself making extreme demands. The results of this process were most obvious in the deterioration of the parties in the Reichstag, where the moderate parties were steadily losing to the extreme demands of clericalism, socialism, anti-Semitism, or agrarianism. The appearance of Rector Ahlwardt on the tribune of the Reichstag was as much a sign of the times as were the Social Democratic interpellations or the Kanitz bill. Since the Reichstag did not govern, and was not responsible, the whole purpose of the political activity of a party in the Reichstag was to force concessions. Thus, more and more, parties came solely to represent special interest groups, and the more extreme and irresponsible the demands, the greater the concessions were likely to be. Speeches in the Reichstag had little bearing on practical political affairs and could thus range from the most rarified utopian idealism to the vilest demagoguery. In this manner the Reichstag was in danger of becoming more of a debating club than a parliament. Naturally, this irresponsibility of the parties in the Reichstag increased the difficulties of the government, as with the Radical and Center opposition to Caprivi's Army Bill and the agrarian opposition to his trade treaties. Thus every important piece of legislation became the occasion for new demands, new concessions, and a new crisis. Government by crisis became the norm.[9]

Caprivi, in assuring the parties in a friendly manner that he would grant all justified demands and carry out useful suggestions "from whatever source," seems to have been thinking of the process of government as one of friendly advice and discussion, as if it were a staff meeting. This procedure might be excellent in a nonpolitical administrative set-up — such as an individual ministry or the army or navy — but politics involves power and the struggle for it by conflicting groups. Somewhere in the process of governing a continuous battle has to be fought. Since the locus of Reich power was not in the Reichstag, and since the important battles had to take place somewhere, they were fought between the Reichstag and the government, within the Prussian Landtag, within the court, between and within the ministries, within the ranks of the bureaucracy itself. In such a state of war of all against all, position and personal influence were very important. Hence the necessity for the government to maintain, in Eulenburg and Holstein, its own official camarilla. This situation contributed strongly to the further weaken-

[9] Cf. *Die Nation*, X, 538–541.

ing and corruption of the bureaucracy. Politics had become per-
sonalized to a certain extent as a natural result of Bismarck's
dictatorship, had been reduced to intrigue and dominated by fear,
hatred, jealousy, and general vindictiveness.[10] After Bismarck's
removal there was no all-directing will to keep these ambitions and
animosities in check and, as a possible substitute, no inspiration
towards coöperation or patriotic endeavor from the top, where the
Kaiser — himself a graduate of the Bismarck school — was proving
just as ambitious, vain, weak, changeable, ungrateful, and petty as
the lowest official. If, to the irresponsibility of the Reichstag one
adds the irresponsibility of the crown, whose authority constitutionally was supreme and whose control of the army, the navy, and
foreign policy was quite independent of the Reichstag, plus the
irresponsibility of the aristocracy and of some officials, it is easy to
understand that it was practically impossible for the government to
conduct a consistent, vigorous policy, since top officials had to spend
most of their time negotiating to avoid the new impending crisis.
The ten serious crises which occurred during the four and a half
years of the Caprivi regime — or an average of slightly more than
one every six months — cannot be attributed merely to the "stubbornness" of the old general or the "immaturity" of Kaiser William
II.

The success of Caprivi's national policy depended ultimately on
a program of reform to reconcile the laboring classes to the Reich
and thus to immunize them against the blandishments of the Social
Democrats. But labor was not to be captured by a mere provision
for Sunday rest or by laws against the labor of women and children.
What they wanted essentially was a share in the power, a recognized
place in the life of the state. The mild and tentative moves made in
this direction by Herrfurth and Caprivi, in the rural government
reform and in Herrfurth's proposed election reform, however, met
with the most harsh and unyielding opposition of the Junker
aristocracy, an opposition which reached its natural culmination in
the movement of the summer of 1894 for new anti-Socialist legislation and for a *coup d'état*. Caprivi was able then to defeat this
reactionary Junker program, but was, in turn, himself defeated by
the Junkers.[11] It was, typically, not the vote of a Reichstag majority
which brought him down, but an undercover battle of personalities
within the court and the government. To the extent that Caprivi,
in this final battle, represented the interests of the Reich and of the

---

[10]Cf. Rothfels, "Lohmann," p. 62.
[11]On Caprivi's victory cf. *Die Nation*, XII, 43–45; on his defeat, *ibid.*, XII, 59–61.

nation, the Prussian Junkers, in forcing him out of office, effectively demonstrated the essential narrowness of their outlook, their egotistical insistence upon placing, at all costs, the interests of their class above the interests of the nation, and, in this fashion, their ultimate incapacity to rule. They could not expect permanently to maintain their position of special privilege while at the same time refusing to serve the national interest.[12]

It was no accident that the conservative general, who had started out with the honest intention of conducting a national program, should end by opposing implicitly the constitution itself. The history of the New Course is something of a cycle. Everything returns to Bismarck. In foreign policy the initial swing away from Bismarckian policy and towards a closer *rapprochement* with England at the expense of Russia returns ultimately to the Bismarckian position of close friendship with Russia. In domestic policy the final year of the New Course brings reconciliation with Bismarck and agitation for a repressive crisis policy led by Bismarck himself.[13] Even Caprivi did not escape the Bismarckian influence, but worked more under its shadow than perhaps he himself was aware. It was never his intention to introduce a basic change in the structure of the Reich which he inherited, to introduce, say, a parliamentary regime. Both in office and later in retirement it was his own loyalty to the Prussian monarchy that hampered him most. His greatest error was that he accepted Bismarck's Reich and tried hard and faithfully to make it work. The bureaucracy operated entirely within the Bismarckian tradition, many of them being Bismarck's men. Holstein, in foreign policy, reasoned from basic axioms culled from Bismarck's textbook — the permanent hostility of England for France, the impossibility of agreement between England and Russia. The Bismarckian tradition was thus codified and followed reverently and rigidly like Holy Writ. This was ironical, since Bismarck's only axiom was his appreciation of and respect for the reality of power, coupled with his own desire to wield it — made clear enough by his final attacks on the dynasty and the nation; the rest was sheer improvisation. At the head of the government edifice the Kaiser and the other princes likewise referred to Bismarckian teachings and precedents — as in the fall of 1894 — for their political guidance. The party leaders, especially those of the middle, Bismarckian parties,

[12]Cf. Geis, "Sturz," pp. 123–124.
[13]Cf. Herzfeld, *Miquel,* II, 186, 287. Holstein suspected that Eulenburg was to set up a caretaker government for Bismarck, letter to Monts, October 24, 1894, Nowak and Thimme, *Errinnerungen u. Gedanken,* p. 348.

Free Conservatives and National Liberals, were lost in confusion
without the strong, restraining hand of the master politician. As
early as July 1890, Kardorff complained fretfully — and loyally —
to Bismarck that Caprivi, with the best of intentions, could never
"electrify" the public and the parliaments, that there did not seem
to be any "strong, energetic will." [14] Public opinion thought for a
while that it had a new "leader" in the Kaiser, but, disillusioned,
soon returned to acclaiming its first love, Bismarck, all the more so
since now the old man was busily engaged in shooting firebrands
into the Reich which he had himself so carefully constructed. The
whole political life of Germany lay helplessly paralyzed, immobile
within the bonds of Bismarckian hero worship and Bismarckian
traditions which, in turn, supported Bismarckian institutions. [15]

It was not only the constitution of 1871 which lay at the root
of the difficulty, but the whole sequence of events in the decade
following 1862. It was the conquest of Prussia by a policy of "blood
and iron" and the subsequent conquest of Germany by Prussia. It
was a solution of the "German problem" that was not a truly national
or German solution, but a convenient means to Prussian — and
Bismarckian — domination. [16] To be sure, the Prussian army had
been necessary to unify Germany, and, since this army was the
vehicle of the Junker aristocracy, the nation created by the army
must serve this aristocracy. But in the process the Junkers were
given a new prestige, a new authority, an exaggerated self-confidence, which made it impossible for them to meet future challenges
with imagination and flexibility. In foreign affairs and in domestic
politics Bismarck had only eighteenth-century solutions to offer.
But at the end of the nineteenth century, in an age of world
economy and world politics, a system of secret agreements and
balance-of-power alliance networks was not enough. In a rapidly
industrializing and democratizing Germany, government by an irresponsible monarchy and an agrarian aristocracy was not enough.
Bismarck's magnificently brilliant creation was a structure as ephemeral, as temporary as the genius that created it. It was, indeed, only
a puppet show after all, a magical construction that had no healthy
life of its own, and that, once it had escaped from the control of its
creator, was doomed to self-destruction. Bismarck's strong and
triumphant German Reich was thus only an incident in the troubled

[14] Thimme, "Bismarck und Kardorff," pt. I, pp. 58–59. Cf. *Die Nation*, XII (1894–
1895), 1–2.

[15] Cf. L. Bamberger, "Zum Jahrestag der Entlassung Bismarcks," pp. 336–340.

[16] Cf. Eyck, *Bismarck*, II, 483–487; F. Darmstaedter, *Bismarck and the Creation
of the Second Reich* (London, 1948), p. 387.

history of the Germans, but one which left pernicious influences behind. The glory of Bismarck's career left Germany with a taste for hero worship and with a tradition of political opportunism and of the unprincipled use of force which the German nation has not yet outgrown. In art, in literature, in music, individual genius is the divine spark leading and inspiring men to greatness, and, as such, is rightly prized. In politics, however, society may sometimes be compelled to pay too high a price for the brilliant but ephemeral achievements of the great man.[17]

[17]Cf. F. Meinecke, "The Year 1848 in German History," *Review of Politics,* vol. 10, no. 4, pp. 478, 489; Darmstaedter, *Bismarck and the Creation of the Second Reich,* pp. 406–407; Shotwell, *Governments,* p. 317.

ALPHABETICAL LIST OF WORKS CITED

Allgemeine deutsche Biographie. 56 vols. Leipzig, 1875–1912.

Anderson, Evelyn. *Hammer or Anvil, the Story of the German Working-Class Movement.* London, 1945.

Arndt, Rudolf, ed. *Die Reden des Grafen von Caprivi im deutschen Reichstage, Preussischen Landtage und bei besonderen Anlässen, 1883–1893, mit der Biographie.* Berlin, 1894.

Ashley, Percy. *Modern Tariff History.* London, 1910.

Bachem, Karl. *Vorgeschichte, Geschichte, und Politik der deutschen Zentrumspartei, 1815–1914.* 9 vols. Cologne, 1927–1932.

Bamberger, Ludwig. *Gesammelte Schriften.* Berlin, 1913.

Barth, Theodor. *Politische Porträts.* Berlin, 1904.

Bergsträsser, Ludwig. *Geschichte der politischen Parteien in Deutschland.* Berlin, 1932.

Berlepsch, Hans Hermann, Freiherr von. *Sozialpolitische Erfahrungen und Erinnerungen.* München-Gladbach, 1925.

Bigelow, Poultney. *Prussian Memories, 1864–1914.* New York, 1915.

Biographisches Jahrbuch und deutscher Nekrolog. Berlin, 1897–1917.

Bismarck, Otto von. *The Kaiser vs. Bismarck.* Translation by Bernard Miall of vol. III of *Gedanken und Erinnerungen.* New York, 1921.

Bornhak, Konrad. "The Local Government of Country Communities in Prussia," *Annals of the American Academy of Political and Social Science,* 3:393–408 (1893).

Brauer, Arthur von. *Im Dienste Bismarcks.* Berlin, 1936.

Brück, Werner F. *Social and Economic History of Germany, 1888–1938.* London, 1938.

Bülow, Bernhard. *Memoirs of Prince von Bülow,* translated by F. A. Voight. 4 vols. Boston, 1932.

Busch, Moritz. *Bismarck, Some Secret Pages of His History.* New York, 1898.

Cambridge History of Poland. Cambridge, 1950.

Caprivi, Georg Leo, Graf von. Caprivi Papers (unpublished). Hauptarchiv, Berlin.

Caprivi, Leopold von. *Die ostafrikanische Frage und der Helgoland-Sansibar-Vertrag.* . . . Bonn, 1934.

Carroll, Eber M. *Germany and the Great Powers, 1866–1914.* New York, 1938.

Cecil, Lady Gwendolen. *Life of Robert, Marquis of Salisbury.* 4 vols. London, 1921–1932.

Clapham, John H. *The Economic Development of France and Germany, 1815–1914.* Cambridge, 1936.

Craig, Gordon A. "Military Diplomats in the Prussian and German Service: the Attachés, 1816–1914," *Political Science Quarterly*, 64:65–94 (1949).

—— *The Politics of the Prussian Army, 1640–1945.* Oxford, 1955.

Crispi, Francesco. *The Memoirs of Francesco Crispi.* 3 vols. London, 1912–1914.

Darmstaedter, Friedrich. *Bismarck and the Creation of the Second Reich.* London, 1948.

Deutsche Revue, eine Monatsschrift. 47 vols. Berlin, 1877–1922.

Deutsche Rundschau. Berlin, 1874 —.

Documents Diplomatiques Français. Paris, 1929 —.

Dorpalen, Andreas. "Emperor Frederick III and the German Liberal Movement," *American Historical Review*, 54:1–31 (October 1948).

Dugdale, E. T. S., ed. *German Diplomatic Documents, 1871–1914.* 4 vols. London, 1928. (Translation of *Die Grosse Politik.*)

Earle, Edward Mead. *Turkey, the Great Powers, and the Bagdad Railway.* New York, 1923.

Ebmeyer, Major von. "Caprivis Entlassung," *Deutsche Revue*, 47(IV): 193–213 (1922).

Eckardt, Julius von. *Aus den Tagen von Bismarcks Kampf gegen Caprivi.* Leipzig, 1920.

Eulenburg-Hertefeld, Philipp, Fürst zu. *Aus 50 Jahren.* Berlin, 1923.

Eyck, Erich. *Bismarck.* 3 vols. Erlenbach-Zürich, 1941–1944.

—— *Das persönliche Regiment Wilhelms II.* Erlenbach-Zürich, 1948.

Fife, Robert H. *The German Empire Between Two Wars, 1870–1914.* New York, 1916.

Geiger, Walter. *Miquel und die preussische Steuerreform 1890–1893.* Göppingen, 1934.

Geis, Robert. "Der Sturz des Reichskanzlers Caprivi," *Historische Studien*, 192 (1930).

Gerlach, Hellmuth von. *Erinnerungen eines Junkers.* (No date.)

Gerschenkron, Alexander. *Bread and Democracy in Germany.* Berkeley, 1943.

Goebel, Heinz. *Die Militärvorlage 1892/93.* Leipzig, 1935.

Goldschmidt, Hans. *Das Reich und Preussen im Kampf um die Führung, von Bismarck bis 1918.* Berlin, 1931.

Goldschmidt, Hans, Kaiser, Hans, and Thimme, Hans. *Ein Jahrhundert deutscher Geschichte . . . 1815–1919.* Berlin, 1928.

Goltz, Theodor, Freiherr von der. *Geschichte der deutschen Landwirtschaft.* 2 vols. Stuttgart, Berlin, 1902–1903.

Gooch, George P., and Temperly, Harold, *British Documents on the Origin of the War.* London, 1926–1938.

Goriainov, Sergei. "End of the Alliance of the Emperors," *American Historical Review,* 23:342–343 (1917–1918).

Gothein, Georg. *Reichskanzler Graf Caprivi.* Munich, 1918.

Gradenwitz, Otto. "Akten über Bismarcks grossdeutsche Rundfahrt vom Jahre 1892," *Sitzungsberichte der Heidelberger Akademie der Wissenschaften,* 12 (1921).

—— *Bismarcks letzter Kampf, 1888–1898.* Berlin, 1924.

Grey, Sir Edward. *Twenty-five Years.* New York, 1925.

Die Grosse Politik der Europäischen Kabinette, 1871–1914 . . . ed. J. Lepsius, A. Mendelssohn-Bartholdy, F. Thimme. 40 vols. Berlin, 1922–1927.

Hale, O. J. *Publicity and Diplomacy.* New York, 1940.

Haller, Johannes. *Aus dem Leben des Fürsten Philipp zu Eulenburg-Hertefeld.* Berlin, 1924.

—— *Philip Eulenburg: the Kaiser's Friend.* Translation by Ethel Colburn Mayne of *Aus dem Leben. . . .* 2 vols. New York, 1930.

Hammann, Otto. *Der Neue Kurs.* Berlin, 1918.

Hartung, Fritz. "Verantwortliche Regierung, Kabinette und Nebenregierungen in konstitutionellen Preussen, 1848–1918," *Forschungen zur Brandenburg-Preussischen Geschichte,* 44:302–373 (1932).

Hasenclever, Adolf. "Geschichte und Bedeutung des Helgolandvertrages," *Archiv für Politik und Geschichte,* 5:507–524 (1925).

Hayes, Carleton J. H. *A Generation of Materialism.* New York, 1941.

Helfferich, Karl. *Georg von Siemens.* Berlin, 1923.

Helldorff-Bedra, Otto von. "Fall des Socialistengesetzes," *Deutsche Revue,* 25(I):273ff., II:43ff. (1900).

Hellwig, Fritz. *Carl Ferdinand Freiherr von Stumm-Halberg, 1836–1901.* Heidelberg, 1936.

Herrfurth, Ludwig. "Die Wahlreform in Preussen," *Deutsche Revue,* 18(II):230–250.

Herzfeld, Hans. *Johannes von Miquel.* 2 vols. Detmold, 1938.

Hicks, John D. *The Populist Revolt.* Minneapolis, 1931.

Hofmann, Hermann. *Fürst Bismarck nach seiner Entlassung, 1890–1898.* 3 vols. Stuttgart, 1914.

Hohenlohe-Schillingsfürst, Alexander von. *Aus meinem Leben.* Frankfurt a. M., 1925.

Hohenlohe-Schillingsfürst, Chlodwig Fürst zu. *Denkwürdigkeiten der Reichskanzlerzeit*, ed. K. A. von Müller. Stuttgart, 1931.

—— *Memoirs of Prince Chlodwig of Hohenlohe-Schillingsfuerst*, ed. Fr. Curtius, translated by G. W. Chrystal. 2 vols. New York, 1906.

Hohlfeld, Johannes. *Deutsche Reichsgeschichte in Dokumenten, 1849–1926*. Berlin, 1927.

Holstein, Friedrich von. *The Holstein Papers*, ed. N. Rich and M. H. Fisher. Cambridge, 1955 —.

Huber, Ernst R. *Heer und Staat*. Hamburg, 1943.

Hüsgen, Ernst. *Ludwig Windthorst*. Köln, 1907.

Hutten-Czapski, Bogdan Graf von. *Sechzig Jahre Politik und Gesellschaft*. 2 vols. Berlin, 1936.

Ibbeken, Rudolf. *Das aussenpolitische Problem Staat und Wirtschaft in der deutschen Reichspolitik, 1880–1914*. Schleswig, 1928.

Jagemann, Eugen von. *75 Jahre des Erlebens und Erfahrens*. Heidelberg, 1925.

Kardorff, Siegfried von. *Wilhelm von Kardorff, ein nationaler Parlamentarier im Zeitalter Bismarcks und Wilhelms II, 1828–1907*. Berlin, 1936.

Kautsky, Karl. *The Class Struggle (Erfurt Program)*. Chicago, 1910.

Kehr, Eckart. "Schlachtflottenbau und Parteipolitik 1894–1901," *Historische Studien*, 197 (1930).

Keil, Friedrich. "Die Langemeinde in dem östlichen Provinzen Preussens und die Versuche, eine Landgemeindeordnung zu schaffen," *Schriften des Vereins für Sozialpolitik*, 43 (1890).

Keim, August. *Erlebtes und Erstrebtes*. Hannover, 1925.

Kladderadatsch; humoristisch-satirisches Wochenblatt. Berlin, 1848 —.

Köhler, Wilhelm, ed. *Revanche-idee und Panslavismus*. Berlin, 1925. (Vol. I of *Amtliche Aktenstücke zur Geschichte der europäischen Politik 1885–1914* [Belgian Archives]).

Krausnick, Helmut. *Holsteins Geheimpolitik in der Ära Bismarck, 1886–1890*. Hamburg, 1942.

Kremer, Willy. *Der soziale Aufbau der Parteien des deutschen Reichstages 1871–1918*. Emsdetten, 1934.

Kröger, Karl H. *Die Konservativen und die Politik Caprivis*. Rostock, 1937.

Langer, William L. *The Diplomacy of Imperialism*. New York, 1935.

—— *European Alliances and Alignments, 1871–1890*. New York, 1931.

—— *The Franco-Russian Alliance, 1890–1894*. Cambridge, 1929.

Lerchenfeld-Koefering, Hugo Graf. *Erinnerungen und Denkwürdigkeiten, 1843–1925*. Berlin, 1935.

Leuss, Hans. *Wilhelm Freiherr von Hammerstein, 1881–1895 Chefredakteur der Kreuzzeitung*. Berlin, 1905.

Lotz, Walther. "Die Handelspolitik des deutschen Reiches unter Graf Caprivi und Fürst Hohenlohe, 1890–1900," *Schriften des Vereins für Sozialpolitik*, 92(II) (1901).

Lowell, A. Lawrence. *Governments and Parties in Continental Europe.* Boston, 1896.

Lucius von Ballhausen, Robert Freiherr. *Bismarck-Erinnerungen.* Stuttgart, 1921.

Maenner, Ludwig. *Prinz Heinrich zu Schoenaich-Carolath.* Stuttgart, 1931.

Meinecke, Friedrich. *Staat und Persönlichkeit.* Berlin, 1933.

——— "The Year 1848 in German History: Reflections on a Centenary," *Review of Politics*, 10(IV):475–492 (October 1948).

Mommsen, Wilhelm. *Johannes von Miquel.* Stuttgart, 1928.

Monts, Anton Graf von. *Erinnerungen und Gedanken des Botschafters Anton Grafen Monts,* ed. K. F. Nowak and F. Thimme. Berlin, 1932.

Müller, Karl Alexander von, ed. "Die Entlassung," *Süddeutsche Monatsheft,* 19:138–178 (1921).

Müller, Wilhelm. *Politische Geschichte der Gegenwart.* Berlin, 1870–1891.

Die Nation, Wochenschrift für Politik, Volkswirthschaft und Literatur. Berlin, 1883–1907.

Nowak, Karl F. *Kaiser and Chancellor.* London, 1930.

Österreichische Rundschau. Vienna, 1904 —.

Oldenburg-Januschau, Elard von. *Erinnerungen.* Leipzig, 1936.

Oncken, Hermann. *Rudolf von Bennigsen.* 2 vols. Stuttgart, 1910.

Petersdorff, Hermann von. *Kleist-Retzow.* Stuttgart, 1907.

Ponsonby, Sir Frederick, ed. and trans. *Letters of the Empress Frederick.* London, 1928.

Potëmkin, V. P. *Istoria Diplomatii.* Moscow, 1945.

Preussische Jahrbücher. Berlin, 1858–1935.

Radowitz, Josef Maria von. *Aufzeichnungen und Erinnerungen,* ed. H. Holborn. 2 vols. Stuttgart, 1925.

Radziwill, Marie. *Une grande dame d'avant guerre. Lettres de la Princesse Radziwill au Général de Robilant 1889–1914.* 4 vols. Bologna, 1933–1934.

Raschdau, Ludwig. *Unter Bismarck und Caprivi, 1885–1894.* 2nd ed. Berlin, 1939.

Reischach, Hugo Freiherr von. *Unter drei Kaisern.* Berlin, 1925.

Rennell Rodd, Sir James. *Social and Diplomatic Memories, 1884–1893.* London, 1922.

Richter, Hubert. "Aus kritischen Tagen," *Deutsche Rundschau,* 190:151ff. (1922).

Richter, Kurt. *Der Kampf um den Schulgesetzentwurf des Grafen Zedlitz-Trützschler vom Jahre 1892.* Halle, 1934.

Rogge, Helmuth. *Friedrich von Holstein Lebensbekenntnis in Briefen an eine Frau.* Berlin, 1932.

Rosenberg, Arthur. *Birth of the German Republic, 1871–1918.* New York, 1931.

Rothfels, Hans. "Theodor Lohmann und die Kampfjahre der staatlichen Sozialpolitik," *Forschungen und Darstellungen aus dem Reichsarchiv,* 6 (1927).

"The Ruler in Berlin." Anon. rev., *The Times Literary Supplement,* December 11, 1948.

Sartorius von Waltershausen, August. *Deutsche Wirtschaftsgeschichte, 1815–1914.* Jena, 1923.

Schlözer, Kurd von. *Letzte römische Briefe, 1882–1894.* Berlin, 1924.

Schmidt-Bückeburg, Rudolf. *Das Militärkabinett der preussischen Könige und deutschen Kaiser . . . 1787–1918.* Berlin, 1933.

Schmitt, Bernadotte. *Triple Alliance and Triple Entente.* New York, 1934.

Schneidewin, Max. "Briefe des toten Reichskanzlers von Caprivi," *Deutsche Revue,* 47(II):136–147, 247–258 (1922).

—— *Ein wenig mehr Licht über Bismarck, Caprivi, und die jüngst erlebte Mobilmachung des Liberalismus.* Berlin, 1892.

Schreck, Ernst. *Reichskanzler Graf Leo von Caprivi.* Düsseldorf, 1891.

Schulte, Dr. von. "Erinnerungen an Graf Caprivi," *Deutsche Revue,* 24(II):229–235 (1899).

Schulthess' Europäischer Geschichtskalender. 79 vols. Munich, 1860–1938.

Schweinitz, General Hans Lothar von. *Briefwechsel des Botschafters General von Schweinitz.* Berlin, 1928.

—— *Denkwürdigkeiten des Botschafters General von Schweinitz.* 2 vols. Berlin, 1927.

Seligman, Edwin R. A. *Essays in Taxation.* 8th ed. New York, 1919.

—— *The Income Tax; A Study of the History, Theory and Practice of Income Taxation at Home and Abroad.* New York, 1911.

Sell, Manfred. *Das deutsche öffentliche Meinung und die Helgoland-Sansibarvertrag.* Berlin, 1926.

Shotwell, James T., ed. *Governments of Continental Europe.* New York, 1942.

Specht, Fritz, and Schwabe, Paul. *Die Reichstagswahlen 1867–1897.* . . . Berlin, 1898.

Das Staatsarchiv, 1861–1914. 86 vols. Leipzig, 1872–1919.

Stadelmann, Rudolf. "Der neue Kurs in Deutschland," *Geschichte in Wissenschaft und Unterricht,* 4:538–564 (September 1953).

Stanwood, Edward. *American Tariff Controversies in the Nineteenth Century*. Boston, 1903.

Statesman's Yearbook. London, 1864 —.

Statistisches Handbuch für das Deutsche Reich. Berlin, 1907.

Stein, August. *Es war alles ganz anders; aus der Werkstätte eines politischen Journalisten, 1891–1914*. Frankfurt a. M., 1922.

Stenographische Berichte über die Verhandlungen des Preussischen Landtages, Haus der Abgeordneten. Berlin, 1848–1917.

Stillich, Oskar. *Die politischen Parteien in Deutschland*. 2 vols. Leipzig, 1908–1911.

Stolper, Gustav. *The German Economy, 1870–1940*. New York, 1940.

Tarbell, Ida M. *The Tariff in Our Times*. New York, 1911.

Taussig, Frank W. *Tariff History of the United States*. New York, 1910.

Taylor, A. J. P. *Bismarck*. London, 1955.

———— *The Struggle for Mastery in Europe, 1848–1918*. Oxford, 1954.

Thimme, Friedrich, ed. "Bismarck und Kardorff," *Deutsche Revue*, 42(I): 46–59, 162–185, 278–288; (II):24–45, 149–168, 262–279 (1917).

———— "Fürst Bülow und Graf Monts," *Preussische Jahrbücher*, 231:193–219; 232:17–34.

The Times. London, 1785 —.

Tims, Richard W. *Germanizing Prussian Poland . . . 1894–1919*. New York, 1941.

Tirpitz, Alfred von. *My Memoirs*. 2 vols. New York, 1919.

Tirrell, Sarah. *German Agrarian Politics after Bismarck's Fall*. New York, 1951.

Townsend, Mary E. *Rise and Fall of Germany's Colonial Empire, 1884–1918*. New York, 1930.

Trappe, Werner. *Dr. Hans Freiherr von Berlepsch als Sozial-politiker*. Bochum-Langendreer, 1934.

Ullstein, Ludwig. *Eugen Richter als Publizist und Herausgeber. . . .* Leipzig, 1930.

Veblen, Thorstein. *Imperial Germany and the Industrial Revolution*. New York, 1915.

Verhandlungen des Reichstages . . . Stenographische Berichte. Berlin, 1871–1938.

Victoria I. R. *Letters of Queen Victoria*, ed. G. E. Buckle. 3rd series. London, 1930–1932.

Wagner, Adolf. "Die neueste Silberkrisis und unsere Münzwesen," *Preussische Jahrbücher*, 54:138–166, 242–284.

Wahl, Adalbert. *Deutsche Geschichte von der Reichsgründung bis zum Ausbruch des Weltkrieges, 1871–1914*. 4 vols. Stuttgart, 1926–1936.

Waldersee, Alfred Graf von. *Aus dem Briefwechsel des Generals Alfred Grafen von Waldersee.* Stuttgart, 1928.

—— *Denkwürdigkeiten des General-Feldmarschalls Alfred Grafen von Waldersee,* ed. H. O. Meissner. 3 vols. Stuttgart, 1923.

Weber, Alfred. "Die Entwicklung der Arbeiterschutzgesetzgebung seit 1890," *Schmollers Jahrbuch für Gesetzgebung, Verwaltung und Volkswirtschaft im Deutschen Reich,* 21(1897).

Wedel, Carl, Graf von. *Zwischen Kaiser und Kanzler: Aufzeichnungen des General-adjutanten Grafen Carl von Wedel aus den Jahren 1890–1894.* Leipzig, 1943.

Wenck, Martin. *Die Geschichte und Ziele der deutschen Sozialpolitik.* Leipzig, 1908.

Werdermann, Johannes. *Die Heeresreform unter Caprivi.* Greifswald, 1928.

Wermuth, Adolf. *Ein Beamtenleben.* Berlin, 1922.

Wertheimer, Eduard von. "Ein kaiser- und königlicher Militärattaché über das politische Leben in Berlin 1886–1895," *Preussische Jahrbücher,* 201:264–282 (1925).

Wertheimer, Mildred. "The Pan-German League, 1890–1914," *Columbia Studies in History, Economics, and Public Law,* no. 251 (1924).

Wilhelm II. *The Kaiser's Memoirs.* New York, 1922.

Wippermann, Karl, ed. *Deutscher Geschichtskalender.* Leipzig, 1885–1934.

Witte, Sergei I., Count. *Memoirs of Count Witte.* London, 1921.

Wolf, John B. "The Diplomatic History of the Bagdad Railroad," *University of Missouri Studies,* 11, no. 2 (1936).

Zechlin, Egmont. *Staatsstreichpläne Bismarcks und Wilhelms II, 1890–1894.* Stuttgart and Berlin, 1929.

Zedlitz und Neukirch, Otto Freiherr von. "Miquel als Finanzminister," *Preussische Jahrbücher,* 105:1–18 (1901).

Ziekursch, Johannes. *Politische Geschichte des neuen deutschen Kaiserreiches.* 3 vols. Frankfurt a. M., 1925–1930.

INDEX